WORLD LITERATURE, TRANSNATIONAL CINEMA, AND GLOBAL MEDIA

With extraordinary transnational and transdisciplinary range, *World Literature, Transnational Cinema, and Global Media* comprehensively explores the genealogies, vocabularies, and concepts orienting the fields within literature, cinema, and media studies.

Orchestrating a layered conversation between arts, disciplines, and media, Stam argues for their "mutual embeddedness" and their shared "in-between" territories. Rather than merely adding to the existing scholarship, the book builds a relational framework through the connectivities within literature, cinema, music, and media that opens up analysis to new categories and concepts, while crossing spatial, temporal, theoretical, disciplinary, and mediatic borders. The book also questions an array of hierarchies: literature over cinema; source novel over adaptation; feature film over documentary; erudite over vernacular culture; Western modernisms over "peripheral" modernisms; classical over popular music; written poetry over sung poetry, and so forth. The book is structured around the concept of the "commons," forming a strong thread which links various struggles against "enclosures" of all kinds, with emphasis on natural, indigenous, cultural, creative, digital, and the transdisciplinary commons.

World Literature, Transnational Cinema, and Global Media is ideal to further the theoretical discussion for those undergraduate and graduate departments in cinema studies, media studies, arts and art history, communications, journalism, and new digital media programs at all levels.

Robert Stam is University Professor at New York University. His books include *François Truffaut and Friends*; *Literature through Film*; *Film Theory: An Introduction*; and (with Ella Shohat) *Unthinking Eurocentrism* and *Race in Translation*. With work translated into sixteen languages, he has taught in France, Brazil, Tunisia, Germany, and the UAE.

WORLD LITERATURE, TRANSNATIONAL CINEMA, AND GLOBAL MEDIA

Towards a Transartistic Commons

Robert Stam

LONDON AND NEW YORK

First published 2019
by Routledge
2 Park Square, Milton Park, Abingdon, Oxon OX14 4RN

and by Routledge
52 Vanderbilt Avenue, New York, NY 10017

Routledge is an imprint of the Taylor & Francis Group, an informa business

© 2019 Robert Stam

The right of Robert Stam to be identified as author of this work has been asserted by him in accordance with sections 77 and 78 of the Copyright, Designs and Patents Act 1988.

All rights reserved. No part of this book may be reprinted or reproduced or utilised in any form or by any electronic, mechanical, or other means, now known or hereafter invented, including photocopying and recording, or in any information storage or retrieval system, without permission in writing from the publishers.

Trademark notice: Product or corporate names may be trademarks or registered trademarks, and are used only for identification and explanation without intent to infringe.

British Library Cataloguing-in-Publication Data
A catalogue record for this book is available from the British Library

Library of Congress Cataloging-in-Publication Data
Names: Stam, Robert, 1941- author.
Title: World literature, transnational cinema, and global media : towards a transartistic commons / Robert Stam.
Description: London ; New York : Routledge, 2019. | Includes bibliographical references and index.
Identifiers: LCCN 2018039396 (print) | LCCN 2019000675 (ebook) | ISBN 9780429428579 (ebook) | ISBN 9781138369573 | ISBN 9781138369573 (hardback :alk. paper) | ISBN 9781138369597(paperback :alk. paper) | ISBN 9780429428579(ebk)
Subjects: LCSH: Literature and transnationalism. | Motion pictures and transnationalism. | Mass media and globalization.
Classification: LCC PN56.T685 (ebook) | LCC PN56.T685 S73 2019 (print) | DDC 809--dc23
LC record available at https://lccn.loc.gov/2018039396

ISBN: 978-1-138-36957-3 (hbk)
ISBN: 978-1-138-36959-7 (pbk)
ISBN: 978-0-429-42857-9 (ebk)

Typeset in Bembo
by Taylor & Francis Books

CONTENTS

Acknowledgments   *vii*

Introduction: The terms of debate   1
1   Goethe and *Weltliteratur*   16
2   The theory of World Literature   20
3   From World Literature to alternative modernisms   24
4   The cosmopolitanism of the Periphery   35
5   Columbus, *El Nuevo Mundo*, and Postcolonial Studies   40
6   French postcoloniality and *litterature-monde*   51
7   Sibling disciplines: Literary Studies and Cinema Studies   58
8   From literature to film: A study in ambivalence   64
9   The cinema and the World Literature canon   69
10   The gains of (film) translation   75
11   Adaptation, remix, and the cultural commons   84
12   From adaptation to remix   91

13	World cinema: The pre-history	100
14	The theory of World Cinema	103
15	World music and the commons	110
16	Transmedial music in Latin America	119
17	The transnational turn	130
18	Transnational cinema	136
19	The coefficient of transnationality	141
20	Transnational reception, gender, and aesthetics	147
21	Transnational film schools and pedagogy	156
22	Minor cinema, the indigene, and the state	163
23	The rise of the "woods": From Hollywood to Nollywood via Bollywood	169
24	Globalization, political economy, and the media	176
25	Aquatic tropologies	185
26	Technologies of intermedial flow	191
27	Globalization: The mediatic resistance	196
28	Transoceanic currents: The red, black, and white Atlantic	202
29	Global indigeneity and the transnational gaze	208
30	The media's "deep time" and the planetary commons	221
31	The commons and the globalized citizen	226
32	Terminological reflections	230
33	Toward a "trans" methodology	237
Notes		*240*
Index		*260*

ACKNOWLEDGMENTS

Although I have been engaged by the issues raised in this book for a long time, going back to a collection co-edited with Ella Shohat (*Multiculturalism, Postcoloniality, and Transnational Media*, Rutgers 2003), its concrete origins and gestation trace back to its first conceptualization as part of the planning for a conference on "Transnational Cinema/Media Studies" that Ella Shohat and I organized at NYU-Abu Dhabi in 2014. I would like to thank the NYU-Abu Dhabi Institute for sponsoring that Conference, and to thank all of the participants, first the members the organizing committee—Dale Hudson, Sheetal Majithia, Seunghoon Jeung, and Jung Bong Choi, and secondly to all those who came to Abu Dhabi and presented superb papers which enriched our knowledge of the transnational cinema field: Talal Al-Muhanna, Nezar Andary, Dudley Andrew, Shohini Chaudhury, Jean-Paul Colleyn, Amalia Cordova, Armida de la Garza, Thomas Elsaesser, Zoe Graham, Inderpal Grewal, Edward Akintola Hubbard, Dina Iordanova, Lena Jayyusi, Gina Marchetti, David Martin-Jones, Minoo Moallem, Onookome Okome, Surya Parekh, Richard Pena, Sandra Ponzanesi, Arvind Rajagopal, Rasha Salti, Viola Shafiq, Helga Tawil-Souri, Shouleh Vatanbadi, Joao Luiz Vieira, and Zhen Zhang.

I would like to thank those who read the MSS in its entirety or in part, namely: Dale Hudson, Marina Hassapopoulou, Ella Shohat, and the anonymous readers for Routledge, most recently, and earlier for Wiley-Blackwell. As Mikhail Bakhtin and Roland Barthes point out, all writing is hybrid, crowded with the voices and discourses of others. We academics would not survive or hopefully thrive without the support of an imagined and real community of scholars who we see as ideal readers. In this sense, I would like to give a shout out to the following friends, helpers, colleagues, and collaborators: Awam Amkpa, Arjun Appadurai, Finn Brunton, Vincent Carelli, Luiz Antonio Coelho, Marc Cohen, Amalia Cordova, Sérgio Costa, Manthia Diawara, Michael Dinwiddie, Steve Duncombe, Chris Dunn, Patrick Erouart, Arturo Escobar, Marcelo Fiorini, Faye Ginsburg, Inderpal Grewal,

Esther Hamburger, Peter Hulme, Randal Johnson, Caren Kaplan, Jason King, Ivone Margulies, Marc Michael, Surya Parekh, Richard Pena, Mary Louise Pratt, Alessandra Raengo, Jolene Ricard, Renato Rosaldo, Ilda Santos, Werner Sollers, João Luiz Vieira, Robert Young, and Ismail Xavier.

The intellectual conversations promoted by various Centers at NYU have been an endless source of stimulation and inspiration. Here I would like to thank Frederic Viguier from *La Maison Française*; Juan Fernandes, Omar Alejandro Dauhajre, and Ana Dopico at the Juan Carlos of Spain Center, Jill Lane from the Center for Latin American and Caribbean Studies, Culture and History, along with the Comparative Race Studies Group led by Pamela Calla; Diana Taylor and NYU's Hemispheric Institute of Performance and Politics, with its spectacular *encuentros* in Monterrey, Mexico, Lima, Peru, Rio de Janeiro, Brazil, and New York City; and Faye Ginsburg and the exciting events offered at the various Centers that she has founded and directs, such as The Center for Media, Culture and History and the Center for Religion and Media.

I would also like to acknowledge the many institutions and individuals who invited me to address some of the topics discussed here at Conferences or in brief courses or lecture series, and express appreciation for the comments and suggestions made by members of the audiences at such events. Moving from present to past, these include thank yous to Awam Amkpa and Deb Willis for an invitation to present a paper on "Blackness, the Favela, and the Media Spectrum," at the Conference on the Black Mediterreanean at the University of Palermo, Palermo, Italy (June, 2018); Vinzenz Hediger and the Goethe University, Frankfurt Germany for a Keynote for Conference "The Other 1968" at the Museum Angewandte Kunst in Frankfurt (May, 2018); Pamela Calla for her invitation to present "Protocols of Eurocentrism" for the "Comparative Race Study Group" in CLACS (May, 2018); Mark Sandberg for inviting me to lecture at U.C. Berkeley on "The Remixed Avant-Gardes: or How I learned to Stop Worrying and Love You-Tube" (April, 2018); Stefan Solomon and Lucia Nagib for inviting me to form part of a Panel-Presentation on the Tropicalia Movement at the Tate Modern, London (November, 2017); Lucia Nagib for inviting a Keynote Lecture for the Conference on Intermediality at the University of Reading (November 2017); Consuelo Lins and Denilson Lopes for my Lecture Series (in Portuguese) on Aesthetics and Politics in the School of Comunications at Federal University of Rio de Janeiro 2017: (April, 2017); Esther Hamburger for a Lecture Series (in Portuguese) on Aesthetics and Politics in the School of Communications at the University of Sao Paulo (March, 2017); Sergio Costa for inviting me to present "Variations on a Transatlantic Theme" as opening Lecture for the series "Minor Cosmopolitanisms"; and for Conducting a Graduate seminar with the Minor Cosmopolitanisms Research Training Group, University of Potsdam, Potsdam, Germany, October 28, 2016, as well as for inviting Ella Shohat and myself to participate in a book launch panel on the occasion of the German translation of *Race in Translation* at the Freie Universität Berlin, Germany (October 27, 2016); Messias Bandeira for inviting me to offer a Lecture Series (in Portuguese) on Alternative Media at the School of

Communications at the Federal University of Bahia, Brazil (June, 2015); Ismail Xavier, Christian Borges, and Esther Hamburger an invitation to present a Lecture Series (in Portuguese) on "Aesthetics and Politics" at the School of Communications at the University of Sao Paulo (June, 2014); Ilda Santos for inviting me to offer a Lecture in Portuguese on the "Lusophone Red Atlantic" at the Sorbonne Nouvelle, Paris III (April, 2012); Shannon Welles-Lassagne and Ariane Hudelet for an invitation to give a lecture on "Transmutations of Adaptation" at the Third International Conference on Film Adaptation, University of Bretagne, France (June, 2011) which subsequently became part of their collection *Screening Text:*

Critical Perspectives on Film Adaptation (London: McFarland, 2013); Dora Baras for suggesting a keynote on subversive aesthetics at the Subversive Film Festival in Zaghreb, Croatia (May, 2011); Professor Bravo and Denilson Lopes for an invitation keynote lecture on "Carandiru and the Discursive/Mediatic Spectrum" at the "Recoveries of the Real" conference in NYU Buenos Aires (June, 2010); Joao Luiz Vieira for an invitation to offer a lecture on "Theory and Practice of Adaptation" lecture at Federal University Niteroi, Brazil (May, 2010). Other invitations include a lecture on "The Red Atlantic" at the *Casa de Saber* in Rio de Janeiro (May, 2009); a presentation on "The Red Atlantic: Tupi Theory and the Franco-Brazilian-Indigenous Dialogue" at the Shelby Cullom Davis Center, Princeton University (April, 2009); keynote at the "Adapting America/America Adapted" conference, Bogazici University, Istanbul (2008); thanks to Jacques Aumont and Phillippe Dubois for an invitation to offer a series of lectures in French at la Sorbonne Nouvelle (Paris III) concerning "Literature and Cinema" (October–December, 2008); Caroline Cappucin for an invitation for a lecture in French on "Critical Representations of First Contact" at *L'Institut d'Amerique Latine* in Paris (November, 2008); Armida de la Garza for an invitation to give a keynote lecture on "Globalization and Aesthetics from Below" at the "Asia and Latin America Conference" in Puebla, Mexico (August, 2008); and Deane Williams for an invitation to give a lecture on "The Aesthetics of Brazilian Documentary" at Monash University, Melbourne, Australia (June, 2008); Manuela Ribeiro Sanchez for the invitation to give a keynote "Tupi or not Tupi a Tupi Theorist" at the "Europe in Black and White" conference, University of Lisbon (May, 2008). Finally, my thanks to Armida de la Garza for her invitation to give three Lectures—"Literature and Adaptation," "Brazilian Modernism" and "Politics and Aesthetics" at Nottingham University in Ningbo, China (November, 2006).

Although most of the material in the book is new, it does inevitably revisit earlier work, as noted in the end notes, but almost freshly milled, within new frames, with new inflections and changes in emphasis, in relation to altered landscapes and morphing issues and discourses. (I have noted most of these "revisits" in the endnotes). The material on the asymmetrical power relations between Global North and Global South revisits some of the issues raised in a different way in *Unthinking Eurocentrism: Multiculturalism and the Media* (Routledge, 1994) but now from the perspective of 2018 and in relation to World Literature, Transnational Cinema, and Global Media. The material on filmic adaptations of novels revisits concepts and texts elaborated in *Literature through Film: Realism, Magic, and the Art of Adaptation*, but this time in relation to David Damrosch's stipulations about precisely what constitutes World Literature. The section on Francophone Literature builds on and modifies and supplements an essay (with Ella Shohat) "Postcolonial Studies and France," published in *Interventions* (Spring, 2012) and subsequently included in *Race in Translation: Culture Wars in the Postcolonial Atlantic*. The material on Isaac Julien's film on Franz Fanon borrows from my "Fanon, Algeria, and the Cinema: The Politics of Identification" in Shohat/ Stam eds. *Multiculturalism, Postcoloniality and Transnational Media* (the Depth of Field Series, Rutgers University Press, 2003). Some of the material on revisionist adaptations formed part, but with differences, of an essay entitled "Revisionist Adaptation: Transtextuality, Cross-Cultural Dialogism, and Performative Infidelities," included in Thomas Leitch, ed., *The Oxford Handbook of Adaptation Studies* (Oxford, 2017). Some of the material on the Red Atlantic and indigenous thought appeared in very different form in the essay "The Red Atlantic Dialogue: Response 1" (with Ella Shohat), our dialogue with the 10th Anniversary edition of Sandy Grande's seminal book *Red Pedagogy: Native American Social and Political Thought* (Rowman & Littlefield Publishers, 2015).

I am also grateful for the help of various assistants over the period of gestation, notably Sally Weathers, Jennifer Kelly, and Benjamin Min Han, along with the indispensable technical assistance I have received at various stages from a digital genius named Joseph Modirzadeh. I would like to express my appreciation, finally, for the warm, gracious, and extremely efficient work of Routledge editor Natalie Foster and editorial assistant Jennifer Vennall.

I would like to thank Reindert Falkenberg, Gila Waels, and Nora Yousif at the NYU-Abu Dhabi Institute.

INTRODUCTION

The terms of debate

At this point in the history and theory of the arts, terms like "World Literature," "Transnational Cinema," and "Global Media," along with their myriad permutations (World Cinema, World Music, Global Film, Global Art Film, Transnational Literature, Transnational Media and so forth), and their minoritarian variations (exilic, diasporic, minor, peripheral, hybrid, accented, indigenous) have proliferated in literature, film, and media studies. They have become baggy-monster concepts, signifying too much and too little. As sliding signifiers, they share partially overlapping referents but also carry distinct cultural associations and disparate discursive histories. The terms differ widely in their genealogies, their disciplinary affiliations, and their political affect. Each carries its own historical freight and intertextual baggage; each coaxes us in specific directions.

This book explores the genealogies and vocabularies, and to some extent the actual scholarship, orienting a number of neighboring artistic and mediatic fields that to some extent share their objects of study and their methods of interpretation, yet rarely speak to or learn from one another. My goal, therefore, is to orchestrate a complexly layered conversation, a kind of polylogue, between arts, disciplines, discourses and media. Through a transdisciplinary map of the changing lexicon of the three cognate fields (and four if we include my excursus on World Music), I hope to multiply and enrich perspectives on the academic study of world/transnational/global literature, cinema, and media as they move through and across all kinds of borders—spatial, temporal, disciplinary, political, cultural, and theoretical.

But beyond mapping the fields, I hope to perform the concept of border-crossing itself through a kind of recombinant choreography of trans-disciplines. Crossing borders always entails anxiety because it means leaving the comfort zones of communities, and nations, and disciplines. But crossing borders can generate transformation, just as arts, media, and disciplines can transform one another. Resnais' art documentaries like *Guernica*, for example, transform Picasso's painting through film.

Through a theorized practice of mutual embeddedness and impact, I hope to explore the rhizomatic interfaces across arts, media, and disciplines, to suggest that they are invested in one another, that literature is "in" the cinema (and vice versa), that philosophy is "in" literature, and that music and cinema are "in bed with" all the other arts in what can become a fruitful *ménage à mille*. The arts and the disciplines intermingle, as in the following passage from John Dunham Peters: "Music and astronomy concern the heavens, and arithmetic and geometry the earth, and arithmetic is the foundation of music as geometry is of astronomy … Arithmetic and astronomy study the eternal, and music and geometry the perishable."[1] Any art can serve as a gateway drug into the ecstasies of the other arts and the *jouissance* of their intercourse. More broadly, time and space are chronotopically mingled; the past is in the present (and vice versa), the transnational is in the national (and vice versa), the Global South is in the Global North, and so forth.

This text is "transartistic" in that it treats a number of arts—literature, cinema, and music. But this "trans-artistry" is also part of the individual arts. Cinema as a medium, for example, is inherently transartistic, in that the audio-visual media have the tremendous advantage of being multi-track, consisting, at least prior to the advent of the digital, in Christian Metz' "five tracks," each of which makes potentially available the arts affiliated with that track: the music track potentially inherits the entire history of music; the image track embeds and rearticulates the history of visual representation and the pictorial arts; the sound track absorbs the history of theater, speech and performance, and so forth. All media, in this sense, have been endlessly enriched by their dialogue with all the other arts. In this sense, film has a millennial rather than a single-century history, since it inherits all the temporal arts (music, narration, etc.) and spatial arts (painting, photography) not only within but also across national traditions. Digital media expand these possibilities exponentially, since they facilitate and even encourage the combination of arts and media into new configurations. Indeed, 21st-century arts and culture offer a form of "deep Remixability" (Lev Manovich), whereby digital environments become the hosts not only all the arts but also of all formats and styles, resulting in a systematic hybridization. Instead of the classical "five tracks" of cinema, we find an infinite *combinatoire* of "variables" susceptible to infinite juxtapositions, interfaces, and cross-fertilizations, whereby a variety of aural and visual materials—live action, motion graphics, musical performance, archival footage, computer animation, composited images—can be woven together in a continuous constantly mutating flow.

I will begin with a few caveats.

First, the book does not claim an impossible "coverage" of a corpus, e.g. a survey of all the relevant World Literature or Transnational Cinema films and texts. Rather than a survey, the book is at once a metacritical mapping of fields, a personal and at times speculative essay, and an overview of the kind of work performed under the various rubrics. This is not a book that will tell you about "everything that is happening in World Literature or World Cinema," but I hope it will tell you something about the relations between those fields and the theories that underlie them.[2] Rather than an exhaustive treatment of the three titular topics the book is a meditation on the relations between them.

Second, my analyses of specific texts are not all-encompassing; they only serve to illustrate or illuminate the issues outlined in the introduction.

Third, our key terms and the fields they designate are not easily isolatable from one another. The projects implied by the terms "World," "Transnational," and "Global" all share, for example, a desire to transcend the nation-state as the taken-for-granted unit of analysis. Books on World Cinema/Literature, Transnational Cinema/Literature, and Global Cinema/Literature sometimes cover much of the same ground. Although a Venn diagram of their fields of reference would show substantial overlap, the very point is to go beyond the typical segregation of disciplines by insisting on their family resemblances and differentiated commonalities.

Fourth, the key terms discussed are analytical and post facto rather than professional; i.e. they were coined by academics rather than by arts and media practitioners. Thomas Elsaesser's observation that directors do not "set out to make World Cinema ... it is a label given to a film by someone else ..."—applies equally to the "transnational" and "global."[3]

Fifth, the terms do not refer to intrinsic properties or essences belonging to the objects studied. It is not a question of proving that a given film should be labeled "transnational" or "global"; the same film could be seen simultaneously as "global" in one dimension, "transnational" in another, and "worlded" in still another. The debate is not about correct labels but about the productivity of the concepts and grids.

Sixth, the meanings and reach of the terms vary widely depending on national, academic, and disciplinary entanglements. Different constituencies invest the terms with distinct hopes, desires, and fears. The words reverberate differently for different hearers in different parts of the world. As situated, conjunctural utterances, their political valence varies with historical context, political-economic conjuncture, and the psycho-social investments of those deploying the term.

Threaded throughout the book are a number of recurring issues and debates. First, all the terms, and the projects associated with them, are shaped by developments of late capitalism summed up in the word "globalization." This massively complex phenomenon might be summed up as a process of acceleration and intensification of previously existing trends, intensifying cross-border exchanges of all kinds, whether of goods, people, capital, services, information, or ideas. "Globalization" serves as a metonym for a polyvalent historical moment characterized by a number of related trends: the collapse of Communism, flexible accumulation, financialization, privatization, market idolatry, austerity programs, time-space compression, and the spread across borders of unequal economic conditions.

Although globalization is the long-term product of millennia of historical change, some key "recent" dates in this process might include: 1976 and the Nixon-managed Jamaica Accords that led to the abandonment of the postwar Bretton Woods protocols of financial exchange; 1978 and the economic opening toward China; 1979–1980 and the Reagan/Thatcher-led wave of privatizations; 1989–1992 and the end of the Cold War and of the Soviet Union, in tandem with the invention of the World Wide Web; 1999 and the anti-globalization protests in Seattle; 2001 and the World Trade Center attack as opening up a period of asymmetrical warfare and terrorism; 2007–2009 and the "subprime" financial crisis and a narrowly averted freeze of the economy, "saved" through massive aide to the "too-big-to-fail" banks; 2017 to the present, with the rise, in many countries, of Marine le Pen-style or Trump-style nativism, white-backlash *ressentiment*, and what is looking ominously like a kind of "Global Weimar" moment.[4]

The key actors within globalization, meanwhile, are the transnational corporations, the manipulators of financial markets, pension funds, hedge funds, central banks, rating agencies like Standard and Poor; global enterprises like McDonald's and Big Oil; international fora like the G20 and G8; international economic institutions like the IMF, the World Bank, and the WTO; globally dispersed media such as CNN, BBC, Murdoch, Disney, Time Warner; the new media corporations like Apple, Google, Samsung, Amazon; and NGOs like Amnesty International, Greenpeace, and Doctors without Borders; along with mobile elites (tourists, international students) and the equally mobile subalterns (refugees, migrants) and criminal perpetrators (terrorists, scam artists).[5]

In popular and mass-cultural terms, globalization evokes the intensified interconnectivities implied by the Internet, Social Media, Facebook, Hollywood blockbusters, along with low-cost air travel, smartphones, and Starbucks. What one thinks of globalization partially has to do with what one thinks of these phenomena and whether a person or group sees itself as a winner or loser within the new globalized world order. Schematically speaking, the ordinary "winners" would include all those who enjoy any of the phenomena listed above and especially the technical "goodies" afforded by the Internet and all it has brought in terms of easier contact between individuals and peoples. Globalization also brings prosperity in certain parts of the world and for certain sectors of their population, along with the digital revolution and all it has brought in terms of easier contact between individuals and peoples and so forth. At the same time globalization has brought immiseration, ecological disaster, identity-theft, and the digital divide in ways that disproportionately disadvantage the Global South and minorities in the Global North.

The most powerful financial winners are transnational corporations and the very rich (the 1% within the 1%) and all those who enjoy the power of ownership over resources of all types which allows them to take full advantage of the newly freed flows of capital and information. This privileged group includes the countries of the historically advantaged West, followed by those countries like the Gulf States and Singapore that have "sovereign funds; then the "Asian Tigers," and slightly lower on the scale, certain Global South countries with "emerging markets" like the BRICS countries (Brazil, Russia, India, China, South Africa), and to a lesser extent the MIST countries (Mexico, Indonesia, South Korea, Turkey). The victims of globalization, meanwhile, include the resource-poor nations of Africa and Asia, exploited and manipulated by debt and IMF austerity programs, the indigenous peoples threatened by ecological devastation and loss of land, along with all those raced, gendered, and classed minorities surviving within the richer countries but condemned to lives of poverty and social ostracism. Those at the top of the world's food chain control the resources and networks of the global system while those at the bottom experience the collateral damage of exclusion, unemployment, and impoverishment. At the same time, the consequences of these very same global privatizing forces have triggered a global collaborative response in terms of such diverse issues as climate change, financial regulation, and pandemic illnesses.

Globalization in its dominant form goes hand in hand with neo-liberal ideology and the Thatcherite-Reaganite version of this ideology, embodied in a savage capitalism that combines, as Naomi Klein puts it, "privatization of the public sphere [and] deregulation of the corporate sphere."[6] Neo-liberal policies reinforce global inequalities by redistributing wealth toward the top. These globalized conditions are widely shared but lived unevenly by those, in Zizek's words, "who circulate capital" as opposed to those whom "capital circulates,"[7] or in more colloquial language, the difference between "those who make money, and those whose money makes money." The perennial struggles between Capital and Labor have now morphed into the battle between the too-big-to-fail banks and the too-likely to-fail individuals mired in debt (Deleuze's "dividuals"). Updated for the digital age and the concomitant "virtualization" of economic exchange, the social gap becomes that between those who tell computers what to do by dictating their algorithms, and those who are told by computers what to do, those who write the codes and those that obey them.

A second concern in this text is to see all the arts and media not in temporally provincial "presentist" ways but rather within the *longue durée* of "deep time." Shallow ahistorical analyses of globalization, for example, treat it as a recent phenomenon rather than a longstanding trend. Exactly when globalization began remains an open question. Andre Gunder Frank and Barry Gills formulated the question in the title of their 1993 volume "*World System: 500 Years or 5000?* Armand Mattelart, in *Histoire de L'Utopie Planétaire; De la Cité Prophétique à la Societe Globale*, answers the question by tracing the global back to earlier and earlier incarnations of empire, from the 20th century's Pax Americana, back to the 19th centuries Pax Britannica, to the 15th century's Pax Iberica, back to the Pax Romana and the earlier Alexandrine Greek hegemony. Amartya Sen, reversing the usual directionalities of knowledge, traces globalization back to the year 1000 and a process of the circulation of science that moved not from West to East but rather from East to West.[8]

Moving even further back into the past, analysts have deployed geological and archeological tropes of "deep media." For John Durham Peters, contemporary media, understood very broadly as the means by which meaning is communicated, are layered over unrecognized forms of media that carry meaning but do not speak as such. Poet John Keats discerned "huge cloudy symbols of a high romance" by reading the "night's starred face." The ancient trope of the world-as-a-book, similarly, suggests that the world itself conveys meaning. Present-day media, in this very broad sense, embed ancient forms. As Peters puts it:

> Digital media resurrect old media such as writing, addresses, numbers, calendars, timekeepers, maps, and money. They give life to age-old practices such

as navigating, cultivating, stargazing, weather forecasting, documenting, and fishing ...[9]

Digital media, in this sense, "revive ancient navigational functions; they point us in time and space, index our data, and keep us on the grid."[10] Peters warns us that we should never talk as if media are a recent invention dating back only a century or two. For a long time, the word "medium" suggested an element (like water) or an environment, or a vehicle. But even before civilization, "humans had media such as graves, baskets, stars, families and fire."[11]

The subtitle of Siegfried Zielinski's *Deep Time of the Media* reads: "*Toward an Archaeology of Hearing and Seeing by Mechanical Means.*"[12] The goal is to "dig out" the deeper strata of the media in such a way as to include early geological time from its "beginnings" on up to the contemporary instrumentalization of the sky itself for "signal traffic," where space junk becomes a mobile geological stratum orbiting around our planet. Media archeologists, in the words of Erkki Huhtamo and Jussi Parikka, have "begun to construct alternate histories of suppressed, neglected, and forgotten media that do not point teleologically to the present media-cultural condition as their "perfection."[13] Some historically aborted technologies or "dead media" are evoked in the classics of World Literature, as when William Power, in *Hamlet's Blackberry*, compares the erasable "writer's tables" in Shakespeare—"... from the table of my memory/I'll wipe away all trivial fond records"—to contemporary tablets and smartphones.[14]

Bruce Sterling and Richard Kadrey's "Dead Media Project," for its part, aims to use the Internet to catalog and study extinct forms of human communication, much as scientists study fossils to discern extinct forms of animate life. Sterling mentions the *quipus* of the Inca in pre-Columbia Peru, i.e. color-coded fabrics used as accounting devices (for example for the census) and historical record. The Spanish conquistadores tried to destroy the memory of the *quipus* by condemning them to be burned at the Council of Lima in 1583, yet roughly 400 survived the Spanish onslaught.[15] Recently, in a case of what might be called "archaic digitalization," these ancient forms of communication have been resurrected in "the Quipu Project," an interactive documentary and web interface concerned with women and men who were sterilized in Peru in the mid-1990s. The site enables voices from these marginalized communities to be heard and responded to anywhere in the world.

Scholars such as Zielinski have also challenged the notion of a linear progression of technological advancement leading inexorably toward the present-day configuration of global media, privileging instead a history of unanticipated interruptions, false starts, unexpected detours, dynamic spurts, and illusory turning points. In *A Geology of Media*, Jussi Parikka envisions the media through geology as

> the science about the ground beneath our feet, its history and constitution, the systematic study of the various levers, layers, strata, and interconnections that define the earth ... [foregrounding] the importance of the nonorganic in

constructing media before they become media: the literal deep times and deep places of media in mines and rare earth minerals.[16]

In an extremely long view, some scholars trace the "global" even farther back, to the history of the planet itself, in a revisionist temporality that would reduce the Annales school *longue durée* to a mere instant in time, whereby nations and nation-states would come to seem like very recent and ephemeral phenomena. We could even trace global movements and migrations back to the tectonic plate movements that created the "continental drift" that fractured Pangaea, when the earth consisted of a single land mass, and sent earthworms, animals, and proto-human beings scrambling around the earth's surface.[17]

A third commonality of the fields discussed here is that they are all shaped by the uneven power relations between the Global North and the Global South, relations informed, as a discursive corollary, by Westocentric assumptions and the resistance to them. This book distances itself from Eurocentrism in the various disciplines. Despite a common misunderstanding, *Eurocentrism* does not refer to Europe in its literal sense as a continent or a geopolitical unit but rather to an intellectual orientation rooted in colonial power, to a kind of political Unconscious, an interlocking network of buried premises, embedded narratives, and submerged tropes which construct Europe (and the Neo-Europes spread around the world like the U.S. and Australia) as universally normative. The problem, in short, is not the "Europe"—at this moment a relative haven of liberal democracy and tolerance—but rather the "Centrism." In fact the term "Eurocentrism" in a sense misleads since it stipulates a geographical locus for a discourse which now permeates much of the globe; it could equally well be called "coloniality" (Anibal Quijano), or "occidentosis" (Jalal al Ahmad) or "European planetary consciousness" (Mary Louise Pratt), or "the colonial mindset," or "Euro-hegemonism" or "Western hegemony," or "occidental worldview,"[18] Cherokee author Thomas King calls it the "unexamined confidence in Western civilization."[19] For the coloniality/modernity project of Arturo Escobar, Enrique Dussel, Ramon Grossfuguel, Santiago Slabodsky, and Walter Mignolo, coloniality forms the inseparable dark side of modernity, just as postcoloniality forms the dark side of postmodernity.

Global North-centered economic history in the Weberian tradition attributes the West's spectacular success to its ethical probity and enterprising spirit, forgetting that European advantages in many ways derived from the wealth that flowed to Europe from the Americas and from other colonized regions. Jason W. Moore speaks of the easy availability to Western powers of the "Four Cheaps" that facilitated Western domination—labor, food, energy, and raw materials.[20] In its various discursive iterations—mercantilism, free-trade imperialism, laissez-faire capitalism, modernization take-off theory, and neo-liberal globalization—metrocentric political economy develops a diffusionist "trickle-down" economics on a global scale. Just as wealth supposedly trickles down from rich to poor *within* nation-states, so the wealth of the Global North, thanks to "free trade" and Western investment, is imagined as trickling down from the North to irrigate and fertilize the Global

South with the fecundating manure of investment. European progress is seen as self-generated, autonomous, unrelated to the appropriation of wealth or ideas from the formerly colonized regions, while investment-based progress in those regions is seen as an altruistic gift from Europe. The North is seen as the Creditor, and the South the Debtor, as if the North owes nothing to the South. Westocentric economic history does not acknowledge that this unidirectional narrative can be reversed, that the West can be seen as indebted in the sense of owing its own prosperity to the precious metals, fertile land, and the enslaved and indentured labor provided by the non-West.

The verbal skirmishes triggered by identity politics, Affirmative Action, the canon, multiculturalism, anti-imperialism and anti-globalization and the like, as Ella Shohat and I argued in *Race in Translation*, are but the surface ripples of a deeper oceanic struggle to decolonize power structures and epistemologies constructed over centuries.[21] If in one sense the culture wars emerged in the post–World War II period, in a much longer view they participated in the five-century process by which the European powers reached positions of economic, military, political, and cultural hegemony in much of Asia, Africa, and the Americas. Some of the major corollaries of this colonial process were the massive expropriation of territory; the large-scale destruction of indigenous peoples and cultures; the enslavement of indigenous Americans and Africans; and racism within the colonized world and within the West itself. Although resistance to colonialism has existed since the very beginnings of colonization, that resistance reached critical mass in the post–World War II period, generating the paradigm shift in scholarship that contested Eurocentric narrativizations of history, established racial hierarchies, and canonical modes of knowledge production.

All of the academic and artistic trends addressed here—World Literature, World Cinema, Transnational Cinema, and Global Media—have been impacted directly or indirectly by key 20th-century events—World War II, the Jewish Holocaust, and Third World decolonization—which conjoined to relativize the West as axiomatic center of reference and to affirm the rights of non-European peoples emerging from the yoke of colonialism. Although resistance to colonialism has existed since the very beginnings of colonization, this resistance reached critical mass in the postwar period. In the wake of centuries of struggles, decolonization achieved climactic expression with Indian independence in 1947, the Chinese revolution in 1949, Algerian independence in 1962, up through the independence of Mozambique and Angola in the mid-1970s. If Nazism, fascism, and the Holocaust revealed in all their horror the "internal" sickness of Europe as a site of racism and totalitarianism, Third World liberation struggles revealed the "external" revolt against Western domination, provoking a crisis in the taken-for-granted narrative of European-led Progress. Just as newly independent Third World nations tried to free themselves from colonial subordination, so First World minorities challenged the white-supremacist protocols of their own societies. The present-day white backlash suggests that many of these protocols have not disappeared and constantly resurface and risk becoming hegemonic.

World Literature, World Cinema, and World Music, along with Transnational Cinema and Global Media, have also been impacted, albeit unevenly, by what Ella Shohat and I have referred to as the postwar "seismic shift" in political and intellectual life.[22] The seismic shift brought to the surface the tensions inherent in centuries of literal and discursive struggle. Western Europe, Latin America, and North America all had their anti-imperialist, anticapitalist, antiracist, antisexist, and antiauthoritarian movements. Such projects were not only allied metaphorically but also concretely linked in transnational networks of activism. The movements varied in their emphases, however, depending on whether they took place in the formerly imperial and authoritarian France of de Gaulle, or in a neocolonized Latin America oppressed by U.S.-supported dictatorships, or in what José Martí called the "Belly of the Beast" (the United States). In France, the vociferously Third Worldist May '68 movement offered its support to revolutions (in China, Vietnam, Cuba, Algeria, Cuba) and to minority U.S. "internal colony" movements such as the Black Panthers, the American Indian Movement, and the Young Lords, seeing them as partial models for First World revolutionaries. A "tricontinental" united front combined a left-tinged revolutionism with an ardent anticolonialism. It was also in this postwar period that Global South intellectuals influenced by dependency theory, especially in Latin America, began to speak of their nations as "dependent," "peripheral," and "neocolonized." Dependency Theory generated widely read and similarly titled books like Walter Rodney's *How Europe Underdeveloped Africa*, Eduardo Galeano's *The Open Veins of Latin America*, and Manning Marable's *How Capitalism Underdeveloped Black America*.

The earlier Third Worldist and tricontinental movements, and the later critical race, multicultural, ethnic studies, and postcolonial studies form the conceptual infrastructure of the seismic shift. Many scholars began to rethink their disciplines in terms of the global changes triggered by decolonization and by minority struggles, in ways that have massively impacted the study of literature, cinema, and the media. Disciplines in which the West was assumed to be both the speaking subject and the object of study were subjected to critique and perspectival shifts. Critical and even insurgent proposals were expressed in recombinatory coinages such as "third world literature," "third world cinema" "revisionist history," "critical law," "radical philosophy," "reflexive anthropology," and "critical pedagogy,"—where the qualifiers suggested a reconceptualization of a canonical discipline from the periphery and from below. The thrust was doubly critical, first of the *presence* of Eurocentric perspectives and second of the *absence* of non-European and nonwhite faculty, students, perspectives, and cultural topics. Decolonizing projects called for more inclusionary educational systems, more culturally diverse political representation, more racially equitable justice systems, and greater indigenous, immigrant, gay, lesbian and women's rights (which later morphed into LGBQT+). In national terms, the goal was to create egalitarian social formations, where the state was not dominated by a single ethnicity but rather represented the totality of its citizens, all with an equal claim to both recognition and redistribution. This inevitably meant taking into account the historical practices that had generated the structural inequalities in the first place.

Many disciplines, in a later iteration of this decolonizing process, took a strong "multicultural turn" in the late 1980s, followed by a strong "transnational" turn in the 1990s. Within American Studies, for example, scholars questioned the American exceptionalist Anglo-normativity that had informed the field, calling attention to U.S.-based literature written (or spoken) in languages other than English, including in indigenous languages, and exposing the imperialist (and anti-imperialist) undercurrents even in the canonical texts of Melville, Thoreau, and Twain.

A fourth throughline in the book has to do with the ways that our conceptualizations of "World," "the Transnational," and the "Global" are figured through the metaphors, whether conscious or unconscious, that quietly undergird and shape and "orient" our thinking. Rather than the "metaphors we live by" (George Lakoff), I have in mind the "metaphors we think through," or better, the figurative constellations and apparati that "think us," even without our realizing it. In this sense, I will be concerned with the tropologies of analysis. Given that metaphor can serve as a cognitive instrument, a producer of knowledge, our collective project as scholars consists on one level in a quest for the most finely tuned and productive metaphors to illuminate the subjects at hand. What are the political and intellectual implications of such metaphors? The literature on engaged in this book offers a veritable constellation of tropes, both explicit and implicit. Recent scholarship has been inundated, as it were, by acquatic metaphors— "global flows" (Appadurai), liquid modernity (Bauman), "circum-Atlantic performance" (Joe Roach), "tidalectics" (Kamau Brathwaite), "media archipelagos" (Joshua Neves) "piracy" (Sandar Baskhar), and of course the "Black Atlantic" (Robert Farris Thompson, Paul Gilroy)—giving expression to a poetics of flows and eddies and currents. The metaphors themselves, as we shall see later, become symbolic dissolvents of borders and stratifications, part of a search for a more fluid and egalitarian language of analysis.

The transnational and global literature, according to Jung Bong Choi, displays a polarity opposing two kinds of tropes; a negative pole emphasizes metaphors tied to stasis, land, territory, roots, enclosure, boundaries, restricted spaces (barbed wire, fences, trees, homestead, hermetic dealing, isolation, ghettos). This family of negatively connoted tropes tends to be associated with stigmatized abstractions such as essentialism, binarism, inertia, nationalism, tradition, and so forth. The other, more positive pole, entails metaphors of connection and mobility—water, routes, waves, interfaces, connectivities, attractions, liaisons, transits, diasporas, switchboards and networks, and movement across boundaries, all associated with freedom, openness, routes, and convivial intersubjectivity. I would add a third more reflexive type of trope to Choi's schema, having to do with the "meta"-perspectival tropes which evoke the theories and concepts through which we perceive our object of study, whence the omnipresence of optical-conceptual tropes like prisms, grids, modes, lenses, optics, windows, maps, perspectives, standpoints, parallax views, ways of seeing, polyperspectivalism, and so forth.[23] Indeed, for Friedrich Kittler, media studies was not an object-oriented field but rather a "way-of-seeing" field.[24] And for John Durham Peters, "all media are active metaphors in their power to translate experience into new forms."[25]

The metaphorics of writing about these issues also relay a flexible political— aesthetic attitude and rhetoric very much open to ambiguity and contradiction. Since it is difficult to posit a single political drift or valence to something as multi- faceted as globalization, for example, analysts appeal to rhetorical figures of con- tradiction as a way of acknowledging its contradictory effects. The oxymoron, for example, fuses opposite affects and tendencies, resulting in coinages such as "glocal" or paradoxical phrases such as "local cosmopolitanism," "complicitous critique" (Meeghan Morris), and "antagonistic mutuality" (Thomas Elsaesser). One of the foundational oxymorons of media studies as a field, coined already in the 1960s was, of course, McLuhan's "global village" with its linkage of small-scale community with global reach. Globalization discourse also favors antinomies, the term used in Kantian logic and epistemology to explain the unavoidable tension between what is rationally true and what is empirically experienced; e.g., "time is infinite and time has a beginning" or "human beings are both free and deter- mined." Given its contradictory effects and interpretations, as we shall see later, globalization analyses often deploy tropes that evoke the paradoxical simultaneity of apparently opposite trends and effects, for example that globalization engenders both homogenization and differentiation, nativism and globalism, gregarious con- viviality and sadistic trolling.

Many tropes maintain a zone of ambiguity, as when Joshua Neves and Bhaskar Sarkar, in the context of Asian video culture, speak of the "penumbra of the global" with its dusky connotations of a semi-dark belt created by eclipses and with the "magical figurations of Hindu mythology."[26] Such troubled metaphorics become a way, for these authors, of upsetting pseudo-universal "grids of intellig- ibility" derived largely from "Anglo-US and continental European contexts and protocols."[27] Such figures emphasize the contradictory, the ambiguous, and the dissensual even while they cut through rigid polarities to reveal subterranean affi- niities and "linked analogies" connecting disparate poles and spaces. At the same time, Bakhtinian terms such as *dialogism, polyglossia, pluristylism, heteroglossia, chron- otopes, exotopy*, and *excess seeing* stress pluralistic heterogeneity and the mutual illu- mination (and relativization) of cultures. Deleuzian terms such as *rhizome, molecular, becoming other*, similarly, show a systematic option for the plural, the relational, the mutating, and the transformational, fostering an openness to multiple, Enlighte- ments, modernities, and cosmopolitanisms.

A fifth throughline threaded through the book is the issue of artistic and mediatic specificity and methodological self-awareness. At various points, I will conduct what linguists call "commutation tests," in reference to the procedure developed by the Prague School linguists, whereby the analyst examines the ways that changes in the signifier trigger changes in the signified. Substituting a dif- ferent art for "literature" within the World Art paradigm, for example, triggers linguistic alterations. While it seems meaningful to speak of "transnational fund- ing," it would seem non-sensical to speak of "World Funding," since the World as such does not fund films, or to speak of "postcolonial funding," since post- coloniality is a critical concept and not a funding agency. Of the three keywords, only "transnational"—transnational literature, transnational cinema/television, transnational media—seems appropriate to virtually all of the cases. There are reasons, I hope to show, why specific rubrics and prefixes work for some media but not for others, but that is to get ahead of our story.

A sixth throughline revolves around the idea of the Commons. At once archly traditional and hyper-contemporary, the root-metaphor of the "commons" has appealingly multiple resonances, evoking everything from ancient patterns of communal land ownership– what Percy Bysshe Shelley called the "equal participation in the commonage of nature"—to the contemporary digital commons of the "copy left" movements. The notion of commonly held land forms a social norm shared by diverse social formations ranging from the 13th century England of the "Great Charter of the Forest" to the longstanding social systems of countless indigenous peoples. The term evokes a cornucopia of socio-political ideals –Tom Payne's "Common Sense," Marx's "primitive Communism," the "Boston Commons," the "Common Wealth," the "common people," the Paris Commune, the "Creative Commons," and the indigenous "common pot." The commons is not composed of dead "things" or "resources" but rather of social relations of cooperation and solidarity. Vesting property in the community and emphasizing the collective dimension of ownership, the commons evokes "communism," but without its Stalinist baggage, and "socialism," without the bloodless social-democratism that so easily turns it into capitalism-with-a-human-face.[28] The *commons* counters the individualist, capitalist fetishizing of exclusive proprietary rights that fuels the corporate drive to privatize everything from Amazonian bio-diversity and Bolivian water to the beats of Hip-Hop and the lyrics of "Happy Birthday." It also counters the "dark money" that soils American politics. Two brothers inherit a fortune based on oil-wealth and now, thanks to the Citizens United decision by the Supreme Court, play a decisive role in American politics, able to infuse any campaign with money or sponsor ads of dubious origin. To paraphrase an Indian nationalist song provoked by the British colonial take-over of the *dharma khandams*, or community commonlands:

> He claims all the oil is his
> Did his father create the oil?[29]

Currently proliferating in the writing of figures as diverse as Naomi Klein, Slavoj Zizek, Vandana Shiva, Elinor Ostrom, David Graeber, David Harvey, and Peter Linebaugh, the term *"the commons"* reflects a growing tendency, since the 1990s, to haunt privatizing neo-liberalism through the specter of egalitarian communalism. Linebaugh calls the commons the "red thread" joining centuries of class struggles.[30] The *commons* evokes resistance to "enclosure" in all its forms, whether in its early proto-capitalist form of fencing in commonly shared land, or in its contemporary forms of marshalling judicial restraints such as "patent" and "intellectual property" to police the ownership of ideas. As the antithesis of the commons, Enclosure is often a form of thievery which criminalizes the commons. Linebaugh cites an anonymous English poem which tells the story:

> The law locks up the man or woman
> Who steals the goose from off the common
> But lets the greater villain loose
> Who steals the common from the goose.[31]

In the wake of the fall of Communism and the crisis of Capitalism, the "*commons*" evokes the planetary struggle to reclaim the "common wealth." Public parks, in this sense, form leafy vestiges of the traditional forest commons. For Michael Hardt and Antonio Negri, the "common is not only the earth we share but also the languages we create, the social practices we establish, [and] the modes of sociality that define our relationships ..."[32] For Jacques Rancière, "politics is the sphere of activity of a *common* that can only ever be contentious."[33]

The trope of the commons is highly relevant to our three major categories. First, World Literature and World Cinema form part of the broad, uncopyrighted commonwealth of human artistic intelligence that we have called the "cultural commons." When John Keats wrote "When I have fears that I may cease to be / *before my pen has glean'd my teeming brain* ..." [italics mine] he was alluding to the gleaning of the Forest Commons referred to in the "English Charter of the Forest" (the companion document to the *Magna Carta* in 1217). The idea of the commons is transnational in that it is a broad social concept that forms part of the genealogy of most human societies rooted in common land, and one that is also potentially (albeit unevenly) theoretically available to all societies.[34] In this text, I will explore variations on the commons theme—the natural commons, the cultural commons, the intellectual commons, the digital commons, the political commons and so forth.

Finally the debates revolve around what Benjamin Peters calls "terminological technologies."[35] Language, we know, is not a transparent medium; it is the very material with which we constitute our worlds. Language is immersed in history and politics, and specific words can become depleted or be revived for new uses. Terminology, as Armand Mattelart puts it, forms a "terrain of struggle between groups and classes, development projects, and societies."[36] The terms point, in Jamesonian language, to "master codes" in which "competing discourses fight it out within the general unity of a shared code."[37] In political terms, each term-code arguably has its left, right, and centrist wings, which is not to say that the codes per se cannot "tack right" or "tack left." Since political struggle, as Bakhtin and Voloshinov taught us, always passes through language, we must address a series of questions to each term.[38] What is at stake in these acts of naming? What is each term's genealogy and reach? What kind of work does the term do? To whom is it addressed? For whose benefit? Whom does it include or exclude? Whom does it aggrandize or diminish, empower or disempower? What are its disciplinary and transdisciplinary affiliations? Its key thinkers and gurus? What political perspective or social positions does it imply? Are some terms intrinsically more progressive than others? What does each term obscure or illuminate, screen out or bring into focus? Which terms stimulate creative energies and which shut them down? Why do words like "World," "Transnational" and "Global" resonate differently depending on the location, time, art, and discipline in question?

I do not aim here to offer an exhaustive survey of the work that goes on under the various rubrics, and much less to create a new canon or orthodoxy. Rather, what interests me is hosting an open forum for diverse voices in order to catalyze a conversation about the challenges and opportunities in diverse fields and from a wide array of vantage points. How do the issues appear when we multiply the cross-border "looking relations" (Jane Gaines), informing the world, the transnational, and the global?[39] Why are films seen so differently from different locations and vantage points? Why would *Black Orpheus* be seen as quintessentially Brazilian outside of Brazil, but as suspectly French within Brazil itself? Why are some Iranian films seen as typically Iranian when screened at festivals abroad and yet disdained by Iranian audiences themselves as pandering to the tastes of Western film festivals? What can we learn from this cross-border "excess seeing" or the complementarity of perspectives (Bakhtin)? Why would the British TV series *The Tudors* be regarded as historically inaccurate in England but as gospel truth in Turkey? Why would *Slumdog Millionaire* be a huge hit outside of India but a failure within India. The question is not only of "ways of seeing" but also of "ways of understanding" and "ways of hearing." I am especially interested in perspectives and voices emerging from the periphery, or from scholars not yet translated into English, or in relation to under-recognized film movements and under-valued theories. My ultimate goal might be summed up, in this sense, as a kind of deprovincialization of the mediatic gaze.

Mingling discursive history with textual analysis, speculative essay with critical overview, this book addresses diverse disciplinary constituencies. As a disciplinary hybrid, the book develops a syncretic, even anthropophagic methodology. Diverse concepts and leitmotifs relevant to many disciplines—Postcolonial Discourse, Indigeneity, Intermediality, Core and Periphery, the Commons—are woven into the diverse sections, creating a kind of musical echo effect whereby cognate themes resurface in different contexts, so that the diverse sections reverberate together. In structural terms, the book passes border controls to migrate from country to country, from field to field and from medium to medium—while lingering at the borders, moving from literature per se to literature on its borders with cinema, then from cinema per se to the convergence of the literary and cinematic worlds in the Worlds of Music, then to cinema and music on their borders with the transnational, then to the transnational on its borders with global media and world music and so on. The real action, I am suggesting, is to be found in the interstitial in-between of the various terrains; rather than segregation and disciplinary purity, miscegenation, impurity, and mutual invagination.

Although this book does not try to perform the impossible by giving an exhaustive survey of a vast corpus of texts, I will turn on many occasions to specific films or novels or pieces of music, in order to crystalize a larger concept or exemplify a salient trend. While acknowledging the overlapping specificities of the various arts and media, I will also grant myself a flaneur-like cultural-studies-style freedom to stroll through various disciplinary and artistic neighborhoods, wandering across disciplines, texts, and discourses, ancient and contemporary, "low" and "high." Throughout, I will invoke a full mediatic spectrum that includes feature films, short films, documentaries, music videos, Cable-TV sketch comedy, web-series and so forth. In the final section, I will propose a methodology oriented around a series of "trans" words, beginning with "transnational" but also including transdisciplinary, transmediatic, transtextual, transregional, and transartistic.

1
GOETHE AND *WELTLITERATUR*

We can begin, then, with the "Worlds." Alongside the infinity of historically consecrated "Worlds"—"World's Fairs," "World Series," "World Wide Web," "World Trade Organization," the "World Social Forum"—we find the artistic Worlds—World Literature, World Cinema, and World Music, all of which I will touch upon in the ensuing pages. The relation between "the World" and the Arts is reciprocal and mutually reinforcing; the "World" adds value to the Arts, while the Arts also add value and prestige to the World.

Unlike World Cinema and World Music, World Literature has a generally acknowledged tutelary figure—Johann Wolfgang Goethe. Thus the concept of World Literature is usually traced back to Goethe's neologism *Weltliteratur*, most notably in a diary entry in January 31, 1827, as well as in scattered references elsewhere. The theorists of World Literature almost invariably pay homage to Goethe as totem and patron saint. The initial essays in *The Routledge Companion to World Literature*, for example, spend considerable energy spelling out what Goethe might have meant by *Weltliteratur*. Much as all of philosophy has been seen as "footnotes to Plato," World Lit can be seen as a series of "footnotes to Goethe." For Goethe, the notion of a purely national literature had become obsolete; "the epoch of world literature," he famously wrote, "is at hand, and everyone must strive to hasten its approach."[1] A basic ambiguity, however, as Theo D'haen, David Damrosch and Djelal Kadir point out, has haunted World Literature since Goethe, an oscillation or hesitation between on the one hand a restrictively elitist and ethnocentric definition of World Literature, consisting of on the one hand of European canonical masterpieces cherished by an enlightened coterie, and on the other a more open and democratic World Literature as potentially embracing all literary works by writers everywhere and of every origin.[2]

World Literature inevitably inherits some of the occidento-centrism of its founding figure. The Euro-diffusionist Goethean model envisioned Western literature as expanding from Europe into the larger world and providing the model for literary study elsewhere. Traditionally, World Literature, and the Comparative Literature for which Goethe was a midwife, emplotted literary history, à la Auerbach, as emerging out of biblical Hebraism and classical Hellenism, all retroactively projected as "Western." A provincial narrative saw the novel as beginning in Europe—with *Don Quixote* and *Robinson Crusoe* often posited as texts of origin, respectively for Southern and Northern Europe. Yet one could just as easily see the novel, defined as fiction in prose, as emerging from *outside* of Europe and then spreading *to* Europe. What Arjun Appadurai called the "Eurochronology" problem embeds the axiomatic categories, typologies, and periodizations drawn largely from Western literary history.[3] Canonical literary criticism, in this sense, tends to plot artistic history, like history in general, "North by Northwest"—or as some would have it "Plato to Nato"—in a trajectory that leads inexorably from foundational texts such as the Greek epics and the Jewish Bible to literary realism and artistic modernism. But given that the Bible was rooted in Mesopotamia, Canaan, and Africa, given that classical Greek culture, as Martin Bernal has demonstrated, was deeply impacted by Semitic, Phoenician, Egyptian and Ethiopian cultures, one wonders why the Jewish Bible and *The Odyssey* should be seen as univocally "Western?"[4]

If one defines the novel, à la Margaret Anne Doody, simply as "prose fiction of a certain length," then the genre can be traced much farther back to the great prose narratives of antiquity such as the Egyptian, the Arab, the Persian, the Indian, and the Syrian.[5] The novel was the product of combinatory contact between Southern Europe, Western Asia, and Northern Africa. Discovered papyrus fragments of novels have even suggested that novel reading was popular among 2nd-century Egyptians. Nor is it an accident that the title of Heliodorus' *Aithiopika*, the longest of the surviving Greek novels, means "Ethiopian Story." A Renaissance Italian writer like Boccaccio found it normal to draw on the Eastern repertoire of the *Fables of Bidpai* and *Sindbad the Philosopher*. Writers like Cervantes and Fielding were quite aware of and influenced by this heritage. "Whoever has read *Pamela* or *Tom Jones*," as Doody puts it, "is in contact with Heliodorus, Longus, Amadis, Petronius" and we too are in contact with them when we "read authors of the nineteenth or twentieth century [such as Salman Rushdie] who have read other authors who read those works."[6] In his essay "World Literature and Philology," Michael Holquist makes similarly broad claims for one of the source disciplines for World Literature—philology—which he traces back not to modern Germany, the site of its latter-day flourishing, but rather to the Fertile Crescent thousands of years ago: "The priests and scholars who kept the wisdom of the Sumerian past alive in the second millennium BCE, through annotations, bilingual texts, and translations," he writes, were "the first philologists."[7]

Goethe's approach to literature was in some ways not so much Eurocentric as *Greco*-centric, in that he insisted that the literati trace World Literature not to any contemporaneous literature such as the Chinese, the Serbian, or the German, but rather "to the ancient Greeks, in whose works the beauty of mankind is constantly represented."[8] In this sense, Goethe's thought is aligned with a discourse that sees Greece as the "place where it all began," that traces political democracy to Athens and philosophical thinking to the "Greek miracle," a working out of the problematics formulated from the pre-Socratics up to the present. World History has no single point of origin—World History is polycentric—yet the Greco-centric vision posits history, including literary history, as "beginning" in Greece.[9] Yet even during the so-called classical period, literary history was played out around the globe, in China, in the Indus Valley, in Mesopotamia, in Egypt and Ethiopia, and in Meso-America and Turtle Island in indigenous North America. When Greece was falling under Roman hegemony, the Adena culture of what came to be called the Americas had been flourishing for over a millennium.

Unlike the language-haunted 20th-century theory, Goethe's 19th century was dominated by historical/diachronic modes of thinking which emphasized temporal evolutionary processes ordered around progressive change, a pattern common to Hegelian idealism, Marxist dialectical materialism, the Grimm Brothers Comparative Linguistics, and Darwin's evolution of the species. As Foucault put it in "Of Other Spaces: Utopias and Heterotopias":

> The great obsession of the 19th century was, as we know, history: with its themes of development and of suspension, of crisis and cycle, themes of the ever-accumulating past, with its great preponderance of dead men and the menacing glacialization of the world.[10]

Historicism was also at the basis of the Comparative Linguistics which traced contemporary European and extra-European languages (Sanskrit, Farsi) to a common trunk of an Indo-European *Ur-sprache*. In this sense, the "World" in "World Literature" has a distinctly Germanic ring, one indissociable from Marx and Hegel and the 19th-century German historical imaginary. As Emily Apter points out, *Weltliteratur* rhymes with all those other German *Welt* words—*Weltgeist* (world spirit), *Weltanschauung* (world view), *Weltkenntnis* (world knowledge), and *Weltshmerz* (world-pain).[11] The term carries the distant memory, I would further argue, of the stagist elitism of Hegel's concept of "world-historical peoples," a hierarchal concept that ranked privileged peoples and literatures as "world-historical" and relegated those who lacked nation states (for Hegel, Africans and Jews) to a bare existence "outside of history."

World Literature in Goethe's sense also has a touch of the Faustian overreacher (although to identify it with a Nietzschean Will to Power would be too much). Who apart from God, or Hercules, after all, could grasp something as all-encompassing as the "World?" Both the advocates and the critics of World Literature note the field's outlandish ambition. In the 1970s, even formalist literary scholar Rene Wellek complained that the "World Literature" category was simultaneously too indiscriminately inclusive in embracing all of literature and too narrowly exclusive in emphasizing canonical masterpieces.[12] David Damrosch, although from a different school of thought, similarly, has recognized the chimerical, Sisyphean nature of the task of dealing with such an impossibly broad topic, given that it requires many years to develop a deep familiarity even with a single culture. Another World Literature advocate, Franco Moretti, registers the melancholy truth that even the most voracious and polyglot scholar can realistically survey only a few national literatures.[13]

The more skeptical Emily Apter, meanwhile, speaks of the "gargantuan scale of world-literary endeavors."[14] To truly master the literary world would require not only knowing all of the worlds' literatures and the languages in which they were spoken and written but also knowing all the cultures that generated those literatures. Even multi-lingual philologists such as Ernst Curtius and Erich Auerbach, well-schooled in ancient and contemporary languages, restricted their ambitions to mastering only the "important" European classical and modern languages and literatures. Even granted total access to all of the world's literature, Moretti suggests, the most polyglot scholar would still miss the "other 99.5 percent."[15] Like Woody Allen's Zelig, ashamed of never having finished *Moby Dick*, literary intellectuals are always *en manque*, haunted by the White Whale of what Margaret Cohen, in a different context, calls "the great Unread."

2

THE THEORY OF WORLD LITERATURE

In a key text for our discussion, David Damrosch has defined "World Literature" as encompassing "all literary works that circulate beyond their culture of origin, either in translation or in their original language." Damrosch distinguishes between World Literature as 1) an established body of classics, and 2) an evolving canon of masterpieces. To avoid an overly capacious definition, Damrosch stipulates a series of requirements for World Literature status. Apart from simply circulating beyond national borders, World Literature must have 1) the quality of "gaining" in translation, and 2) the capacity to "estrange" us from the axiomatic norms of our home culture. Damrosch has also pointed to the reflexive "meta" dimension of World Literature, seeing it less as a fixed canon of works than "a mode of circulation and of reading"[1] and as "multiple windows on the world."[2]

Alongside "Third World Literature" and "Postcolonial Studies," "World Literature" continues the project of deprovincializing literary studies as it had conventionally been taught in the West. Damrosch begins his book *How to Read World Literature* by defining the temporal stretch of a World Literature which reaches back in time over nearly five millennia, and extends in space to almost every inhabited region of the globe. Damrosch avoids Goethe's Greco-centrism by opening up a space for Sumerian poetry, Indian *rasa* aesthetics, the Pyramid texts of ancient Egypt, and what he calls the "exquisite" body of poetry issuing from the pre-Columbian Aztec empire.[3] Significantly, Damrosch's choice for "the first true work of world literature"—the *Gilgamesh Epic*—is not Greek but Mesopotamian.[4] Damrosch also takes swipes at the Eurocentric assumptions orienting literary anthologies, criticizing the *Norton Anthology of World Masterpieces* for mapping a literary "World" (at least up to the 1985 edition) basically comprised West Europe and the United States, and where even the 1992 edition included only a "handful of non-western authors."[5] An admirable sense of cultural relativism, moreover, animates Damrosch's call for us to understand "the different literary assumptions made in different cultures, including assumptions to what is literature itself …"[6]

Damrosch moves easily from Sophocles' *Oedipus Rex* to Kalidasa's *Shakuntala* as two masterpieces of world drama, "products of ancient, polytheistic societies, in which numbers of gods were believed to act in all areas of earthly life."[7] Practicing a kind of comparative cross-cultural criticism, Damrosch dances gracefully from epic to epic across the globe, leaping with great stylistic and analytical agility from literary vine to literary vine, from the *Iliad* to the *Ramayana*, from Homer to Walcott, from Dante to Amiri Baraka, from the Bible to Gilgamesh. The cultural counterpoint is not that of Said's "contrapuntal reading," however, since in Damrosch's case there is no agenda of "haunting" one chronotopic space/time with another space/time as a part of a deconstructive postcolonial project, or for that matter with any political project beyond reforming and pluralizing the literary curiculum.

"World Literature" in some ways occupies the functional slot of Matthew Arnold's "best that has been thought and written." In this sense, "World Literature" has a curatorial vocation to gather under its umbrella the most important works. It necessarily invokes, if only tacitly, an idea of aesthetic standards, of works that merit the status of a "world-class" literature. Damrosch is obviously not suggesting that *all* texts, from those of James Joyce to those of Stephen King, that circulate beyond their linguistic and cultural points of origin qualify for entry into the sphere of World Literature. In this sense, we might spell out a distinction—valid for the other arts as well—between those works that *manage* to circulate thanks to specific configurations of power, for example from elite patronage or from massive corporate or mediatic promotion, and those that circulate because they *deserve* to circulate thanks to their indisputable aesthetic and narrative excellence. The passage from local to global is not rigid, however, and some works—*Ulysses* and *Lolita* come to mind—first gain a reputation for excellence and only later receive massive institutional support).

At times, World Literature, or at least literature enjoying worldwide marketability, meets the World Wide Web, as when Paulo Coelho, in a literary enterprise with mystical overtones, maintains a website in thirteen languages, and includes an FAQ where he answers questions submitted by his international fans. Unlike Cultural Studies, with its penchant for analyzing and in a way redeeming "low" popular cultural phenonema through the grid of "high" theory, World Literature does not usually deign to pay attention to massively popular authors like Coelho. The term World Litcrature, in this sense, serves as a certificate of quality, premised on the gatekeeping role of cosmopolitan experts, i.e. those who can read with a "detached engagement with worlds beyond our own place and time" and who are thus equipped to discern the difference between long-lasting masterpieces and pop-cultural ephemera.[8]

Unlike "World," terms like "Transnational" and "Global," are not essentially honorifics; they do not imply an aesthetic standard, even if the projects associated with these terms do not completely foreclose aesthetics either. World Literature advocates also stress the salutary effect on humanistic minds generated by a sumptuous variety of literary pleasures and cultural experiences. Damrosch attempts to go beyond narrow Euro-nationalism and Anglo-centrism by expanding the kinds of literature and culture to which scholars, students, and general readers are to be exposed. The "we" subject that is learning and enjoying and expanding its consciousness—its *Bildung* in the Kantian sense of human beings emerging out of their immaturity and provinciality—is assumed to be a collective Western "we," endowed with immense cultural capital, whose sophistication has been further burnished by exposure to new "minor" currents of thought and new voices from the Global South. In a kind of trickle-down humanism, professors and their students "universalize" themselves. The melioristic project is at once a personal one rooted in Enlightenment tempering of the self and a collective one dedicated to constructing a canon of prestigious cultural figures, whereby worthies parlay with other worthies in a virtual symposium of the Greats on the Olympian heights. (The literary gods have historically preferred to congregate on Mount Olympus rather than on Mount Kilamanjaro or Mount Fuji). In still another sense, World Literature sometimes adopts a somewhat culinary attitude toward art, seeing it as an object of individual consumption, reminding us of Bakhtin's critique of Formalist poetics as inadequate to the specifically social nature of the literary phenomenon.[9] The problem, for Bakhtin, is not pleasure in the aesthetic per se—his own prose revels in the gregarious pleasures of the carnivalesque and the Menippea—but rather in its a-social and private character.

The notion of "circulating beyond borders" at times becomes conflated with tropes of transcendence, redolent of an individualistic rising above the common mediocrity by going beyond restrictive barriers, in ways that recall Stephen Daedalus' desire to "fly past the nets" of nationalism in order to achieve cosmopolitan universality. Susan Sontag echoed Daedalus when she wrote; "To have access to literature, world literature, was to escape the prison of national vanity, of philistinism, of compulsory provincialism, of inane schooling, of imperfect destinies and bad luck. Literature was the passport to enter a larger life, that is the zone of freedom."[10] The works that reach the status of World Literature, and the critical texts that explicate that literature, are thus seen as triggering a move beyond suffocating provincialities to achieve a free-breathing universality. Rather like the dirigible in *Around the World in Eighty Days*, such works rise above their fenced-in local ground to ascend into the higher atmosphere of World Literature. The "universal" Shakespeare rises, while the "local" Marlowe crashes and burns.

Although World Literature as a field of criticism is not generally Marxist, what the French call "Marxizing" currents have been present from the beginning. Building on Goethe's economic tropes of "market exchanges" and "intellectual commerce" to evoke the commercial circulation of literature, Marx and Engels themselves correlated the rise of World Literature with the rise of the capitalist mode of production. In words that anticipate the discourses of globalization, they write in *The Communist Manifesto* that:

> ... in place of the old local and national seclusion and self-sufficiency, we have intercourse in very direction, universal interdependence of nations. And as in material, so also in intellectual production ... National one-sidedness become

more and more impossible, and from the numerous national and local literatures, there arises a world literature.[11]

Marx and Engels are in a sense being more transnational in their thinking than Goethe, in that Goethe did not think of *Weltliteratur* as transcending the nation; rather he saw the necessity of Germany developing a unified national literature alongside other culturally specific national literatures. At the same time, in an anticipatory literary equivalent of "socialist internationalism," Marx and Engels stressed the social-collective dimension of moving beyond national narrow-mindedness. In this reading, both Goethe and Marx were advocates of World Literature, but in Marx's and Engel's case the advocacy involved both the critique and the affirmation of the "world market" as at once a destructive and constructive force. *The Communist Manifesto* seems even to anticipate the Internet and the "Creative Commons" when it speaks of the process by which the "intellectual creations of individual nations become common property."[12] In this sense, World Literature in Marx's conception anticipates a John Lennonesque artistic world without borders, a utopian public sphere or imagined global community, at the same time that it foresees the disastrous effects of laissez-faire economics on culture.

Marxist currents also enter the World Literature field through figures such as Franco Moretti. Building on Braudel and the Annales School idea of a world economy as well as on later dependency theory, Moretti's "world-systems" model draws on the Marxist-inflected thought of such figures as Andre Gunder Frank and core/periphery and world-systems theory of Emmanuel Wallerstein and Samir Amin. These theorists argue that a hierarchical global system dominated by metropolitan capitalist countries and their multinational corporations simultaneously generates, as opposite sides of the same coin, the wealth of the Global North (formerly known as The Third World) and the misery of the Global South. Moretti views World Literature as the "literature of the capitalist world-system" which molds a "world literary system," characterized by systematic power imbalances between Core and Periphery."[13] The literary world, like the world of political economy, for Moretti, is "one but unequal," generating simultaneously an empowered Western "Core" and a disempowered non-Western "periphery.

In the realm of political economy, as we shall see later, Dependency and World Systems theories have been subjected to multiple critiques pointing to: a metrocentrism that accords substantive agency only to the Center; an incapacity to conceptualize the dynamic interplay of the global and the local; a failure to acknowledge the residues of communal pre-capitalist formations; and a blindness to the "relative autonomy" of the cultural sphere. 1970s Dependency theory was sometimes accused of a kind of left Prometheanism which saw the Global North as the all-powerful Prime Mover of world events, and the Global South as passive worshipper at the Altar of the Global Center. Despite its origins in a theory that was theoretically pro-Global South, Moretti's deployment of World Systems Theory remains Euro-diffusionist in that it assumes a one-way movement of literary innovation from Center to Periphery.[14]

3

FROM WORLD LITERATURE TO ALTERNATIVE MODERNISMS

In "Conjectures on World Literature," Moretti speaks of "the law of literary evolution" that dictates that the "diffusion" of the modern novel, in "cultures that belong to the periphery of the literary system," arises "not as an autonomous development but as a compromise between a Western formal influence (usually French or English) and local materials."[1] Whenever "a culture starts moving toward the modern novel," Moretti claims, "it's *always* as a compromise between foreign form and local materials."[2] Moretti's rather capacious "periphery" conflates a heterotopic assembly of nations which includes the colonized, formerly colonized, and neo-colonized spaces of the globe—the Near East, South Asia, Latin America, and West Africa—alongside the merely dominated or peripheralized countries and regions such as Turkey, Southern Europe, and Eastern Europe. His account unfortunately erases crucial historical differences between those peripheries that experienced the racialized conquest of indigenous peoples, the transoceanic slave trade and chattel slavery (for example in the Americas) and those that did not share these historical cataclysms.

Two inter-related binarisms haunt and trouble Moretti's law of literary evolution. First, Moretti's formulation resuscitates the form/content binarism thoroughly dismantled by Bakhtin, Jameson, Benjamin, Brecht, Derrida, Rancière, and countless other theorists. In so doing, he reflects what Rancière calls the "representative regime," which understands artistic activity on a highly gendered and Promethean model of an active form that imposes itself and fecundates inert matter and subjects it to its representational ends, as opposed to the "aesthetic regime of art," which:

> ... rejects the idea of form willfully imposing itself on matter and instead identifies the power of the work with the identity of contraries; the identity of active and passive, of thought and non-thought, of intentional and non-intentional.[3]

Secondly, this initial form-content binary becomes linked to the broader binarisms of a Westocentric artistic discourse that assumes the West as generative of a clearly sequenced series of aesthetic paradigm shifts giving birth to realism, naturalism, modernism, and collage, which then spread, belatedly, to the "rest of the world." The non-West, for its part, provides unsigned "raw" materials to be refined and "cooked" by named Western artists like Picasso. Western cultural institutions, meanwhile, have largely retained the power not only to possess and exhibit non-Western artifacts but also to establish the canon and define what qualifies as "Art" with a capital A and what qualifies as lower-case "folklore." In strictly theoretical terms, the Core, symptomatically, generates "form," seen as the quintessence of literary creation, while the Periphery is the passive source of inert "materials." A corollary of this attitude was the idea that the peoples of the Global South were just "sitting on" their material and cultural wealth, not making it productive, not redeeming it through the "form" of the commodity.

It is hard to ignore the extractive undertones buried in the notion of the formal "refinement" of metaphorical raw materials, strongly reminiscent of the ways that the colonized world historically provided literal "raw" materials along with symbolic materials– like the masks of Benin or the polyrhythms of Africa—to be processed, refined, manufactured, monetized, and subsequently analyzed and synthesized in the Global North. But in the domain of culture there is no such thing as "raw" materials; no matter how disreputable their origins the materials are already "cooked" by the pre-existing intertext. To paraphrase Derrida, there is nothing outside the intertext. Indigenous legends, and hip-hop lyrics, are no less intertextual than the most refined exempla of canonical literature. Which is not to deny that peripheral literature cannot be colonized or derivative. In the context of cinema, Glauber Rocha drew a clear distinction between the artistic texts that might fit Moretti's imitative description as cases of "coconut milk in a Coca Cola bottle," while he saw Cinema Novo films as "coconut milk in a coconut," informed by a "palm tree" aesthetic. Playing on the Spanish word for South (Sur), Glauber called for a *Sur-realismo Magico*, a surrealism worthy of the Global South.

In a later self-correction ("More Conjectures") Moretti acknowledged that his Core-Periphery formulations were inadequate because they "erased from the picture the transitional area (the semi-periphery) where cultures move in and out of the core"[4] But even this course-correction, and the addition of a third "Semi-Periphery" category leave in place a number of problematic binaries, beginning with Core and Periphery itself. What are now three categories are still seen as static spaces into which a culture "moves," when in fact all cultural spaces are always already unstable, mixed, and in constant motion, without any stable ground. Economic maps, moreover, are not necessarily congruent with cultural maps. Nor are the Core and Periphery of political economy necessarily isomorphic with the Core and Periphery of literature and aesthetics, spheres where all the sites have been mixed for a very long time. Latin Americans, as Brazilian cultural critic Paulo Emilio Salles Gomes famously said about Brazilians, are simultaneously "occupiers and occupied," in other words both Core and Periphery.

This "mixedness" becomes very clear in the case of Brazilian modernism in the 1920s. While it is tempting to the uninitiated to see the movement as a pale derivative of the European avant-garde movements such as Futurism, Surrealism, Dada, and so forth—and the connection is definitely there—the movement was much more innovative than derivative. No one refutes the "pale copy" idea of Global South modernism than poet-novelist-philosopher-provocateur Oswald de Andrade, the key figure in the Modern Art Week in Sao Paulo in 1922. On one level, Oswald was indeed inspired by the European avant-gardes. On his visit to Paris in 1922, he described the impact of the avant-garde movements, in racialized terms, as an "incredible destruction of the respectable behavior of the white supposedly civilized adult."[5] But after this initial impression, Oswald took avant-garde ideas in completely new directions. For example, with the possible exception of the Surrealists, the European avant-gardes were not terribly concerned with the issue of colonialism. With Oswald, in contrast, colonialism was at the very kernel of his preoccupations. In the present day, when the word "postcolonial" has been partially eclipsed (or more accurately supplemented) by the term "*de*-colonial" favored by the Coloniality/Modernity Project, it is striking that Oswald anticipated this discursive mutation over six decades earlier, in that his manifestoes employed the same pre-fix "de" as part of an aggressive decolonization—"*De*-Cabralize," "*De*-Columbusize," "*de*-Vespucci-ize"—as a way of demystifying the colonial conquerors of the Americas.

"Anthropophagy" formed the equivalent of a decolonizing form of transtextuality within a neo-colonial context. The goal was to devour the artistic techniques of the super-developed countries to avoid being swallowed up by them, thus turning the imposed culture back, transformed, against the colonizer. Thus we find a profoundly anti-colonialist thrust in de Andrade's work. Yet it would be misleading to speak of a "post-colonialism avant la lettre, in the sense that Oswald's conceptualizations on one level cut deeper even than the postcolonial critique of the 1980s. While those movements tended to emphasize the latter day colonialisms/imperialisms such as the French, the British, and the American, Oswald stressed the foundational imperialism—the Iberian imperialism—that made the other imperialisms possible.

In comparative terms, I would argue that Brazilian modernism—which is rarely even mentioned in the hundreds if not thousands of books on artistic modernism—is the movement that actually has the most to say to our present circumstances, for a number of reasons: 1) in its anti-colonial thrust, it was the least Eurocentric of the modernist movements; 2) it placed the indigenous question at the center of its project, seven decades before the UN recognition of the rights of indigenous peoples; 3) Oswald's emphasis on native communal ownership of land anticipates the contemporary emphasis on the "commons"; 4) in terms of art history, Oswald rejected the Eurocentric narratization of modernism itself as in his provocative labelling of surrealism as the "best *pre*-anthropogic movement," a jab, as I see it, against Hegelian-style stagism in the narration of artistic history; 5) the movement questioned the notion of "progress" by suggesting that Brazil already enjoyed a past-perfect utopia before Columbus, in what Marshall Sahlins would later call "the original affluent societies" and "societies of abundance"; in other words the "Discovery" did not bring happiness but misery; 6) while most European avant-gardes were highly masculinist, Oswaldian modernism was *symbolically*, if not always personally, feminist in its emphasis on matriarchy as embodied in the Tupi Ur-matriarchy of Pindorama; 7) in *The Crisis of Messianic Philosophy* Oswald denounced patriarchy as the *primum mobile* of oppression in the world;[6] 8) Oswald was post-Marxist in his friendly critique of Marxism, pointing out that Marxism did not fit societies without proletariats such as Brazil; 9) for Oswald, Marxism shared with capitalism its penchant for a productivism that was harmful to human environmental health, thus anticipating Baudrillard's critique of productivism in *The Mirror of Production* in the 1970s and the parallel indigenous critiques of the ecocidal implications of productivism by Ward Churchill and others, a critique especially germane in the era of the Anthropocene. 10) Oswald anticipated Marcuse's idea of leisure as a realm of freedom rather than necessity in his indigenously oriented praise of *sacer-docio*—etymologically "sacred leisure"—as opposed to the Puritanical angelization of labor and productivity;[7] 11) Oswald called for an all-embracing revolution that was at once social, political, literary, religious, and cultural. Anthropophy, in his view, would "devour" all previous revolutions and go beyond them, as is suggested in an suggestive entry in the Cannibal Manifesto:

> Filiation. The contact with caraiba brazil[i.e. the indigenous peoples of Brazil]. The place where Villegagnon landed [i.e. the Protestant founder of the French colony in Brazil that lasted from 1555 to 1600]
> The natural man. Rousseau.
> From the French revolution to romanticism, to the Bolshevik revolution, to the surrealist revolution to the kayserlings technized barbarian.

This astonishingly dense entry evokes four centuries of social and intellectual history that link indigenous social thought and praxis to progressive movements in Europe.

Oswald calls for a revolution infinitely "greater than the French Revolution," that is the "Carib revolution," without which "Europe would not even have its meager declaration of the rights of man."[8] Oswald's concept of an all-encompassing revolution, as Beatriz Azevedo points out, constitutes a kind of revolution in the very conceptualization of revolution itself, one thought from an indigenous imaginary.[9] Oswald's critique of the "meager" Rights of Man, I would suggest, has to do with the fact that the French *Les Droits de L'Homme* and the U.S. Bill of Rights, important as they are, are still based on a competitive notion of individual rights, of *my* right to property, of *my* right to free speech, rather than on a more gregarious *communal* conception rooted in a notion of the commons.

The Brazilian tropes of anthropophagy, the Carib revolution, and the *indio tecnizado* (the high-tech Indian) were very different from the primitivism of European modernism or the cannibalism of Picabia or the surrealism of Breton. As Brazilian literary critic Antonio Candido points out:

> In Brazil primitive cultures were mixed up with everyday life and were living reminiscences of a recent past. The provocations of a Picasso, a Brancusi, a Mx Jacob, and a Tristan Tzara, in the end, had more to do with our own Brazilian cultural inheritance than it had to do with theirs. We were accustomed to black fetishism and *calungas*, and spiritual magic and folkloric poetry, which made it easy for us to assimilate artistic processes which in Europe, unlike Brazil, presented a profound rupture with the social milieu and its spiritual traditions.[10]

The Cannibal Manifesto of the Dadaists, with its endless repetitions of the word "nothing," looks quite weak and impoverished when compared to Oswald's Cannibalist Manifesto. As Augusto de Campos puts it, the "nihilism" of the *Manifesto Canibal Dada* "has nothing to do with the generous utopia of our anthropophagy."[11] For my part, I would even argue that Brazilian modernism, in its emphasis on the aboriginal Tupi matriarchy of *Pindorama*, in its non-instrumental approach to Nature, and in its celebration of communal indigenous social arrangements, has much more to say of relevance to contemporary society than the masculinist, elitist, and often ethnocentric provocations of a Breton or Tristan Tzara.[12]

To see Latin America as "peripheral" is to confuse political economy with cultural expression. Although economically dominated, in cultural terms Latin America is an amalgam of Core and Periphery. On one level it is thoroughly Western: it is located in the Western Hemisphere; it is called "Latin," a term redolent of the Vatican and the Holy Roman Empire; its dominant languages are European; its Republican constitutions are modeled on those of the U.S. and France; its elites are largely Euro-descended, and its dominant modes of sociality are Western. At the same time, Latin America is not *only* Western; it exists "in excess" of the Western, with but also over and against the West. The very label "Latin" America is a misnomer which elides most of the Brazilian population. First introduced by the French in the 19th century, and associated with Emperor Napoleon III's campaign to promote the unity of all Latin peoples, French intellectuals and state officers brandished *Latinité* as an antidote to the surging power of the "Anglo-Saxons," imagined as a cohesive group in counterdistinction to the "Latins."[13]

Walter Mignolo and the other members of the Coloniality/Modernity group have underscored the Janus-faced character of this concept of a "Latin" America that served to restore European, Meridional, Catholic, and Latin "civilization" in South America and simultaneously to produce serious structuring absences (Indians and Afro-diasporics). "Creole consciousness," as Mignolo puts it, "was indeed a singular case of double consciousness: the consciousness of not being who they were supposed to be (Europeans)." The critical consciousness of Afro-Creoles and indigenous people, meanwhile, emerged not from not being considered Europeans but from not being considered *human*. As an irredeemably mixed site, in sum, Latin America might better be characterized not as "Latin" but as indigenous-Euro-Afro-Asian.

A number of criticisms of World Literature have been raised within literary studies, quite apart from the field's vexed relation to Postcolonial Studies that we will discuss later. One major critique can be found in Emily Apter's *Against World Literature: On the Politics of Untranslatability*. While acknowledging World Literature's welcome expansion of the canon and its salutary preoccupation with translation, she laments the field's "reflexive endorsement of cultural equivalence and substitutability, and its celebration of nationally and ethnically branded "differences" that have been niche-marketed as commercialized "identities.""[14] The "Eurocentrism" of World Literature, for Apter, discriminates against smaller nations by favoring critical lexicons that hail from the dominant ones."[15] She proposes instead a "translational transnationalism" as a critical praxis that adjusts literary technics—interlinear translation, exegesis—to the exigencies of a contemporary language politics marked by linguistic diasporas, the internationalization of North American literary studies and the English language, the ecologies of endangered languages, the impact of accents and code-switching and so forth.[16] She draws especially on Glissant's notion of "opacity," associated for her with "untranslatability," the right of subalternized peoples to guard some of their secrets and the need of the dominant powers to acknowledge that not everything can be "mastered" and forced into the Procrustean Bed of a Westocentric epistemic system.

Other objections to World Literature have to do with its insufficient attention to the assymetrical power arrangements underlying the "circulation" of World Literature. In the context of 19th-century France, Balzac's *Illusions Perdues* brilliantly anatomized the impact of power relations on literary publishing *within* a single country. Needed now is a new Balzac, like Moretti but without his ethnocentrism, capable of charting the complex power-inflected artistic relations between North and South. Cross-border "circulation" in literature and in the arts generally depends on being wired into an empowering agency—a hegemonic nation, a stable government, a mighty corporation, an economic force –with the capacity to enforce and guarantee circulation. Any unidirectional diffusionist view of circulation risks naturalizing the cultural hegemony of the Global North. Historically, the work of many Global South writers richly *deserved* to circulate beyond its linguistic and cultural borders but could only be empowered to circulate when it was "discovered" by Global Northern gatekeepers and "sponsors"—Susan Sontag for Machado de Assis, and Helene Cixous for Clarice Lispector. One could make a similar case, as we shall see later, for World Music in terms of the role of figures like Paul Simon, David Byrne, and Peter Gabriel as mediators for the music of the Global South. Something similar happens in the world of cinema when filmic "scouts" come up with auteurs who fit within a Westocentric model; thus Elia Suleiman is the Palestinian Godard; Jean-Pierre Bekolo is the Camerounian Spike Lee; Kunle Afolayan is the "Scorsese of Lagos."

The cognitive handicap of the cultural Center is to imagine that, first, it knows and has sole custody of "the best," and second, that it has unlimited access to the best that has been created, when in many cases, Global South writers never had the good fortune to be "discovered" at all, and thus remained "mute and inglorious." Or, the writers were "discovered" only belatedly and even then only by a minority of scholars within specific Area Studies fields. The formally brilliant and thematically innovative Brazilian novelist Machado de Assis, if he had written in a hegemonic language, could easily have been an internationally recognized author like James Joyce or Marcel Proust. Long a fringe writer known mainly to Brazilians, Machado was "discovered" almost a century after the publication of key novels like *Memorias Postumas de Bras Cubas* (1881) and *Dom Casmurro* (1899). Yet later Machado came to be compared to Kafka (by Allen Ginsburg) and to Beckett (by Philip Roth). In her introduction to Gregory Rabassa's translation of *Bras Cubas*, Susan Sontag calls Machado "the greatest writer ever produced in Latin America," surpassing "even Borges" while Harold Bloom calls him "the supreme black literary artist to date." Many commentators find his work uncannily contemporary; for Woody Allen Machado's work so modern that it seemed to "have been written yesterday."[17]

The Brazilian writer Mário de Andrade, to take another example, published his *Macunaíma: The Hero without Character* in 1928, nevertheless the novel has yet to enter the bloodstream of "World Literature." *Macunaíma* could be called "the Mother of all Magic Realist novels" (and of all postcolonial-hybridity novels as well) in the sense that it was written decades before the Latin American "Boom" and even more decades before the wave of "postcolonial hybridity." Unfortunately, the (execrable) English translation of the novel is long out of print and has rarely been read, while the novel is known and referenced usually only by Brazilianists and Latin Americanists, remaining relatively unknown in the Anglo—American, and even in the Spanish American, literary world.

That Mário de Andrade is not recognized as a major literary figure like James Joyce or Marcel Proust, or for that matter like Gabriel Garcia Marquez, whose poetic universes are in no way richer than his own, is largely a matter of historical accident and of writing in the "wrong" language. As a multilingual polymath, at once musicologist, composer, poet, and novelist, Mário came equipped with the language skills of a German philologist, the investigative skills of an anthropologist, the musical talents of a composer, the eye of a photographer, and the *jeu de l'esprit* of a French essayist. The possessor of immense cognitive-cultural capital, De Andrade compiled European, Amerindian, and African legends to create *Macunaíma*. He called his text a "rhapsody" both in the musical sense of a free fantasy on an epic, heroic, or national theme, and in the etymological sense of "stitcher" since the novel "stitches" tales to form a kind of artistic crazy-quilt. Viscerally anti-colonialist, de Andrade opposed Portuguese tutelage, Anglo-American imperialism, and French cultural paternalism. Against the Brazilian predilection for seeing France as cultural mentor, Mário wrote in a letter, in a kind of artistic declaration of independence, that he wanted not only to end the "grammatical domination of Portugal" but also to "cut the umbilical cord that ties Brazilians to France."[18]

Moretti's divison of Core and Periphery, which gets superimposed on the Form/Material binary, simply does not account for texts such as *Macunaíma*. First, De

Andrade's text itself forms an integral part of the literary Core in that many of its sources spring from the World Literature canon. De Andrade himself always insisted that he was writing in the tradition of Apuleius, Petronius, Rabelais, Cervantes, and Lazarillo de Tormes, in short in the tradition of a fundamental current within "World Literature" that Bakhtin called "Menippean Satire." Although one can speak of Core and Periphery in terms of the *circulation* of a novel like *Macunaíma*, the text itself, at least in cultural terms, absorbs the Core while peripheralizing it, in an epistemologically asymmetrical context where the Periphery tends to know the Core, while the Core usually does not know the periphery.

Pascale Casanova, in a deprovincializing spirit, sees the lack of French interest in translating *Macunaíma*—the novel was published in France only in 1979, more than a half-century after its publication in Portuguese—as "the proof of the critical ethnocentrism of the Centers."[19] Speaking more broadly, she scores the critical blindness that derives from "the denegation of the *rapports de force* specific to literary battles."[20] While the writers of the Periphery have to besiege the fortress of the Center to get in, the writers of the Center are locked inside the fortress. As a result, she argues, the writers of the Center suffer from a defect of vision. Naturalizing the power hierarchies that guarantee their privileges, they fail to perceive the structure of World Literature: "They are as if blind by definition: their very point of view on the world hides the very world that they believe is reduced to the tiny part that they are able to see."[21] In a kind of dependency theory of cognitive capital, she argues that it is this "constitutive ethnocentrism that produces literary exoticisms."[22]

Like James Joyce, de Andrade's polycentric and polyglossic vision integrates the erudite and the popular, the literary and the colloquial. In what amounts to a miscegenated *feijoada* of mythologies, de Andrade combines the World Literary tradition with the popular culture of oaths, nursery rhymes, proverbs, along with the indigenous legends collected by German anthropologist Theodor Koch-Grunberg in the headwaters of the Orinoco between 1911 and 1913 (published in his two-volume *Vom Roroima zum Orinoco: Ergebnisse einer Reise in Nord Bresilien und Venezuela in den Jahren 1911—1913* in 1923).[23] According to Koch-Grunberg, Macunaíma was a mythic figure, a kind of mischievous trickster figure, whose name means "Great Evil"; indeed, the natives found it amusing that the missionaries translated Macunaíma as "God." (Reportedly, people of the region still tell the stories about Macunaíma and his brothers). Unlike many ethnologists of his time, Koch-Grunberg's goal was not to study and measure the Indians but rather to understand their stories. He speaks of their generosity and openness, their "idyllic life" and their "deep love of humor and mockery," and their "penchant for nicknames based on physical appearance or bizarre behavior."[24] (In 1911, Koch-Grunberg also made a film – available on You-Tube – entitled *Aus Dem Leben der Taulipang* which portrays a happy and self-sufficient community).

Drawn from what might be called the indigenous mythological commons, the legends were more than just "raw material" for Mário de Andrade. Much of the humor of the book comes directly from the legends, for example the idea that the sun became yellow because Macunaíma threw an egg at it, or that Macunaíma "left his conscience on the island of Maroja." Both Koch-Grunberg and Mário de

Andrade admired the collective craft of the tales, and the novel conveys real sadness that "No one on earth could speak the language of the tribe, or recount those juicy episodes [leaving] an immense silence [slumbering] on the banks of the Uraricoera." In a letter to fellow poet Carlos Drummond de Andrade, Mário spoke of his "artistic interest" in the Indians and their "stupendous" tales. Rejecting any primitivist attitude, Mário adds:

> I believe this propensity of mine [for indigenous legends]is not just of the moment or the result of fashion. I always had it and for me these great traditional legends of the tribal peoples are the finest histories, tales, and novels there can be.[25]

The very language of *Macunaíma* is syncretic, weaving African, indigenous, and Portuguese words; its imagined speech carries the linguistic genes, as it were, of the Indians, African, and European immigrants of Brazil. We are reminded that the Odyssey too began as a stitching together of legends and formulaic phrases.

Mário's attitude toward his sources was what would later be called "postmodern." When Amazonian folklorist Raymundo de Moraes "defended" Mário from charges of plagiarism, Mário rejected his "help" using the classical "great artists steal" argument:

> Yes, I copied, my dear defender. What shocks me—and I find this supremely generous—is that my detractors forgot all they know, restricting my copying to Koch-Grunberg, when I copied them all. And even you, in the Boiunna scene. I confess I copied, and copied sometimes verbatim. You really want to know? ... I took whole sentenCes from Rui Barbosa, Mario Barreto, and the Portuguese chroniclers, and I tore apart the ever so precious and solemn language used by the contributors to the *Revista de Lingua Portuguesa*.[26]

At the same time, the book is richly indebted to the European avant-garde and to the Futurists—de Andrade was known in Brazil as the "Futurist" poet—and the French avant-gardists, some of whom, such as Blaise Cendrars, were the author's friends and whom he "invited" into the book as characters in search of the "marvelous." Significantly, he calls the Surrealists *macumbeiros*, or followers of the Afro-diasporic possession religions such as *candomble*, thus inviting them into the club of those I have elsewhere called the "trance-modernists."[27] Within de Andrade's archaic modernism, the anti-realist aesthetics, discontinuous characters, and spiral temporalities of indigenous narrative mate easily with modernist trans-realism. Here "form" and "materials," native and foreign, are inextricably wed in a synchresis, thus revealing the limitations of Moretti's idea of a sterile "compromise" between Western form and non-western content.

Just as the European avant-garde became "advanced" by drawing on the "primitive," so Mário de Andrade drew on the "archaic" elements of indigenous Brazilian culture, elements less "pre-modern" (a term that embeds modernity as *telos*) than "para-modern." The distinction between archaic and modernist, in the case of *Macunaíma*, is non-pertinent, since both modernism and indigenous narrative arts eschew the conventions of mimetic realism. It is thus less a question of animating inert non-western "materials" with fecundating injections of Western "forms," as the Moretti account would suggest, or of merely juxtaposing the archaic and the modern; it is rather, a question of deploying the archaic in order, paradoxically, to modernize, within a dissonant temporality which combines a past imaginary communitas with an equally imaginary future utopia.

These mixed temporalities rhyme with oxymoronic formulations such as "revolutionary nostalgia"—Walter Benjamin's idea that the past can be mobilized as a vital resource for transforming the present—and Negri's "*futur anterieur*," or Bennet and Blundell's "strategic traditionalism" as referring to indigenous media,[28] all of which defy linear history by conveying the paradoxical temporality of using the old to construct the new. Magic Realist texts, in a similar way, fashion a sense of non-linear palimpsestic time, where different temporalities co-exist. Isabel Allende's *Eva Luna* tells us that "While you and I are speaking here, behind your back Christopher Columbus is inventing America, and the same Indians that welcome him in the stained-glass window are still naked in a jungle a few hours from this office, and will be there a hundred years from now."[29] Thus magic realism encodes the multiplicity, the malleability, and the superimposability of time.

Macunaíma, "the hero without any character," as the novel's subtitle has it, lacks character not only in the conventional moral sense but also in lacking the psychological "coherence" of the autonomous ego and the sociological coherence of the verisimilar character. Ethnically, he is at once black, white, and Indian, and ethically he is by turns selfish, generous, cruel, sensual, and tender. Seven years before the publication of *Macunaíma*, interestingly, a "Core" writer, the Austrian novelist Robert Musil, began to write his never-completed yet ultimately published novel—*The Man without Qualities*—a book whose title recalls the subtitle of *Macunaíma*. The Musil novel also concerned a man of ambivalent morality, lacking in any essential traits that would allow us to narrativize his life as a recognizable type, but in the Musil case the issue is *eth*ical rather than *eth*nical; there is no recognizable racial or multicultural dimension to his quality-lessness, whereas *Macunaíma* stresses the ethnic/racial instability of its protagonist. Whereas the European text one stresses the subjective polyphony of voices within the psyche, the Brazilian text explores a complex *cultural* polyphony which typifies both the psyche and the culture. (Over fifty years later, Woody Allen produced his own version of a "man without qualities" and a "hero without character" in his *Zelig*, a story about a bizarre chameleon-conformist with an uncanny talent for taking on the accent and ethnicity of his interlocutors, set like *Macunaíma* in the 1920s in another immigrant city).

The largely unidirectional official traffic of culture from Center to Periphery, especially in terms of translation, continues apace even in the present. Lawrence Venuti points out that in 1977 Brazilian publishers brought out over 1500 translations from English, while publishers launched only 14 translations of Brazilian literature in England and the U.S.[30] The meritocratic assumption in the West, however, is that truly great literary works will somehow inevitably wend their way into English and thus transition into World Literature status, just as it is assumed in the realm of cinema that all truly great films, despite the myriad cultural and institutional obstacles thrown in their path, will inevitably make their way to North Atlantic film festivals. A kind of cognitive divide generates asymmetrical awareness between Core and Periphery, including in terms of language mastery. In the Global South, in contrast with the Global North, multilingualism for intellectuals is virtually mandatory. Given the unnevenness of power, comparison and the awareness of cross-cultural comparabilities become the norm, one of the "advantages of disadvantages" that ends up engendering what might call the paradoxical sophistication of the periphery, in tandem with, at times, the unacknowledged provinciality of the Center.[31]

It is for this reason that some scholars see World Literature as subtly legitimizing entrenched hegemonies, whether of West European culture in Goethe's time, or of the Global North in the age of neo-liberal globalization. In *Death of a Discipline*, Gayatri Spivak denounced a "hegemonizing hermeneutic" and the global marketing of a monolingual World Literature in widely disseminated anthologies which ignored cultural specificities in an ahistoric accumulation of texts where extra-European classics are reduced to tasty snippets for Western consumption. Like Harold Bloom's *The Western Canon*, the World Literature anthologies sometimes promote a kind of "Europe-plus" approach, where a few Global South authors (Tagore, Achebe, Neruda) form a belated supplement to the sacrosanct European canon. *The Norton Anthology of World Literature*, as noted by World Literature scholars themselves, until recently consisted of Anglo-American and European classics supplemented by a sprinkling of works from Asia and Africa.[32]

Chris Andre, meanwhile, argues that World Literature tends to function as ideological justification for whatever power position it speaks from, usually on behalf of those who have accumulated cultural capital, whether it be the heirs of German cultural supremacy in Goethe's time, or of Anglo-American hegemony at the time of the Latin American "Boom," or the present-day supposedly "post-hegemonic" system of global capitalism.[33] To be fair, these asymmetries have been duly noted by some World Literature scholars. For Sanja Bahun, a World Literature approach favors a "rigid synchrony whose axial points are the development of nation-states and international capitalism."[34] For Djelal Kadir," the West performs the "worlding" in that the West is "where the fixed foot of the compass that describes the globalizing circumscription is placed."[35]

4

THE COSMOPOLITANISM OF THE PERIPHERY

Blind to the dynamic cultural agency to the Periphery, Moretti fails to see the Periphery as a constitutively generative field of artistic energy that endlessly impacts and transforms the Center, including in formal terms, even as it being transformed by that Center. Indeed, Latin American, Caribbean, and Afro-diasporic artists, pace Moretti, rather than merely imitate European formal innovations, have been extremely fecund in *formal* innovation and neologistic aesthetics: De Andrade's "*anthropophagy*," Carpentier's *real maravilloso Americano*, Glissant's "*diversalite*," Rocha's "*aesthetic of hunger*," Sganzerla's "*aesthetics of garbage*," Espinosa's *cine imperfecto*, Henry Louis Gates' "*signifying-monkey aesthetic*," Tomás Ibarra-Frausto's *rasquachismo*, Arturo Lindsay's "*Santeria aesthetics*," Guillermo del Toro's "termite aesthetic," Paul Leduc's "*salamander* (as opposed to dinosaur) *aesthetic*," Teshome Gabriel's "*nomadic aesthetics*," Kobena Mercer's "*diaspora aesthetics*," Gloria Anzaldua's "*border aesthetics*," not to mention the most celebrated of all—*realismo magico*.

Cultural exchange and aesthetic innovation, in sum, are multidirectional and to some extent reciprocal. As the product of five centuries of surprising cultural remixings, the art of the Americas are almost inevitably "original." But even "the core of the Core," let us say the North Atlantic countries, are themselves syntheses of Western and non-Western cultures, thoroughly infiltrated by the "minor," the "peripheral," and the "subaltern." They are all, to use Caetano's words about the United States, "inevitably mestizo" (*fatalmente mestizo*). The notion of a pure Western Core is premised on crucial exclusions, such as the African and Semitic influences that shaped classical Greece, the osmotic Sephardic-Judeo-Islamic culture that played a crucial role in the Middle Ages and the Renaissance, and the Moorish influence on the poetry of courtly love. The African influence on painting and music, the impact of Asian forms (Kabuki, No drama, Balinese theater, ideographic writing) and so forth. Both Core and Periphery are mixed sites, omnivorous mélanges of cultures. The Periphery did not simply mimic the Core;

the two were, in contemporary academic parlance, "mutually constitutive; "in short, they are "inside" each other.

Within the transoceanic "crossings" of literary texts and ideas, Global South countries have operated at a severe disadvantage. Some of Brazil's disadvantages, for example, derive from domestic factors, such as widespread non-literacy and the weakness of the publishing industry. But other disadvantages derive from arbitrary external factors, for example: the Portuguese prohibitions on publishing in its colonies, the relative lack of prestige and dissemination of the Portuguese language (even as compared with Spanish), along with Brazil's relegation, by the powers that be, to the cultural periphery, within a racially skewed division of international intellectual labor. Indeed, Mário de Andrade himself reflected on the processes of cultural discrimination that devalued the work of Brazilian artists, thus anticipating the "cultural dependency" debates of the 1960s and 1970s. While declaring himself "very optimistic about the creativity of our literature and other contemporary arts," Mário de Andrade doubted Brazilian texts would ever win the applause they deserved due to "factors which have nothing to do with artistic merit." Some countries—and here he anticipates both systems theory and Moretti—he pointed out:

> ... weigh in with great force in the universal scale; their currency is valuable or pretends to be valuable, and their armies have the power to decide in the wars of the future ... the permanence of the arts of any given country in terms of the world's attention exist in direct proportion to the political and economic power of the country in question.[1]

Here de Andrade anticipates Casanova's economic metaphor of the literary Stock Market. Just as the prices of Latin America's raw materials were once set in Amsterdam, London, or New York, so the value of its cultural goods still tended to be calibrated outside of Brazil, again in those very same world capitals.

The mutually constitutive character of Core and Periphery becomes especially evident in the case of magic realism. The movement has been variously defined in terms both of its magical and marvelous themes and in terms of its polyperspectival forms of narration. Magic realism bypasses the formal conventions of dramatic, illusionistic realism in favor of such alternative modes as the carnivalesque, the anthropophagic, the reflexive-modernist and the resistant postmodernist.[2] Its aesthetics are often rooted in non-realist, often non-western cultural traditions featuring other historical rhythms, other narrative structures, other views of the body, sexuality, spirituality, and the collective life. At the same time, the spirit of the movement existed in germ in Cervantes *Don Quixote*, which orchestrated a dialogue between the reality principle—embodied in Sancho Panza—and fantasy, incarnated and performed by Don Quixote. By incorporating non-modern traditions into clearly modernizing or postmodernizing aesthetics, it problematizes facile dichotomies such as traditional and modern, realist and modernist, form and content, and Core and Periphery.[3]

The temporalities of art are necessarily enfolded and temporally mixed. The distinction archaic/ modern, for example, is often not pertinent, in that both modernist and para-modern aesthetics challenge the protocols of mimetic realism and the ideal of the verisimilar imitation of phenomenal appearance. In their attempts to forge a liberatory language, alternative cultural traditions make artistic use of *para-modern* materials such as popular religion and ritual magic—phenomena that exist outside of the tradition/minority and culture/folklore binarisms. The fashionable talk of hybridity" and "syncretism" usually associated with postmodernism and the postcolonial theory of the 1970s and 1980s, for example, forgets that artists/ intellectuals in Latin America and the Caribbean were thematizing hybridity over a half-century before the postcolonial writers formulated their theories.

The contribution of Franco-Cuban writer Alejo Carpentier to the theorization of literature was to territorialize magic realism by rooting it firmly in the Afro-indigenous cultural soil of the Americas. Carpentier spoke in 1949 of *lo real maravilloso americano* (the marvelous [Latin] American real), which he contrasted with European surrealism in terms of a specifically Latin American fantastic rooted in the cultural mixtures typical of Latin America. Carpentier first coined the phrase "the marvelous American real" in his preface to *El Reino de Este Mundo* (in 1949) to evoke the mestizo magic of a continent. Although the precise meaning of the phrase is somewhat elusive, it points to a number of themes and leitmotifs: the prodigious, uncanny qualities of Latin American social reality; the continent's syncretisms of indigenous, African, and European cultures; the botanical/meteorological sublime of rainforests, hurricanes and volcanos; the tragic heroism of Latin American history as incarnated in figures like Montezuma in Mexico and King Henri Christophe in Haiti; murderous cross-cultural clashes such as Cortez' entrance into Tenochtitlan. Unlike the cool, cerebral, and in some cases Europhile magic realism of a Borges or Cortazar, Carpentier saw "the marvelous American real" as based in popular cultural practices and collective beliefs typical of the indigenous and subaltern populations of the "New World." Rather than emerging from the juxtaposition of an umbrella and a sewing table, the New World marvelous comes from a dissensual multiculturality and the counterpointing of cultures.

A man of immense culture, Carpentier was deeply familiar both with Europe, where he spent much of his life, and with Latin America, where he also lived and which he studied passionately. *Concierto Barroco* forms a pan-Latin American allegory which mingles a critique of the cruelty of the Spanish/Portuguese conquista with an exaltation of the miscegenated culture which formed the long-term cultural precipitate of conquest. In fact, an annoyed sense of Latin American fatigue with European condescension, informs many of Carpentier's observations. "Our 19 century," Carpentier writes, "offers characters who are much more interesting than a little Scottish king like Macbeth."[4] Carpentier contrasts what he sees as the labored efforts of the European avant-gardists to engineer the marvelous through techniques of dislocation, with the marvelous as it inheres in Latin American quotidian reality itself.

If the Old World were going to patronize the New World as artistically "young" and "infantile," in the manner of the early European "naturalists" like

Buffon who found even New world nature "immature" and "barren," the New World artists and intellectuals would deploy its trump card by going back before 1492 and the European conquest to locate a pre-Columbian legacy in indigenous culture, as a way to forge a peculiarly Latin American sense of "deep time." Writers of the Americas "looked to re-enchant the fallen world by drawing on indigenous spirituality and forms of knowledge unknown to Europe."[5] Although the very phrase "marvelous American real" locates this aesthetic in the contemporary Americas, at times Carpentier finds its aesthetic antecedents in earlier times—in the pre-Columbian past of mythological texts like *Popol Vuh* and *Chilam Balam* for example—or in distant locations, whether in Hindu and Persian literature or in the Europe of Ariosto, Rabelais, Cervantes, and Shakespeare. As Pascale Casanova points out, Octavio Paz tried, in the 1950s, in the *Labyrynth of Solitude*, to "found and ennoble Mexican national identity by reestablishing a lost continuity between all the historical legacies—and notably by reconciling the pre-Columbian heritage with the history of Spanish colonization and the social structures it implanted."[6] Forty years later, upon receiving the Nobel Prize, Paz describes a kind of séance or dialogue with the dead, between contemporary Latin American artists and the indigenous past: "Pre-Columbian Mexico," Paz asserts," with its temples and its gods, is admittedly on one level a pile of ruins, yet the spirit which animates them is not dead. It speaks to us in the coded language of myths and legends, of ways of living, of popular arts and customs. To be a Mexican writer is to listen closely to what this the present/presence tells us."[7]

Some of the most innovative narrative in Latin America has drawn on the storytelling commons of indigenous myth and legend. Miguel Angel Asturias Nobel Prize-winning novel *Hombres de Maiz* (1949) draws on the *Popol Vuh* (the Mayan encyclopedia of theogony, cosmogony, and astrology that Asturias himself had translated). Leslie Marmon Silko's *Almanac of the Dead* (1991) revolves around an attempt to rescue a Mayan almanac hidden from the Spanish by a native guardian. Carlos Fuentes, similarly, insists on a cultural continuity, despite the violent rupture created by 1492 and the conquest, between pre-Conquest and post-Conquest Mexico: "This heritage goes from the ruins of ChichenItza and Machu-Pichu tto the indigenous influence on modern painting and architecture. And from the baroque art of the colonial period to the literary works of our contemporaries like Jorge Luis Borges or Gabriel Garcia Marques ... Few cultures in the world possess such riches."[8]

Further south, meanwhile, the Brazilian modernists too tried to deploy and reanimate and actualize the ancient legends of Amazonian tribes within a proto-post modernist collage aesthetic. The modernist 1920s trope of contemporary Brazilian artists becoming Tupi, a group that the modernists mistakenly thought to be extinguished by conquest, was another very Brazilian way of asserting a cultural continuity whose beginnings predated 1492. Recent attempts to see North American literature as multilingual, as expressed in other European languages like German, French, Italian, and Portuguese, as well as in dialects like Yiddish, and in indigenous languages like Ojibwe (also known as Chippewa) and Comanche, in contrast, give pride of place to indigenous literature, including indigenous "orature."[9]

Magic Realism can be seen as transnational in a narrow, continental sense as an aesthetic and narrative anti-aesthetic shared by certain Latin American writers, or it can be seen as transnational, in an even broader sense, as a general globalized postcolonial phenomenon, a kind of base-line aesthetic for some members of the Global South.[10] Aesthetic innovation generally arises, not exclusively but importantly, from the transnational mingling of multicultural knowledges and practices. While it has become a commonplace to speak of the exhaustion of the avant-garde, in my view transnationally remixed aesthetics promise an infinite combinatoire based on innovational transtextuality. Innovation emerges from the transnational rendezvous of incommensurable cultural paradigms, from the encounter of a Picasso with African sculpture, from the comings and goings between Europe and Latin America of an Alejo Carpentier, from the encounter of a Mário de Andrade with surrealism, on the one hand, and Amazonian legend on the other, or from Villa-Lobos' simultaneous encounter both with European modernist music and with *sertaneja* melodies. In no case can one relegate one side of these equations to mere "materials" and the other side to "form"; the two are indissolubly wed.

5

COLUMBUS, *EL NUEVO MUNDO*, AND POSTCOLONIAL STUDIES

If we are going to speak in any historical depth about the "World" in World Literature, we would do well to trace current discussions to the set of events that made it possible to speak, for the first time accurately, of a single "World." This world, that we now think of as *the* World, has its long-term origins in colonial modernity and the seismic transformations summed up in the date 1492. In that year, Columbus connected the two formerly estranged halves of the world making it possible to speak of the "World" that eventually turned into the "World" of "World Literature." For Chickasaw scholar Jodi A. Burd, 1492 and the Conquest "served to reworld lands and reciprocal relationships into property and conscripted labor."[1] Long before the advent of Systems Theory, both Adam Smith, the patron saint of capitalism, and Marx, the patron saint of Communism, had seen the "long 1492" as the initial impetus for capitalist modernity. Adam Smith wrote in *The Wealth of Nations* (1776) that the "Discovery of America, and that of the East Indies via the Cape of Good Hope, are the two greatest events recorded in the history of mankind."[2] Marx and Engels, less than a century later, wrote in *The Communist Manifesto* that "The Discovery of America, the rounding of the Cape, opened up fresh ground for the rising bourgeoisie [leading to] the increase in the means of exchange and in commodities generally, [giving] to commerce, to industry, an impulse never before known …"[3] 1492 and its sequels were seen as marking the creation of the "world system" in what Marx in *The Communist Manifesto* called "the rosy dawn of primitive accumulation."[4]

The encounter between the European and the indigene also triggered various streams of utopian thought, with immense catalytic impact on what we know as the Western "left." As Oswald de Andrade put it:

> To know that on the other side of the earth there had occurred an encounter with human beings knowing neither sin nor redemption, without theology or

hell, produced not only utopian dreams but also a general shock to the consciousness and culture of Europe.[5]

The 1492 date forms a metonym for a series of inter-related historical processes, including the Edicts of Expulsion against the Jews and Muslims, the Inquisition against *marranos*, the Conquest of the "New" world, and the Transatlantic slave trade. As Ella Shohat and I argued more than two decades ago in *Unthinking Eurocentrism*, a series of interlinked "questions"—the colonial/modernity question, the slavery question, the Jewish, Muslim, "Indian," Black, and African questions—can all be partly traced back to that cataclysmic moment. In this sense, the entire world, including the literary, cultural, and mediatic world, still lives under the shadow of 1492. Indeed, many contemporary quarrels reverberate across time with what might be called the "long 1492." The debates in 1550 between the conservative jurist Sepulveda and the pro-indigenous priest Bartolome de las Casas about whether Indians enjoyed *derechos humanos* still echo today, to the point that author/screenwriter/dramaturg Jean-Claude Carriere, four and a half centuries after the original debate, could stage, and later film, the famous *controversy* verbatim, in full knowledge that it would resonate with contemporary audiences aware of burning issues of indigenous rights. The current discussion of the "commons" and "corporate enclosure" can be traced back to the enclosure and liquidation of the indigenous commons which began in 1492 and continues to the present day. Colonialism itself can be seen as a foundational theft of the commons. By "understanding colonialism as the theft of the commons, "Nandita Sharma and Cynthia Wright argue," the agents of decolonization as the commoners, and decolonization as the graining of a global commons, we will gain a clearer sense of when we were colonized, who colonized us, and how to decolonize ourselves and our relationships."[6]

Needless to say, I am not positing an eternal Manichean struggle between Good and Evil, with brutal armies of diabolical colonialists neatly arrayed against angelic *indigenes* and their proto-postcolonial allies. The question is not one of individual morality at all, but rather of the public contest of discourses and practices, some favoring cultural equality and reciprocity, and others naturalizing hierarchy and domination. The various positions within these debates are not static or transhistorical. The debates have taken different forms depending on geographical space—whether they took place in France, or in Haiti, or in Brazil—and on historical period. The debates are staged differently depending on what field and medium is being addressed and how facts are narrated, arranged, and sequenced through an (often) unacknowledged and assumed set of paradigms and grids.

A crucial yet often absent conversation, in this sense, has to do with how the field of World Literature might be mapped across the cognate field of what is variously called "Postcolonial Theory," "Postcolonial Critique" and "Postcolonial Studies." Despite partially overlapping concerns, the two fields engage in what Bakhtin would have called an unspoken "hidden polemic." What, then, are the points of tension and what the opportunities for mutual illumination and theoretical interfecundation between the two fields? As an interdisciplinary domain of inquiry, Postcolonial Theory explores the colonial archive and postcolonial identity, in order to offer what Brett Christopher calls a "wide-ranging critique of the political-economic conditions and the ways of thinking, seeing and representing that empire instilled, and which ... continue to persist to one degree or another after the formal dismantling of empire."[7] While World Literature à la Damrosch seems to be agnostic or neutral on globalization, Postcolonial Critique tends to be more frankly critical in that it breaks with any idealized versions of history, in this case with idealized versions of World Literature as well as with any euphoric account of globalization by always reminding us of the colonial and neo-colonial processes that laid the groundwork for globalization and for globalizing arts and media.

As an interdisciplinary project, Postcolonial Studies explores the colonial archive and postcolonial identity, often in work inflected by the various "posts," and especially by poststructuralism. Postcolonial Theory incorporates while also tweaking and criticizing anti-colonial discourse. In this sense it embeds the historical memory of decolonization while also marking a discursive shift from anti-colonial to postcolonial discourse.[8] If the key axes of discussion during decolonization had been empire and nation, postcolonialism multiplied the intersection of axes including race, gender, class, region, religion, sexuality, and ethnicity, without nation and empire ever disappearing from view. The genealogy of the field traces back to the anti-colonial struggles themselves and to the accompanying debates about post-independence policies and theories. The postcolonial existed in germ in the anti-colonial. The "Pitfalls of National Consciousness" chapter in Fanon's *The Wretched of the Earth* (1961), written during the twilight of French colonialism in Algeria, constituted an anticipatory gesture toward the postcolonial field. And while Fanon mobilized, and critiqued, the theoretical idioms available in his day—phenomenology, psychoanalysis, Marxism, and so forth—postcolonial discourse has mobilized the theoretical (largely poststructuralist) idioms available in its period, later artists have mobilized the idioms available to later generations.

Few films register this discursive shift more revealingly than Isaac Julien's essay-film *Black Skin, White Masks* (1995). Typifying a postcolonial moment, Julien's film opens up Fanon's corpus to the grid of intersectionality (Kimberly Crenshaw) whereby multiple axes of difference (nation/ race/gender/sexuality/ generation, and ideology) mutually inflect and complicate each other, axes which are not reducible to each other and which confound any simplistic notions of any essential identity. In what might be called an audio-visual-textual dance of positionalities, race is gendered, sexuality is raced, class is sexualized and so forth. A corollary of this open-ended dance is a pushing-the-envelope audacity, a constant flirtation with "incorrect" images, for example the choice of a gay Langston Hughes to "represent" the African American community.

At the same time, *Black Skin, White Masks* offers a fairly cool "post" take on Fanon's incendiary prose, conveying both identification with and distance from Fanon, while deploying a carefully calibrated ironic distance from Third Worldist rhetoric. In a sense, Julien is a symbolic "son" of Fanon. Like Fanon, Julien is a man of Caribbean origin who moved to the metropole. Just as Fanon's work emerges from the independence movements against colonialism in the 1960s, Julien's work came out of the black British art movements and the uprisings against discrimination and police brutality in the 1970s and 1980s. If Fanon embodied the theory and practice of Third World nationalism, Julien embodies the theory and practice of *postcolonial postnationalism* in the metropole. Just as Fanon mixed genres and discourses in his writing, mingling psychoanalysis, sociology, poetry, literary criticism and so forth, Julien mixes cinematic genres in his film, mingling archival footage, interviews with Fanon's family members and with Fanon's psychoanalytic colleagues (Azoulay), scholars (Françoise Vergès, Stuart Hall), along with quoted fiction films, stylized fantasy sequences, and direct-to-camera soliloquys by the actor (Colin Salmon) playing "Fanon." Julien also cites *Battle of Algiers*, especially privileging the torture sequences, scenes perfectly relevant to Fanon as the psychoanalyst treating both the torturers (the French) and the tortured (the Algerians). In a kind of subliminal musicality, Julien deploys a trilled flute, borrowed from *The Battle of Algiers* soundtrack but detached from its image track, as a kind of minimalist leitmotif, an acoustic synecdoche for the situated, vibrating tension of the colonial agon.

The Julien film picks up on a striking feature of Fanon's work—its constant preoccupation with the clash of gazes or what might be called, paraphrasing Jane Gaines, colonial looking relations.[9] In *Wretched of the Earth*, Fanon casts colonialism itself as a painful crossing of looks: "I have to meet the white man's eyes." The colonist trains on the colonized a look of desire, of appropriation, of surveillance. He overlooks, surveys, and oversees from above, without being looked at, surveyed, or overseen, while the look of the native on the settler town "is a look of lust ... to sleep in the settler's bed, with his wife if possible." The colonialist's greatest crime, meanwhile, was to make the colonized see themselves through colonized eyes. And in the wake of Sartre, de Beauvoir, and Fanon, Julien's film thematizes the racialized, sexualized look. Like that other filmic allegory of voyeurism, Hitchcocks *Rear Window*, the Julien film proliferates in words having to do with looking: "see," "regard," "the desiring gaze," "field of vision," "scopophilia," "voyeurism," the "look that fractures," the "sexualized nature of the look." Indeed, the film constitutes a theorized orchestration of looks and glances, captured and analyzed in all their permutations: "Fanon"'s direct look at the camera/ spectator; de Gaulle's paternal look at Algeria as he parades through Maghrebian streets (edited in such a way that veiled women shield themselves from his regard, thus evoking the theme of "Algeria Unveiled"); the dumb uncomprehending look of French soldiers on Algerian women, their misinterpretation of the hermeneutics of the veil; the aerial surveillance performed by French helicopters over the casbah; the sympathetic look of the woman observer (cited from *Battle of Algiers*) who cries as she witnesses torture and empathizes with the victim.

The Isaac Julien film exemplifies the idea that the "postcolonial" is only in part a temporal marker—the end of colonialism—and is more fundamentally the marker of a discursive shift. In the 1960s within anti-colonial discourse, one category—the nation—wielded overweening authority; everything else was subordinated to it. But in the 1980s, to take the case of France and Algeria in the wake of the civil war in Algeria and social tension in France, religion, ethnicity, and sexuality come to the fore, in a situation where ethnic tensions with colonial overtones are quite obvious. The visible official checkpoints of *The Battle of Algiers* turn into the invisible and unofficial barriers between *banlieue* and city center in the France of Mathieu Kassovitz's *La Haine* (1995) and Mahmoud Zemmouri's *100% Arabica* (1997). The footage of Parisian rebellions at the beginning of *La Haine* seems like an updated version of the demonstrations at the end of *The Battle of Algiers*. Within the reconfigured socioscape, the colonial fracture is now to be found on both sides of the colonial divide. With postcolonial discourse, nations on both sides are discursively recognized as characterized by what Bakhtin calls heteroglossia, or sociocultural "many-languagedness." The Algerian nation is progressively recognized as gendered (given the worsening oppression of women after independence, as ethnically divided (Arab vs. Amazigh), and as religiously divided, not only between Islam and other faiths (or between secular and religious) but also between the culturally religious and the theologically/ideologically religious. France, for its part, also comes to be seen as what it always was, itself multi-ethnic and multi-faith, now with a population that is one-fifth Muslim, within a moment of a certain "racialization" of religious affiliation.

In a sense, Postcolonial Studies and World Literature, as well as World Cinema studies, all emerged, but in distinct ways, from the commingled ashes of the Three Worlds model and the unified nation model. The Three Worlds model was initially conceived by French demographer Alfred Sauvy during the era of decolonization in the late 1950s, by analogy to the "three estates" in the pre-revolutionary France of the *ancien regime*, i.e. the commoners or the Third Estate in contradistinction to the First Estate (the Royalty and Nobility) and the Second Estate (the Clergy). Retrofitted and globalized for the 20th century, the term posited three worlds: the colonial/capitalist First World of the West (Europe, the U.S., and Australia); the Second World of the "Socialist Bloc" (with or without China); and the Third World of the colonized, decolonized, and neo-colonized countries, as the tricontinental "Commoners" or transnational people. (The three estates metaphor could be seen as Francocentric in the sense of universalizing a French historical experience based on the Revolution and the Republican political model).

This tripartite model came into crisis when two of the "Worlds" began to lose their firm outlines as geo-political formations. The "Second World" expired dramatically in 1989 with the collapse of the Soviet Empire and the end of the Cold War. The "Third World," for its part, entered into a different more slow-working kind of existential and nominational crisis, not as a formal group of states like the "Socialist Bloc" but rather as a loose conceptual alliance at once political, cultural, and terminological. In the 1990s, the term "Third World" came to be seen as an antiquated relic of a more militant "tricontinental" period. From a Marxist perspective, Aijaz Ahmad argued that Third World Theory was as "open-ended ideological interpellation" that papered over class oppression in all three worlds, while limiting socialism to the (now extinct) Second World.[10] While the First World was defined by its imperial domination, and the Second World by its socialist solidarity, the Third World, for Ahmad, was largely defined by its *lack* of agency, as "having experienced" or "suffered" the externally imposed phenomenon of colonialism. Three Worlds theory, it was argued, flattened heterogeneities among Third World nations, masked contradictions and conflicts between nations (Pakistan vs. India, Ethiopia vs. Eritrea, etc.). The Three Worlds also obscured shared commonalities within their differences, for example the common presence of "First peoples" aka the Fourth World of indigenous peoples, in much of the Third World. Since the three worlds were not neatly separable or ghettoizable, analysts called for an idiom of mutual imbrication between the worlds, leading to such formulae as "the First World is in the Third World" (and vice versa), the North is "in" the South, and vice versa, while indigenous peoples inhabit all the worlds.

The flowering of Postcolonial Studies in the late 1980s partly derives from the entry of intellectuals from the formerly colonized countries into the Anglophone academy as well as from the increased visibility of immigrant-descended populations in the United States and Europe. Although Francophone thinkers such as Césaire and Fanon were seminal thinkers for postcolonial thought, many French intellectuals have until recently been reticent about the project. Latin American intellectuals, meanwhile, have been somewhat ambivalent, saying in effect that postcolonialism for them is "old news." If Latin America was in some ways "behind" Europe—for example, in technology or industrialization—in other ways it was culturally "ahead" of European thinking, having the ambiguous advantages of the double parallax vision that comes with knowing both the Center and the Periphery. The Anglo-American—Indian orientation of much of Postcolonial Studies, unfortunately, too often relegated Latin American and Latin-Americanist intellectuals, not to mention indigenous critique, to the theoretical sidelines. At the same time, Latin American and Latino scholars (Enrique Dussel, Fernando Coronil, Walter Mignolo, Arturo Escobar, Anibal Quijano, Nelson Maldonado-Torres, and Ramón Grosfoguel, among others) have been formulating the "colonial/modernity project," which takes the critiques developed by indigenous peoples, and by Latin American anti-imperialists, as fundamental to any thoroughgoing postcolonial project.[11]

The British Empire/Commonwealth orientation of Postcolonial Theory, meanwhile, has sometimes led to the overlooking of the long-term antecedents of hybridity discourse in the work of Latin America and Caribbean intellectuals. A 1971 essay by Brazilian novelist/literary critic Silviano Santiago calling attention to the "in-between of Latin American culture," for example, clearly anticipated Homi Bhabha's formulations concerning the "interstitial," the "in-between" and the "third space of negotiation."[12] While the wide circulation of race/postcolonial work is partly due to the global reach of the English language and the power of the Anglo-American academy, it would be misleading to chart a linear trajectory whereby these movements "originated" in Anglo-America and then "traveled elsewhere." Conquest, colonialism, slavery, Anglo-American imperialism, military interventions, expulsions, immigration, and the "brain drain" brought a translocated and hybridized mix of peoples and ideas, helping to shape the various progressive projects. Despite the frequent location of Postcolonial Studies in the Anglo-American academe, in discursive terms these projects were impacted by anticolonialist discourse generally, by the poststructural theory associated with France and Francophone world, by the black British cultural studies associated not only with the United Kingdom but also with South Asia and the Caribbean, by the subaltern studies associated not only with India but also with postcolonial diasporas, by the hegemony theory associated with Gramsci and Italy, by the dependency theory and coloniality/modernity project associated with U.S. Latinos and with Latin America, and by the center/periphery and world systems theory associated with many different sites.

A supersessionist narrative suggests that the waxing popularity of World Literature arguably coincided with a perceived waning of Postcolonial Studies and a crisis within Comparative Literature. James Graham, Michael Niblett and Sharae Deckard, in *Postcolonial Studies and World Literature*, call World Literature the "spectre" haunting postcolonial literary studies. But although World Literature is sometimes said to be a strategic reaction against a Postcolonial Studies perceived as running out of steam, in reality postcolonial style-scholarship continues in force, and furthermore, has constantly moved into new disciplinary fields. Moreover, World Literature and Postcolonial Studies do not usually confront each other directly. (For the Amazonian natives with whom Lévi-Strauss worked, the *absence* of relation was a *hostile* relation.) Moreover, the two are not completely separable; there are many overlaps and points of contact. "Both fields seek," as Robert Young puts it, "to move the study of literary texts beyond the confines of European literature."[13] Two key figures in the Postcolonial Studies and World Literature fields (Edward Said and David Damrosch) both draw, to some extent, on the same legacy of philology à la Ernst Curtius, Leo Spitzer, and Erich Auerbach. While both valorize literature, the postcolonial critic is more likely to simultaneously (directly) deconstruct and (indirectly) exalt classic texts. Postcolonial writing is not given to adulatory adjectives or aesthetic compliments, it honors texts simply by selecting them for analysis. Said's contrapuntal reading of Austen's *Mansfield Park* does not question the artistic quality of the novel; rather, it assumes that quality but opens up its submerged subtexts and shadowy meanings. While World Literature usually highlights the worthiness of the literature it studies—Moretti with his "distant reading" here being the exception—Postcolonial Studies à la Said simply takes the literary worthiness for granted; in fact, in a kind backhanded compliment, Said would not waste his deconstructive, or better "contrapuntal," energies on an unworthy object.

It was Said's "opening up" of the Austen text that allowed Patricia Rozema to create her revisionist film adaptation of *Mansfield Park* which filtered the novel through the prism of Said's analysis in *Culture and Imperialism*. The adaptation counterpoints the estates of upper-middle-class England with the Big Houses of the colonized Caribbean, using the Sir Bertram character as a link to the slavery backgrounded in the novel. The film's audacious reimagining of the novel through a postcolonial grid outraged critics who found its emphasis on slavery "unfaithful" to the original. The scene in which Fanny Price discovers Tom Bertram's pornographic sketchbook of sadistic scenes from the Antigua plantation was seen by some Austen devotees as an anachronistic and politically correct rubbing of slavery in the noses of (the presumably white) fans of the novel. But as Tim Watson points out, the adaptation can be productively seen within the context of two debates which were centuries apart, i.e. the debates about slavery at the time of the novel's production, and those about reparations at the time of the film's release. The adaptation simply "unsilences" the critique of slavery elided in the novel, where Fanny's question about the slave trade remains unanswered.[14]

It would be wrong to overstate the opposition between World Literature and Postcolonial Studies, given that a number of scholars "swim" in the mingled currents of the two fields. Pascale Casanova, with her crucial book *The World Republic of Letters*, for example, is a major reference in both fields. David Damrosch, meanwhile, can make occasional respectful nods to Edward Said's work. Said's own texts, Jonathon Arac points out, have not only been incorporated into World Literature, but have themselves reshaped comparative literature in ways that enabled "the recent renewal of World Literature as a live topic."[15] The co-edited anthology *World Literature in Theory* includes many names—Edward Said, Gayatri Spivak, Aamir Mufti, and Françoise Lionnet among them– who could be just as easily regarded as Postcolonial Studies Scholars as World Literature scholars. Indeed, Section III of the volume ends with a friendly dialogue between Damrosch and Spivak, surprising since Spivak had been a vocal critic of the globalized market of World Literature in English translation). Another key figure linking World Literature with Postcolonial Studies is Djelal Kadir, who has helped the journal *World Literature Today* becomes a crucial site of encounter of the two currents, with major attention paid to writers such as Kamau Brathwaite, Assia Djebar, Maryse Conde, and Joao Cabral de Melo Neto.

Postcolonial literary studies is defined both as *for* critical anti-colonial and postcolonial perspectives—and *against* Eurocentric assumptions and perspectives and an overly narrow Western canon. At the same time the field both privileges and contests "Commonwealth Literature," much as Glissant, as we will see later, contests the category and practice of "Francophone literature." World Literature would seem to be *for* whatever qualifies as world-class literature. While the corpus of World Literature can at times coincide with that of Postcolonial Literature, the perspective, and the stakes, are dramatically different. Both fields practice hermeneutics—the theory and method of interpretation—but hermeneutics of a different kind. While World Literature practices, for better or worse, a hermeneutics of Endorsement, Postcolonial critique practices, again for better or worse, a hermeneutics, if not of Suspicion, as the caricature would have it, but at least of simultaneous critique and celebration, where the two become inseparable.

If there is a "World" in a postcolonial perspective, that world is not single and it is not a quiet unified realm of contemplative adoration. Rather, it is a world informed by what Robert Young calls "the remainders and the reminders" of colonialism, forming an unequal, fractured set of "worlds," existing within highly hierarchical power relations and stratifications. While World Literature can be comparative and international, Postcolonial Studies is inescapably *trans*national in that it invokes by definition the fraught and uneven relationalities, at a minimum, between, at a minimum, two nations—colonized nation and metropolitan nation-state. It often goes farther to analyze the broader interface between what we now call, in another gesture of arbitrary line-drawing, the Global North and the Global South. On both sides of the colonial fracture, one must add, the nations in question might in fact be nations-of-nations or multi-nations or transnations. India is a multi-nation transected by various ethnic, religious, and linguistic groups. All the nation-states of the Americas, similarly, are in fact multi-nations, in that they orchestrate indigenous nations, the descendants of African slaves and European and broad Asian and Latin American immigrant populations.

The expansion of temporal scope characteristic of World Literature, according to Bruce Robbins, allows for and enables "depoliticization," in that World Literature appeals to "canons of non-European literature, like those of India or China, that predate colonialism and may have nothing to do with unequal power between the world's nations and regions."[16] In terms of spatial scope, meanwhile, World Literature is of the two categories "the more comprehensive geographically" since postcolonial analysis limits itself to areas of the world impacted by colonialism.[17] However, if one takes a longer view of colonialism as beginning with Columbus and the Conquest, people everywhere live under the shadow of Columbus and the "Columbian exchange" of plants, vegetables, minerals, goods, and peoples. "Contact between the two disconnected halves of the world five centuries ago," as native American writer Paul Chaat Smith puts it, was "the profoundest event in human history … [one] that changed the planet and created the world we live in today …"[18] For John Durham Peters, 1492 also had serious consequences for media in the "deep media" sense:

> The world-spanning sea voyages of Portugal and Spain in the fifteenth and sixteenth centuries went together with the invention of paper machines for inventories and populations—the trial, manifest, lading and management of cargo, identity papers, and related forms of visual, numerical, and verbal data management.[19]

As a transdiscipline, Postcolonial Studies can be seen in metaphorical terms as simultaneously both "younger" and "older" than World Literature. It is younger in the sense that while World Literature dates back to Goethe's *weltliteratur* coinage in 1827 in terms of its critical nomenclature, and thousands of years back in terms of the corpus studied, Postcolonial Studies presumably goes back only to the period after independence and decolonization, and the emergence of postcolonial critique within literary studies in the late 1980s with Said's *Orientalism*. But in another sense the critique of colonialism itself goes back to the very beginnings of colonialism, inaugurated by the active resistance of the indigenous peoples targeted by colonialism and the discursive resistance of their European and Euro-American allies from Bartolome de las Casas to Jean-Paul Sartre. Furthermore, postcolonial critique is not restricted to the colonial or postcolonial periods; it can take as its objects of study periods before the advent of Western colonialism per se. Postcolonial critique can extrapolate its arsenal of reading strategies backward in time, for example, to the literature of ancient empires as exempla of "proto-colonialism" or "proto-imperialism." Liberation theologians in Latin America, for example, read the biblical literature, and especially the Pauline epistles and Revelations, as critiques of the Roman Empire and Pax Romana, which they analogize, in an Auerbachian "figural" manner, with U.S. imperialism and the Pax Americana.[20]

Although Postcolonial Studies and World Literature Studies can both be politically critical, Postcolonial Theory and Coloniality/Modernity theory are self-declaredly critical in their very definition, more inclined to theorize, deeply imbricated as they are in the various "post" discourses, be they poststructuralist, post-modernist, post-Marxist, or post-nationalist. Moreover, Postcolonial Studies usually embeds the various "turns" (the linguistic, cultural, feminist, queer, and transnational turns, and so forth). Whereas World Literature is capable of being political yet tends to be disinterested (almost in a Kantian sense), Postcolonial Studies is by definition interested and engaged. While postcolonial critique attempts to convey a sense of urgency, World Literature à la Damrosch at least, conveys an affect of tasteful delectation rather than activist intervention. While postcolonial critique is given to an infinite rondelay of self-critique and self-redefinition, World Literature is more relaxed about its mission and not especially given to auto-critique.

World Literature seems to make more gestures of inclusion toward Postcolonial Literature than the reverse, but that is perhaps a symptom of magnaminity in victory. Yet the apparent triumph of World Literature in terms of academic fashion in some ways constitutes a pyrrhic victory. By definition, World Literature is concerned primarily with a single art/medium—literature—and thus limited to a single field of study. Although many of its tutelary figures, such as Edward Said, Gayatri Spivak, Homi Bhabha, and Robert Young, emerged from literary studies, Postcolonial Studies, in contrast, is much more ecumenical, expansive, and even Protean in its interests and methodologies, and thus more easily extrapolatable to other fields. Since Postcolonial Studies is not tethered to a specific corpus or to any specific discipline dedicated to that corpus, it can easily cross-pollinate with virtually any discipline, displaying a chameleonic adaptability which allows it to have a major impact on disciplines like history, geography, anthropology, and other disciplines in the humanities and the social sciences.

As a result, the postcolonial perspective has by now "spread across almost all the disciplines in the humanities and social sciences, from the classics to development theory to law to medieval studies to theology—even sociology, under the encouragement of postcolonial-minded scholars such as Arjun Appadurai and Paul Gilroy ..."[21] Postcolonial Critique can contribute even to the history of the natural sciences by critiquing Eurocentric accounts of the history of science and by recalling the non-European origins of innumerable scientific breakthroughs in astronomy, mathematics, navigation and so forth. (See for example anthropologist Arturo Escobar's work on indigenous science among native peoples in South America.)[22] Despite the 2007 PMLA interrogative "obituary," whose title "The End of Postcolonial Theory?" would seem to bespeak a desire for its demise, the field continues to unsettle through its endlessly probing questions. The larger point, to my mind, is that any analysis of Literature that does not take colonialism, neo-colonialism, and postcolonialism into account is lacking in political seriousness, just as any account of World Cinema, as we shall see, that does not reflect on the various Worlds that colonialism made is necessarily very historically shallow and politically vacuous.

6

FRENCH POSTCOLONIALITY AND *LITTERATURE-MONDE*

France and the Francophone world play a special and in some ways unique role in relation to issues of cultural prestige in the realms both of literature and cinema. In her thoroughgoing *La Republique Mondiale des Lettres*, Bourdieu-influenced literary scholar Pascale Casanova points to the international aura of Paris as "the capital of that Republic without frontiers, the universal homeland without any narrow patriotism ... a transnational site whose only imperatives are those of art and literature—the Universal Republic of Letters."[1] French exceptionalism has been traditionally wedded to the idea of the French Revolution and its Republic as a universal model for the world. In this sense, France represents *"liberte, egalite* and *fraternite,"* not only for its own citizens but also for all those who seek freedom in France as a *terre d'asile* (land of political asylum) and a *terre d'accueil* (land of refuge). Secular French nationalism, like U.S. nationalism, sees itself as beyond the national, as Universal. In the cases of both French and U.S. Republicanism, the particular national interest has the trait of claiming to be universal, resulting in what Pierre Bourdieu calls "two imperialisms of the universal."[2]

Both French and American nationalism evoke their universal mission through metaphors of light, the U.S. as "beacon to the world," and France as the beacon whose Enlightenment ("les lumieres") and *rayonnment* (shining out) spread out and illuminate the world. The torch held by Lady Liberty, a French gift to the U.S., forms a stony embodiment of this diffusionist trope of the outward spreading of light. The pretension of universality of the two *republiques soeurs*, in the cases of France and the U.S., form a kind of national "symbolic capital" (Bourdieu) that can be deployed in the service of two forms of cultural imperialism—the aggressively brash Pentagon-Hollywood kind, and the soft-spoken seductive French "cultural exception" kind. Both have exercised hard as well as "soft" power.

This claim to being a non-nationalist nation plays out in the ways France interacts with the world in cultural terms. There are few parallels in the U.S., in this sense, to the ways that the French cultural establishment (and government) honor and support not only their own cultural achievements but also those of other nations. To put it succinctly, while Hollywood bullies the world, French cultural institutions seduce it and "patronize" it. Already in 1984, Jean Guiart, from the *Musée de l'Homme*, had spoken of the new "mission" of French ethnology: "to valorize the cultural riches of each non-European people."[3] One finds this welcome valorization of non-European cultures in many manifestations of French cultural policies, whether in the area of the "World Republic of Letters," with the key French role, stressed by Casanova, as Gatekeeper or World Bank for Literature, or in World Music, of which France is a main producer, or in World Cinema, where France has helped finance emerging cinemas not only in Francophone Africa, Asia, and the Middle East but also in other parts of the world, making Paris the capital, in some ways, of Global Art cinema; to Hollywood's commercial "franchise-ization," France answers with auteurist "Frenchification."

Although France on one level has challenged Hollywood hegemony, it has also had to walk a fine line between a generous pluralism and a subtle paternalism. Indeed, there is a Gaullist aspect to this patronage of the arts in the Global South. In the heyday of *la Francophonie*, De Gaulle presided over the demise of the French empire, and then shortly thereafter fabricated the image of France as the defender of the Third World against those the French so inaccurately call—reducing diverse peoples to two Germanic tribes—"les Anglo-Saxons."[4] Although France could no longer pretend to be a superpower, it could at least speak for "the rest" as the sponsor of an alternative universality, rallied against the false universalism of the "hyper-power." The obvious problem, of course, was that the entire schema presumed that the recently decolonized Third World could not speak for itself; it needed a white European mediator like France.

The global configuration of cultural power has implications for the status of postcolonial studies in France vis-à-vis the English-speaking world. Anglophone-centered postcolonial studies tends to neglect the French-speaking world, while for a long time France tended to neglect, or even resist, postcolonial studies. The relation of French intellectuals to the postcolonial, in this sense, presents a paradox. On the one hand, France and the Francophone zones formed crucial sites in the postwar paradigm shift in thinking about race and colonialism in the postwar period. The related rebellions summed up in the date "May 1968" forming the high-water mark not only of anti-capitalism but also of Third Worldism. While de Gaulle pursued his independent path between the United States and the Soviet Union, the left mounted massive demonstrations, along with an immense intellectual production in support of Third World revolutions and the resistance movements in the West, especially in the United States.

The postwar period also witnessed the emergence of an embryonic black movement ensuant to the arrival in France of a new generation of African and West Indian students, often on scholarships, leading to a substantial intellectual community. France, and especially Paris, served as a key node in the network of Third Worldist thought, contributing to the postwar critique of dominant trends in the human and social sciences as reflecting the economic and cultural imperialism of the European colonial powers. In the 1970s, the Laboratory for Third World and African Studies at University of Paris VII, for example, combined African, Asian, and Latin American studies. The fact that postcolonial studies at first found little purchase on the French intellectual scene was thus partly due to the fact that the postcolonial field was seen as *already* occupied by anticolonial and anti-imperialist writing and activism therefore seemed, despite the new theoretical wrinkles, a case of "déjà vu all over again." Present-day postcolonial studies in France, in this sense, cannot be seen as merely as an epigonic or belated copy of work performed outside of France; rather, it must be situated intertextually, in relation to the anticolonial corpus fashioned by these earlier writers.

What could be called "proto-postcolonial" work was also performed by Arab intellectuals in France, in what might seem like a surprising institutional site: French "Oriental" studies. French-speaking Arab intellectuals formed part of a linguistic, cultural, and scholarly continuum. As insiders/outsiders, they resembled the British-educated "white but not quite" colonial elites, or the English-speaking Arab scholars in Middle Eastern studies in the United States. Beginning in the 1950s, Oriental academic institutions in France began to recognize the independence struggles in the Arab world, while also absorbing a few Arab intellectuals into their ranks. In 1963, a decade and a half before Edward Said's seminal book *Orientalism*, Anouar Abdel-Malek published "Orientalism in Crisis" in the journal *Diogenes* (vol. 44, Winter 1963). For Abdel-Malek, Third World independence struggles inevitably impacted Oriental studies by turning those who had been "objects of study" into sovereign subjects. "The hegemonism of possessing minorities, unveiled by Marx and Engels, and the anthropocentrism dismantled by Freud [had been] accompanied by Europocentrism in the area of human and social sciences, and more particularly in those in direct relationship with non-European peoples7."[5] A decade later, Abdallah Laroui's *La Crise des Intellectuels Arabes* (1974) denounced the Orientalist penchant for "speaking for [Arab] others" and attacked the Orientalists as a bureaucratic caste.[6]

Despite these currents, until recently postcolonial theory formed a structuring absence in French Left discourse. This absence contrasted not only with the Anglo-American academic world but also with other parts of Europe (the Netherlands, Germany, Scandinavia, Iberia) and with Latin America and with many parts of Asia and Africa, all sites where postcolonial studies have been a significant presence for decades. In France, in contrast, the word "postcolonial" functioned largely as a chronological marker, a synonym for "postindependence" rather than as an index of a discourse or field of inquiry. For complex reasons, many French intellectuals ignored at best, and maligned at worst, a constellation of interrelated projects such as postcolonial studies, cultural studies, and critical race studies. There was a manifest hostility to what were perceived as Anglo-American currents in general, whether these currents came in the form of multiculturalism (associated with that mythical ethos known as the "Anglo-Saxons") or cultural studies (associated initially with the United Kingdom and later with the United States) or postcolonial theory (associated with India, the United States, the United Kingdom, and the Anglophone zone generally), and especially with postcolonial intellectuals well-installed in the Anglo-American academe (Edward Said, Gayatri Spivak, and Homi Bhabha).

The French literary field had long been dominated by the discursive formation of *la Francophonie*. Less a critical theory than an officially mandated post-independence reformatting of the *mission civilisatrice*, *la Francophonie* can be seen as a Gaullist cultural, diplomatic, and commercial project partially aimed at Anglo-American rivals for influence in the Third World. This situation generated an ambiguous status, at once privileged and marginalized, for Francophone writers. In words that in some ways apply as well to Francophone filmmakers, Pascale Casanova pinpoints their awkward situation: "Paris had never been interested in the writers from its colonial territories; in fact, it has for a long time scorned and mistreated them as provincials, too close for their differences to be recognized or celebrated yet too far to simply be perceived."[7] The Caribbean writers, for example, come to be seen as too Caribbean to be French and too French to be Caribbean. Much of the postcolonial "air" was thus sucked up, at least in literature departments, by *la Francophonie* and Francophone literature.

Yet the very concept of *Francophonie* has been challenged both by the critics and by the writers themselves, who prefer such formulation as "world literature in French." Glissant's concept of *litterature-monde* emerged in the context of writers from the former French colonies in Africa and the Antilles who were eager to shed the paternalism of "Francophone" literature. Although the term on one level simply translates Goethe's *weltlitteratur*, on another level it transforms it through the translation into French, and through a hyphen which suggests an equation between two substantives. The phrase was devised as an antidote to the peripheralization of Global South artists in general, and in particular the paternalism of post-Independence Francophonie which tethered Francophone writers to the French metropole even in the postcolonial periods. Despite the power of the hyphen in unifying/splitting two substantives, *litterature-monde* does not completely avoid the difficulties of World Literature. By literally translating *Weltliteratur*, Françoise Lionnet has argued, the advocates of *litterature-monde*, despite their subversive intentions and practices, were ironically recentering everything that they had meant to decenter.[8]

Like the concept of "Ethnic Music" and "World Music"—as musics of "the Rest"—the concept of *Francophonie* also had a racial subtext. The term supposedly referred to all those writers from outside Hexegonal France who spoke and wrote in French, for example the writers from Africa and the Caribbean. Yet white European writers like Ionesco and Beckett, who undeniably fit the literal definition, were strangely excluded from the category. The tacit racial hierarchy resemble that underlying the difference between the French word *étranger*—assumed to refer to Western foreigners in France—*and immigrés* –implied to be immigrants of color from the formerly colonized or peripheralized countries. The former, like their textual productions, could "circulate" easily, while the latter encountered practical obstacles, bureaucratic hurdles, glass-ceilings, and *la double peine*.

As a result of this difference in academic categories and genealogies, what in the Anglophone world would have been called "postcolonial," and which would usually have been pursued in the diverse "studies" programs such as "cultural studies," "race studies" and so forth, in France might be simply named in relation to traditionally enshrined disciplines "history" or "anthropology" or "economics" or "literature." "Postcolonial literature," similarly, might be called in France "literature of development" or "emergent" literature. Such work was often critical of colonialism in theory and practice, even if it did not sufficiently unpack such infantilizing terms as "emerging" and "developing." Already in 1971, anthropologist Georges Balandier, for example, anticipated Homi Bhabha's notions of "sly civility" as a coping mechanism within colonialism by speaking of "collective reactions that could be called clandestine or indirect" or of "calculated manifestations of passivity" as subtle ways of undermining colonial domination.[9] What was most lacking in the French academic work, perhaps, was the metatheoretical and transdisciplinary thrust of postcolonial studies, even though that thrust in many ways had been fueled and energized by French critical theory.

A number of poignant ironies, as Ella Shohat and I point out in *Race in Translation: Culture Wars around the Postcolonial Atlantic*, hover around the initial reluctance of French intellectuals to embrace postcolonial studies. The first and most obvious is that postcolonial studies itself has been very much shaped by Francophone anticolonial discourse. Many key sets of questions (*problematiques*) within postcolonial studies trace back to Francophone intellectuals such as Césaire, Senghor, Fanon, Memmi, Glissant, and Anouar Abdel-Malek. The second irony is that "French Theory," as Robert Young pointed out in *White Mythologies*, was shaped by the colonial situation and by the fact that many of the leading theoreticians (Derrida, Althusser, Lyotard, Cixous, Bourdieu, Foucault) were biographically or experientially linked to North Africa. The third irony is that French poststructuralism has had massive impact on leading postcolonial thinkers—one thinks of Foucault's influence on Said, Derrida's on Spivak, Lacan's on Bhabha—and on the postcolonial field in general, manifested in myriad references not only to Derrida, Foucault, and Lacan but also to Deleuze, Guattari, Irigaray, Cixous, Lyotard, Glissant, and de Certeau. (This poststructuralist aspect of postcolonial theory is all the more striking given the fact that the leading poststructuralist thinkers themselves, perhaps with the exception of Balibar, rarely engaged in any systematic way with issues of colonialism and race and rarely cited anticolonialist texts.)

A fourth irony about the aversion to postcolonial theory revolves around the fact that France in the 1960s and early 1970s had been the epicenter of "Third Worldism," precisely the tradition that postcolonialism was both embedding and superseding. With the postwar dismembering of the French empire, colonialism and decolonization were necessarily at the core of many polemics, even if only by implication. Indeed, much of the French contribution to the seismic shift stems from these early battles, as Third Worldist writers such as the Antillais Césaire, Fanon, Maryse Condé, and Glissant alongside African writers such as Leopold Senghor, Amílcar Cabral, Cheikh Diop, and Mongo Beti, at times in conversation with radical African-American expatriates such as Richard Wright or Arab/Maghrebian/ African/Francophone writers such as Albert Memmi, Gisèle Halimi, Anouar Abdel-Malek, Mohammed Harbi, Alioune Diop, Hamidou Kane, Amadou Hampaté Bâ, and Assia Djebar found Hexagonal allies in figures such as Edgar Morin, Maxime Rodinson, Claude Lévi-Strauss, Jean-Paul Sartre, Simone de Beauvoir, Henri Alleg, Pierre Vidal-Naquet, François Maspero, Yves Bénot, Francis Jeanson, Alice Cherki, Yves Bénot, and so many others, In this sense, Anglophone postcolonial scholars would do well to "deprovincialize" themselves.

Somewhat belatedly, the past two decades have generated a substantial body of postcolonial work in France, founded, according to Marie-Claude Smouts, on three propositions long accepted in the "Anglophone" academe: (1) that the colonial fact forms an integral part of the history of the French present; (2) that colonialism has thoroughly transformed not only the former colonized societies but also the colonizing society itself; and (3) that France, in order to shape a more inclusive republic, has to recognize the legacy of its colonial past.[10] Despite the initial resistance in France to postcolonial theory in the academic sphere, the political debates about colonialism became much more part of the public sphere in France than was the case in the United States and the United Kingdom. It would therefore be wrong to see the issue in a stagist and linear way, as if it were merely a question of French intellectuals getting up to speed or "catching up" with the Anglophone sphere. "The temporalities and historicities of different languages," as Rada Iveković puts it, "do not always coincide."[11] Some of the French hesitations about postcolonial studies derived, as we have seen, from a pride in France's status as a privileged terrain for anticolonial, anti-neocolonial, and anti-imperialist writing by both French and Francophone writers within and beyond the Hexagon. This anticolonial and anti-imperial work later morphed, it could be argued, not so much into the postcolonial academic field but rather into the activism associated with the alter-globalization movements. The World Social Forum, for example, began as a collaboration between progressive Workers Party Brazilians and the anti-imperialist leftists of *Le Monde Diplomatique*. So while there has been less postcolonial academic production in France, there has also perhaps been more political activism related to the latter-day sequels of colonialism and imperialism.

The past decades have seen a veritable explosion of postcolonial studies in France in the 21st century and especially after 2005. In the late 1990s and in the first decade of the 21st century, we witness a major engagement in France itself with postcolonial studies. Numerous conferences and special issues of journals such as *Esprit, Labyrinthe, Rue Descartes*, and *Mouvements* treat "the colonial fracture," "the sequels of colonialism," and "the wars of colonial memory." Many of the recent publications thematize the historical delay itself through a quasi-ritualistic acknowledgment of the French hesitation in joining the postcolonial trend.

While only some of the work is performed under the rubric of the "postcolonial," it is all directly or indirectly related to colonialism and its aftermath. In terms of basic trends, first, a large body of current work focuses on the hidden history of French colonialism and the contradictions inherent in "republican colonialism": Bernard Mouralis's *Republic and Colony: Between History and Memory* (1999); Rosa Amelia Plumelle-Uribe's *White Ferocity* (2001); Yves Bénot's *Colonial Massacres* (2001); Marc Ferro's edited volume *The Black Book of Colonialism* (2003); Olivier Le Cour Grandmaison's *Colonize/Exterminate: On War and the Colonial State* (2005); Nicolas Bancel, Pascal Blanchard, and Françoise Vergès's *The Colonial Republic: Essay on a Utopia* (2003); and Jean Pierre Dozon's *Brothers and Subjects: France and Africa in Perspective* (2003).

Second, another body of work, in what in the U.S. would be called a "cultural studies" manner, treats colonial/imperial popular culture as consumed by the French populace within the Hexagon: Nicolas Bancel, Pascal Blanchard, Gilles Boetsch, Eric Deroo, and Sandrine Lemaire's *Human Zoos* (2002); Pascal Blanchard and Sandrine Lemaire's *Colonial Culture: France Conquered by Its Empire, 1871–1931* (2003) and *Imperial Culture: The Colonies at the Heart of the Republic, 1931–1961* (2004); and Pascal Blanchard, Nicolas Bancel, and Sandrine Lemaire's *The Colonial Fracture: French Society Seen through the Prism of Its Colonial Heritage* (2005). These books address the ways in which ordinary French people could enjoy the spectacles provided by "imperial culture" as manifested in colonial expositions and "Human Zoos"—portrayed in the Abdellatif Kechiche's film *Black Venus*—where colonials were displayed for the delectation of the European and American populace.

Third, some work—Romain Bertrand's *Memories of Empire: The Controversy about the "Colonial Fact"* (2006), Benjamin Stora's *The War of Memories: France Faces its Colonial Past* (2007), and the collective work *An Unfortunate Decolonization: France from the Empire to the Banlieue Riots* (2007)—critically explores the "war of memories" spiraling around colonialism. Fourth, postcolonial texts treat the corollary theme of the history and memory of slavery: Françoise Vergès's *Chained Memory: Questions about Slavery* (2006) and Édouard Glissant's *Memories of Slaveries* (2007). The work on slavery presents an ambiguous relation to a postcolonial field that too often brackets slavery, as if it were not also at the very kernel of the colonial question. These texts seek to demonstrate a clear continuity between colonialism and slavery, including in the form of fervent abolitionists, such as Victor Schoelcher, who subsequently metamorphosed into equally fervent colonialists.

Fifth, there is work on postcolonial literary studies per se: Jean-Marc Moura's *Francophone Literatures and Postcolonial Theory* (1999) and Jacqueline Bardolph's *Postcolonial Studies and Literature* (2002). Although Pascale Casanova's massively informed *The World Republic of Letters* certainly engages writers who could be called "postcolonial," she generally avoids the idioms of postcolonial theory in favor of political and economic metaphors—the "stock market" of literary values, literary "currency exchanges" and "the Republic of Letters"—drawn from Bourdieu's concepts of cultural capital and literary distinction. In any case, probing questions about race and postcoloniality are now being asked in contemporary France, posed both along a spatial axis—concerning whether colonialism is internal or external to French history—and along a temporal axis, concerning whether colonialism still shapes contemporary French history.

7

SIBLING DISCIPLINES

Literary Studies and Cinema Studies

Although World Literature and World Cinema are seldom brought into conversation, it is obvious to film scholars, at least, that the two have a close kinship. If not exactly siblings, they are at least cousins tracing their lineage back to a common set of ancestors. Indeed, in many ways, Cinema Studies has historically operated in tandem with Literary Studies. First, many of the pioneers of Cinema Studies—at least prior to the professionalization and what Bourdieu would call the "autonomization" of the field beginning in the late 1960s—were trained in English Literature, Romance Languages, and Comparative Literature. Founded in 1959, the Society for Cinema Studies (initially called the "Society of Cinematologists") was self-consciously intended "to be to film what the Modern Language Association was to literature."[1] Second, many of the field's axiomatic concepts—authorship, genre, realism, intertextuality, the canon—were drawn from Literary Studies. The protocols of close-reading and *explication de texte* were also shared, even if those protocols were constantly being transformed and mediatized and adapted for the newer medium. Third, the founding ontological query of the discipline—summed up in Andre Bazin's title: *What is Cinema?*—was a remediated twist on the same theoretical question posed decades earlier by the Russian Formalists in relation to literature i.e. the question of artistic specificity or "literariness," now transposed into the Metzian semiotic question of the "specifically cinematic." Fourth, the two fields have generally shared the same theoretical trends and *maîtres a penser*, by turns absorbing, reshaping, and extrapolating the theoretical trends affecting the humanities in general– Merleau-Pontian phenomenology, Saussurean semiology, Piercian semiotics, Lacanian psychoanalysis, Althusserian Marxism, Derridean poststructuralism, Lyotardian postmodernism, Jamesian post-culturalism, Saidian and Spivakian postcolonialism, Deleuzian rhizomatics and so forth.

Literary Studies and Cinema Studies, and World Literature and World Cinema differ, however, in terms of the political orientation and disciplinary legacies of their departmental "hosts." The topic of World Cinema is largely housed in "Film and Media Studies" departments which were from the beginning more friendly toward, in the beginning, Third World Studies, Ethnic Studies, and Women's Studies, and later toward left-inflected transdisciplines like Postcolonial Studies, Cultural Studies, Multicultural Studies, a friendliness which has much to do with the fields' geneses as disciplines. Literature departments, like literature itself, enjoy the prestige of anteriority, but they also bear the burdens of that anteriority in the form of the persisting power of totemic figures and inherited paradigms. Unlike Literary Studies, which was challenged in the 1960s by its "Young Turks," Cinema Studies itself was founded in the 1960s *by* Young Turks and *allied* with the Young Turks of other fields. (In fact the New Wave director/critics so admired by Cinema Studies scholars were literally called "the Young Turks). The field of Cinema Studies began as a dissident, avant-garde friendly discipline where Soviet revolutionary films, Vertovian montage, "Third Cinema," and the various "New Waves" enjoyed pride of place. As a "breakaway" formation from more traditional disciplines like History and English, the field flourished in tandem with other "breakaway" transdisciplines such as Ethnic Studies, Women's Studies, and Third World Studies. What these trends had in common was the fact that they all operated in the interstices of the traditional departments and were relatively unencumbered by the "weight" of older figures and paradigms.

Cinema Studies emerged in the 1960s during the heights of first-phase structuralism and semiotics, and was intimately linked to artistic, political, and theoretical currents in France. My own Department of Cinema Studies at NYU was founded, significantly, in 1968, the year associated with revolutionary movements around the world, and especially with the May 68 protests in France. In terms of film, the late 1960s and early 1970s proliferated in radical movements of political, artistic, and cinematic renovation. In the wake of Italian Neo-Realism and the French New Wave, the period saw the emergence of many radical national film movements: Cinema Novo in Brazil, New Latin American Cinema, Nueva Ola in Mexico, Neues Deutsches Kino in Germany, New American Cinema in the U.S., New Indian Cinema in India, and Giovane Cinema in Italy. The events of 1968 had momentous repercussions for the arts generally and for film specifically. The events of May were foreshadowed, in a sense, by film-related events in February, specifically the *L'Affaire Langlois* and the February protests against the Gaullist regime's attempt to fire Henri Langlois, the director of *la cinemateque francaise*. Many of the films, and the debates around them, concerned a "struggle on two fronts": the political and the aesthetic, and the issues in the vanguard of Cinema Studies, at that time, revolved around aesthetics and politics, and highly fraught questions of bourgeois ideology, Marx, Althusser, the "political film" and the like.

1960s radical film theory and semiotics anticipated and came to form part of the Cultural Studies that came later with its penchant not only for debating the concept of "radical film" but also for deploying "high" theory to analyze "low" popular objects of study such as B-films, pop genres and advertisements. Radical journals such as *Cinetique Cinemaction* and post-68 *Cahiers du Cinema* in France,

Jump Cut, *Camera Obscura*, and *Cineaste* in the U.S. and *Screen* and *Framework* in the U.K were widely read by film students and cinephiles in general. A key intermediary between French film theory and the American academe was *Le Centre Americain d'Etudes du Cinema* in Paris—which later morphed into *Le Centre Parisien d'Etudes Critiques*—where many American film scholars studied with theorist/scholars like Christian Metz, Raymond Bellour, Thierry Kuntzel, Pascal Bonitzer, Marc Vernet, and Michel Marie. The roster of such scholars includes many key figures in the field: Dana Polan, Constance Penley, Hilary Radner, Judith Mayne, Sandy Flitterman-Lewis, Rick Altmann, Maureen Turim, David Rodowick, Howard Besser, Janet Bergstrom, Ed Lowry, Kelly Conway, Richard de Cordova and many others.[2]

The *Cahiers* critics who subsequently formed the nucleus of the French New Wave—itself a favored topic for Cinema Studies writing and curriculum—meanwhile, were deeply impacted by literature. Ambivalent about literature's established institutional power and cultural charisma in France, the critic-directors saw literature both as model to be emulated and enemy to be abjured. Haunted by the overweening prestige of literature in a country that had always venerated its writers, the *Cahiers* critics forged the concept of the filmmaker as *auteur* as a way of transferring the millennial aura of the established art of literature to the fledgling art of film. Novelist/filmmaker Alexandre Astruc prepared the way with his landmark 1948 essay "Birth of a New Avant-Garde: the Camera-Pen," where he argued that the cinema was becoming a new means of creative expression analogous to painting or the novel.[3] In the postwar period in France, film discourse, like literary discourse generally, came to gravitate around such literary concepts as "textuality," and "intertextuality" and filmic *ecriture*. A graphological trope—from Astruc's camera-pen (camera-stylo) to Robbe-Grillet's *cine-roman*, to Varda's *cine-ecriture*—informed a wide spectrum of coinages. This fondness for scriptural metaphors was scarcely surprising given that many of the New Wave directors began as film critics who saw writing essays and making films simply as two variant forms of artistic expression. Not only did the New Wave directors practice literary adaptation in the literal sense, usually of non-canonical novels, they also made films where literature exercised a strong but quiet presence. Even when the films did not actually adapt novels or novelists, they were yet imbued with their spirit, whence the pervasive influence of Balzac on Chabrol, Truffaut, and Rohmer, or Faulkner and Jarry and Rimbaud on Godard, or Proust on Resnais. In this sense, Resnais's obsessive search for lost cinematic time makes him a "Proustian" director, even though he never actually adapted *A la recherche du temps perdu*. (This literariness is not unique to the NewWave, of course; Jane Campion's *The Piano*, by the same token, is often called "Brontean" in its sensibility, while Lucretia Martel's *La Cienega* is seen as "Faulknerian").

French intellectuals were firm believers in the philosophical dignity of cinema. Indeed, a remarkable number of illustrious French writers—for example Marguerite Duras, Jean Cayrol, and Alain Robbe-Grillet—took up filmmaking, or wrote about cinema—for example Roland Barthes, Gilles Deleuze, Alain Badiou, Jean-Luc Nancy, and Jacques Rancière. (This cross-art and cross-disciplinary migrancy can partially be explained by the nature of Paris, and especially certain neighborhoods like the Latin Quarter, as artistic-intellectual "clusters of clusters" featuring densely packed concentrations of Universities, libraries, bookstores, cinemas, theaters, and cafes). Philosopher Jean-Luc Nancy, for his part, has not only written about film, for example in his *The Evidence of Film* but also through his text *L'Intrus*, which formed the basis for French director Claire Denis's film of the same name. (Nancy also crossed over to the production side himself by developing films in conjunction with artist-filmmaker Phillip Warnell).

Speaking more generally, the artistic cross-overs between cinema and literature as cultural practices have been multi-faceted and multi-directional—novelists who become screenwriters (William Faulkner, F. Scott Fitzgerald, Vladimir Nabokov); screenwriters who become filmmakers (Charlie Kaufman, Paul Schrader); novelists who become filmmakers (Hanif Kureishi); filmmakers who become novelists (Elia Kazan); celebrated novelists who write film criticism (Carlos Fuentes, Gabriel Garcia Marquez); film critics who become filmmakers (all of the *Cahiers* directors—Godard, Truffaut, Rivette, Rohmer, Chabrol—plus Olivier Assayas, Pascal Bonitzer, Glauber Rocha, and Kleber Mendonca Filho); film theorists who become filmmakers (Laura Mulvey, Peter Wollen); and film academics who draw on World Literature theory to frame their own World Cinema theory (Dudley Andrew, Lucia Nagib).

But apart from these direct links between the two arts/media, we find art-historical synergies between the history of literature and the history of filmic fiction. Although the cinema's technological razzle-dazzle bestows the shine and sheen of modernity, its dominant aesthetic was firmly grounded in the 19th century, in that it inherited the mimetic aspirations of 19th-century literary realism and naturalism of Dickens, Balzac, and Zola. However "modern" in the sense of belonging to technological and industrial modernity, the dominant forms of cinema were not modernist in an aesthetic sense. The beginnings of cinema in the 1890s coincided with a crisis within the veristic project as expressed in the realist novel, in the naturalist play (with real meat in Antoine-staged butcher shops), and in obsessively mimetic exhibitions. Comprised of those movements in the arts (both inside and outside of Europe) which emerged in the late 19th century, artistic modernism flourished in the early decades of the 20th century, and which became institutionalized as "high modernism" after World War II, in contrast, promoted a trans-realist, non-representational art characterized by abstraction, fragmentation and aggression. Unsurprisingly, the most bitter disappointments, on the part of literate readers, have had to do with filmic adaptations of modernist novels like those of Joyce, Woolf and Proust, precisely because in such cases the aesthetic gap between source and adaptation seems most startling, less because of any inherent deficiency in the cinematic medium but rather because of the conventional option, within dominant cinema, for a pre-modernist veristic aesthetic.

The Worlds of Literature and Cinema are thoroughly commingled. Just as literature is deeply embedded in cinema, so the cinema is embedded in literature, even in literature that antedated the invention of cinema. I am speaking here of the phenomenon of the "proto-cinematic." Although the term usually refers to those optical devices—such as the magic lantern, the mutascope, zoetrope, the stereoscope, the thaumatrope, the Phenaktistiscope, and so forth—that preceded the cinema, I use the term to speak of literary anticipations of cinematic technique.[4] Werner Herzog, interestingly, uses the same expression of "proto-cinema" in relation to the 30,000-year-old drawings found in the Chauvet cave, registered in his film *Cave of Forgotten Dreams* (2010). For Herzog, these images from the cavernous deep time of the Palaeolithic period are uncannily reminiscent of "frames from an animated film … almost a form of proto-cinema." By comparing the cinematic apparatus to Plato's Cave, 1970s film theorists like Jean-Louis Baudry, similarly, were also highlighting a philosophical form of the proto-cinematic.

More typically, the word "proto-cinematic" is used imprecisely in relation to literature as meaning anything and everything that is sharply visualized, or emotionally impactive, or featuring physical action. I use the term to refer not to optical devices but to the technologies of narrative, characterization, and point of view in literary fiction, but here I am speaking of more precise anticipations of filmic devices and procedures. Flaubert's *Madame Bovary*, for example, is proto-cinematic in manifold ways: 1) the film-script like precision in the notation of gestures and attitudes; 2) the use of literary props such as Charles' silly cap or Rodolphe's riding crop; 3) the acute sensitivity to a multi-planar and 3-dimensional evocation of sound; 4) the montage, already noted by Eisenstein, of contrasting discourses and speech genres (political and amorous) in the Agricultural Fair Sequence ("les comices"); 5) the use of *le style indirect libre* as a kind of "dolly in" to Emma's consciousness, in an indeterminacy of narrative voice that mingles distance with interiority; 6) the frequent precise articulation of physical vantage point, like a setup in film, linked to the perspective of various characters, including minor characters beginning with the "nous etions au coin" of the first paragraph and toward the end the "curieux"looking at Charles from over the hedge; 7) the dispersal of point of view, à la Hitchcock, to numerous characters both major (Emma, Charles) and minor (the students, two gossips); 8) the manipulation of distance and focal length between close shots (of Emma's flower) and distance ("une femme descendit"); 9) the literary equivalents of subjective travelling shots conveying the kinesthetic passage of a carriage through space; and 10) the destabilized portraiture as a flow of impressions in time.[5]

I will return to adaptation in a moment, and specifically to cases where World Cinema actually adapts the canonical favorites of World Literature, but my very specific goal in what follows is to "test" the concept of World Cinema against Damrosch's requirements for World Literature status, to recapitulate: 1) that it must "*circulate*" beyond its homeland; 2) that it must "*gain in translation*," and 3) that it must "*estrange*" its readers from their own culture. Damrosch's prerequisites are relevant, in some ways, to cinematic adaptations of the World Literature canon, but in surprising and illuminating ways. We can begin with Damrosch's basic definition of World Literature as "literature that circulates beyond its linguistic and cultural point of origin, whether in translation or in the original." The "circulation" requirement as defining World status, as we saw earlier with literature, can be posed as a question of quality—i.e. works in either media must exhibit the artistic excellence or cultural complexity that allows them to transcend their culture of origin—or as a question of power, the *realpolitik* capacity to make "content" circulate around the world, quite regardless of quality. The criterion of circulation, when it fails to distinguish between quality and power, quietly discriminates against a good deal of deserving art.

"Circulation," moreover, does not operate in the same way in literature and film. Although virtually all contemporary artistic production is filtered through what the Frankfurt School critics called the "culture industry" and what Bertolt Brecht and Walter Benjamin called the "apparati," a historically shaped distinction separates the two arts/media. Put simply, no apparatus or agency within World Literature wields anything like the overweening *puissance* of Hollywood within the film world. While Hollywood, whether seen as an integral part of World Cinema, or as its ideological and aesthetic opposite number, or as "just another other" cinema, forms an inescapable backdrop in any discussion of World Cinema, no comparable entity or agency or institution holds similar sway within World Literature. Readers and spectators around the world are much more likely to have heard of 20th Century Fox (now 21st Century Fox) and Paramount Pictures (now owned by Viacom) and Warner Brothers (now Time-Warner) than they are to have heard of the conglomerates that dominate the book trade such as Thomson Pearson, Bertelsmann, and Hachette Lure. The only equivalent in the literary field to the quite literal hegemony of Hollywood would be something much more limited and modest—e.g. the cumulative infrastructural power of publishing conglomerates—or something more abstract and metaphorical– the hegemonic presence of the English language, or the symbolic power of an abstract construct like the "canon." On the other hand, this difference between cinema and literature is eroding in the age of media convergence and financial concentration, especially with corporations like Amazon that now produce and distribute all kinds of what they rudely call "content," as long as it is profitable, including in the form of films and books, many of them based on the World Literature canon.

8

FROM LITERATURE TO FILM
A study in ambivalence

In historical terms, a difference in aura and prestige separates literature from film. While World Literature claims a multi-millennial tradition, World Cinema claims only slightly more than a century. Yet in aesthetic terms, the cinema emerges from artistic "deep time" in that it inherits, thanks to its multiple tracks, the millennial histories of all the temporal and spatial arts. It is heir to the entire history of theater and the performance arts through its image and sound tracks, the entire history of the pictorial arts through the visual track, the entire history of music through the music track and so forth. One of the first serious treatments of the cinema in English, poet Vachel Lindsay's 1915 book *The Art of the Motion Picture*, emphasized the absorption by the "seventh art" of Cinema of its "sister arts" like poetry, painting, sculpture, and music. The study of cinema therefore becomes impoverished when it is isolated from its ecological relation to the other arts. As Alain Badiou puts it:

> Cinema is the seventh art in a very particular sense. It does not add itself to the other six while remaining on the same level as them. Rather, it implies them—cinema is the "plus-one" of the art. It operates on the other arts, using them as its starting point, in a movement that substracts them from themselves.[1]

Summas by their very nature, both the novel and the fiction film, are open to all cultural forms. Their essence is to have no essence. The cinema has resources unavailable to the novel; it can literally include painting, poetry, and music or it can metaphorically evoke the techniques and procedures of those artists; it can display a Cubist painting, or emulate Cubist techniques, cite a jazz performance, or emulate jazzistic improvisations and create polyrhythmic montage sequences.

The relations between film and literature have often been wary and ambivalent. On the literary side, World Literature theory has existed in a state of denial about the intimate connection between World Literature and World Cinema. The website of the Belgrade Department of World Literature, in a symptomatic example, expressly aspires to treat World Literature in a historical-intellectual perspective "untainted" by media studies, as if media studies were irremediably tarnished and beyond the pale of the "historical-intellectual."[2] The *Routledge Companion to World Literature* ignores cinema generally and cinematic adaptations specifically, with the exception of one welcome essay by Jan Baetens which stresses the role of remediations in rescuing literature from oblivion.

Behind such patronizing attitudes toward the cinema, I have argued elsewhere, lies a supercilious sense of superiority—which in the past became quite obvious in the dismissive attitudes toward film and film adaptations of novels within the field of literary studies. The widespread assumption was that film adaptations had somehow always done a disservice to literature. Until relatively recently, the conventional language of adaptation criticism, both in journalism and in academic writing, had often been profoundly moralistic. Terms like "infidelity," "betrayal," "deformation," "violation," "bastardization," "vulgarization," and "desecration" proliferate in adaptation discourse, each word carrying its specific charge of opprobrium. "Infidelity" carries overtones of Victorian prudishness; "betrayal" evokes ethical perfidy; "bastardization" connotes illegitimacy; "deformation" implies aesthetic disgust and monstrosity; "violation" calls to mind sexual violence; "vulgarization" conjures up class degradation; and "desecration" intimates religious sacrilege and blasphemy.[3]

Although the illusory force of the putative superiority of literature to film can be partially explained by the undeniable fact that many adaptations **are** indeed mediocre or misguided, it also derives, I have argued, from deeply rooted and often unconscious assumptions about the relations between the two arts. The once regnant doxa concerning adaptation's inferiority derived, in my view, from a constellation of substratal prejudices that I have elsewhere summed up as: 1) **seniority**: the assumption is that older arts are necessarily better arts. Literature profits from a double "priority"; a) the general historical priority of literature to cinema, and b) the specific priority of novels to their adaptations. As Mitchell Stephens argues, "new media are criticized and old media are cherished";[4] 2) the **dichotomous thinking** which presumes a bitter rivalry between film and literature, entangled in a Darwinian struggle to the death; 3) **iconophobia**, the culturally engrained prejudice against the visual arts (traceable not only to the Judaic-Muslim-Protestant prohibitions of "graven images" and to the Platonic depreciation of the world of phenomenal appearance), whereby the allure of the spectacle is seen as overwhelming reason;[5] 4) **logophilia**, or the valorization, typical of cultures rooted in the "religions of the book," of what Bakhtin calls the "sacred word" of written texts. Hovering over adaptation, one might speculate, is the Book of Revelation's threat against anyone who dares to alter the text with the plagues it describes (Revelation 10.35); 5) **anti-corporeality**, a distaste for the unseemly "embodiedness" of the filmic text with its inexorable materiality, its incarnated, fleshly, enacted characters, its real locales and palpable props; its carnality and visceral shocks to the nervous system; 6) **class prejudice**, a socialized form of guilt by association. The cinema, perhaps unconsciously, is seen as degraded by the company it keeps—the great unwashed popular mass audience, and with its lower-class origins in "vulgar" spectacles like sideshows and carnivals; 7) **parasitism,** the idea that adaptations are seen as parasitical on literature—they burrow into the body of the source text and drain its vitality—or even vampiric—fatally sucking the life-blood from its source. But adaptations can resuscitate novels that were forgotten or on life-support. As Linda Hutcheon puts it, they can "keep that prior work alive, giving it an afterlife it would never have had otherwise ... adaptation is how stories evolve and mutate to fit new times and different places."[6]

The field of adaptation studies, according to Thomas Leitch, has gone through three phases: 1) Adaptation Studies 1.0, from the 1960s through much of the 1990s, which established the field, and which centered on medium specificity arguments—e.g. film's vocation for realism—and on fidelity to the literary text; 2) Adaptation Studies 2.0 from the late 1990s into the 2000s where intertextuality became the key word rather than fidelity; and 3) Adaptation Studies 3.0, which stressed the innovations introduced by digital technologies.[7] Prior to the move from the fidelity paradigm to the intertextuality paradigm that began in the late 1990s, the standard rhetoric in adaptation studies had often deployed an elegiac discourse of loss, lamenting what had been "lost" in the transition from novel to film, while ignoring what had been "gained." Those of us who see gains in the process therefore appeal to the positive Darwinian meaning of "adaptation"—e.g. the beauty of orchids as celebrated in *The Orchid Thief* and in the Kaufman/Jonze *Adaptation*—or to more positive metaphors such as "fertility," "expansion" and "transformation." The discourse of loss goes back to the silent period. In a 1926 diatribe, Virginia Woolf, for example, excoriated adaptations for reducing a novel's nuanced idea of "love" to "a kiss," or for rendering "death," in a literal-minded fashion, as a "hearse."[8] Too often, adaptation discourse subtly reinscribed the axiomatic superiority of literature to film. Many of the complaints about adaptation, it should be added, were addressed to Hollywood adaptations in the studio period, when novels were filtered through standardizing protocols: highs production values, the star system, streamlined narratives, the censorship by the Hayes Code and so forth. Much has changed in a period where highly literate filmmakers like Ang Lee meet as equals with cine-literate writers like Atom Egoyan, James Schamus, or Sherman Alexie. Too much of the discourse, I have argued, has focused on the rather subjective question of the *quality* of adaptations, rather than on the more productive issue of the *analytical* productivity of adaptations, including in the Damroschian sense of "gains in translation."

Obviously germane to both literature and film, the concept of intertextuality—the multifaceted relations between texts—has gone through myriad transformations over the centuries, going back to and including: Montaigne's 16th-century conceit that more books are written about other books than about any other subject; the 19th-century historicist tracing of literary "influences"; T.S. Eliot's 20th-century invocation of "Tradition and the Individual Talent";

the historical avant-gardes' penchant for Cubist "collage"; Bertolt Brecht's "refunctioning"; and the Situationists's *detournement*, or the subversive high-jacking of pre-existing texts. The "transtextual turn" gained momentum with the advent of structuralism and semiotics in literary and film studies and later with the dissemination of Bakhtin's ideas about "dialogism" and "embeddedness"; Kristeva's about "intertextuality"; Genette's five types of "Transtextuality"; Henry Louis Gates' "Signifying," and Andre Gaudreault's "intermediality." The digital turn, meanwhile, has generated a massive proliferation of terms in the same vein: sweding, transcoding, reformatting, mashups, remixes, remediations, and memes. In *Remix*, Lawrence Lessig distinguishes between "reading only" culture, and a digitally enabled "reading/rewriting" culture, as manifested, we would add, in revisionist adaptations and remixes.[9]

Some of the celebrated "remix films"—the construction of entire films out of materials drawn from other films—can be seen as second-degree rewritings of novels which resemble experimental *ecriture*. David Claernout's *The Pure Necessity* (2016) re-edits the animated classic *The Jungle Book* (1967), based on Kipling, in such a way as to eliminate all traces not only of human beings but also of anthropomorphic representations, leaving us only with the sights and sounds of the jungle. Anne McGuire's *Strain Andromeda The* (1992), meanwhile, re-edits Robert Wise's sci-fi classic *The Andromeda Strain* (1971), based on a Michael Crichton techno-thriller, so as to be seen in reverse so that the entire last shot appears first and the entire first shot appears last, in a *Hop-Scotch* style Switcheroo à la Julio Cortazar. Matt Bucy's *Of Oz the Wizard* (2004) alphabetizes every line of dialogue from *The Wizard of Oz*, beginning with the sound "ah" and proceeding to an onomatopoetic scream of "Aaiee!" on to the end of the alphabet, reminding us of the experimental writing of Georges Perec and his novels, based on arbitrary constraints such as writing an entire novel while avoiding the letter "e," or of Raymond Queneau's 99 retellings of the same story in his *Exercises de Style*.

Adaptation is of course a paradigmatic form of transtextuality, defined broadly by Genette in *Palimpsestes* as "relations between texts." More specifically, adaptation forms an instance of Genette's "hyper-textuality" in the sense of being transtextual variations on pre-existing texts (hypotexts). A single hypotext, for example, *The Odyssey*, can be seen as spawning a series of hypertextual spin-offs ranging from Virgil's *Aeneid* and Joyce's *Ulysses* to Godard's *Contempt* (1963) to Derek Walcott's *Omeros* (1990), on to the Coen Brothers' *O Brother, Where Art Thou?* (2000) and Guy Madden's *Keyhole* (2011), which compresses Odysseus' journeys across the wine-red seas into the narrow confines of a single domicile. Filmic adaptations of novels inherit and reconfigure a double constellation of transtexts, first the literary legacies that inform the source novel and secondly the cinematic and artistic legacies embedded in or mobilized by the filmic adaptation. The highly praised adaptation of Henry Fielding's *Tom Jones* by Tony Richardson, for example, incorporates many of the genres and techniques already present in the novel (epic, pastoral, historical, direct-address to the reader and so forth) but superimposes them on the genres and techniques available to film. The opening sequence, for example, alludes to silent cinema through archaic iris-in techniques, melodramatic intertitles, and hyperbolic acting, all combined with procedures such as the hand-held camera techniques drawn from contemporaneous film movements such as the French New Wave. (A 1997 BBC TV documentary about the Fielding novel has the putative author make a cameo as the narrator, when he is rudely cut off by the director).

9
THE CINEMA AND THE WORLD LITERATURE CANON

Since I have addressed adaptation at length elsewhere, I will stress here only the relation to films which adapt the canon of World Literature, and only in relation to the issues raised by Damrosch—circulation, translation, and estrangement. Through adaptation, literature and cinema share a considerable portion of the literary canon, for the simple reason that a very high proportion of feature films, especially A-list features, adapt prestigious literary works, self-designated as such through formulae such as "based on," "inspired by" and the like. This tendency is found world-wide. To take the example of India, hundreds of films and TV series have been based on Indian classics like the *Ramayana* and the *Bhagavad Gita*. Many Indian films have been based on the novels, plays, and short stories of a highly regarded figure in World Literary Studies—Rabindranath Tagore –going back to *Balidan* (Sacrifice) in 1927 up through *Detective* in 2017, based on a Tagore 1898 short story, and the 2015 TV series *Stories*, with 26 episodes based on the Bengali author's short stories.

Although at first regarded by many writers as an enemy and rival of literature, the cinema can also be seen as *saving* literature by popularizing it through adaptations. While translations into other languages certainly help usher novels into the privileged realm of World Literature, translations into audio-visual form are perhaps even equally consequential. Various branches of the mass media—radio, film, television, video, the Internet—have both used literature and been used by it. If the copy, as Derrida suggested, creates the prestige of the original, the endless iterations of novels like *Don Quixote, Robinson Crusoe,* and *Madame Bovary* in the form of films, animated cartoons, installations, video games, theme parks, mashups, and interactive-web sites have clearly kept those novels alive by maintaining and even swelling their prestige. When Google honored Borges with a "doodle" celebrating his 112th birthday, showing him facing a simulacral Library of Babel, that too is a kind of homage. Adaptation can be a historically sensitive barometer—at once technological, aesthetic, and ideological—of changes in the social atmosphere.

(Lucy Mazdon points out that the same argument could be made for remakes, but that few scholars have noted it.)[1]

We find a vivid example of this barometric function in the interminable series of adaptations of *Robinson Crusoe*. Even prior to and alongside the advent of the cinema, an endless array of literary and social commentators, some of them celebrated writers like Karl Marx and James Joyce, even before the wave of post-colonial studies, noted the novel's deep entanglement with colonialism and slavery. The film adaptations of *Robinson Crusoe* began with the Méliès version in 1902, and continue unabated up through the present day. If one moves from the 1719 novel to all the 18th- and 19th-century Robinsonnades on to the century of film, one discerns a series of striking mutations. From the playfully (only inferentially) racist 1902 version by Méliès up to the latest online games loosely based on the novel, we witness in many cases a slow deconstruction of the figure of Crusoe as hero and the ongoing construction of Friday as hero. The 1932 Hollywood film *Mr. Robinson Crusoe*, produced during the depression but at the heights of American imperialism in the Caribbean and the South Pacific, shows an almost sadistic relation between Mr. Crusoe—a Wall Street-style tycoon-adventurer who abandons his yacht to swim to a South Pacific island (a region less associated with slavery in the Americas)—and the savage headhunter Friday, whom he virtually drowns (in contemporary parlance "waterboards") all in good imperial fun. But the film also provides exactly what is missing in the novel—a woman—quite logically named "Saturday". To reconcile the titillation of a romance with an exoticized "Polynesian" character (played by a Spanish actress), with the taboo against East/West miscegenation—never the Twain shall love—the film has Crusoe take Saturday back to New York to make her a Josephine-Baker style "jungle" star on fabulous Broadway.

The Surrealism-inflected 1954 Bunuel version two decades later "improves" the novel by making Crusoe less racist and Friday more critical, while leaving the civilized/savage binarism more or less intact. Racing over decades we note both continuities and discontinuities. For example, many of the adaptations, including even the 1960 Disney "family entertainment" version of *Swiss Family Robinson*, prolong a tradition of colonial massacres of people of color. The 1995 version with Piers Brosnan provides a romantic frame and "improves" the Crusoe–Friday relationship by making it more "equal," yet stays faithful to the trope of the "regenerating violence" of an "integrated" colonial extermination of masses of people of color. Ultimately, the film obeys Kurtz' recommendation in *The Heart of Darkness*—"Exterminate the brutes!"

The 1964 sci-fi film *Robinson Crusoe on Mars*, under the impact of NASA on the one hand, and the Civil Rights movement on the other, turns Crusoe into a white liberal space explorer and Friday, in line with Defoe's characterization of a definitely not black straight-haired fine-nosed indigene, into an Indian-presenting Martian nobleman. In the finale, rather than Crusoe saving Friday—the original pretext for enslavement—it is Friday who saves Crusoe's life. Four years later, in the revolutionary year of 1968, the Disney cartoon, *Rabbitson Crusoe*, perhaps under the impact of the *zeitgeist* of drugs, rock n roll, and insurrection, turns Crusoe himself into the cannibal who wants to devour the "Injun" Bugs Bunny, who outsmarts him in the classic B'rer Rabbit manner.

The 1975 Jack Gold *Man Friday*, under the impact of Third World decolonization and the metropolitan counter culture, turns the colonial "boy" Friday into a Man and the titular hero, and Crusoe into a dottering colonialist. The 1999 *Castaway*, made in the giddy heyday of globalization, begins in Russia with the tearing down of a statue of Lenin, thus invoking a key moment and an iconic trope for triumphant neo-liberalism. Hanks' Crusoe—allegorically named Chuck (as in "throw") Noland (as in "no-land")—neglects love and family as he slaves away for the highly globalized Federal Express corporation. Friday becomes into a mute volley ball imaginary-friend, while the new Crusoe reveals the dehumanizing effects of globalization. The Reality Show "Survivor," the original European title of which directly referenced *Robinson Crusoe*, meanwhile, underscores an Ayn Randian eliminationism and Social Darwinism. (If we combine the survival-of-the-fittest ethics of *Survivor* with the dog-eat-dog politics of *The Apprentice*, we get an advance glimpse of what was to become political Trumpism). At the same time, we find an opposite current in the 2016 animation film, based on *Robinson Crusoe*, entitled *Wild Life*. Without exaggerating the film's progressiveness, it does reflecting the impact of ecology and the Anthropocene; the point of view is now not from the ship from the shore, where animals await the arrival of the clueless Crusoe. Nature-loving animals dominate the perspective, while a parrot becomes the narrator, and Crusoe becomes the strange klutzy unknowing savage whose folkways the very civilized animals find passing strange.

Much as the cinema has aided literature by popularizing its texts, the cinema has indirectly helped literature departments in the sense that literature courses increasingly rely on filmic adaptations of literature to swell enrollments. In a cultural studies era where professors increasingly poach on each other's domains, this opportunism has provoked some resentment among cinema studies scholars when literature professors untrained in the history and theory of cinema teach film in a thematic rather than specifically cinematic manner."[2] But in the end, the two fields need each other: literature departments benefit from the buzz and excitement of cinema, while cinema studies departments benefit from the aura of literature. Many teachers have used film, Marty Gould points out, as "a treat or reward for "students for making it all the way to the end of a long novel, or as a bit of respite between encounters with difficult texts …"[3] Even when adaptation is not a "formal component of the curriculum," he adds, "its shadow looms over the English classroom to the point that] it is increasingly difficult to segregate literature and film into separate courses."[4] Indeed, many states have adopted Common Core standards that include film adaptation. Thomas Leitch, for his part, makes a strong theoretical defense of adaptations as not only appropriate but even *essential* to the English curriculum.[5]

The issue of adaptation is crucial in part because a high proportion of Oscars for Best Picture—85% in 1992—go to film adaptations of literature. Adaptations make up 95% of American miniseries and 70% of movies of the week that win Emmies.[6] The books in question tend to be middle-brow fictions like *The Godfather* or *The Silence of the Lambs*, with rare forays into the upper ranges of World Literature such as *Hamlet* in 1948 and *Tom Jones* in 1963, or more recent works such as *Out of Africa* and *The English Patient*, or literary derivatives and remediations like *The Life of Emile Zola* (1937), *Oliver!* (1968), *Man of la Mancha* (1972), and *Shakespeare in Love* (1998). Despite what many would regard as "mistakes" in choices both for the Oscars and the Nobel Prizes," where ephemeral modishness was confused with aesthetic excellence, at this point in history there are few texts prized by World Literature scholars that have *not* been turned into film.[7]

A glance at the ranks of Nobel Prizes in literature, meanwhile, shows that many of the writers honored—Rudyard Kipling, Rabindranath Tagore, Thomas Mann, Luigi Pirandello, Herman Hesse, William Faulkner, Ernest Hemingway, Albert Camus, John Steinbeck, Gabriel Garcia Marquez, Naguib Mahfouz, Toni Morrison, Jose Saramago, Gunter Grass, and Mario Vargas Llosa, have first been honored by becoming literally translated, and thus enabled to form part of World Literature, and second by being translated in a figurative sense, in the form of filmic adaptations, often in *multiple* filmic adaptations. The *Ramayana*, the *Iliad*, *The Odyssey*, *A Thousand and One Nights*, *Beowulf*, *The Tale of Genji*, *Canterbury Tales*, *Don Quixote*, *Madame Bovary*, *A la Recherche du Temps Perdu* and virtually all of Shakespeare, Dickens, and Balzac, have been rendered in filmic form, often multiple times, even scores or hundreds of times.

At times adaptations take the form of filmo-biography. The life of Keats formed the subject of *Bright Star* (2009), the life of Emily Dickenson is the subject of *A Quiet Passion* (2016), the Lesbian romance of Elizabeth Bishop and Brazilian architect Lota de Macedo Soares forms the subject of *Flores Raras* (Reaching for the Moon, 2013), while *The Hours* (2002) deals with the impact of Virginia Woolf's Mrs. *Dalloway* on three generations of women. In the Arab world, Poets Jalal Ul-Din Rumi and Abu Muhammad Muslih al-Don bin Abdallah Shiraz have been adopted for film, while William Carlos Williams is discreetly homaged in Jim Jarusch's *Paterson*. Even the *Popol Vuh* has been turned into a partly animated documentary by Patricia Amlin—entitled *Popol Vuh: the Creation Myth of the Maya*—featuring as its lead commentator none other than World Literature Doyen David Damrosch himself! In fact, Damrosch has participated in videos concerning *The Epic of Gilgamesh*, *The Odyssey*, and the *Bhagavad Gita*. Even Disney has worked to disseminate the World Literature canon, copyrighting the cultural commons through animations derived from *A Thousand and One Nights*, *Treasure Island*, and *Don Quixote*. Donald Duck and Mickey Mouse have been enlisted in animations of *The Odyssey*, the King Arthur cycle, *Don Quixote*, various Shakespeare plays, *Gulliver's Travels*, and *Les Miserables*.

The top-down cannibalization and enclosure of the world's cultural commons by the Disney Corporation, meanwhile, has not gone without critical notice. The remix video "Fair(y) Use Tale"—an obvious play on "fair use" and "fairytale"—produced by Bucknell University professor Eric Faden together with his media-savvy students, attacks Disney as one of the most notorious practitioners of copyright abuse. Through a jiujitsu tactic, the short film obeys the letter of copyright law as a platform to both explain Fair Use doctrine and to denounce the most litigious of entertainment corporations. Fair Use law requires the creation of something new, which "Fair[y] Use Tale" conspicuously manages to do. Using over 400 very short clips and snippets of dialogue drawn exclusively from Disney animations, the film becomes a critical treatise on copyright and the Disney attempt to "enclose" the planetary cultural commons. A demonstration of the possibilities of satirical pedagogy, the video has been seen by millions of viewers on line, and is even used in law schools to explain copyright law.

The issue of literary adaptation plays a special role in "minor" nations, where adaptations can become a "heritage" genre for the Global South. Adaptations can serve multiple purposes: a means for outwitting censorship through strategic allegory, advancing national prestige, or simply providing viable stories. Brazil has a proud tradition of brilliant literary figures worthy of transnational attention. Over its more than a century of history Brazilian cinema has adapted scores if not hundreds of classical novels by Brazilian writers of World Literature quality (if not necessarily in terms of reputation and status). Some of the earliest adaptations, during the silent period, were of Indianist classics such as Jose de Alencar's *Iracema* and *O Guarani*. After the advent of sound, we find filmic and televisual adaptations of novels by Machado de Assis, Mario de Andrade, Jose Lins do Rego, Raquel Queiroz, Jorge Amado, Clarice Lispector, Nelson Rodrigues, Guimaraes Rosa, Milton Hatoum, Raduan Nassar, and many others.

This fondness for the adaptation of canonical texts is equally true of Brazilian Television, as exemplified in the remarkable figure of a true televisual auteur—Luis Fernando Carvalho, whose entire career, with the exception of the single feature film *Lavoura Arcaica* (Ancient Tillage) itself based on a novel by Raduan Nassar—has been dedicated to directing adaptations of canonical Brazilian plays and novels for television.

The dominant attitude toward the relations between Television and Cinema on the part of the Brazilian intelligentsia, as Eli Lee Carter points out, was 1) an Adornonian posture that condemned television as an ideological tool that alienated the masses; and 2) an elitist attitude that saw TV as a wasteland completely devoid of legitimate culture.[8] In this sense Luis Fernando Carvalho's work presents a parodox, since throughout his career, Carvalho has worked within Globo's massively industrial system and yet resisted what Carter calls "the industry's tendency toward factory-like production and the resulting lack of audio-visual experimentation."[9] Carvalho has maintained firm artistic control in work comparable in experimental audacity to the work of the Cinema Novo directors and to non-Brazilians such as Tarkovsky, Visconti, and Raul Ruiz. Among the Brazilian and Portuguese classics that he has directed for Globo are: *Riacho Doce* (Sweet River) a 40-chapter miniseries based on the work of Jose Lins do Rego; *Uma Mulher Vestida de Sol* (A Woman Dressed in the Sun), *O Auto de Nossa Senhora da Luz* (The Play of Our Lady of Light), and *A Pedro do Reino* (Stone of the Kingdom) all based on the work of Ariano Suassuna; *Alexandre e Outros Herois* (Alexander and Other Heroes), based on Graciliano Ramos; *Capitu*, an extremely experimental operatic collage version of Machado de Assis' *Dom Casmurro: Dois Irmãos* (Two Brothers) based on the homonymous novel by Milton Hatoum; and *Os Maias*, based on Portuguese writer Eca de Queiros.

Speaking more generally about literature itself, it is hard to ignore a certain Rise of the Literary Rest in terms of literary prizes and prestige. In Britain, the Booker Prize has since the 1980s been dominated by writers linked in various ways to the former colonized world: such as Keri Hulme, Ben Okri, Michael Ondaatje, and Arundhati Roy. While no African writer had won the Nobel Prize before the mid-1980s, four have won it since then: Wole Soyinka in 1986; Naguib Mahfouz in 1988; Nadime Gordimer in 1991; and J. M. Coetzee in 2003. Carribean writers Derek Walcott and V.S. Naipaul won it in 1992 and 2001 respectively, while African-American Toni Morrison won it in 1993. Latin America has a longer history of winning Nobel Prizes—Gabriel Mistral in 1945; Asturias in 1967; Neruda in 1971; Marquez in 1982; and Octavio Paz in 1990. In French and Francophone literature, the prize-winners include Assia Djabar, Sony Labou Tansi, Patrick Chamoiseau, Maryse Conde, and countless others.

10
THE GAINS OF (FILM) TRANSLATION

In what follows, I will be dealing with three distinct questions concerning the role of translation within the sibling worlds of World Literature and World Cinema: 1) How is the role of translation, in the *literal* sense, different with regards to literature as opposed to literary films? 2) How do novels, in general, "gain in translation" in the *mediatic-metaphorical* sense of translating a text written in a single-track medium for a multi-track medium? 3) How do novels in the *cultural* sense, finally, "gain in translation" in the form of transnational and transcultural adaptations?

By way of historical background, translation has not garnered the same status or operated in the same way in the two media. In the case of literature, the translators of canonical texts are presumed to be highly literate and deeply knowledgeable about the author and text in question, and thoroughly conversant with both source and target languages. Some translators are themselves celebrated writers; one thinks of Baudelaire translating Edgar Allen Poe, or Walter Benjamin translating Proust. Well-known translators like Gregory Rabassa, Richard Howard, and Haroldo de Campos, meanwhile, rather like Bollywood playback singers, who are as well known as the performers they dub, are famous in their own right. Yet it is difficult to find a case where a translator of film dialogue from a film adaptation of a literary work, even one based on a classic of World Literature, has become famous in his or her own right. In the case of film adaptations, even when the film is literally quoting narrative passages or actual dialogue from the source novel, little care is taken to find truly qualified translators. While publishers would presumably never engage a hack journalist to translate *À la Recherche du Temps Perdu*, film distributors regularly hire incompetents to translate adaptations of prestigious authors, including adaptations based on the World Literature canon, and even where the dialogue or the off-screen narration of the adaptation is directly taken from the novel. When the very same words, when transposed into a more "vulgar" latecomer medium, somehow cease to be "literature" worthy of competent translation.

As a result, translated titles and subtitles often reflect serious miscalculations due to insufficient mastery of the source or target language or culture. A Romanian translator-bureaucrat, for example, misled by the phonetic and scriptural resemblance between the Italian musical term *moderato* and the Romanian word *moderat* (cautious), and the similarity between *cantabile* and *comtabil* (accountant) construed *Moderato Cantabile*, the musical title of the Marguerite Duras novel adapted by Peter Brook as *The Quiet Accountant*, leaving confused spectators waiting for a Godot-like titular character who never appeared. Torn from its usual linguistic environment, even the literally translated title enters into a booby-trapped field of what Bakhtin calls "prior speakings." The English phrase "Horse's Mouth," for example, forms part of a paradigm of colloquial expressions that include "straight from the horse's mouth" and "don't look a gift horse in the mouth," a point lost on the Polish translator who rendered the title of the film adaptation of the Joyce Cary novel as an overly literal *Konsky Pysk* ("Mouth of the Horse"). Since the same colloquial associations do not exist in Polish, the title became an architextual miscue, leading baffled viewers to expect a horse that never materialized on the screen.

In historical terms, translation has had a very diverse history in the two media. To take first the point of literal translation, cinema in its earliest incarnations knew a condition completely unknown to literature— absolute wordlessness. Spectators were happily astonished simply to witness the arrival of a train or the fluttering of leaves in the wind. Silent era film theorists called the cinema a form of "visual Esperanto" a new language which would democratize and internationalize the arts by offering a universal language immediately understandable by everyone.[1] Early on in the silent period, however, wordlessness gave way to various forms of verbal mediation—presentational lectures, singers-behind-the-screen, and, most prominently, intertitles to convey dialogue and plot. The fact that spectators could read intertitles in their own language allowed them to imagine that the actors/characters as well were speaking that same language, that Greta Garbo was not speaking Swedish-accented English but rather French, Farsi, or Hindi, or whatever language the spectator happened to be reading through the subtitles.

This phantasmatic utopia came to an end with the advent of sound, which offered words to be heard and images to be seen in perfect synchronization. But even in that case a crucial difference remained between the written and the cinematic presentation of speech. While written transcription has to use special devices or differential spelling ("Good Lawd!") to convey an accent or intonation, the sound-film is incapable of representing speech *without* accent or intonation. Indeed, it was this literalness of accent that engendered difficulties during the transition from silence to sound and from country to country. Rather than phantasize some ideal voice conjured up by their own imagination, spectators were obliged to confront the actually existing voices of their favorite stars. French spectators were disappointed, *evidemment*, that Charlot was not French. Greta Garbo, film fans discovered, had a charming Swedish accent, while leading man John Gilbert revealed an annoyingly "reedy" voice, triggering massive desertion on the part of his fickle fans. (Some of these transition-to-sound glitches are depicted in comic terms in such films as *Singin' in the Rain* and *The Artist*).

Conventional cinematic discourse, as Rick Altman stressed in his paradigm-shifting issue of *Yale French Studies* (1980) on "Cinema/Sound," privileges the eye and downplays the ear.[2] The constant "ocularcentric" portrayal of film as a "visual medium" seen by "spectators" leads us to forget that cinema is actually a visual-aural-linguistic-digital medium that is heard and felt as well as seen. Sound, in this sense, brought many "gains" in the cinematic translations of novels. As a multi-track medium, cinema is especially equipped to deal with the mise-en-scène of speech communication. Cinema provides an environment, a dialogic backdrop for communicative speech. It can draw out the visual implications of speech by correlating word with gesture, dialogue with facial expression, verbal exchange with corporeal dynamics. In the cinema, whole sequences and even entire films can be structured by wordplay and sound-image relations. Hitchcock, for example, constantly exploits the power of the interface of word and image. The overture sequence of *The Wrong Man*, for example, can be seen as structured in its entirety by the quibbling sentence "Manny plays the bass." The protagonist plays the bass, quite literally, in the Stork Club. But he also plays the "base" when he is falsely accused and prodded by the police to mimic the actions of the actual thief. The opening sequence of *Strangers on the Train*, similarly, based on a Patricia Highsmith novel, similarly, is structured around verbal-visual puns, where dialogue expressions such as "doubles" and "double-crossing," whiskey "doubles," and tennis "doubles" coincide, thanks to the editing, with shots of crossed legs, crossed tennis racquets, criss-crossed train tracks, lap-dissolves as a criss-crossing of shots, and so forth. Hitchcock's cameo shows him get on the titular train carrying what is known as a "double bass." Such cross-film-track play would have been virtually impossible in a verbal medium, thus offering a certain "gain in (mediatic) translation."

With sound cinema, spectators could hear the original language while literate spectators could also read the subtitles and intertitles in their own language. Some spectators feel "exiled" by subtitles, experiencing them as a legible sign of their own foreignness:

> The inevitable duality of something made in one place and to be seen both at home and abroad stands out in every film that is subtitled or dubbed. It stands otherness is continually and unmistakably present at the bottom of the screen.[3]

In some countries, foreign films are thus as much "read" as seen. While those fluent in the language of the film see it and hear it and understand it, the linguistic "exiles" read it. Intertitles and subtitles were not the universal norm, however; only some countries allowed postsynchronization, thus generating the sub-vs.-dub debate. As Tim Bergfelder points out, while English audiences found dubbing an annoying break in cinematic verisimilitude, German audiences generally accepted dubbing, giving birth to "technologically advanced subsidiary industry to which prestigious actors, writers and directors lend their names and voices."[4] French audiences, meanwhile, generally enjoyed the luxury of choosing between V.O. ("version originale") and postsynched films. In the case of postsynchronization, the spectator, ignorant of the original words, remains unaware of her own "foreignness," unaware, even, that a translation has taken place. In India, the screen is ofen crowded with multiple layers of subtitles from multiple languages such as English, Hindi, Tamil and so forth. At times, multilingual conversations in cosmopolitan circumstances in the filmic narratives, are homogenized into a single language in the subtitles.

With the advent of the Internet, we encounter the phenomenon of fan subtitling as a labor of amateur love dedicated to prized but relatively unknown films. The Internet has also resuscitated the practice of situationist *detournement* by facilitating the substitution of ironic or politically radical subtitles, as in the case of the anti-globalization titles superimposed on the trailer of *The Lord of the Rings* [*of Free Trade*]. Some artists exploit the *lack* of subtitles for artistic purposes. For example, some films about the European conquest of the Americas feature dialogue in indigenous languages, without subtitles, to reproduce the feeling of linguistic exclusion and vulnerability on the part of Europeans confronting indigenous "opacity." Much of the dialogue of Dos Santos *How Tasty was my Frenchman* (1971) is in the Tupi language, so that the film required subtitles virtually everywhere it was screened, including in Brazil itself, thus giving the spectator a visceral sense of what it felt to be a European in Brazil at a time that Tupi was the lingua franca. The title of Glauber Rocha's *Der Leone Have Sept Cabecas* (1975), meanwhile, pointed to the transnational character of colonialism by referencing the language of five of African's European colonizers. In the film, Glauber stresses their ultimate inter-changeability through non-literal, identity-scrambling casting, by having an Italian play the American, a Frenchman play the German and so forth. The implied conflation and ethical leveling of the various colonizers went against the grain of the tradition of intercolonial narcissism which insisted that one own nation's colonialism was more humane or civilized than those of the other, thus France claimed a mission civilisatrice, Portugal pointed to its racial flexibility, and the U.S., with its imperialism of military bases, lauded its lack of interest in actually conquering land.

The advent of globalization and the emergence of World Cinema as a category favored a new interest in the somewhat neglected topic of the role of translation, subtitles, and postsynchronization. In the wake of a 1985 essay entitled *The Cinema after Babel: Language, Difference, Power* (authored by Ella Shohat and myself)—I am not suggesting influence—a number of scholars such as Abe Mark Nornes, Egoyan and Balfour, and Natasha Ďurovičová have creatively pursued the topic of the changing role of translation in film. In a comprehensive study entitled *Cinema Babel* (2008) Abe Mark Nornes underscores the exploitative side of subtitling and postsynchronization that forms part of a search for world markets. In many ways, the Internet has further strengthened the hegemony of the English language. Global Cinema, for Nornes, is "Translator's cinema." In the new situation, translation powerhouses generate the biblically named "genesis files" which he defines as:

... essentially an English language scenario/spotting list—a compilation of all dialogue [which] is annotated with precise timings of the subtitles ... Upon completion of the file, the company sends the computer file to its translators as an e-mail attachment. These translators simulteously open the genesis file and substitute each line of dialogue with a translated subtitle in their own language. After the substitutions are complete, the new titles are sent back to the translation house by e-mail, where they are converted into discrete subtitle tracks on a single DVd, or any format from theatrical release to television broadcast to the World Wide Web."[5]

The problem is that the default language of translation is always English, leading to subtitling that amounts to translations of translations. The whole operation is mechanical and merely verbal, in the sense that the translators often do not see the source text in the original language. For Nornes, the "very name of the master file—"genesis"—holds within it a "neo-imperial translation project positioning English as the source of all meaning."[6] Thus subtitling ends up reinforcing the domination of English, to the point that even German language films tend to be subtitled in English as the "universal" language.

In the case of indigenous or minor-language media, film offers an advantage simply not available to literature. First, in practical filmmaking terms, non-literate ethnic groups can pass easily from an oral culture to an audio-visual culture, without necessarily passing through literacy. Second, the use of subtitles also offers a "gain" by providing a solution to the challenge posed by Ngugi wa Thiongo's call for linguistic decolonization. Ngugi urged African writers to write not in the colonizing languages of the West but rather in African languages like his native Kikuyu. But for filmmakers it is possible to have dialogue in Kikuyu or any other "minor" language, with subtitles in Western languages, allowing both insiders and outsiders to have their linguistic cake and eat it too. For Kikuyu-speaking spectators of an English film, meanwhile, the subtitles can be in Kikuyu. (This "solution" excludes, unfortunately, all those not fluent in both Kikuyu and Western languages). But even without subtitles or dubbing, spectators can get a sense of the feel, the "grain," the social affect and the musicality of the language, its characteristic sounds and intonations, and, since basic facial expressions of fear, joy, and anger are similar in most cultures, even of the relation of words to emotions and to corporeal expression. Through tone and body language, they can detect emotions such as love or hatred, or social attitudes such as arrogance or servility, and learn about how emotions are expressed, in a kind of mediated apprentissage in the affective codes of another culture. In this sense, the cinema offers a feeling of transcultural intimacy denied to literature, where we imagine, but do not actually hear "the grain of the voice," or literally witness the postures, attitudes, and movements of the character.

Writers like Ngugi are responding to a problem—the world-wide hegemony of English and more broadly the hegemony of West European languages—which bears relevance both to World Literature and World Cinema. "Translation," both in World Literature and in World Cinema, primarily means translation into English. Although all languages are in principle equal in the sense of being attuned to their ambient culture, some languages, both in literature and in the cinema, have been made "more equal "than the others. To the adage that "a language is a dialect with an army and a navy," Alexander Beecroft has added that a language is also a "dialect with a literature."[7] Nuclear weapons, or a strong currency, can generate a shift from "minor" to "major." For Beecroft, "the three dominant facts of the literary world in our time ... are the general preponderance of English, the presence of a comparatively lively circulation of translated texts among European languages, and the general isolation of even very populous non-European languages from any kind of global literary system."[8] The lack of translation out of non-European languages, for him, "represents the single greatest barrier to the free flow of literature and ideas around the world."[9]

Inscribed within the play of power, languages get caught up in hierarchies rooted in cultural hegemonies and political domination. As the heir of the global power of Pax Britannica and of the American neo-imperialism of bases, English has long been the vehicle of the projection of Anglo-American power, technology, finance, and popular culture. As a result, Hollywood films have often betrayed a linguistic *hybris* bred of hegemonic domination. Presuming to speak of and for others in its native idiom, Hollywood proposed to tell not only its own American stories but also the stories and legends of others, and not only to Americans but also to other nations, and only in English. In Cecil B. De Mille epochs, both the ancient Egyptians and the Israelites spoke English, and so, for that matter, did God. In the classical Hollywood film, the Greeks of the *Iliad*, the Romans of *Ben Hur*, Cleopatra of Egypt, Anna Karenina of Russia, and Jesus of Nazareth all had as their lingua franca the English of Southern California. In terms of Latin America, Evita Peron, Carlos the Jackal, and Frida Kahlo, have all been obliged to address the world in English. The trailers of some internationally distributed films, such as *Central Station*, meanwhile, sometimes mask their national origin through dialogue-free trailers which rigorously avoid the "local" language, in this case Brazilian Portuguese.

At times, a power struggle takes place within English itself, with the emergences of a broad range of "Englishes" such as Indian English, or Nigerian, or Jamaican English which have achieved a kind of local autonomy. A parodic mashup, entitled "Mean Sketels" (Mean Sluts) superimposes clips from the super-white bourgeois series "Mean Girls" on top of dubbing which renders the dialogue as funky Jamaican patois. Languages get detached from nation and ethnicity, as French and English literary prizes go to writers who are not ethnically French or English in the traditional ethno-nationalist sense. Moreover, struggles over linguistic hegemony do not always involve tensions between the "West and the Rest." In the arena of mass-media circulation, terms like "transnational" and "global" have been used to highlight South-South connectivities, both within regions (e.g. Turkish telenovellas popularized in the Arab world) and beyond regions (Latin American telenovelas exported to Europe and Asia). At times the point of official policy is to undo pre-existing connectivities, as when post-Ottoman Turkey under the rule of Kemal Attaturk, for example, systematically worked to "de-Arabize" and partially Westernize foreign films through a top-down form of "Turkification." Until the late 1940s, as Zeynep Dadak points out, cinema in Turkey was primarily based on the consumption of imported films, notably American and Egyptian.[10] Arab films were screened in a reception context shaped by a Kamelism that mandated the use of the Latin instead of Arabic script, in a social climate that was hostile to Arab culture generally and to popular Egyptian films and music in particular.

The most successful Arab films were therefore adapted/translated/transformed for the Turkish screen. Egyptian music tracks were replaced with music by well-known Turkish composers like Saadettin Kaynak, whose fame partly derived from the use of dubbed Turkish music to replace Egyptian film soundtracks. After the first sound-film studio was opened in 1932 by İpek Film, dubbing into Turkish became *de rigeur*, allowing for more comprehensive studio-style control. A 1939 decree banned foreign languages from film soundtracks to be replaced by clear and proper Turkish. After songs in Arabic were officially banned from films in the same year, the "Turkification" of soundtracks became a common practice. While the melodies might be kept more or less intact, for example, the lyrics would be translated into Turkish and performed by a Turkish singer. This "Top-Down-Turkification," as Dadak points out, was Janus-faced and ambivalent in that it simultaneously represented an oppositional Turkish alterity toward the West combined with a disdainful othering of the Arab oriental within Turkey itself.[11]

In many ways, the very nature of "translation" shifts its meaning when we turn our attention to a different medium. Film adaptations of literature, for example, are doubly "translations." When distributed abroad, they are (often) translations first in the literal sense, i.e. the intertitles and dialogue of their source films are translated through subtitles or through post-synchronization (dubbing). But they are also translations in a second metaphorical sense, in that even prior to the translation in the literal sense, they have "translated" a source text through the expressive resources of a different medium, where the specificity of each medium derives from its respective materials of expression. To use semiotic language, literature, cinema, and music all have specific "materials of expression"—verbal in the case of literature, musical (and at times verbal when including lyrics) in the case of music, and multi-track in the case of cinema. The novel has a single material of expression—the written word. That word can be materially expressed on stone, parchment, papyrus or as digital information, but the basic substance remains the same—words as materialized in phonemes and morphemes.

The cinema, in contrast, has at least five tracks: moving photographic image, phonetic sound, music, noise, and written materials. In this respect, the cinema has not lesser but rather greater resources for expression than the novel, and this quite independent of what actual filmmakers have actually done with these resources. Indeed, in evaluative terms one could credit literary fictioners with accomplishing marvelous feats using nothing but mere words, while censuring filmmakers for doing so little with such opulent resources. (The issue is not one of superiority of talent or achievement, in sum, but rather one of wealth and complexity of resources.) The shift, in adaptation, from a single-track, uniquely verbal medium such as the novel, which "has only words to play with," to a multi-track medium like film, which can play not only with words (written and spoken) but also with music, sound effects and moving photographic images, explains the unlikelihood, and even the undesirability, of literal fidelity to a novelistic source.

Filmic adaptations of novels, as I have argued elsewhere, involve myriad metamorphoses, as source-novel hypotexts are transformed by a complex series of operations: selection, amplification, concretization, actualization, critique, extrapolation, popularization, reaccentuation, indigenization, transculturalization, remediation and so forth—all of which allow for, but in no way guarantee, "gains in translation." The source text forms a dense informational network, a series of verbal cues which the adapting film text can then selectively take up, amplify, ignore, subvert, or transform. The filmic adaptation of a novel performs these transformations according to the protocols of a distinct medium, absorbing and altering the available genres and intertexts through the grids of ambient discourses and ideologies, and as mediated by a series of filters: studio style, government censorship, ideological fashion, political pressures and economic constraints, auteurist predilections, charismatic stars, cultural values and so forth.

Every dimension is enriched and amplified by cinema, and some would say *too* enriched, leaving nothing to the imagination. While a writer can offer a detailed description of a country estate, the adaptation can pan over its actual facades or zoom into the nooks and crannies of an actual museum, as in the case of *The Russian Ark*. Novelists are exempted from many of the tasks that beset filmmakers. While writers need not spell out how a character is dressed, for example, film adaptations, at least adaptations in a realistic mode, usually feel obliged at all times to dress their characters, specify weather conditions and so forth. While a writer can describe the buzzing vitality of a world-famous square, a film can simply film it *in loco* in surround sound, immersive mise-en-scène, and 360 degree cinematography. In this sense, film remediates and actualizes reception theory in literature à la Iser or Jauss, for which a text is an event whose indeterminacies are completed by the imaginative work of the reader. By filling in such lacunae, adaptations, in this sense, offer multi-track amplifications of the cues of their source novels.

Thanks to its multiple tracks, the combinatory riches of cinema are infinite, since it feeds on the perennial legacy of the cultural and artistic commons. Although Robbe-Grillet once falsely praised cinema for knowing only the present tense, his "praise" was unwarranted, since the film medium has all the tenses and an infinity of other ways of marking the passage of time. First, the cinema has language in the most literal and banal sense of dialogue, intertitles, and voice-over narration, and therefore has all the tenses available to "natural language. But a film can also communicate tense and the passage of time in myriad ways: lap-dissolves, flashbacks, changes in lighting, altered color, filters, undercranked cameras, cosmetic rejuvenation or aging of characters, artificially "aged" footage; period costume, paintings, vintage props and so forth, all without mentioning the possibilities opened up by digital post-production and CGI effects. Furthermore, the cinema enjoys a unique capacity to "congeal" past time and movement in the form of archival footage, i.e. images (and sometimes sounds) literally registered in the past. While the Kundera novel *The Unbearable Lightness of Being* refers to the "motion pictures ... stored in archives around the world" showing the 1968 Soviet invasion of Czechoslovakia, the Philip Kaufman adaptation of the same novel simply includes the actual widely seen TV reports of the invasion.

Although Nabokov's Humbert in *Lolita* expressed envy of the expressive resources of the cinema, film too has its own severe limitations, especially in terms of the fragility and even the perishability of the text in its material form. In the early days of film schools, a perennial haptic ritual for beginning students involved physically handling a short film strip, where the teacher would ask the student to feel and smell the celluloid itself:

> The students are then asked to place the film, emulsion side up, between their lips. As the tacky emulsion sticks to their top lip, laughter ripples through the class as the students encounter the substance and materiality of the medium. This initiation into the world of celluloid—its tangibility, tactility, and texture—introduces one of the medium's most intrinsic qualities: its physicality.[12]

In literature, the physical condition of a book is of interest to historians and archivists, but it is not of primordial importance to literary scholars. As long is there is a single copy of the book, it does not matter if the pages are yellowed or singed, as long as the words are legible, they can be reprinted and disseminated.

In film, in contrast, the sheer physicality of the materials of the text matters in ways difficult to imagine in literature. While Flaubert's stylish *mot juste* remains forever *juste* even when the pages are frayed, such is not the case with films. A literary text retains all of its semantic riches; the phrase "luminous blue" in literature will remain forever luminous, but the blue of a Technicolor print is liable to literally decompose. If the text is readable, by the same token, the format or font of a novel does not matter, but a colorized film noir, shorn of its expressionist *chiaroscuro*, is no longer the same film. While telespectators accept colorized TV versions of films, or changed aspect ratios to fit the TV screen, thus eliminating a substantial part of the image, it is hard to imagine readers of *War and Peace* tolerating a Kindle version reformatted in such a way as to eliminate a third of every sentence. Speaking more generally, the digital revolution has transformed every aspect of cinema—all the way down, as the expression goes—from scripting, filming, editing, sound design, exhibition, and reception.

The digital revolution has not had any equivalent cataclysmic effect on writing per se; the changes have mainly impacted the dissemination and reception of the texts, not the texts themselves. In cinema, in contrast, recent debates revolve around the question: "when does a film cease to be film." Does film expire with digitality and the long-announced imminent demise of theatrical exhibition, or is film now omnipresent on a multitude of new formats and venues.

11

ADAPTATION, REMIX, AND THE CULTURAL COMMONS

Damrosch's other requirement for a text to qualify as World Literature is that it "estrange" readers from the habitual assumptions and ideological frames of their "home" culture. Revisionist film adaptations of the canonical works of World Literature, in this sense, can estrange us by dramatically transforming and revitalizing their source texts through provocative changes in locale, epoch, casting, genre, perspective, performance modes, production processes, and even basic formats. In this sense, to adapt Damrosch's formulation, they potentially "gain" in *cinematic* translation by distancing us from our own culture and, just as importantly, initiating us into another. (Of course, this estrangement can also operate in purely literary rewriting, but without the multi-sensory haptic density available to the cinema.)

A high proportion of feature films consist of filmic adaptations drawn from the literary commons of classic texts, the rich domain of non-copyrighted or public domain material. One of the sections of Thomas Leitch's indispensable *Oxford Handbook of Adaptation Studies* is entitled "Adapting the Commons."[1] Adaptation in this sense can be seen as a form of textual poaching, a metaphor redolent of the agricultural commons, described by Michel de Certeau in *The Practice of Everyday Life* as comparable to the poor poaching their way across Medieval fields. Agnes Varda's *Les Glaineuses* ("The Gleaners and I," 2000) examines the practice by common people of gathering leftover crops after the harvest. The film evokes the *literal, natural commons* in its original meaning as the forest land available for purposes of gathering food, wood, and other necessities. Varda has male and female legal authorities, dressed in robes, explain the complex laws—we are reminded of the "Charter of the Forest" that accompanied the Magna Carta—regarding gleaning. We also meet the representatives of *enclosure*. As a parsimonious landowners explains, gleaning must be forbidden; grapes must be left on the ground to rot because the gleaners can too easily become competitors, and one "has to protect one's capital." Classically portrayed in Millet's painting *Les Glaineuses*, the metaphor of poaching was borrowed by Henry Jenkins to apply to the subcultural appropriation of mass-culture, referring to procedures whereby the consumer absorbs the scraps of mass-mediated culture to become a producer. As a form of cross-artistic file-sharing, adaptations "stretch" verbal texts to fit a multi-track medium which can draw on all the arts integral to the cinematic medium, resulting in the amplification of intertexts. An insistence on strict fidelity in adaptation, in this sense, can constitute a form of hermeneutic "*enclosure*" that asserts ownership on the meaning of a text, as opposed to a view open to transtextual remodelings of a source text.

Revisionist adaptations of canonical texts, in this sense, sample source texts drawn from the *literary commons*, available to be poached, borrowed, transformed, parodied, and reinvoiced for the aesthetic and social needs of a new time and place. The endlessly protean adaptations of Shakespeare's plays, in the theater, the cinema, and on television, offer vivid examples of innovative remediation, even if only by communicating a sense of the wide range of possible performative and cultural "readings" of a canonical text. To speak only of the 20th century, such Shakespeare remediations in film go at least as far back as J. Stuart Blackton's *As You Like It* in 1912. Over two decades later, in the theater, Orson Welles' staged his controversial *Voodoo Macbeth* in 1936 in Harlem, where Welles transformed the racial affect of Shakespeare's play through an all-black cast, deploying black performance to completely re-envision a canonical masterpiece.

But quite apart from what might be considered the "gimmick" of an all-black cast, Welles radically reinterpreted Shakespeare by transposing the location and time of the play from 11th-century Scotland to 18-century Haiti, while also transposing the performance of the play from the white downtown to the black uptown of Harlem's Lafayette Theater. The Welles version generally respected the literal text of *Macbeth* but deployed costumes, sets, and performance to evoke the most radical of the Republican revolutions—the Haitian revolution—a revolution which was at once political, social, and racial. Welles took elements familiar from European history and concretely present in the Shakespeare play—witches, charms, magical thinking –, but reimagined them through their Afro-diasporic correlatives. Collaborating with African opera singer, dancer, and dramaturg Asadata Dafora, Welles restructured the adaptation through the sequencing of Haitian rituals, as evoked by drummers of Sierra Leone. Hecate, the witch goddess, metamorphosed into a male Vodun priest, associated in the Yoruba tradition with Exu-Legba, the trickster spirit of crossways and entrances, and, for Henry Louis Gates, linked to translation, semiosis, and adaptation.[2]

Voodoo Macbeth shows that ethocentrism is less a matter of corpus or the epidermic identity of the artist than a way of seeing a canonical text through a non-Eurocentric grid. Contemporaneous debates, in this sense, can be staged around the corpus of Shakespeare. Indeed, Shakespeare himself seeded his plays with what would later "sprout" as "multicultural" elements; Shakespeare's Globe was indeed global. Welles opened the way for an endless pageant of the filmic and theatrical "Africanizations" of Shakespeare. Moreover, Shakespeare has often been radically "multiculturalized" both in literature and film, whether through non-traditional casting (Julie Taymor's 2010 version of *The Tempest*) or through indigenous rewriting, as when Cherokee writer William Sanders, in "The Undiscovered," has Shakespeare himself shipwrecked off Virginia and ultimately adopted by the Cherokee who rename him "Speareshaker" and who teach him the Cherokee language, and stage a revisionist version of *Hamlet* as a comedy complete with folkloric songs and dances. In the wake of *West Side Story* (1957), which set *Romeo and Juliet* in a stylized Manhattan Latin "slum," Lúcia Murat's 2008 film *Maré, Nossa História de Amor* (*Maré, Another Love Story*) resets *Romeo and Juliet* in the actual Rio de Janeiro slum named in the title.

Brazilian dramaturg Jose Celso Martinez Correia, meanwhile, has reprocessed Shakespeare through the grid of the Brazilian 1920s modernist trope of anthropophagy. That trope referred, as we saw earlier, to the cannibalistic devouring of the European historical avant-gardes as a way of absorbing their power without being dominated by them, just as the Tupinamba Indians devoured European warriors to appropriate their strength. This aesthetic was famously captured in the witty modernist slogan: "Tupi or not Tupi: That is the Question," i.e. whether the Brazilian artist should be proudly Indian (anti-colonial) or be shame-faced colonized mimics. The cannibalistic twist on the most famous phrase from *Hamlet* was enacted in a 2009 six-hour version of Shakespeare's play by Jose Celso's Oficina Theater Company. The play begins with all the performers, and the audience, singing a musical version of the "Tupi or not Tupi slogan." Interestingly Oswald had pointed out that there is no verb "to be" in Tupi, whence the substitution of "Tupi" for "to be." Some Islamic philosophers, such as Souleymane Bachir Diagne, claim that much of Western philosophy has revolved around about a verb that does not even exist in many languages, leading to endless debates about essential and accidental attributes, essence and existence and so forth.[3] The famous Shakespeare quote is also relativized by the fact that in Portuguese the speaker has to choose between "ser" (for more or less permanent states such as national identity) and "estar" for more transitory states such as illness or momentary feelings. Ze Celso chooses the existential openness and immediacy and becomings of "estar" over the ontological essentialisms of the verb "ser." Further amplifying the carnivalesque hybridities already present in the play itself, the performance is interspersed with original musical numbers, in a variety of styles and genres, related to the themes and characters: "Ophelia's *Fado*," "Polonius Blues," "Guildenstern's Ballad," "Canticle of the Furies" and so forth. Henry Louis Gates, meanwhile, offers another culturally inflected twist on transtextuality theory with his concept of signifying linked, once again, to the Yoruba trickster figure Exu-Legba, the spirit of the crossroads and a figure for semiosis, translation, and adaptation.[4] Although the Oficina version of the play is available in a box set of DVDs, it is more than "filmed theater." Rather, it is a case where film transforms theater and theater transforms film, where filming is already part of the theater production, where cameras and camerapersons are present in every performance, with their work displayed on giant screens as with rock concerts.

Speaking more generally, revisionist readings of Shakespeare have disinterred the latent critique of anti-Semitism in *The Merchant of Venice*, the implied scoring of racism in *Othello*, the sly questioning of colonialism in *The Tempest* and so forth. Tim Blake Nelson's *O* (2001), for its part, turns Othello into a black basketball star in an American high school who dates the Dean's daughter. Michael Almereyda's 2000 *Hamlet*, meanwhile, turns the Castle of Elsinore into the headquarters of the "Denmark Corporation" as a critique of capitalism in the era of globalization. *Te Tangati Wahi Rawa o Weniti* (*The Maori Merchant of Venice*, 2002), the first feature film spoken in the Maori language, constitutes, according to its director (Don Selwyn), an act of reverse colonization, an attempt to "colonize Shakespeare." As Houston Wood points out, the film calls attention "to the parallels between how the Jews and the Maori have been treated by white Christians."[5] In this sense the film correlates the twinned oppressions of Europe's internal and external others, through what might be called, riffing on Raymond Williams, "analogical structures of feeling."[6] The list of Global South indigenizations of Shakespeare is a long one, but would have to include: the Brazilian *Merry Wives of Windsor* (*As Alegres Comadres*, 2003); the Venezuelan *Macbeth* (Macbeth-Sangrador, 2000); the Chinese *Hamlet* (*The Banquet*, 2006); the Tibetan *Hamlet* (Prince of the Himalayas, 2006); the parodic Singaporean *Romeo and Juliet* (*The Chicken Rice Wars*, 2000); the Burkina Faso *Juliet et Romeo* (2011); the Japanese *Ran* based on *King Lear* (1985) the German-Yemini *Macbeth* (Someone is Sleeping in My Pain, 2002), to name just a few.[7]

Within these encounters between a writer of one national origin and the work of a director of another national origin, we encounter various patterns of transformation. One pattern is top-down Hollywoodeanization: the American Minnelli adapts and Americanizes, or better "MGMizes," the French *Madame Bovary*; or the Disney Studio adapts the Arab *A Thousand and One Nights*. But the traffic of adaptation is often more lateral and multidirectional: the Brazilian Bia Lessa adapts Thomas Mann's *The Holy Sinner* in *Crede-Mi*; the Frenchwoman Claire Denis adapts the American Melville in *Beau Travail*; the Italian Visconti adapts the German Thomas Mann in *Death in Venice*; the French Bresson adapts the Russian Dostoevsky; the Anglo-Indian Gurinder Chadha adopts the Englishwoman Jane Austen in *Bride and Prejudice* and so forth. Within these cross-border gazes, critics have occasionally felt that the "native" writer has been better "understood" by the "foreign" filmmaker. The question is not one of officially assigned or epidermic identity, but rather of a transnational capacity for cross-border identifications and affinities. The Egyptian critic Kamel Ramzy, for example, found the Jorge Pons Mexican version of Egyptian Nobel Prize winner Mahfouz's novel *Midaq Alley* more true to the novel than the Egyptian version by Hassan El-Imam. Critics can also find the foreign writer more *simpatico* than the "home" writer, as when the Mexican Paz Alicia Garciadiego encouraged her husband Arturo Ripstein to adopt Mahfouz's *The Beginning and the End*, feeling the Egyptian novel to be closer to her as a Mexican than any novel by a Mexican author.[8]

Texts evolve over what Bakhtin calls "great time;" undergoing surprising "homecomings," as every age and culture "reaccentuates in its own way the works of [the past]."[9] Bakhtin's insight, although not addressed to film—a subject he rarely addressed—is rich in implications for our discussion. Cross-national film adaptations based on canonical works create an interface across multiple times and cultures. As such, they can potentially function as sensitive socio-cultural barometers registering discursive fluctuations and intellectual trends. In a double timeframe, each filmic recreation of a novel reveals and at times unmasks aspects not only of the period and culture of origin of the novel, but also of the period and culture of the adaptation. Adaptation, in this sense, is a work of transnational reaccentuation, whereby a source work is reinterpreted through novel grids, discourses, and perspectives. The potential result is what Bakhtin calls "excess seeing." Taking as his root metaphor the situation of a literal dialogue, where one interlocutor sees what the other does not see—for example what is in the background, the expression on the interlocutor's face and so forth—excess seeing" could be compared in cinematic terms to the shot/counter shot structure in filmic editing, but this time in the realm of cognition and awareness so as to apply to the complementarity of perspectives not just of persons but also of genres, media, and cultures.

On another level, to invoke another Bakhtinian term, the cross-referenced culture can provide a salutary "exotopy," Bakhtin's term to evoke the distance—or in Damrosch's terms the "estrangement"—necessary to sympathetic understanding. Many prestigious novels such as *Don Quixote, Robinson Crusoe*, and *Madame Bovary* have been adapted scores of times, in scores of countries, and in countless formats (features, shorts, TV series, animated cartoons, music videos, video games, and installations), and staged by directors from diverse national origins working in diverse "alien" languages. These kinds of transformations are sometimes encapsulated in awkward yet useful "post" concepts which connote transformation, especially in "ization" process words such as actualization, indigenization, racialization, Africanization, relocalization, dialogization and so forth. Just as Mehta "indigenizes" *Madame*, Anglo-Indian director Gurinder Chadha "transnationalizes" *Pride and Prejudice* in her own *Bride and Prejudice* (2004) by translocating the Bennet sisters to India, but globalizing them through involvements with the U.S. and the U.K., Mexican director Alfonso Cuaron, in his 1998 adaptation of *Great Expectations*, meanwhile, actualizes and translocalizes Dickens by setting the novel in contemporary Miami. Brazilian Television, meanwhile, frequently practices "telenovelization" by turning canonical Brazilian novels like *The Slave Isaura* (1875) into Globo Network TV series and *telenovelas*.

The adapters of novels are like scholars consulting ancient books. As Tang Dynasty scholar Do You put it: "Whenever one consults the books of the ancients, it is because one wishes to reveal new meanings and form institutions in accordance with present circumstances."[10] Every cross-cultural adaptation of a novel, in this sense, filters its source text through a specific reconfiguration of a culturally inflected set of genres and discourses. In Ketan Mehta's *Maya Memsaab* (1993)—an Indian rewriting of *Madame Bovary*—the French culture of the source-novel is mediated and transformed by the adapting Indian culture. The transposed names of the characters already serve to indigenize Flaubert's story. The lead character's name "Maya," for example, shares the same phonemes as "Emma" but adds a philosophical connotation, since Maya is Hindi for "illusion." Within the process of indigenization, Mehta systematically substitutes things Indian for *la chose française*. He replaces Flaubert's Rouen with the picturesque resort town of Shimla, exploiting the town's association with the British Raj and with adulterous playboys and mistresses. Rouen cathedral becomes "Scandal Point," while Flaubert's indefatigable tour guide is transformed into a hustler pushing drugs and cheap hotels. The religious associations of the Rouen Cathedral's "Last Judgment" tableau, as Flaubert's ironic religious commentary on a sordid affair, give way to a crudely secular sleaziness. In the novel, Leon and Emma's lovemaking takes place in a horse-drawn carriage, but in the Mehta version the carriage becomes a train, with shades drawn as in Flaubert, while sexual congress is conjured up through a cinematic *clin d'oeil*, evocative of intercourse, to the train entering the tunnel in the final shots of Alfred Hitchcock's *North by Northwest* (1959).

Thus *Madame Bovary* is mediated through a different industry, different favored genres, and different cultural norms. Although relatively realistic within Bollywood norms, *Maya* also features the extravagant musical production numbers typical of Bombay cinema. Through a generic division of labor, the non-musical episodes represent life in a fairly verisimilar manner, while the songs represent life as dreamed and fantasized, thus proving a platform for something like Flaubert's counterpoint of styles. Along with Govind Nihalani, Mrinal Sen, and Shyam Benegal, Mehta belongs to "third way" Indian cinema, a style that negotiates between apparently antagonistic traditions. In this sense, Mehta strives for a "middle cinema" aesthetic located between the fantastic, colorful, dance-dominated, and very popular Bollywood cinema and the austere, low-budget, independent, and programmatically realist new Indian cinema.

Mehta's foiling of genres and style goes hand in hand with his deployment of multiple perspectives and centers of consciousness. Much like Flaubert, who counterpoints the exalted, romantic, metaphoric, grandly literary style associated with Emma, against a flat, banal, metonymic style associated with Charles, Mehta pursues a similar counterpoint, but now filtered through specifically cinematic techniques like lighting, camera movement, editing, and music-image relations. The Mehta version thus forges the filmic correlative of Flaubert's stylistic counterpoint between mimetic realism and bookish fantasy by juxtaposing realistic scenes with Bollywood-style musical production numbers set against sublime scenic backdrops that recall Emma's languorous reveries about Swiss chalets and Spanish castles. Idealizing romantic tropes, as in Flaubert's text, land with a thud in the banal everyday world, in an equivalent to Flaubert's ionic deflation of romantic metaphors. In one marvelous and completely invented sequence, Mehta expands on the story while respecting Flaubert's narrative and aesthetic principles. Inspired by her readings, Maya stages her own death by robbery-cum-murder in order to elicit dramatic declarations of love from her husband. As her own self-staging dramaturg, she scatters the furniture, applies fake blood, places a strategically misleading bloody knife and so forth. The film then counterpoints her romanticized fantasy of the event, where the husband swoons in exclamations of eternal love, followed by the more realistic version, where the husband expresses only irritation at her extravaganza. In short, Mehta creates the cinematic equivalent of Flaubert's *style indirect libre* with alternation of wide-shot veristic representations of events with close-in zooms and dolly in to Emma's fevered literature-fueled romantic fantasies.

12
FROM ADAPTATION TO REMIX

In the age of the Internet, filmic adaptations undergo fascinating mutations, evoked in terms such as "sampling," "remix," "sweding" and "mash-up." Jay David Bolter and Richard Grusin propose the term "remediation" to account for the ways that "new digital media" gain their cultural significance by absorbing and refashioning earlier media and artistic practices.[1] Even before analysts spoke of intermedia, Alain Badiou reminds us, "cinema was itself its own intermedia."[2] Here we are not far from Marshall McLuhan's "rear view mirror" theory, i.e. the view that the content purveyed by each new medium is drawn from the collective inheritance of antecedent media, a logic which suggests that the Internet is the "meta-medium" that will absorb and relay all pre-existing media, with Google as our guide. For John Durham Peters, Google is not only a haven for books but also an incarnation of Hegelian *geist*, "an intelligence fingering its way through documents and coming to know itself, something like Hegel's absolute *Geist* coming to self-consciousness in algorithms."[3]

All arts and media and texts flirt with the various "sister arts" and in this sense could be said to be incestuously and polyandrously "inside" one another. Or as one postmodernist wit put it, "any text that has slept with another text has also slept with all the other texts that that other text has slept with." It is this textually transmitted "dis-ease" that characterizes the intertextual daisy-chain that Derrida called "dissemination." In the digital age, all the arts and media promiscuously mix and mate and remediate one another, with most of them ultimately winding up in some audio-visual-digital form. (Even literature has become interactive and even cinematized in a more than metaphorical sense with books that feature audio and animation and touch-screen gaming design).[4] The mutations themselves multiply exponentially and algorithmically, or to change the metaphor, they metastasize. Henry Jenkins speaks of "media convergence" to refer to the movement of content "across multiple media platforms, the cooperation between multiple media industries, and the migratory behavior of media audiences …"[5] The age of remediation and the refiltering and transmission of products across media obliges us to rethink long-sacrosanct issues of "medium specificity." Contemporary media have become, in Aram Sinnreich's conceptualization, infinitely "reconfigurable."[6] In his summary, they have become: 1) instantaneous; 2) global; 3) multi-sensory; 4) archival; 5) transmissible; 6) permutable; 7) editable; 8) networked; 9) interoperable; 10) and 11) hackable, resulting in an "unprecedented plasticity."[7]

But cross-media intersections did not begin with the digital revolution. Remix practices merely retool and reconfigure what artists, intellectuals, avant-gardists (and everyday people) have done from time immemorial—taking the old and making it new. Improvisation based on repetition and difference had always been the hallmark of Afro-diasporic art, for example. The Afro-diasporic redemption of no-budget materials, even detritus, formed part of the process by which New World blacks, in a situation of extreme scarcity managed to quilt together communities and transmogrify waste products into art. Shorn of freedom, education, and material advantage, Afro-diasporic peoples have teased beauty out of the guts of deprivation, whether through the musical use of discarded oil barrels (the steel drums of Trinidad, the culinary use of throwaway parts of animals); the textile use of throwaway fabrics; and the digital use of musical samples. Although such popular art is not usually seen as avant-garde, the random piling up of found objects is clearly reminiscent of the aleatory collages typical of the historical avant-gardes, evocative of "defamiliarization," "refunctionism"; and "detournement."

The supposedly purely verbal art of literature, Dickens novels, as Kamilla Elliott points out, were not just verbal, in that they were often accompanied by illustrations.[8] Nothing prevents literature from getting mixed up with other arts, even if literature per se remains a medium whose materials of expression are verbal. Today literature is more and more "impure," increasingly remediated as graphic novel, film adaptation, audio book, TV series, performance, installation, interactive website and so forth, without the adaptations ever completely shedding the memory of the original words that constituted the source text.[9] In the wake of the decline of fidelity regimes and the rise of transtextual discourse, literature teachers and teachers of adaptation courses often ask, in a kind of despair, what is to be gained by comparing texts to films, and whether the practice still holds meaning?" Haun Saussy asks in reference to Proust's À la Recherche du Temps Perdu:

> What would Marcel have made of the inaccessibility of Albertine's mind if he had always before him her GPS location, heart rate, probable serotonin level, last 500 Google searches, past year's credit card transactions, status on Friendster, speed-dial list, and 25 most-played songs?[10]

Is the god of "Fidelity" dead, then, or at least moribund, and is all now permitted? The "still" in the question posed by humanities professors as to whether "students still read" embeds multiple subtexts and anxieties felt by scholars in literature and adaptation studies such as a) does comparative analysis of novel and film still hold meaning at a moment of crisis in the humanities in general; and b) does it still hold meaning in a media-saturated and Internet-dominated age when students purportedly see reading long books as a useless "time-suck"; and c) does it still hold meaning in an age of declining enrollments when students feel the pressure of student debt and the search for jobs in an unfriendly economy. Or is it a question of constantly available entertainments; some of the same students who prefer to read Cliff Notes rather than read novels, one notes, have no problem with binge-watching interminable TV series, some loosely based, as it happens, on literature.

In "World Literature in a Postliterary Age," David Damrosch gives voice to these anxieties by asking: "Will classic works of literature soon have only a residual or nostalgic place in an increasingly postliterary age?" Given social media and the endless digital attractions competing for students' time, he adds, "we may wonder whether the modern literatures are fated to disappear beneath the new media flood?"[11] Damrosch adds that "not all the literary classics of the pre-Internet age will survive the transition, but some will." Missed in this formulation is that some classics, such as *Beowulf*, will survive *only* thanks to the media and their translation into Blockbuster films. Without Truffaut's adaptation, similarly, Roche's novel *Jules and Jim* would have remained in literary limbo. Indeed, Damrosch adds reassuringly, "millions of viewers have heard Gilgamesh's story retold by Star Trek's Captain Jean-Luc Picard to a dying Tamarian on the distant planet of El-Adrel."[12] Damrosch mentions the video game based on *Dante's Inferno*, where Dante's poem becomes a kind of "prequel" to the game. (One could easily multiply examples of this "gamification" of literature). It is better to engage with the new media, Damrosch concludes, "than to retreat into a paleontological stance of regret …"[13]

These processes of transformation and remediation of literature often result in a kind of textual diasporization and amplification of a single source text. Thus a celebrated novel (Paulo Lins' *City of God*, 1997) becomes a noteworthy film (Meirelles' *City of God*, 2002), which then generates a TV series (*City of Men*, 2002–2005), and a feature film (*City of Men*, 2007); and a 2013 documentary (*City of God—10 Years Later*). Here we find a 21st-century version of Balzac's *retour des personnages*, wherein characters like Vautrin and Rastignac reappear in various Balzac novels, but in this case characters featured in both the novel and the film *City of God* develop and interact with newly invented characters and situations, without ever completely losing touch with the source text or with the "original" characters, partially because the author Paulo Lins has participated as a consultant in virtually all of the subsequent films and series generated by his novel.

At times the literary source is more or less obscured, as when a Stephen King novel—*The Shining*—becomes a Stanley Kubrick film, which then becomes an analytical documentary-exegesis film-about-the-film (*Room 237*), then a variety of recut trailers (as romcom, as mashup with *Jerry McGuire* and *The Lady and the Tramp*) and even a CNN promo, where the garden maze of the Kubrick film becomes the décor for an ad for "Quest Means Business." Wandering through the maze, Quest addresses the spectator in his usual stentorian voice: "Lost in the maze of choices—stocks, bonds, commodities … raising capital. Turn one corner and economic boom, turn another and recession and bust!" He then offers to be our guide through the financial labyrinth. Embodying the disorientation of the small-scale investor, the ad invokes the haunted Overlook Hotel to conjure up the haunting of the financial world and the "spooked" investor in the aftermath of the 2008 crisis.[14]

Whereas literature teachers are accustomed to teaching literature back to front—from earlier texts to later ones, it is sometimes more effective to teach literature front to back, from *Beowulf* to Baldwin, i.e. to start with materials that students are familiar with—such as recut trailers of films—along with contemporary rewritings and adaptations, and then work back to the source novel. By way of long duree background, one might give a taste of millennia of literature through remixes, mashups, and revisionist adapations. One could begin with the innumerable film adaptations of the sacred texts of the Abrahamic religions, seem as theological remixes and transtextual variations on hypotexts, first, on the Jewish Bible (the Torah), itself already a collage of genres and remix of pre-existing texts and oral traditions, which in turn forms the hypotext for the Christian Bible, which reconfigures the Jewish Bible as Christian allegory by presenting the sacrificial lamb of Abraham and Isaac as a prefiguration of Christ. The Jewish and Christian sacred texts then form hypotexts for the Koran, now a hypertext in which both Moses and Jesus appear as prophets within a remixed Islamic tradition. Here one might screen not only clips from the canonical versions—in every sense of the word "canonical"—but also the more irreverent, even blasphemous, versions of scripture, for example in the form of a remixed trailer presenting DeMille's *Ten Commandments* as a *Grease*-style high school film.

One could follow up with various mashups of the Christian Bible, and especially the filmic recuperations of the medieval tradition of *parodia sacra* (sacred parody) where carnival revelers make fun of the Church hierarchy and even of Christian theology. Together, these riffs on the Last Supper constitute a dispersive diaspora of remediated biblical motifs. Hundreds of films belong to the genre, for example, of the *Coena Cipriani*, i.e. irreverent rewritings of Christ's Last Supper, by Bunuel (*Viridiana*), Tomás Gutiérrez Alea (*La Ultimate Cena*), Mel Brooks (*History of the World*), Monty Python (*Monty Python at the Hollywood Bowl*), Pedro Almadovar (*Dark Habits*) and Stephen Colbert (offering ironic "proofs" of the existence of God), and, of course, the climactic musical-style finale of *The Life of Brian* with its inspiring, theologically incorrect yet biblically rooted celebration of the crucifixion of Brian/Christ alongside a suspiciously numerous array of fellow crucifixees: in the biblical spirit of *felix culpa* (Happy Fall) and the Hollywood musical spirit of "entertainment as utopia" (Dyer), the film's Jesus/Brian exhorts us to "Try to look on the bright side of Death."

One can also offer a History of World Literature through a chronologically arranged series of revisionist adaptations based on texts drawn from the literary commons. This series might include the Spike Lee revisionist update of Aristophanes' *Lysistrata*, in *Chi-raq*, where a female "sex strike," originally set in the Greece of the Peloponnesian Wars, is recast as a sex-strike by black women in

Chicago in the present of gang wars in the inner-city; the Tyler Perry TV series version of Euripides' *Medea* in his comedy about a vengeful woman named "Madea" in his *Diary of a Mad Black Woman*. Advancing in literary time to the 8th century, we have the children's book *Beowulf in Space*, a cross between the Anglo-Saxon saga and *Star Wars*. (When I was studying Anglo-Saxon in order to plumb the depths of "The Wanderer" and *Beowulf*, I never imagined that my students, decades later, would be familiar with the titular epic hero and Grendel thanks to the 2007 3D British-American epic fantasy film directed by Robert Zemeckis.)

Passing over the Elizabethan period and the already-discussed adaptations of Shakespeare, we can move to the 18th century and the 1963 Tony Richardson *Tom Jones* and the 2005 Michael Winterbottom-directed *Tristram Shandy: A Cock and Bull Story*. The Michael Winterbottom version goes much farther than *Tom Jones* by multiplying and "cinematizing" the various levels of reflexivity in a self-conscious 18th century novel. This time it is no longer a question of finding filmic correlatives for the reflexive techniques of the novel, as with *Tom Jones*, but rather of extrapolating these reflexive techniques in a film-about-the-filming of the adaptation of the novel. The film opens with all the trappings of a costume drama in the "national heritage" tradition: a photogenic country estate, an actor in period costume, musical fanfares reminiscent of historical epics, all conveying monumental grandeur, high seriousness and the well-dressed decorum of the landholding elites.

Steve Coogan, who simultaneously plays himself, Tristram Sandy, and Walter Shandy, slowly approaches the camera and begins to directly address the audience with a completely anachronistic citation of Groucho Marx's *boutade* that the problem with autobiography is that "you're not allowed to 'fool around'." Yet on another level the anachronistic citation is completely apt, since Laurence Sterne as author and the novelistic Tristram as narrator and protagonist can be seen as proffering the novelistic equivalent of the digressive self-mockery and sexual innuendo of stand-up comedy. Tristram is a kind of *avant la lettre* stand-up comic. Just as the Sterne novel is itself a kind of fictive autobiography—*The Life and Opinions of Tristram Shandy, Gentleman*—so the Groucho Marx joke becomes a kind of metacritical element, akin to the constant metatextual digressions of the novel itself. If the novel is about the difficulty of telling one's life story in prose, the film is about the difficulty of adapting the novel in the form of images, sounds, and performance. In this film, even the DVD extras are reflexive and literally dialogical, most obviously in the form of the narcisstic and self-aggrandizing audio-commentary by Bryden and Coogan, where the two actors shamelessly exploit the occasion to pitch their talents to a few favored directors, mentioned by name, who might be listening in. Coogan explains to a presumably absent Scorsese, for example, that although he is associated with comic roles, he would potentially also be very good at drama.

Some adaptations combine actualization, relocalization, and social reconfiguration. Moving to France, we find the updated version of an 18th-century play, Marivaux's *Games of Love and Chance*, as adapted by Allouache Kechiche in *L'Esquive* (English title *Games of Love and Chance*, 2004). The film stages a modern-day adaptation of the Marivaux play as a springboard for discussing a French society that is dramatically different from the all-white Franco-Français society of the 18th century play. In a reflexive move, Kechiche does not adapt the play, but rather stages the process of adaptation of the play by students in Paris. But beyond that he stages that process in a surprising location—a present-day high school in the marginalized *banlieu*, literally "suburbs," but more accurately low-income housing projects inhabited by immigrants and their children. Since the students are all relatively poor, the class contrasts so central to the play's mistaken-identity plot become less pertinent, while other issues ignored by Marivaux such as religion (Muslim, Christian, Jewish), nationality, and skin tone, come to the fore. Thus the gap in centuries between source-play and adaptation transmutes into the present-day ethnic-cultural gap—the all-white French personae of the play have become the multi-racial children of a postcolonial France transformed by immigration. While the play retains its contemporary relevance, since the amorous emotions of the young students resemble those of the characters of the play, the crucial class differences in the play are now displaced. The contrast now is between the class assumptions of the play, where noble and servant share a world structured by clear class hierarchies, and those of the film, where the most salient differences reflect the social divides of the postcolonial city—the world of the wealthy French center as foiling that of the world of the impoverished *banlieu*, or what some have punningly called "the place of the banned."

Another 18-century writer, Jane Austen, has inspired a huge outpouring of revisionist adaptations in book, film and other forms. In what Mette Hjort might call "strongly "marked" version of the transnational, where a film is transnational on numerous registers, Gurinder Chadha's adaptation of *Bride and Prejudice* is transnational in funding, personnel, story, and location, directed by the diasporic filmmaker par excellence, by an Anglo-Indian woman who grew up in Kenya, scripted by a Japanese-Basque American screenwriter, enacted by Indian, Anglo-Indian, British, and American actors, filmed in India, the U.K. and the U.S. The film casts a postcolonial-feminist and globalization-conscious gaze on the Austen novel. The film shapes cross-cultural analogies by suggesting certain subterranean affinities between Austen's England and Chadha's India: a similar sexual modesty; the strategic role of dance balls in charting the trajectories of romance; the comparable role of wealth in marriage, whether in the form of western marriages for financial convenience or in the form of Indian arranged marriages.

The intra-national class differences that mark the Austen novel transmute into the transnational cultural differences of the Chadha adaptation, so that the romance between the American Darcy and the Indian Lalita come to homologize the geopolitical romance of India and the U.S. in the period of the film. In a perhaps unduly reciprocal portrayal, both American and Indian have to abandon some of their prejudices. Yet ultimately Lalita becomes the allegorical spokeswoman for some of the Indian complaints about globalization, while the "green-card holder" Kohli character, Chadha's version of Austen's Mr. Collins, comes to satirically incarnate the postcolonial mimicry of the alienated more-American-than-the-Americans Indian bedazzled by the West. In a kind of "compromise-formation," the film reflects a double and contradictory process of simultaneous globalization and indigenization.

Speaking more generally, Jane Austen's work has provided rich material for this constant process of revision and actualization, generating 1) the literary rewritings such as *Pride and Prejudice and Zombies, Sense and Sensibility and Sea Monsters,* and *Death Comes to Pemberley*; alongside 2) fictional biographies (*Jane writes Back* and *Jane and the Damned*) and even *Pride and Prejudice* from a feline point of view (*Pride and Prejudice and Kitties*); plus 3) novelistic actualizations like *The Jane Austen Book Club* and *Lost in Austen*. Curtis Sittenfeld's novel *Eligible* makes Elizabeth Bennet a contemporary writer from Ohio working with a women's magazine and Darcy a brain surgeon. Apart from the multiple film versions of novels like *Emma* and *Pride and Prejudice*, there are films based on Jane Austen's life; along with disguised contemporary actualizations, such as *Emma* remediated as *Clueless* (film and then TV series); plus homages to her work like the *Bridget Jones* books and films; or even the remediations of her work in the form of card games (*Marrying Mr. Darcy: The Pride and Prejudice Card Game*), or interactive websites and the inevitable mashups such as "Jane Austen's *Fight Club*."

The web-series version of *Pride and Prejudice* takes the form of *The Lizzie Bennet Diaries*, whose episodes are filmed as video blogs from Lizzie to her followers. The producers maintain social media accounts for the characters, who interact and produce Facebook posts about their lives. The series begins with "Lizzie" displaying a Tee-shirt on the front on which is inscribed the famous first line of the novel—"It is a truth universally acknowledged that a single man in possession of a good fortune"—and then displays on the back "must be in want of a wife." Lizzie explains that her Mom gave her the Tee-shirt, that she never wears it, that she is a 24-year-old grad student living at home and burdened with a mountain of debt. Although she is eagerly preparing for a career, to her Mom the only thing that matters is that she is single and must be in want of a husband. Lizzie disputes the "universally acknowledged" truth by pointing out that contemporary rich single men are often not looking for wives at all, and that the pool of available males is composed of a dispiriting mix of 22% "sleezeballs and scumbags," 26% men stuck-in dead-end-relationships; 18% men sailing around the world trying to find themselves." Yet according to her mother, "every rich man was put on earth to impregnate her daughter."

The age of what Henry Jenkins calls "participatory culture" has generate a sea-change in the ways that young people can "archive, annotate, appropriate, and recirculate media content in powerful new ways."[15] For the 19th century, examples of revisionist remixed adaptations include the cartoonization of *Heart of Darkness* via *Apocalypse Now* and *Winnie the Pooh* in the mashup *Apocalypse Pooh*, and the rap version of *Moby Dick* by MC Lars, featuring a Pequod crew as multi-racial as Melville's own. Some of the lyrics:

> Call me Ahab ... on the hunt for this mammal that once took my leg. With my worn down cred and my man Queequeeg ... This scar that you see that

runs down my face / Has scarred my soul and inspired this chase ... Full speed ahead! This is American fun / There is wisdom that is woe ... Towards thee I sail, thou unconquering whale. To stab my spear into your white tail ... Now excuse me while I go be melancholy in my room![16]

A cause for optimism about the future of literature is found in phenomena like Def Poetry Jam on Cable TV, slam poetry, and now the Instagram poets who work at the intersection of artistic media and technologies by combining words and images. Another cause for optimism about participatory literary culture is what seems to be a wave in many countries of high school students making performed video-adaptations of the novels assigned in school. These adaptations can even take on an activist edge, as occurred when Latino students studying literature at Still Waters in a Storm, a one-room schoolhouse in Brooklyn, thoroughly frightened by the wave of Trump-led anti-Latino hatred, decided to re-incarnate Don Quixote as a group of Spanish-speaking immigrants in contemporary New York. According to Valeria Luiselli, they turned the project into a musical "The Travelling Serialized Adventures of Kid Quixote," which they performed in homes, offices, and college classrooms: "The troupe arrived with props, a keyboard, a ukulele, a disarmingly humorous script and a handful of deeply moving songs the children had written."[17]

Linda Hutcheon has noted that "there is now a secondary educational industry devoted to helping students 'make the most' of the adaptations."[18] The digital era also brings with it a revisionist mode of literary criticism in the form of the Internet series "Thug Notes," an audio-visual-performative smarter version of "Cliff Notes" where "Sparky Sweets Ph.d," played by comedian Greg Edwards, offers concise summaries and astute analyses of the classics of world literature in the form of black slang glosses. The series logo begins with parodically PBS-style gravitas, with well-stocked shelves of books as backdrop and classical music as soundtrack. The summary of *Hamlet*, to take just one of scores of examples, speculates about whether the protagonist is "wack" by mistreating his "Breezy" (girfiend) and using "Elizabethan Hatorade" (i.e. poison) to fell his enemies. The frequency of disease imagery, Sweets points out, is a metaphor for the "something that is sick" in the Kingdom of Denmark. The analysis, sprinkled with cartoonish illustrations, brings up the classical questions: is Hamlet afflicted with an Oedipus complex (i.e. wants to "get down" with his mother), or is Hamlet divided between Christian principles and the law of vengeance. Since the play is so full of doubts and unresolvable questions, Sweets points out, it turns the spectators themselves and the critics into indecisive Hamlets.

Another entry in the series of technologically enabled revisionist adaptations is the video game based on Henry David Thoreau's *Walden*. The choice is surprising in that Thoreau is often seen as a Luddite, moving to Walden Pond to "detox" from over-mechanized modernity but living in dialogical solitude in his cabin. What could the man who advised "Simplify, simplify" have to do with the constantly accelerating high-tech world of gaming? The game answers this question by following the rhythms of the seasons, beginning in summer and ending a year later.

As a subtle reproach to the competitive *frenesi* of the typical video games, *Walden* stresses austere simplicity and quiet contemplation, coaxing the players into collecting arrowheads and fishing in tranquil ponds. The game's pastoral-intellectual attractions include building cabins, planting beans, sending articles to Horace Greeley, collaborating with the "Underground Ralroad," and chatting with Transcendentalist philosopher Ralph Waldo Emerson,[19] In his book *If Hemingway Wrote JavaScript*, finally, Angus Croll envisions twenty-five celebrated novelists, playwrights, and poets, including Jorge Luis Borges, Charles Dickens, Hemingway, Virginia Woolf, and Tupac Shakur translating their works into code.[20]

The age of the Internet opens up rich pedagogical possibilities. Adaptation Studies and World Literature themselves have to "adapt," if literature is to "still" have meaning" for our students. It was in this same spirit of actualization and remediation that I offered to my NYU students, some of them filmmakers, my proposal for a covert revisionist and de-Gallicized adaptation of *Madame Bovary*. To disguise the French origins of the story, I suggested giving a misleading title such as "The Erotic Adventures of Mia Jones," while giving the other characters a motley series of names drawn from multiple ethnic origins, as would be more typical of the contemporary United States. In my version, the farmer's daughter from Normandy would be a farm girl from upstate New York, where she has been shaped by binge-watching Soap Operas and telenovelas. Still young and naïve, she marries a male nurse from Utica, but soon becomes bored. In the wake of Woody Allen's substitution of film for literature in *The Purple Rose of Cairo*, where Allen replaced one form of escapism—Flaubert's romantic literature—with another—Depression-Era escapist movies, I proposed a technical-mediatic upgrade and change of format by granting Emma/Mia an active online fantasy life. After moving to Brooklyn, Mia would successively fall in love, thanks to Internet dating, first with an artsy Leon-type accountant from Williamsburg and then with a suave Rodolphe-like Don Juan, manager of a Wall Street hedge fund. Ultimately disillusioned with both lovers, she subsequently becomes obsessed with Tinder, culminating in a disastrous series of dates crystallized in a vertiginous montage—reminiscent in its rhythms of the ball sequence in the Minnelli film—of rightward swipes on images of handsome male faces. Subsequently disenchanted with Tinder masculinity, she would move—and here I take my cue from Spike Jonzes' *Her*—to interactive games and fall in love with an Avatar on Second Life. In a nod both to the source text and to contemporary socio-economic realities, she would die less from unreciprocated love than from her Shop-till-you-Drop addiction to credit card debt, resulting in the brutal foreclosure of her home triggered by the 2008 financial crisis.[21]

13

WORLD CINEMA

The pre-history

Having discussed the analogies and disanalogies between World Literature and World Cinema, we can now turn to World Cinema on its own terms, or at least to its international precursors. Long before academics and curators were speaking about "World Cinema" or "Transnational Cinema," politically conscious directors from the various "Worlds" were carrying out projects that at that time were called "international" or "tricontinental" or "pan-African." In the post-World War II period, a kind of politicized auteurism surfaced with Italian Neo-realism and then spread around the world, inspiring directors like François Truffaut in France, Nelson Pereira dos Santos in Brazil, Tomás Gutiérrez Alea in Cuba, Satyajit Ray in India, Youssef Chahine in Egypt, Elia Kazan in the U.S. and so forth. Many auteur-directors from the Third World studied filmmaking in the West. In the 1960s, the Senegalese Sembene studied filmmaking in the U.S.S.R.; the Mozambican (later Brazilian) Ruy Guerra studied at IDHEC in Paris; and a host of Latin American filmmakers—Fernando Birri from Argentina, Tomás Gutiérrez Alea, and Julio García Espinosa from Cuba and Triguerinho Neto from Brazil—studied at the Centro Sperimentale in Rome.

In this period, leftist filmmakers belonged to and hoped to strengthen a "world" of socialist solidarity. Although many "Western" directors have dedicated themselves to international left causes—Agnes Varda, Jean-Luc Godard, Rene Vautier, Ken Loach, and John Sayles come to mind—Joris Ivens and Chris Marker stand out even from this internationalist crowd. Speaking of Ivens, Tom Gunning writes that "no other filmmaker pursued cinema's possibility of portraying global space as tirelessly as Ivens did in his sixty-year career."[1] Many directors were active participants or fellow-travellers within a kind of socialist-communist internationale of filmmakers. Dutch filmmaker Joris Ivens, at times together with his French wife Marceline Loridan—the woman who spoke of her father and the concentration camps in the Rouch/Morin *Chronicle of a Summer* (1961)—made a host of anti-fascist and pro-communist films in more than a score of countries, including the Netherlands/ Indonesia (with the anti-colonialist film *Indonesia Calling*), the U.S. (in collaboration with Pare Lorentz), Spain (supporting the Republican side in the Civil War in *The Spanish Earth*), the U.S.S.R., Germany, Chile, Australia, Poland, Hungary, China, and North Vietnam (with *17th Parallel: The People's War*)

Chris Marker, as internationalist cine-activist par excellence, meanwhile, helped Latin American filmmakers such as Silvio Tendler from Brazil and Patricio Guzmán from Chile. Marker's own films, such as *Sans Soleil*, offer inexhaustible samples of transnational connection, as they operate on, between, and across the borders of many nations, as well as in the interstices of documentary, experimental cinema, and fiction. Marker's career embodied an ardent search for political utopias, the germs of which he found, or hoped to find, in revolutionary Cuba, Maoist China, and the Chile of Unidad Popular, but his wide-ranging enthusiasm was tempered over time by his dry-eyed lucidity about the limitations of actually existing political projects.

A man of the independent non-Stalinist and anti-colonialist left, Chris Marker was in Albert Memmi's terms "the colonizer who refuses." As a progressive anti-authoritarian internationalist intellectual, he was skeptical about his own (or anyone's) capacity to speak "universal truths." Nevertheless, an implicit global utopia of anti-authoritarian socialism haunts many of Marker's films. This is especially true of *Le Fond de l'Air est Rouge* (*A Grin without A Cat*, 1977, with a "reactualized "English-language" version released in 1993) which portrays, in a kind of transnational chronotope of radicality, various left vs. right radical struggles across the globe. The two parts of *Grin without a Cat* bear witness to the melancholy drift from the utopian hopes of the 1960s to the waning of radical affect and the disenchantments of the subsequent period. Shuttling between decades and nations and regions in a kind of transhistorical montage, Marker threads together scenes of revolt from different periods in France, Chile, Germany, Brazil, and the U.S. In a radicalization of Kuleshov's "creative geography" in the 1920s, which had Moscow-launched javelins land in the sporting fields of Washington, D.C., Marker's edits are *literally* and politically transnational. Linking rebellions in various periods and locations, graphic and kinetic matches join gestures and movements across national space as a kinetic assemblage of demonstrators throw paving stones and other objects at the police, By gleaning images of rebellion from around the world, *Grin without a Cat* can be seen as creating what Deleuze calls a "world memory," where "the different levels of the past no longer relate to a single character, a single family, or a single group, but to quite different characters as to unconnected places which make up a world memory."[2] In a way, this internationalist wave of films played an essential political role, paving the way for a more complex, if in some ways less radical vision, later encompassed in the word "transnational." (One could easily imagine a contemporary Marker-style assemblage film, now facilitated by the digital revolution, threading together the latter-day protests that began first in Iran and then with the Tunisian "jasmine" revolution, and subsequently migrated to Egypt, Spain, the U.S. and so forth).

Given that globalization has eroded the notion of the "international" as referencing a list of putatively equal nation-states, the word "international" itself, for many contemporary media scholars, now seems redolent of the musty smell of UN-style aggregations of nation-states in the post-war era, an outmoded throwback term tied to a merely simulacral equality that hides massive asymmetries of power. Yet for film historian/theorist Nicole Brenez, the term "international" retains aspirational pertinence by evoking forms of cross-border left solidarity that one would do well to resurrect, which have reappeared in forms such as the Jasmine revolution in Tunisia or the Occupy Wall Street movement in New York. Jose Miguel Palacios, in his exhaustive research on Chilean exile cinema, demonstrates that in historical terms "internationalism" remains highly relevant to specific moments in film history. It was the self-declaredly internationalist solidarity of socialist and social-democratic countries in the 1970s, Palacios argues, that helped give birth to Chilean exile cinema in the wake of the 1973 *coup d'état*. For Palacios, the key word is "solidarity," as the name for an idea, a set of practices, and a "mode of political subjectivity":

> ... solidarity is a way of being moved by the events shaping the world, together with the desire to act within and to transform the world. This desire—both an ethos and a political affect—can be traced back to the history of internationalist movements, frequently attached to the association of Communist and Socialist Parties and militias on a global scale. Solidarity ... is in fact unthinkable without an invocation of internationalism.[3]

In sum, the concept of internationalist solidarity was and remains pertinent in scholarship dedicated to the historical period of the Cold War, proxy wars, U.S. support for Third World dictatorships and so forth, and therefore indispensable for addressing not only the particular corpus of Chilean exile cinema but also exile cinema generally.

14

THE THEORY OF WORLD CINEMA

The phrase "World Cinema" on one level replaced phrases like international cinema and Third World Cinema. Hardly limited in use to academic analysis, the term has become a commonplace in the language of film festival brochures and catalogues, with film journalists and film scholars, and among hardcore cinephiles and even casually cosmopolitan filmgoers. World Cinema has thus been understood in extremely diverse and even opposite ways, and gradually came to gather under its wide umbrella earlier categories such as "foreign films," to "international art cinema," or to "non-Hollywood film," and "international auteur cinema." In German, the word, *Weltkinematographie* combines echoes of Goethe's *Weltliteratur* with the memory of the Lumiere Brothers' *cinematographe*, but in practice it tends to refer to global art cinema. It is not always clear, however, whether the term World Cinema refers to a specific corpus of films, or to a pantheon of directors, or to a distinct cinematic style, or to a mode of production. At times, the categorization of the film can change with time and circumstance, so that the films of an Ousmane Sembene or Souleymane Cisse can be successively categorized within a national category ("Senegalese filmmaker," "Malian Filmmaker"), then move into a pan-continental category ("African Film") and be finally "promoted" to the category of "World Cinema."

An interesting phenomenon occurs with these films in terms of "circulation." As Michael Talbot points out:

> While on the surface the terms connote appealing images of inclusiveness and unfettered audiovisual circulation, this cinema—the sort that fills outs the programs of North Atlantic film festivals—is a realm firmly governed by exclusivity and limited access. Despite the positive images of cultural circulation the terms invoke on a surface level, the films they describe do not freely circulate the world, but move unidirectionally from the Global South to niche

markets in the North. World Cinema films are intended, often from the level of conception, for consumption by North Atlantic audiences, financially supported through multiple phases of production largely by European funding, and distributed via the network of North Atlantic film festivals, arthouse theaters, and DVD releases.[1]

In terms of academic curricula and academic publications, the situation is equally murky. An undergraduate "History of World Cinema" course at one college, as Talbot points out, might explore a vastly different corpus than a similarly named course at a different institution or location. One textbook, such as Geoffrey Nowell-Smith's *The Oxford History of World Cinema*, employs the term to designate the total global sum of film production, while Shohini Chaudhuri's *Contemporary World Cinema* limits its survey to films from "Europe, the Middle East, East Asia and South Asia." The same confusion reigned in the classifications of that now virtually extinct entity the "Video Store," where "foreign" videos might be classified as "World Cinema" in the UK, but filed under a national category (French Film) or continental (Latin American Film, African Film) or under national, genre, or auteur rubrics. (Kim's Video in Greenwich Village in Manhattan abbreviated "Godard" to an idolatrous "God," in transparent homage to the divinity of the most venerated of Auteurs).

As occurred with World Literature, the study of World Cinema incorporated the insights of earlier work performed under various rubrics such as "Third World Cinema," "Minority Cinema," and "Postcolonial cinema." Building on the already-mentioned internationalist cinema, what has variously been called "World Cinema," "Transnational Cinema," and "Global Cinema" has helped deprovincialize the film canon by opening it up to minority, women, and Global South directors. In works of polymathic erudition, scholars like Dudley Andrew, Lucia Nagib, and in a more skeptical and oblique manner, Thomas Elsaesser, have given us stellar demonstrations of the productivity of a World Cinema approach. While "World Cinema" existed as a rubric long before its recent renewed popularity, it tended to be equated with Western art cinema, ethnocentrically assumed to be the only cinema of interest. At times, World Cinema became synonymous with "non-English speaking film" or "foreign film." An early modest break with this tendentious provincialism can be found in a 1987 volume edited by William Luhr, *World Cinema since 1945*, followed later by the 1996 Geoffrey Nowell-Smith edited volume *The Oxford History of World Cinema*, and the Aristides Gazetas-edited volume *Introduction to World Cinema* and the John Hill and Pamela Church Gibson edited *World Cinemas: Critical Approaches*, both from the year 2000. In these collective projects, Western and non-Western cinemas were treated more or less respectfully, side by side, in a roughly egalitarian manner.

It was only in the 21st century that World Cinema began to be theorized in depth, in ways both similar to and different from its usages in World Literature studies.[2] Lucia Nagib, a key figure in the debates, and an editor in the I.B.Tauris World Cinema Series, invested the cinematic "World" with new energies and perspectives by reformulating the relation between Hollywood and World Cinema. Prior to Nagib's intervention, Hollywood was seen in opposite ways, either as the enemy and rival of World Cinema, or as an integral part of it. Rather than see World Cinema as "not Hollywood," Nagib suggested a World Cinema continuum where Hollywood would take its rightful place as one cinema alongside others. Rather than excoriate Hollywood for its own "otherizations," Nagib simply "anotherized" Hollywood itself as "just another other cinema." Pitting World Cinema against Hollywood, Nagib warned, still positions Hollywood as the primary interlocutor to whom all alternatives are addressed, the language in relation to which all other cinemas are mere subaltern "dialects." Rather like Damrosch in relation to literature but with a much more progressive political agenda, Nagib opts for defining World Cinema not as a corpus but as "a method, a way of cutting across film history, according to waves of relevant films and movements, thus creating flexible geographies."[3] David Martin Jones, meanwhile, has usefully suggested a pluralization of the term to evoke a "world of cinemas." (A logical amendment would further pluralize that expression with a double plural—"worlds of cinemas.")

Nagib and her co-authors (Chris Perriam and Rajinder Dudrah) reconfigured "World Cinema" through the concept of "polycentrism" (an idea generously acknowledged to having been borrowed from our *Unthinking Eurocentrism*, where Ella Shohat and I had ourselves borrowed it from Samir Amin, for whom it was an economic term, which we expanded into an epistemological-discursive-cultural concept) as a way of denormativizing Hollywood. Polycentrism, they write: "… allows us to move fom the uniformizing, opposition and negative understanding of world cinea, and a starting point to question Eurocentric versions of the world and of cinema's place within it …"[4] This "reset" avoids a series of traps such as (1) a *normativization* that would erect Hollywood as the paradigmatic "real" in relation to which other cinemas form the subaltern shadow"; (2) a *Manicheanism* that would demonize Hollywood as "bad" and other cinemas as "good" without recognizing all cinemas as ideologically mixed and conflicted sites traversed by contradictions of class, nation, gender, race and so forth; and (3) a premature *homogenization* that would create a factitious unity on both sides of the equation.[5] In *Theorizing World Cinema*, Nagib, Chris Perriam, and Rajinder Dudrah continue the "polycentric approach" while elaborating on the overlappings and nuances that both join and separate "World Cinema" and "transnational cinema." The authors surround "World Cinema" with some necessary caveats, without which "World Cinema" and "Hollywood and the World" would sound too much like a new iteration of "the West and the Rest," even when the conceptualization is in principle pro-"Rest."

Another key figure in charting the territory of World Cinema has been Dudley Andrew. In "An Atlas of World Cinema" (2004) –the title echoes Franco Moretti's *Atlas of the European Novel*—Andrew critically extrapolated Moretti's methods as a partial model for analyzing World Cinema. Andrew argues for a "dynamic and comparative" approach that would "track a process of cross-pollination that bypasses national directives." Andrew's "Atlas" proposes multiply superimposed maps: political, demographic, linguistic, and topographical:

> Why not conceive an atlas of types of maps, each providing a different orientation to unfamiliar terrain, bringing out different aspects, elements, and dimensions [offering a] ... model, a set of approaches, just as an atlas of maps opens up a continent to successive views: political, demographic, linguistic, topographical, meteorological. marine, historical.[6]

For Andrew, "World Cinema" names both the global reach of Hollywood and the resistance to its domination. Superimposing Moretti's method on comparative linguistics, Andrew intriguingly compares the classical Hollywood model to a kind of hegemonic "Latin," with peripheral cinemas as local "vernaculars." (One is reminded of Bakhtin's enthusiastic endorsement of the ever-changing European vernaculars over against the static, frozen canonicity of Latin).

In "Time Zones and Jet Lags: the Flows and Phases of World Cinema," Andrew highlights the Eurocentric pattern whereby Western festivals, critics, and funding agencies remain the gatekeepers and the literal judges and juries of World Cinema. (The cinema in this sense follows a trajectory similar to that of "World Literature" as charted by Pascale Casanova in *The World Republic of Letters*, whereby the West, and in her view especially France, remains the arbiter in the world Stock Exchange of literary value). Large-scale appraisals of cinematic value, Andrew claims, have been made by and for the West, with the "Prime Meridien" running through Hollywood or Paris, as if the value of 'foreign' cinemas could only be assessed by Western critics attending Western festivals. Andrew does not abandon the notion of aesthetic value, however. Texts like his "China and Africa in the Changing World of World Cinema" proliferate in words and phrases that convey aesthetic judgment, as in his frequent descriptions of films as "stunning" or "notable" or "strong" or "great films." Nor is Andrew apologetic about exercising such evaluative judgment, since in his quite reasonable view the cinema must be treated "both as an artistic and a sociological phenomenon."[7]

Andrew's periodization charts a series of distinct shifts, between the pre-WWII, post-WWII and post-1968 periods, that help to clarify the nature of the changes in scope and character of World Cinema. The first *cosmopolitan phase* of silent cinema was characterized by the coexistence of multiple and roughly equal models of filmmaking. During the second *national phase*, spanning the interwar years through the end of WWII, the advent of sound anchored the cinemas in their linguistic contexts of production, just as critics attempted to identify distinct national styles and industries within each geopolitical location. International circulation during this period, for Andrew, was governed by what would later be called "center-periphery" protocols, with the center being the North Atlantic, extended at times to include the U.S.S.R., and even Japan.

What Andrew dubs the third *federated phase*, extending from the end of World War II through the 1960s, saw the formal networking both of film producers and institutions through such groups as the *Fédération Internationale des Associations de Producteurs de Films*—and for film critics, the *Fédération Internationale de la Presse Cinématographique*. North Atlantic film festivals and the film critics associated with them established themselves as the advocates and arbiters of "quality," often in assumed opposition to the Hollywood "quantity" purporting to foster "both equality and difference in artistic expression" while remaining attentive to "cultural distinctiveness." While these efforts institutionalized European Art Cinema as a counter to Hollywood's economic dominance, they did little to incorporate new nations or regions or auteurs into the realm of World Cinema. A fourth, final *world cinema phase* incorporated a series of "second waves" in the 1980s, and in this sense opened the way to the *global cinema* phase, in the wake of 1989 and the fall of the Berlin Wall and the end of the Soviet empire, a period marked by the swelling strength of globalization.

Shekhar Deshpande and Meta Mazaj, building on the concept of "polycentrism" (Shohat/Stam, Lucia Nagib), lend considerable concreteness and scholarly density to the concept of World Cinema by focalizing major "power centers" in World Cinema—1) Hollywood; 2) Indian Cinema; 3) Asian Cinemas (Japanese, Chinese, Hong Kong, Taiwanese, and South Korean); 4) European Cinema; and 5) Nigerian and Nollywood. These power centers form a "collective snapshot of World Cinema" and present the following features: 1) a high level of cinematic activity; 2) the formation of their own infra-national and supra-national spheres of influence; 3) a tradition of indigenous perspectives and scholarship (what Metz in the 1970s called the "linguistic appendage" of the film industry.[8] This extremely useful schema powerfully decenters Hollywood as just one node of the world production of films.

"World Cinema" sometimes evokes a kind of top-down patronage of the films and filmmakers from the Global South, including the "South" of Europe itself. The brochures and promotion materials of the Festivals and Funding Agencies that support films from the Global South often deploy an infantilizing language of "development," borrowed from economic "take-off" theory, a trope which implies that the underdeveloped Third World toddler can hopefully learn how to walk with the aid of First world investors. As Talbot points out, Film Festival and Foundation brochures and websites, whatever their good intentions and good effects, are pervaded by the outdated and paternalistic language of "development." The Cannes Film Festival, for example, describes the function of its World Cinema Pavilion/Pavillion les Cinémas du Monde as promoting films from "developing" countries so "they can participate in the Cannes International Film Festival."

In the realm of film preservation and distribution, Martin Scorcese's "World Cinema Foundation" deploys a similar discourse in aiming "to help developing countries preserve their cinematic treasures," which in practical terms has had the very positive effect of restoring films from Morocco, Brazil, Romania, South Korea, Senegal, Turkey, Egypt, Taiwan, Mexico, India and Bangladesh to allow for exhibition later at Cannes. The Berlin Film Festival's World Cinema Fund, one of the most prominent sources of festival-affiliated film production funds, similarly, describes itself as "committed to the development and support of cinema in regions with weak film infrastructure," specifically Latin America, Africa, Middle East, Central and Southeast Asia and the Caucasus. For Michael Talbot:

> Such paternalistic language calls to mind the efforts of endangered wildlife support efforts, as well as the often problematic justifications behind Third World humanitarian aid. In characterizing the nations that they support, these funds return us to the biologizing and infantilizing rhetoric of dependency theory, describing *developing* nations, *emerging* and *endangered* film cultures, *lack* of film industries and the political and economic *crises*, implying immaturity or failure on the part of Global South cinemas, and justifying the intervention of European aid.[9]

The branding of global art cinema, for Talbot, is a two-sided coin. On the one hand branding can fabricate rigid badges of identity, and potentially a mindless conformity. On the other hand, festival culture can potentially serve to "increase the visibility of the work, prompting the festival-goer, the critic and the sales agent to take note of a film that would otherwise slip under the radar.[10] In "World Cinema: Realism, Evidence, Presence," Thomas Elsaesser argues that European art/auteur cinema (and by extension, world cinema) has always diacritically defined itself against Hollywood on the basis of a claim for greater realism, whether in the form of Italian neorealism, French *cinema vérité*, Bergmanesque psychological realism. Ingmar Bergman's psychological realism, or Dogma's veristic chastity. In the emerging cinemas of the Global South, we find documentary-style engagements with ordinary people and normal quotidian rhythms.[11]

In "Film Festival Networks: the new Topographies of Cinema in Europe," Elsaesser describes the process by which the gatekeepers of the international film festival circuit confer cultural capital on a new kind of auteur in the context of Hollywood hegemony and global cultural flows. By globalizing Western auteur cinema, "the Festivals created not only a self-sustaining, highly self-referential world for art cinema, the independent cinema and the documentary film" as well as an alternative to "the Hollywood studio system in its post-Fordist phase."[12] In "European Cinemas as World Cinema: A New Beginning," Elsaesser suggests that World Cinema can be considered a latter-day iteration of "Third World Cinema." And indeed, if "World Cinema" is meant to refer only to politically resistant films produced outside of the United States, the term would form a latter-day sublimated version of what was once called "Third Cinema" and "Tricontinental Cinema," but in a situation, I would add, where the radical gun-wielding Che Guevara of Glauber Rocha's films has morphed into the relatively innocuous Globo populist of Walter Salles' *Motorcycle Diaries*, a film which foregrounds the saintly *pueblo* but backgrounds the power structures that oppress them.

If "World Cinema" refers to non-Western cinema, one wonders where cinemas partially modeled on Hollywood, including in the Global South, fit into the picture? In the wake of the first successes of Hollywood studios, the Hollywood industrial model spread around the world. In the 1920s and 1930s, many countries developed their own national Hollywood-style equivalents—Babelsberg-UFA in Berlin,

Mosfilm in Moscow, Taikatsu and Shochiko in Japan, Pinewood in the U.K., Cinecitta in Rome, etc. Even in the late 1940s and 1950s, a group linked to Sao Paulo's industrial bourgeoisie founded the Vera Cruz film company along Hollywood lines. Their luxurious studios modeled everything—the contract star system, compartmentalized specialization, hierarchical production, elaborate lighting—on the Hollywood model. The studio's six sound stages were literally modeled on those of MGM, at a time, ironically, when the studio model in the US, threatened by technological change and the end of vertical integration, was in acute crisis. Ultimately, such an expensive model did not work in a Third World country like Brazil—the company lasted only from 1949 to 1954—and the model was challenged both by the ever-popular musical comedies (*chanchadas*) from Rio, and increasingly, by the emerging Cinema Novo movement, with its Third Worldist politics, low-budget production methods, and "aesthetics of hunger." One perhaps unintended drawback of the term "World Cinema," in this context, is that it perhaps inadvertently favors the feature film—since the word "cinema" is more likely to evoke feature fiction films than short films or documentaries—leaving little room for "minor" and more affordable low-budget forms and modalities of the cinema of the "disempowered."

In *European Cinema: Face to Face with Hollywood* (Amsterdam: AUP 2005), Elsaesser advances an "emulation/emigration" model to explain why European directors like Roland Emmerich and Wolfgang Peterson might adopt a Hollywoodean style in order to attract the notice of studios.[13] In open emulation of Hollywood, "their dream was to make films that either found a large popular audience or pleased an American distributor, in order then to set off and emigrate to New York and Los Angeles."[14] Over more than a century, Hollywood has been progressively Germanized, Italianized, Asianized, and most recently Latinized (by the *tres amigos* del Toro, Ignarittu, and Cuaron, for example, and by Brazilians like Jose Padilha). If the World needs Hollywood, Hollywood also needs the World, whether as supplier of stories and landscapes, or of markets and talent. In cultural and corporate terms, Hollywood has practiced a kind of top-down cannibalism by devouring and patenting world culture in all its infinite variety, sometimes trying to "enclose" elements of works like *Thousand and One Nights* that rightfully belong to the world-wide cultural commons.

At the same time, we cannot equate American Cinema with Hollywood, since some avant-garde cinema in the U.S. sees itself as virulently opposed to Hollywood. Even Hollywood itself, according to trade journals, now sometimes shies away from funding projects that are "too American" because they lack overseas sales values.[15] Elsaesser has also challenged the "Europe-versus-Hollywood" dualism which equates Europe with High Art and Hollywood with crass entertainment. Elsaesser notes that it is "difficult to point to possible European innovations (e.g. multi-strand narratives, layered temporalities, frank depiction of sex) that the Americans themselves are not capable of, or have not imported."[16] Asian cinemas, meanwhile, have clearly absorbed Hollywood, leading to the Hollywoodeanization of Asia and reciprocally if not equally, the Asianization of Hollywood via figures such as Quentin Tarantino, Ang Lee, and Justin Lin.

15

WORLD MUSIC AND THE COMMONS

Media studies is intrinsically a form of comparative studies, since "without other media," as John Durham Peters puts it, "a medium is not a medium."[1] In other words, we can only define a medium differentially, in relation to what it shares or does not share with another medium. In the case of inter-mediality or transmediality, it is not as if a pure medium simply encounters another medium; both media are to some extent always already intermedial before their meeting. Some scholars argue that the arts are *ontologically* intermedial.[2] The arts, then, are transmedial "all the way down."

In this section, I would like to address the inseparabilities and fusions of the various "Worlds" as they converge within popular music. Of all the arts, perhaps none is so universal, so embedded in the cultural commons and in "deep time" as music. While cinema has a one-century history, the origins of music go back before recorded time. Unlike literature, which requires literacy, and unlike cinema, which depends on a complex material infrastructure, music inhabits our minds and bodies. The vast majority of human beings are born not only with a capacity for speech but also for an appreciation of music; music thus forms part of humanity's "commons." It is no accident that Christopher Small entitled his homage to popular music *Music of the Common Tongue*. As a maverick scholar trained in classical composition transformed by his encounter with African-American music, and as someone deeply familiar with European symphonic music, Small was a Western "insider" who ended up favoring the "outsider" music. For Small, music is not a thing but a socially situated activity whose relationalities concerned not only notes and scales and meters but also people and communities. Through music, people and peoples introduce aesthetic order into their lives and explore and celebrate their sense of self and community. Music, in Nina Simone's words, communicates what it "feels like to be free." Through the process of "musicking"—spirituals, blues, jazz, rap—African-Americans managed to survive. Improvising in art as in life, the enslaved created hybrid forms that nourished and got them through the day, through generations, through centuries.

Although Small retains his love for classical music, he detests the social environment in which it thrives. In *Musicking: the Meaning of Performing and Listening*, Small analyzes the social ethos of Western classical music.[3] Small begins by noting a paradox, that Western classical music is seen as "universal," as the very acme of intellectual and spiritual achievement, yet it appeals only to a tiny minority of initiates. Small examines a typical symphonic performance, starting in the lobby of the concert hall and proceeding to a meta-analysis of the musical experience as channeled through elite institutions. He contrasts the stuffy formality of the concert hall—with its ostentatious grandeur, its domineering architecture, its ideally silent and immobile audience, and its rigid division of labor—with the rhythm-propelled conviviality of African shared performativity.

For Small, the concert hall is authoritarian, masculinist, and hierarchical in its very structure. The musicians obey the commands of a conductor, who himself—and it usually is a "he"—obeys the music of "master works" as written by an anointed genius composer. The audience is expected to repress its corporeal needs, whether to cough or to pee, in the name of the ideally perfect performance. Literate composition and notation demands that singers be imprisoned in the rigid categories of soprano, alto, tenor and bass, when many Afo-diasporic singers rudely fly by the limits of such categories. Written notes are meant to be "pitch-perfect"; to be played, but not to be "played with." The performance takes place in a social vacuum: "the presence of others listeners is a best an irrelevance and at worst an interference in the individual's contemplation …"[4] Like the theorists and practitioners of fidelity discourse in Adaptation Studies, I would add, the conductors believe in "sticking to the script" of the music as written. (Johannes Brahms famously once refused an invitation to attend a performance of Mozart's *Don Giovanni* saying he would prefer to read it at home).

Small sees music not as the written score, regarded as Platonic ideal, but rather as a communal ritual which enacts social relations and communication, existing more in the performance than in the score. Much as Socrates was suspicious of writing in its fixing of meaning, Small is suspicious of written musical notation. Afro-diasporic music, for Small, models a very different kind of social relations; it brings into being, if only during the time of the performance, "a society whose closest political analogy is with anarchism … a society in which government is not imposed from the top or from the center, but comes from the individual, who is most fully realized in contributing to the well-being of community—- the polar opposite, one might think, of the symphony concert."[5]

Although "World Music" has its German counterpart in the expression *Weltmusick*, coined by German music theorist George Capellen at the beginning of the 20th century, the term became truly popular only toward the end of the same century. And although "World Music" inevitably carries a faint echo of Goethe's neologism, the World Music movement is not at all invested in Goethe as a tutelary figure, unless one imagines Peter Gabriel, David Byrne, and Ry Cooder as the

"Goethes" of World Music. Nor is World Music interested in finding classical musical correlatives to Goethe such as Beethoven and Brahms. If World Music were to create a canon, that canon, unlike any literary or cinematic canon, would presumably be less interested in singular masterpieces or named artists-geniuses than in musical movements—"Afro-Pop," "World Fusion," "Worldbeat," "Tropicalia," "Free Jazz." World Music has no equivalent to a pantheon of composers analogous to the World Literature pantheon of writers extending centuries back into the past, partially because World Music is concerned with relatively recent global popular music in the era of, first, mass mechanical reproduction and now of mass digital reproduction.

For various reasons, including World Music's perceived association with corporate interests, "World Music" lacks the auratic pedigree of World Literature and to a lesser extent, that of World Cinema. Although presumably coined by ethnomusicologist Robert E. Brown in the early 1960s with his World Music concert series, a tradition carried on by the World-Music-style *Fetes de la Musique* in France beginning in 1982, the World Music tag was officially adopted by the music industry in the late 1980s as a marketing label to refer to "commercially available music of non-Western origin" circulating in "the West."[6] Formally endorsed at a 1987 summit of record label and industry professionals as a way of selling the products of musical artists from outside the Euro-American sphere, the phrase soon became a standard rubric for music journalists, retail outlets, and Billboard charts.

Record labels releasing World Music, not unlike the latter-day specialty divisions of major studios, or the beverage monopolies like Anhauser-Busch that market pseudo "craft" beers, have typically been specialty divisions tied to conglomerates, cleverly masking the corporate financing to flatter consumers into imagining themselves as choosing an alternative to the mainstream North Atlantic music industry. At the same time, commerciality is not necessarily in itself a stain, since in the modern world, all music, including classical music, is on some level immersed in commercial process in that it almost always depends on economic support to be disseminated and, depending on the music in question, even to be produced. Opera depends on subventions from officialdom and from the moneyed elite; it escapes the taint of the commercial because both the funding and the art are upscale and thus deemed worthy of the label "High Art." Yet black popular music, including in its upper reaches, has often been dismissed as "merely" commercial. The former enjoys the aura of high culture, while the latter has the putative "vulgarity" of top-40 hits and the "underclass."

As an elastic term to account for a protean phenomenon, "World Music" variously annexes and absorbs neighboring styles such as folk music, ethnic music, Worldbeat, ethnic fusion, global fusion, and so forth. World Music also has a distinct relation to the notion of medium specificity in comparison both to World Literature and to World Cinema. As an art form, music has always been harder to stabilize and pin down and "enclose" than a verbal literary text, since the vast majority of musical forms were never transcribed, and even transcribed music really comes into full existence only when performed. Unlike the cinema's (usually) two-dimensional images, the sounds accompanying those images are by definition three-dimensional. Unlike literature, whose "materials of expression," to use formalist-semiotic language, have always been verbal; the materials of expression of music have been constantly expanding from the base of musical notes to noise in *musique concrete* to silence (John Cage) to percussive scratching (hip-hop).

John Durham Peters points out that "sound appears and disappears; its being is in time. No purely sonic entity ever endures."[7] This characteristic of music allows for endlessly fluid combinations with others forms of music. For Kevin Kelly, music was the first art/industry to achieve "liquidity," precisely because "music itself is so flowing—a stream of notes whose beauty lasts only as long as the stream continues."[8] In the digital age, this liquidity allows music to be unpacked, reassembled, and unbundled from commercial formats to be archived, filtered, shortened, lengthened, and generally reconfigured. In the post-Napster age, popular music, as Kelly puts it, was not only set "monetarily free; it was freed from constraints [allowing for] a thousand new ways to conjure with those notes."[9] Music has come to so thoroughly occupy social space that popular music is now omnipresent in our social life, raining down, often unheard as music, "while we exercise, while we are vacationing in Rome, while we wait in line at the DMV."[10] Rarely does the moving image come unaccompanied by music; feature films, documentaries, Podcasts, on-line games, newscasts, commercials, You-Tube mash-ups, political remixes, public service announcements, jingles—all need soundtracks.

Unlike World Literature, but like World Cinema, World Music is also potentially multitrack; it can include language through lyrics, whether in the elite form of German *lieder* or the putatively "low" form of popular music, but it also exceeds language by being imagistic, performative, corporeal, and potentially spectacular. Music can be inferentially verbal, as when a composer like Charles Ives or Aaron Copeland or Heitor Villa-Lobos evokes a folk song or popular tune, or when an instrumental version of a song calls up the lyrics in the listener's mind. The spectacularization of music reaches its apotheosis, meanwhile, in the High Art form of Wagnerian opera conceived as a *Gesamtkunstwerk* (total artistic synthesis). But spectacularization can also take the form of the putatively Low Art form of the "street opera" of Brazilian carnival pageantry propelled by hundreds of samba percussionists.

In fact, the notion of the *Gesamtkunstwerk* can be expanded beyond the Wagnerian conception to apply to religious ceremonies such as a Catholic Mass or to Afrodiasporic spirit ceremonies like those of candomblé, which embraces all the senses and all the arts—narrative, poetry, dance, music, costume, and cuisine—which is why these religions were so attractive to those I call the "trance-Modernists" like Wole Soyinke, Maya Deren, Jean Rouch, and Glauber Rocha. The *Gesamtkunstwerk* lives again in the form of Broadway musicals, Hollywood musicals, Bollywood musicals, and in artistically ambitious music video-films. Janelle Monae's Afro-futurist "cyber soul" songs and videos constitute a pan-artistic extended allegory about black history. Her short "Many Moons," for example, features "Cindi Mayweather" as dancer-entertainer at an Android Auction, in a layered allegory that anachronistically mingles the erudite and the popular, the past of the slave auction and the future of science fiction, the utopian and the apocalyptic, in a spectacular mix of visual arts and musical styles. We find another example in the multi-art productions of the Carters (Beyonce and Jay-Z). The "Apeshit" video which accompanies the "Everything is Love" album has the two stars dance and pose with scores of black dancers interacting with the Louvre's paintings and sculptures like the "Mona Lisa," "The Winged Victory of Samothrace," "Venus de Milo," and "the Raft of the Medusa." The official music video conflates a series of contraries, mingling the lofty and the vulgar, the high and the low, the subversive and the cooptive, Afro-centrism and black capitalism, Europe and Africa, social critique and product placement, pop hegemony and artistic resistance. The Carters present themselves as a gender-equal royal couple in parallel to Napoleon and Josephine, while the video becomes an exercise in black-inflected art history which locates moments of transcendent blackness within the canon of Western art. The ode to black beauty subverts a white institution, while largely overlooking the colonial legacy embodied in such institutions. The couple's nonchalance as they stand in front of the Mona Lisa in their pastel-colored shirts recalls the casual footrace through the Louvre of Godard's characters in *Bande a Part*, while hints at an inversion of the white colonial gaze recalls the more explicitly anti-colonialist Marker/Resnais film *Statues Also Die* (1955), banned for twelve years because of its critique of the theft of African art.

The geopolitical mapping and directionalities of World Music differ significantly from those of World Literature. In a paradoxical spatiality, "World Literature," initially associated with the Western cultural "Center," has come to move out to include the "Periphery," at times even becoming synonymous with the Periphery. "World Music," in contrast, is usually seen as emerging from the Periphery, which is then invited into the Center, which, in a feedback loop, then "sponsors" and disseminates the "peripheral" music, thus making it "central." David Byrne, for example, sponsors and promotes Afro-Latin American artists like the Brazilian Margareth Menezes and the Afro-Peruvian Susana Baca. At times, as occurred with Paul Simon's "Graceland" album in the mid-1980s, artistic collaborations mingle sheer love of musical creativity with unequal power situations, where "peripheral" artists benefit, but in a subordinate manner. Simon was lambasted by pro-ANC activists for collaborating with the *apartheid* regime, but he was also praised by others for popularizing the male choral music called *isicathamiya*. Simon's African collaborators, meanwhile, felt doubly penalized, less by Paul Simon himself than by, first, the apartheid regime, and second, by the ANC supporters who boycotted their music in the name of the struggle against *apartheid*.[11]

As Stephen Feld points out, writing on World Music quickly bifurcated into the celebratory and the defamatory. Indeed, the very category "World Music" is reviled by many musicians and musicologists precisely because of its flattening "tone deaf" approach to touchy issues of local sensitivities to cultural colonialism. Given global power asymmetries, Pop Star musicians on both sides of the postcolonial divide have to defend themselves from asymmetrical accusations.[12] The Western collaborator or sponsor becomes susceptible to accusations of "appropriation" and "exploitation," while the non-Western collaborator is accused by his own people of "cooptation," or "selling out," or "colonialism," or even by Westerners themselves, of "westernization."

Long before the advent of the World Music phenomenon, musical instruments, which one would assume to be born as innocent as babes in swaddling clothing, became the objects of demonization, as when folk music fans, in the name of rural "authenticity," booed Dylan's use of an electric guitar at the Newport Jazz Festival in 1965. Three years later in Brazil, in the name of nationalist purity and opposition to the U.S.-supported dictatorship, some leftist musicians and singers, including Elis Regina and Gilberto Gil, denounced the electric guitar as an imperialist North American import. (The same artists adopted electric guitars themselves just a few years later, deploying them with a very Brazilian dexterity). In any case, the electric guitar has multiple origins, and many Brazilians claim that the Bahians Dodo and Osmar invented the electric guitar in 1951 with their "electric trios," even before Leo Fender and Les Paul in 1953.

In some iterations, World Music is unofficially equated with the music of the so-called "ethnic" peoples of the world, a view that leaves the subtly corrosive normativity of whiteness invisible but intact; put simply, either everyone is ethnic or no one is. For its critics, "World Music" evokes a palatable assemblage of deculturated "ethnic musics," a bland concoction that channels music from the Global South into Northern markets, touching lightly on cultural and ethnic difference while dodging sensitive issues of neo-colonial appropriation. Indeed, some of the composer-musicians reflexively associated with World Music do not endorse the label. Distancing himself from the term, Steven Feld calls the term World Music "a label of industrial origin that refers to an amalgamated global marketplace of sounds as ethnic commodities."[13] In a critical gesture that parallels the strategic move of queer critics who speak of "heteronormativity" or "critical race" theorists who "out" the silent hegemony of whiteness, David Byrne has denounced "World Music" as a catch-all marketing gimmick and pseudo-musical term that gathers into a "bin" a hugely variegated array of non-Western musics.

> What's in that bin ranges from the most blatantly commercial music produced by a country, like Hindi film music (the singer Asha Bhosle being the best well known example), to the ultra-sophisticated, super-cosmopolitan art-pop of Brazil (Caetano Veloso, Tom Ze, Carlinhos Brown); from the somewhat bizarre and surreal concept of a former Bulgarian state-run folkloric choir being arranged by classically trained, Soviet-era composers (Le Mystere des Voix Bulgares) to Norteno songs from Texas and northern Mexico glorifying the exploits of drug dealers (Los Tigres del Norte).[14]

Like the Oscar category of "foreign film," the World Music rubric corrals worldwide artistic creativity—the lion's share of music produced on the planet—into a "not us" hodge-podge of everything that does not fit into the Procrustean bed of the Anglo-Western pop universe. (One could extrapolate what Byrne says of American top-40 pop music—that it constitutes the "fast-food" of culture, to

Hollywood blockbusters; restricting one's diet to either is like "eating hamburgers for the rest of your life.")[15]

World Music is linked metaphorically to World Cinema and World Literature, if only by belonging to the broader paradigm of World Arts, acting, as it were, "in concert" and in a mutually impacting manner. Indeed, the express aim of the Sithengi Film Festival, according to T. Hoefert de Turegano, was to "create a viable niche market for World Cinema in the way that a similar market has been created for World Music."[16] World Music is also at times metonymically linked to World Cinema in that music enters the World of film through cross-art collaborations, for example in the form of the composition of soundtracks for feature fiction films. Indeed, Stevie Wonder, Gilberto Gil, Caetano Veloso, Brian Eno and many other popular musicians have composed film scores for many feature films.

But music enters film in countless other ways, whether in the form of concert films (*Graceland: the African Concert*), or music documentaries (*Pangea: Citizens of the World Music Documentary*), or in the omnipresent music videos. And what are music videos, if not transmedial adaptations of music and lyrics? Many music videos are mini-films with aesthetic ambitions, replete with hommages to well-known films and filmmakers. To take a few examples, the visuals and mise-en-scène of the video of the Smashing Pumpkin's "Tonight, Tonight" are based on Méliès' *Voyage à la Lune* (1902); Madonna's "Material Girl" mimicks Marilyn Monroe's performance of "Diamonds are a Girl's Best Friend" in *Gentlemen Prefer Blondes*; the stylized Black and White monochrome décor of Red Hot Chili Pepper's "Otherside" mimics Robert Weine's *The Cabinet of Dr. Caligari*; and Janelle Monae's music videos evoke the android from Fritz Lang's *Metropolis*.

Many music videos could be considered "second-degree" and "third degree" literary adaptations." A fan-made music video of Bruce Springsteen's "The Ghost of Tom Joad," named after the protagonist of Steinbeck's *Grapes of Wrath*, for example, cites specific shots from the John Ford adaptation, as well as some of the famous depression-era photographs (for example those of Dorothea Lange) that inspired both Steinbeck and John Ford. The music video of Annie Lennox's "Walking on Broken Glass" stages the often-filmed *Dangerous Liaisons* by Choderlos de Laclos. Coldplay's "Don Quixote" verbally and imagisticaly references the story and iconography of the Cervantes novel. Gordon Lightfoot's "Don Quixote," for its part, pays homage to Quixote as the bookish righter of wrongs, a "horseman wild and free/tilting at the windmills passing." Lightfoot's Quixote is "wild but mellow," both strong and weak, wise and meek. With "battered book in hand," he stands like a "prophet bold" and "shouts across the ocean to the shore." Celine Dion's "Lolita," finally, defends January-May romance and Lolita's right to love the kind of older man (not the Humbert variety) that Dion herself subsequently married. Other music videos "adapt" not so much a novel but rather the film adaptation of the novel. The music video of "Kiss Me," by Sixpence None the Richer," consists of an evocative pastiche of key scenes from Truffaut's *Jules et Jim*, based on the novel by Henri-Pierre Roche. Blur's "To the End," finally, offers an impeccably edited and wonderfully absurd pastiche/parody of the equally ironic faux-seriousness of the *L'Annee Derniere a Marienbad* itself, adding the non-sensical touch of having lyrics in English "translated" redundantly into English, but where the two texts do not match.

In the era of transmedial convergence, literature is "in" the cinema just as cinema is "in" literature, just as both literature and cinema are "in" music; they are all mutually invaginated in a transartistic remix. The fact that the maxim "Good artists copy. Great artists steal" has been variously attributed to the poet T.S. Eliot, to the painter Pablo Picasso, to the dramatist Bertolt Brecht, and to the composer Igor Stravinsky, suggests that alchemizing the old to create the new has long been common to all the arts. Cross-art comparisons and analogies proliferate in artistic discourses and commentary, reflected in generic rubrics like the "chamber" film (modelled on "chamber music") or in definitions of "cinema is sculpture in motion," or the play of light (in German *lichtspiel*), or in cross-art characterizations of artists— "Godard is the Picasso of the Cinema," or "Proust is the "Debussy of literature," or when a novel is titled a "portrait" (of a Lady, for example), or as a "scene" (of Provincial Life, for example), or when a written text is said to "aspire to the condition of music," or when the films of Lucretia Martel are described as "Flaubertian," or when James Baldwin says he would like to "write the way Aretha Franklin sings" or Stuart Hall claims that Miles Davis was "playing what [he] was thinking."

The term "remix" itself was first associated with practices in popular music but then extended to other arts and cultural practices. Musical remix emerged in the 1970s from a creative environment that used new recording technologies to sample and reconfigure pre-existing pieces from the musical commons, leading to the explosion of phenomena such as sampling and cut-and-mix, along with the corporate attempt to "enclose" such expression. But "remix" as a concept existed long before the digital; Robert Farris Thompson speaks of the "antiquity of the cool" as a "means of putting innovation and tradition, invention and imitation, into amicable relations with one another."[17]

"The ease-of-use of today's creative technologies and networked organization of today's communications infrastructure," according to Aram Sinnreich, "ensure that the tools of media configurability are accessible to hundreds of millions of interconnected individuals."[18] The corporate music world was ill-equipped, however, to deal with the explosive Web-2 "software-ization" of the arts. The explosion of the sampling and cut 'n' mix aesthetic in Hip-Hop brings up the issue of copyright and the *enclosure* of creativity by corporate power. In an early phase, Hip-Hop authorized free-wheeling raids on the musical commons, bypassing the bourgeois proprieties of copyright. Found bits from other songs, political speeches and advertisements were placed in ironic mutually relativizing relationships. Rap music videos, at least in the 1980s, recycled the voices and images of Black martyrs and ancestors such as Malcolm X and Martin Luther King in a "versioning" or remediation which sets up a direct line to African culture heroes, to the African-American intertext, and, as "Black Folks' CNN" (Chuck D's term), to the Afro-diaporic communities. In the film *Corporate Criminals*, Chuck D, who describes Public Enemy's music as an "assemblage of sounds," asks a basic question about the legitimacy of corporate enclosure: can anyone "own a beat?" It is perhaps not a coincidence that those who have ancestors whose very lives and bodies were stolen and turned into property should display a certain skepticism about private property and the morality of stealing). How, one wonders, did a situation arise where the infinitely rich tradition of African and Afro-diasporic percussive polyrhythms could come to be "owned" by a corporation, as if one could parcel off or "enclose" a few drops in the ever-churning sea of circum-Atlantic musicality? Unfortunately, the corporate policing of sampling did manage to partially dam the flood of Hip-Hop creativity, as corporate predators saw the possibility of new revenue-streams derived from musical property rights.

Today "configurability" (Sinnreich) allows anyone with an I-Pod, TiVo, and I-Movie to create what Bill Ivey and Stephen Tepper call the "curatorial me" to select snippets of musical information for creative purposes.[19] The digital revolution has enabled all sorts of musical remixes. In 2006, the Canadian Broadcast Corporation's Radio 2 Channel, which primarily offers erudite music, initiated a competitive "Compose Yourself" series, where listeners were invited to download "the Ride of the Valkyries" from Wagners's "Ring Cycle" and remix it as they saw fit. We find a different incarnation of this irreverent spirit, this time in the realm of popular music, in TradeMarkG and his "Wheel of Mash," modelled on "Wheel of Fortune," where two wheels, one featuring, for example, Public Enemy spontaneously gets remashed with the music of Herb Alpert). But these techniques were anticipated in the analog period by the ersatz opuses of "PDQ Bach," the putative "lost son" of the Bach family and the fictitious composer created by musical parodist Peter Schickele, with his hilarious remixes of hitherto unknown instruments (such as the "pastaphone" made of uncooked manicotti), incompatible musical styles (baroque with Broadway musicals), and startling juxtapositions and remixes of Brahms Second Symphony with "Beautiful Dreamer."

16

TRANSMEDIAL MUSIC IN LATIN AMERICA

In his 1974 novel *Concierto Barroco*, Franco-Cuban writer Alejo Carpentier gave us a foretaste of the convergences of musical worlds by deploying the prose resources of the novel to evoke a miscegenated utopia of classical and popular musics. He first conceived the novel in 1936, when he learned that the Italian composer Vivaldi had written an opera (*Montezuma*) on the conquest of the Americas Carpentier sees "America" itself as a baroque concert counterpointing European, African and indigenous elements, a cut-'n'-mix of highly elaborated melodies and complex African polyrhythms, set in a landscape whose lush vegetation hides the gold and silver which financed European capitalism and *crioullo* luxury. As intimated by its title, the novela's structure is modeled on a baroque concert. Not only are many of the characters musicians, but also the book's very structure is musical. Within an aesthetic of anachronism, Carpentier has the novel's musical jouissance achieve climax in a jazzistic romp at the Venetian festival where Carpentier has musicians from different historical epochs meet in a Menippean dialogue between the dead and the living. A conga-line procession then snakes through the concert hall propelled by a percussive Afro-Cuban chant, generating a Eurocentric complaint from Scarlatti about "cannibal music!" The proleptic anachronism of Carpentier's fantastic Venetian symphony points toward the later-to-be realized Africanization of World Music, whereby Afro-diasporic musical forms like jazz, salsa, samba, reggae and hip-hop, have come to dominate popular culture, providing anticipatory forms of what Paul Gilroy calls planetary conviviality."[1]

World Music, unlike World Literature, has little interest in the "classical" forms of the art. The very term World Music itself connotes contemporary popular music as opposed to classical music. Yet popular music, especially in the Americas, comes with its own kind of erudition. If one includes musician-composers like Duke Ellington, George Gershwin, Heitor Villa-Lobos, and Antonio Carlos Jobim as part of a broader spectrum of music which absorbs the popular and has popular appeal, we see that in the Americas, the line between the popular and the erudite is more blurry than it is in continental Europe. Jazz is sometimes called "American classical music" for example, and many jazz and popular musicians—Thelonius Monk, the Modern Jazz Quartet, Miles Davis, and even more pop musicians like Billy Joel and Ray Charles, were partially formed by their classical music training. Peter Gabriel, Brian Eno, Paul Simon, Joni Mitchel, the Beatles, Ruben Blades, Chico Buarque de Holanda, and hundreds of others, all have exhibited own forms of erudition and experimentation.

In some "entrancing" works of art, all of the categories– World Literature, World Cinema, World Music, Transnational Cinema, Global Media—merge together under the swirling baton of a musical "dominant." Brazilian music, for example, has managed to produce a commercially successful aesthetic synthesis at once national and transnational, popular and experimental, accessible and complex. As the royal road to the depths of Brazil's cultural Unconscious, music is the least colonized branch of Brazilian popular culture, both more Africanized and more confidently cosmopolitan than its cinematic counterpart. Perhaps as a consequence, it is also the most successful in disseminating itself around the world. Unlike Brazilian Cinema, Brazilian music consistently outsells non-Brazilian music. Brazil's "export quality" (Oswald de Andrade) music –and here the export is of a "cooked" and not a "raw" product—in some ways reverses the usual Westocentric currents through musical "counter-flows."

Brazilian music, perhaps more than Brazilian Cinema, has managed to produce an aesthetic synthesis at once national and transnational, popular and experimental. At the same time, it has been more commercially successful. Brazil's "export quality" music reverses the usual currents; it influences World Music, where it is constantly borrowed and plagiarized.[2] In musical terms, Brazilian and American artists meet as absolute equals; when Jobim collaborates with Sinatra, or Milton Nascimento with Wayne Shorter, or David Byrne with Caetano, there is no question of artistic subordination. Obviously the relative success of Brazilian music vis-à-vis Brazilian Cinema and Brazilian literature has to do with many factors: that music does not depend on a vast infrastructure, that popular musical production is less expensive than cinematic production, and more attractive to a mass audience than literature; and that music is inserted in a distinct manner into the global economy. As we have seen with literature, Music has no equivalent to Hollywood. In fact, the music corporations in general have been relativized in the wake of Napster, Spotify, Pandora and the like. Nevertheless, some dimensions of this differential success transcend political economy. Brazilian music is not haunted and dominated by the overpowering aura of a hegemonic aesthetic; in World Music, the dominant aesthetic *is* Afro-syncretic. Indeed, Brazilian music was born syncretic, mingling syncretisms from its various source cultures. A scene in *Joaquim* (2017), a Brazilian film about 18th-century national revolutionary hero Tiradentes, captures the long-term roots of this syncretism by showing an indigenous man, together with a newly arrived African, without a common language but armed with talent and artistic *disponibilite*, making music together by synchronizing and syncretizing their styles to achieve harmonious and percussive mutuality.

A striking feature of Brazilian popular music is its outlandish poetic and literary ambition. And here we must question the hierarchy that sets the written literary word over and above the equally literary sung word (as well as melody and harmony over percussion). After all, music and literature have been linked since time immemorial. The formulaic phrases of the *Odyssey* were originally meant to be sung by bards accompanied by a lyre. The origins of tragedy go back to Dionysian rites where masses of people sung and danced themselves into ecstatic frenzy. The Greek chorus was not called a chorus for nothing. Aristophanes wrote monodies, meant to be sung, into his plays. Although music is often seen as detracting from the prestige of poetry, it might also be seen as adding charm and intensity. Could it be that a kind of Platonic fear or emotion, or a valorization of the virtuality of words versus the corporeality of the voice, plays a role in the devaluation of music by literary intellectuals?

As a multiart movement, the Tropicalia movement led by Caetano and Gil that emerged in the late 1960s, dynamized and reorganized the cultural field, to the point of becoming virtually hegemonic within present-day Braziliam popular culture,. "Pop star intellectuals" such as Gilberto Gil, Caetano Veloso, Chico Buarque, and Zé Miguel Wisnik, to name a few, write books and compose music that comments on the burning issues of the time, often actively intervening in the debates about race and national identity. Gil and Caetano are what in the Anglo-American world would be called "public intellectuals," major commentator-theoreticians on social justice and the arts, known as incisive critics of racism and as musical celebrants of Brazilian conviviality. They embody and perform their theories in very diverse genres and media, ranging from music, books, films, and interviews to happenings and even via public policies, as when Gil became Minister of Culture in the Lula government and embraced the "Creative Commons" movement, including by releasing three of his songs, all with titles beginning with the recombinant prefix "Re" ("Refavela") to evoke repetition with a difference in the spirit of "remix culture" (Lessig).

Both Caetano and Gil constitute Orphic intellectuals. (It is no accident that Vinicius de Moraes wrote "Orfeu de Conceicao," or that Caetano composed the music track for Carlos Diegues' film *Orfeu*, which turned Orpheus into a pop star devoured by his fans.) Riffing on Gramsci's "organic intellectual," Caetano and Gil might be called "Orphoganic" intellectuals; they write books in one moment, lead dancing Dionysian crowds in another, and in Gil's case, serve as Minister of Culture. They both perform and dance and sing popular culture and theorize it. In a multimedia intervention, they enact the cultural debates in visual, sensuous, written, lyrical, percussive, and even institutional-political form. Their music demonstrates art's capacity to give pleasurable form to social desire, to open up new grooves, to mobilize a sense of possibility, to shake the body politic through what Caetano calls the "world's sweetest protest music."[3]

No one has written more brilliantly about the multi-faceted creativity of Brazilian popular music than literary scholar and composer/singer/lyricist Jose Miguel Wisnik. He is the author of an ambitious, non- Eurocentric, theory/history of music entitled *Sound and Sense: A Different History of Music* (1989). Accompanied by cassettes featuring a syncretic mélange of styles of music, the book starts not with the Greeks—the usual habit in such texts—but rather from the body and the pulse. Wisnik announces from the outset:

> This is a book for musicians and non-musicians. It speaks of the human use of sound and the history of this usage. But it is not a "history of music" in the conventional sense: i.e. history of styles and authors, their biographies, idiosyncracies and compositional peculiarities. Nor is it a history of tonal European music seen as the universal music. It is, rather, a book about voices, silences, noises, chords, and fugues in different times and societies.[4]

In his essay "The Happy Science: Literature and Popular Music in Brasil," Wisnik cites contemporary Brazilian popular music as an example of Nietzsche's "*Frohliche Wissenschaft*" (joyful knowledge), or *Le Gai Savoir* as per Godard's film title. (Bakhtin, similarly, spoke of the intellectual-performative openness of carnival's "gay relativity"). Of course, the mix of the popular and erudite existed already in embryo already in the multicultural mix that Brazilian music had always been since the beginnings of colonial conquest. But this mélange of popularity and erudition really took flight when a sophisticated poet and dramatist, Vinicius de Moraes—author of many volumes of poems as well as of the play *Orfeu de Conceicao* (source play for the film *Black* Orpheus)—joined up with the similarly sophisticated Bossa Nova musicians. These musicans integrated very diverse forms of music—the complex polyrythyms of samba, the complex harmonics of French impressionist composers like Revel and Debussy, the jagged inventions of French Modernists like Milhaud and Satie, the cross-over style music of Gershwin and Duke Ellington in the U.S. and Villa-Lobos in Brazil, the lyrical subtlety of the *chanson francaise*, and the modernist chord changes of American "cool jazz."

The result within MPB (Popular Brazilian Music) was a perhaps unprecedented synthesis of "high" and "low" culture. Wisnik notes the "permeability established, beginning with Bossa Nova, between so-called high culture and popular cultural production, forming a field of encounters that cannot be understood within the binary between music of entertainment and creative and informative music."[5] Brazilian post-Bossa Nova music, for Wisnik, combines African, indigenous, and Portuguese roots with jazz, classical music, rock, international pop, and avant-garde experimental music. The music has what I would call a "transartistic" dimension" in its devouring of the other arts, or what Wisnik calls "an intense dialogue with literary, painterly, cinematic and theatrical culture."[6]

Singer/composer/dramatist/novelist Chico Buarque de Holanda, grandson of the creator of the standard dictionary of Brazilian Portuguese (Aurelio Buarque de Holanda) and son of a famous cultural historian and theorist of Brazilian national identity (Sergio Buarque de Holanda) meanwhile, is also a transartistic talent who combines the "high" and the "low," and who should rightly be seen as a major figure in the various artistic "worlds" of World Literature, World Theater, and

World Music. "Chico" has written Brechtian-style musical plays; his *Opera do Malandro* (Hustlers' Opera, staged as a play but also filmed by Rui Guerra) was based on the same John Gay play ("Beggars' Opera") that also inspired Brecht's *Dreigroschenoper*. He has also written widely praised modernist novels such as *Estorvo, Benjamin*, and *Budapest* which have been praised by critics like Roberto Schwarz and translated into many languages.

Chico is best known, however, for writing extremely sophisticated song-poems of the highest poetic level, whence the common claim that poetry in Brazil often takes the form of popular song. Some of Chico's song-poems clearly draw on the taproot of World Literature, discernible, for example, in the myriad references to classical Greek literature and mythology, and specifically to the *Iliad* and *The Odyssey*, in his song-poem "Women of Athens." Indeed, the poem's frequent use of words ending in *"as"* and *"os"* recalls the typical plurals of the Greek language itself. The song was written in 1976, at the torturous nadir of the sexist and brutal Brazilian dictatorship, as part of a play penned by playwright/ dramaturg. and radical performance theorist Augusto Boal, author of the widely translated *Theater of the Oppressed*, The play forms an allegorical indictment of a multi-leveled system of social domination, where the past of classical Greece resonates with the present of contemporaneous Brazil. In Brechtian style, the lyrics call on us to "Contemplate the example / Of the women of Athens" who "live for their husbands / The pride and joy of the Athenian race." When they are loved, the women of Athens "bathe themselves in milk" and "arrange their long locks." When "hounded" by their husbands, they "kneel, they beg, they implore" and "suffer for their husbands," who "represent the power and might of Athens." When the warriors returned from war get drunk, "they seek tenderness elsewhere … but always return/to the arms of their Helens." The song concludes:

> Young marked widows
> Pregnant and abandoned
> They never make a scene
> They dress in black,
> They retire and conform
> And they shrink and dry up
> All for their husbands,
> Pride and Joy of the Race of Athens

Although sometimes wrongly taken as an ode to female subordination, the song and the play—as suggested by the play's title—*Lisa, the Liberating Woman*—and by the lyrics of the song—clearly point to the opposite, a denunciation of male domination and internalized female oppression.

Gilberto Gil, similarly, matches his polymorphic musical styles to "world songs" with global references. Already in the 1980s, Gil was commenting musically on the favored postcolonial theme of cultural hybridity. His song "From Bob Dylan to Bob Marley: Samba Provocation" poetically addresses the transoceanic traffic of ideas back and forth across the Black Atlantic, in this case between Brazil, Jamaica,

North America, and Africa. The song's subtitle designates it as a "provocation samba," a play on the Vargas-era "exaltation sambas" that lauded Brazilian heroes during the carnival pageants. The "provocation" here is to exalt not the nation-state but rather Afro-diasporic hybridity. In the song, Gil explores the "roots" and "routes" of Afro-diasporic culture, ranging easily, in a musical correlative to magic realism in literature, over five centuries and across diverse continents, orchestrating a counterpoint between the early 16th century of Portuguese colonialism in Brazil and the late 20th century era of Bob Dylan, Bob Marley, and Michael Jackson:

> Soon after Bob Dylan converted to Christianity
> He made a reggae album as a form of compensation
> He abandoned the Jewish people
> But returned to them while heading in the wrong direction ...

The allusion to a putative Dylan reggae album through which he returned to the Jewish people clearly references Rastafarianism as an Afro-diasporic religion imbued with Jewish symbologies (the "Lion of Judah," "Babylon," and so forth); Dylan, leaving Judaism, returns to it through the sacred music of Jamaica. The song continues:

> When the peoples of Africa arrived in Brazil
> There was no freedom of religion ...
> As a result, Africans in Brazil adopted Our Lord of Bomfim
> An act both of resistance and surrender

Significantly, Gil's lyrics speak not of "blacks" but of the "peoples of Africa," since the reifying totalization of "blacks" was itself the product of colonialism and slavery. The values of religious freedom and tolerance, Gil reminds us, did not extend to African or indigenous peoples in the Americas, who were obliged to abandon the indigenous god Tupa and the African Olorum and the other gods. Given this lack of freedom of religion, "Africans in Brazil adopted Our Lord of Bomfim, an act both of resistance and surrender."

The refrain goes as follows:

> Bob Marley died
> Because besides being black
> He was Jewish
> Michael Jackson, meanwhile
> Is still around
> But besides becoming white
> He's become very sad

The final refrain indexes two forms of syncretism, one in the activist form of the music of Bob Marley and the other—and here the song, written in the 1980s, was very prescient—in the more melancholy form of Michael Jackson. In sum, the song allegorically stages the relationalities of vast cultural complexes, counterpointing one set of times and spaces through another set of times and spaces, in a suggestive contrapuntal haunting across national and temporal boundaries.

Gil's song is not atypical of the Tropicalia Movement, founded by Caetano and Gil along with Tom Ze, Rogerio Duprat and others, a movement that was transnational, transartistic, and transmediatic from the outset. Its acknowledged inspiration came from the multiart modernist movement of the 1920s with its anti-colonial tropes—rooted in their interpretation of indigenous culture—of "anthropophagy" and the "Carib Revolution." Just as the Modernists devoured surrealism and Dada, Caetano was fond of saying, "we devour Jimi Hendrix and the Beatles." It was as if the Beatles had declared themselves the heirs of the Surrealists. Just as the Modernists believed in devouring the avant-garde culture of Europe, the Tropicalistas, devoured both the dynamic but marginalized popular cultures of Brazil and what they found most exciting and fecund in transnational pop culture.

Veloso's extensive oeuvre offers another example of a transartistic popular singer intimately entangled with the various arts. One cannot analyze Caetano's work in depth without considering his intermedial engagement not only with music—his most obvious sphere of creative activity—but also with the other arts and media as well. That the category of World Music is relevant to Caetano is obvious, since he has won many World Music awards, even though he himself, like his friend and musical collaborator David Byrne, expressed skepticism about the very category of World Music. But beyond that, Veloso's work is also profoundly transartistic, beginning with a longstanding involvement with literature. For purposes of brevity, I will list only a few of the many examples of Caetano's "literariness": 1) scores for many films and miniseries based on novels such as the TV series *Milagres do Povo* and the film *Tieta do Agreste*, both based on novels by Jorge Amado; 2) soundtracks for films (e.g. *Orfeu*) based on plays; 3) music written for the Brazilian theatrical version of Jean Genet's play *Haute Surveillance*; 4) artistic collaboration with some of Brazil's most famous literary theorist-critics, such as Augusto de Campos and Haroldo de Campos; 5) and the "musicalization" of celebrated poems such as Castro Alves' abolitionist classic *Navio Negreiro* ("The Slave Ship") and Fernando Pessoa's "Navegar e Preciso." (Caetano sings and speaks in fluent English, Spanish, and French).

Transnationality and transartistry also characterize Caetano's literary writing. A talented prose stylist, his sinuous long-winding sentences are at times reminscent of his beloved Marcel Proust. The title of his lengthy memoir *Vereda Tropical* was a playful variation on the title of Joao Guimaraes Rosa's monumental (Joycean) novel *Grande Sertao: Veredas*, which sets the Faust story in the Brazilian backlands, much as Joyce set the Odysseus story in Dublin. The memoir constitutes a major statement on various themes: the Tropicalia movement, the relationship between politics and aesthetics, the impact of dictatorship on culture, and Brazilian national identity. In this sense, the book has been compared in Brazil to such landmark texts as Freyre's *Masters and Slaves* and Sergio Buarque de Holanda's *Roots of Brazil*. Journalistic reviewers of the English translation of Caetano's memoir *Tropical Truth* were startled to encounter a pop star who could write knowingly about European, American, and Brazilian culture, in a text where names like Ray Charles and James Brown brush up easily against names like Stockhausen, Wittgenstein, Heidegger, and Deleuze.[7]

A transartistic approach also enables us to address Caetano's deep involvement in cinema. As Caetano himself pointed out, the Tropicalia movement itself was inspired by a film by Glauber Rocha: "that whole Tropicalia thing was formulated inside me on the day that I saw *Terra em Transe*."[8] According to Caetano, "my heart exploded during the opening sequence, when, to the sound of a candomblé chant, an aerial shot of the sea brings us to the coast of Brazil." Without that "traumatic moment," Caetano writes, "nothing of what came to be called tropicalism would have ever existed."[46] Like Glauber, Caetano used multicultural dissonance as a creative resource. Among the many other pieces of evidence of Caetano's deep immersion in the filmic universe, I will offer just a few examples from his artistic and intellectual production: 1) the precocious publication of cineliterate essays on the films of the various "new waves"; 2) acting roles in a number of films, for example the role of samba musician Lamartine Babo in Julie Bressane's *Tabu*; 3) singing performances in feature films ("Cucurrucucu La Paloma" in Almadovar's *Habla com Ella* and "Burn it Blue" for Julie Taynor's *Frida*; 4) the composition of musical hommages to Federico Fellini and Giuletta Masina in the CD *Omaggio a Federico e Giuletta*; 5) musical scores for films, many of them adaptations, such as *Sao Bernardo*, based on the Graciliano Ramos novel.

Caetano has also directed a feature film bearing the reflexive title of *Cinema Falado* (Sound Cinema, or Spoken Cinema, 1986). The film is transtextual and transartistic in the sense that it is structured around the counterpoint of a novel—Cabrera Infante's "polyphonic novel *Tres Tristes Tigres*—and a reflexive popular Noel Rosa song—"There is no Translation"—about cinema and the impact of Hollywood films in disseminating the English language. At the beginning of the film, Caetano informs us that he was inspired by Godard's idea that "films should consist of people telling stories in front of a camera." The film also incarnates Walter Benjamin's idea of a literary text consisting only of quotations. In his synopsis of the film, Caetano describes his collage technique: "Here the experimental mixes with the documental. Spoken texts; prose and poetry, philosophy, written by the filmmaker himself or by his favorite writers. People he likes, actors with whom he has lived. Exercises in sound and photography, some dance and theatre."[9] Caetano is that rare popular singer whose lyrics often reveal what he has been reading. (It is not an accident that one of his CDs was entitled "Livros"). The lyrics of Caetano's stylized rap song "Lingua," (Language) allude to the Heideggerian view of German as the only truly philosophical language: "It is said that one can only philosophize in German/ but I say, if you have a fantastic idea/ It's better to put it in a song." In the film, Caetano literalizes this Heideggerian valorization of the philosophical advantages of German by having a German studies scholar/translator literally "philosophize in German."

In a rare instance of a pop-star homage to a film movement, Caetano, together with Gilberto Gil, wrote a song-essay-poem dedicated to the history and aesthetics of Brazilian Cinema. The song, called simply "Cinema Novo," riffs on the titles of Cinema Novo films, combined with pithy observations about their narrative, aesthetic, and political strategies. In a sense, the song prolongs Caetano's early film critical work, this time in a song-essay which evokes the key films, historical phases, and aesthetics of Cinema Novo. Brecht's "theatre of interruptions," for example, is referenced in the following lyric: "the music interrupted the story / but the music was so beautiful / that noone minded." Or the lyrics pay homage to the sister arts: "The film wanted to say: 'I am Samba'" alludes to Nelson Pereira's *Rio 40 Graus*, and its use of the orchestrated version of Ze Keti's "I am Samba." The phrase "ripped open the cinema screen" alludes to *Black Orpheus*'s opening image of a Greek frieze of Orpheus and Eurydice, optically shredded by an explosion of a samba batucada). A reference to a "land in trance" nods to Rocha's *Land in Trance*). But here the trance takes place in a geographically impossible "backlands of Ipanema," combining through "creative geography" the *sertao* settings of the early Cinema Novo films with the Ipanema of Hirszman's *The Girl from Ipanema*, a film which features a beach celebration of *Candomble*). The lyric "The Samba wanted to say "I am cinema" and "I want to be film, a film-film" pay homage to the strong self-reflexive strain within Cinema Novo, and to the poetic "marginal cinema" where the "film said: 'I want to be poetry." A single verse offers a litany of names—"My name is Orson Antonio Vieira Conselheiro de *Pixote*—which reference Orson Welles, Antonio Conselheiro (the millennial cult leader from Euclides da Cunha's novel *Rebellion in the Backlands*) Vieira (the name both of Padre Vieira, a famous 16th century priest, and of the populist leader in *Terra em Transe*) and finally to the title character of Babenco's *Pixote*. Many of the lyrics refer to filmic adaptations of literature: Graciliano Ramos' novel *Vidas Secas*, Carlos Drummond de Andrade's poem *O Padre e a Moca*, Clarice Lispector's *Hora de Estrela*. In a musical demonstration of transmediality, Caetano deploys the various arts to illuminate and comment on one another. On still another level, Caetano's work, and Tropicalia in general, anticipated 21st-century remix culture (Lessig) in its mashups of musical styles such as *caipira* (hillbilly) and Bossa Nova—i.e. styles that should not work together but somehow do—and its remixing of languages and cultures, of the sacred and the profane, the erudite and the popular, and the archaic and the (post) modernist.

We find another example of transartistic convergence within the Worlds of World Music, World Cinema, and World Literature, in the transmediatic work of Puerto Riqueno artist Rene Perez Joglar, also known as El Residente, founder of the group "Calle 13" Depending on the grid one adopts, Joglar's work qualifies for virtually all of the World Art categories invoked in this book. In his artistically miscegenated oeuvre, the arts and media shamelessly flirt and mix and mate with other arts and media to the point of making him difficult to categorize. The most obvious category—"World Music"—is hardly adequate to his remarkably hybrid creations, which mingle cinema, literature, and music, all the while advancing radical political ideas. At the same time, his work qualifies as World Cinema in the sense not only that he is a trained filmmaker who directs his own films and music videos, which betray the influence not only of the gritty heritage of Third Cinema and *cine-imperfecto* but also the stylistic traces of consecrated World Cinema auteurs like Pedro Almadovar, Joaquim Pedro de Andrade, Glauber Rocha, and Alejandro Jodorovsky.

Multiply transnational, Joglar is a man of transartistic formation (music, cinema, plastic arts), the product of a transnational education (Puerto Rico, the U.S., and Spain), and a participant in transnational musical collaborations, for example with Tom Morello and Zack de la Rocha from "Rage against the Machine," Chad Smith from "Red Hot Chili Peppers," with the Canadian Nelly Furtado, the Israeli-Palestinian Kamilya Jubran, the Argentinian Gustavo Cerati, the Nigerian Seun Kuti, and a long list of others. The Calle 13 music video "Latin America," for example, articulates radical anti-corporate globalization themes in an extremely accessible form which mingles vibrant pan-Latin American music with a rapid-fire montage of Latin American singers, faces, and landscapes as part of an alter-globalizing protest against the privatization of everything, combined with an assertion of a pan-Latin American identity reminiscent of Jose Marti's *nuestra America*. As a striking example of pan-Latin Americanism, transnational at once in theme, locale, and performing personelle, the video mingles images of Quechua in the Andes neighboring with representatives of other regions such as the Caribbean, along with cultural icons like the Argentinians Che Guevara and Maradona, the Peruvian Suzana Baca and the Brazilian Maria Rita, alongside the victims of dictatorship, such as the *madres* of the *desaparecidos* from Argentina. The lyrics inventory the inalienable rights of nature and the "natural commons," including the wind, the sun, the rain, the heat, the clouds, the colors, happiness and pain, everything that is not for sale ("no se vende"), everything that should not be prey to the extractive predations of transnational corporations.

Most recently Joglar has explored transnational musical genetics by making music based on his own genome. Since his DNA, like that of many people in the Americas, and especially in Afro-indigeno-Latin America, traces back to Africa, Europe, Asia, the Middle East, and indigenous America, back in short to a proto-transnational genome that preceded even the formation of nation-states, Joglar decided to collaborate with musicians with whom he shares DNA. This global gallery includes much of the world, ranging from the Tuareg guitarist Bombino in Burkina Faso, Chinese opera musicians in Beijing, Goran Bregovich's brass band in Serbia, a Chechen Choir, the actress/chanteuse Soko in France, and Dagomba trbial singers in Ghana. DNA. His tastes are globally omnivorous: hip-hop, salsa, native American chants, Irish Jigs, klezmer. The images he gathers for his website and music videos are often not from the picturesque tourist sites but rather from the dark places of the world, places of poverty and devastation.

The first music video from the Multi-Viral album is "Somos Anormales," which features a carnivalesque celebration of the grotesque and deformed as part of a cornucopia of imagistic variations on birth and human life. The opening sequence features the birth of an outsized child from giant simulated vagina of a black mother. The shot reminds us in its audacity of the opening shot of the film

Macunaíma where a 50-year old white man in drag gives birth to an equally improbable 50-year old black baby. We are reminded of Bakhtin's "pregnant hag" bringing new life, seen as the paradigmatic image of carnivalesque corporeality. A five-minute summing-up of human history and genetic heterogeneity, the videoclip immerses us in redeeming filth, sublime mud, and amniotic fluid, as we move from birth in Africa through to tribal warfare, to scenes of a profoundly miscegenated *l'amour fou* and an orgiastic *menage à mille*.

The video of *Somos Anormales* was filmed in the South of Siberia and features members of the group Chirgilchin, well-known for its Central Asian harmonies. The video itself recalls the fantastic imagery of magic realist novels. Joglar's work is transnational in its themes, and *transmediatic* in its venues as well as in its production. The artistic manifesto on his website calls for an art that perpetually renews itself, where concepts (à la Deleuze) generate the music, where artists document their creative process, and where aesthetics and social militancy go hand in hand. Joglar's videos also show that going transnational does not mean abandoning the national; some of his earliest work supports the Independence of Puerto Rico, and his "LatinoAmerica" can be seen as a transnational coalitionary pan-defense of Latin America generally. At the same time, his music, lyrics, and activism practice transnational solidarity by supporting undocumented workers ("Somos Todos Ilegales"), Palestine ("Multi-Viral"), oppositional movements ("Occupy," "Yo Soy 132") and human rights organizations (Amnesty International). In Joglar's work, in a *ménage à mille*, the Genetic Commons meets the Musical Commons meets the Transnational Commons.

17

THE TRANSNATIONAL TURN

We can begin our discussion of the "transnational" by distinguishing between the 1) transnational *phenomenon*, on the one hand, and its 2) *theorization* on the other, that is between the transnational *fact*, and the transnational *project*. The transnational fact is hardly a historical novelty. In historical terms, virtually all nations are, in the end, transnations, indelibly marked by the presence and pressures of other nations, both neighboring and distant. The cultural borders between national zones have always been porous, confounding "inside" and "outside." Phenomena imagined to be unique to one nation are in fact often shared with close and distant neighbors. The idealized imagined community of Benedict Anderson, the "we" of the nation, to make a broader point, almost always exists in relation to other countries and other cultural regions, in relation to which they have defined their own slowly morphing identities. The first nation imagines itself in relation to another nation or nations, and the same imaginary operates on the other side; it is as if they were looking at each other in an infinite regress of two or more distorting mirrors. To the imaginary "we" corresponds an imaginary "them," In situations of conquest, colonialism, or occupation, the morphing becomes violently accelerated within fast-changing structures of power, generating such phenomena as forced assimilation, cooptation, sly subversion and resistance. Although the very idea of the nation is premised on demarcating a populace and a territory vis-à-vis other communities and territories, nations exist "in relation;" like individuals, they affirm their identity diacritically, through a mirror-like play of national self and foreign other. They attain self-identity and self-awareness through a comparative process, with and against and through their neighbors, their enemies, and their victims.[1] The Mexican aphorism "So far from God and so close to the United States" encapsulates the kind of wary ambivalence involved in such "neighborly" relationships).

The concept of the "transnational" seems to have initially emerged in the 1970s from the fields of business and corporate culture, and only later became part of critical cultural analysis. In the corporate world, "transnational" belongs to a paradigm that has to do with the scope and degree of interaction with a corporation's operations outside of their "home" country. Its initial reference was to national corporations whose affiliated operations were increasingly dispersed across diverse countries. Within these operations, "international" corporations are importers and exporters who do not emphasize investments outside of their home country. "Multinational corporations" have investment in other countries, but do not have coordinated product offerings in each country. Rather, they are more focused on adapting their products and service to individual local markets. "Global corporations," meanwhile, have invested in and are present in many countries. They market their products through the use of the same coordinated image/brand in all markets, although one corporate office is responsible for global strategy. "Transnational corporations," finally are more complex and centrifugal; they invest in foreign operations, have a central corporate facility, but give decision-making, Research & Development, and marketing powers to each individual foreign market.

In a broader sense, the "transnational turn" is regarded by many analysts as a response to the intensification and acceleration of longstanding processes of globalization and the need to go beyond binary oppositions between the national and the foreign, the local and the global. Aihwa Ong defines transnationality as a "condition of cultural connectedness and mobility across space" which has "intensified under late capitalism".[2] In this sense, the new stress is on the complex flows of populations, capital, technologies, cultures and media products across borders, while underscoring the "multispatial, multilayered, hybrid identities and cultures that coexist at cross-border, regional, and global levels."[3] For Garcia-Canclini, globalization "reorders differences and inequalities without eliminating them."[4] In the realm of cultural theory, Arjun Appadurai spoke in *Modernity at Large* (published 1996) of the processes of "deterritorialization" that were unmooring local populations, as they were buffeted about by the contradictory forces of globalization, engendering both fragmentation and recomposition.

Mel van Elteren concisely sums up the Janus-faced "dialectical interplays of globalization" as generating antinomies and interplays between apparently contradictory transnational trends: 1) *universalization vs. particularization*, whereby globalization universalizes some phenomena, e.g. production, management, and marketing, while particularizing others to articulate local uniqueness; 2) *homogenization vs. differentiation*, whereby globalization combines a pastoral-folkloric nostalgia for the rural and the local with the production of a superficial sameness of urban institutional appearances—anticipated by Jacques Tati's film *Playtime* where tourism posters feature identical airports, hospitals, high rise residences, and cookie-cutter office buildings; 3) *integration vs. fragmentation*, whereby ever-widening spheres of unification (e.g. the European Union, NAFTA) coexist with increasing fragmentation and racial division; and 4) *centralization vs. decentralization*, whereby centripetal concentrations of power and capital and corporate mergers coexist with centrifugal decentralizing counter-forces.[5]

In order to unpack the contradictions embedded in the "transnational," we have to first unpack the contradictions already embedded in the "national" itself.

Nations, like states, Ernest Gellner has argued, "are a contingency, and not a universal necessity."[6] Long before the nation-state form, there were nations, along with complex debates about their character. For Anthony Smith, a nation or ethnic group is distinguished by four features: 1) a sense of unique group origins; 2) a sense of group history and destiny; 3) a sense of distinct cultural traits; and 4) a sense of unique solidarity.[7] Such impressions of cultural uniqueness, solidarity, and special destiny are partially constructed of course. Although nations like to cultivate a sense of antiquity and of continuity, a felt relation between the contemporary and the ancient, most nations are partially fictional constructions based on invented pasts. Twentieth-century and 21st-century historical processes, meanwhile, led to the phenomenon of "new nations" and a desire for autonomy in the wake of two post-War World II phenomena: 1) decolonization in what used to be called the "Third World," on the one hand, and 2) the dissolution of what used to be called the Second World—the Socialist Bloc—and the end of the Soviet Union on the other.

The transnational turn also took the form of the transnational feminist studies represented by scholars such as Caren Kaplan, Inderpal Grewal, Chandra Mohanty, Minoo Moallem, Ella Shohat, Radha Hegde, Jacqui Alexander among others. The theory termed "transnational feminism" was first developed by Inderpal Grewal and Caren Kaplan in 1994 in their seminal text *Scattered Hegemonies: Postmodernity and Transnational Feminist Practices*, and further elaborated three years later in M. Jacqui Alexander and Chandra Mohanty's *Feminist Genealogies, Colonial Legacies, Democratic Futures* in 1997. In *Scattered Hegemonies* Kaplan and Grewal define transnational feminism as "critical practices linking our understanding of postmodernity, global economic structures, problematics of nationalism, issues of race and imperialism, critiques of global feminism, and emergent patriarchies."[8] They also speak of "transnational feminist alliances," and "affiliative groups" and transnational linkages.[9]

Transnational Feminism offers a powerful grid for examining the gendered nature of cross-border flows of people and cultural information around the world, especially emphasizing the hierarchical and gendered "channels" of these flows. Transnational feminism examines the ways that globalizing capitalism impacts human beings across races, classes, genders, nations, and sexualities. Drawing on postcolonial feminist theory, critical race theory, and post-Marxism, transnational feminism moves beyond notions of a nation-state based "International" feminism, to emphasize not only the role of patriarchal capitalist power structures, but also differentiated subjectives as instantiated in the perspectives of women of color. As scholars in other fields began to cite and incorporate the insights of ethnic studies and transnational feminist scholars, issues of race, gender, colonialism, and multiculturality came to be seen as relevant to all fields of inquiry and to all communities, even if the issues were experienced in uneven ways.

The frequent ambivalence about the political valence of transnationalism reflects the inevitable ambiguities of any complex phenomenon or concept which is thoroughly traversed by social contradiction. It is thus hardly surprising that buzzwords like "transnational" leave the academe aflame with controversies, as the terms themselves come to trigger left and right takes on the issues, with both utopian and dystopian inflections. These symptomatically ambivalent responses remind us of the Marxist understanding of capitalism as both marvelously creative and horribly destructive, representing the "power of money," as Caetano Veloso put it in a song lyric (*Sampa*), "to both create, and destroy, beautiful things."

Very diverse ideological formations are friendly to globalization, just as diverse forces are hostile. Visionary artist/theorist Hito Steyerl speaks of the "political montage" which serves populist mobilization." What does it mean for the articulation of protest, she asks, when:

> ...nationalists. Protectionists, anti-Semites, conspiracy theorists, Nazis, religious groups, and reactionaries all line up together at antiglobalziation demos in a dispiriting chain of equivalences?[10]

It all depends, in the end, on the angle of critique and the view of the nation-state. One can distinguish among at least four kinds of politically-inflected critiques of globalization: 1) critiques of the nation-state from the neo-liberal center right or the WTO—motivated by the desire to pressure nation-state governments to favor free trade, privatization, and de-regulation policies; 2) critiques of the nation-state from Marxist or systems theory perspectives, which see the state as concentrating economic power in the hands of the corporate and financial elites from the Global North, or 3) critiques of globalization from a leftist perspective which see the nation-state as the protector of the welfare state and the *Etat-Providence* from globalizing forces which erode those social gains; 4) critiques of the nation-state from left-Anarchist perspectives, which emphasize the states' inherently coercive nature; 5) critiques from the nativist-populist right à la Marine Le Pen, where the movement is not necessarily against the welfare state per se but rather opposed to sharing its benefits with the unwashed immigrant masses. All of these groups critique globalization but they do so for very different reasons; and 6) critiques from a nativist-populist perspective which wants to destroy the welfare state and "emtitlements." Anti-globalization catalyzes strange bedfellows. Both the right-wing nativist Steve Bannon and the editorial staff of the leftist journal *Le Monde Diplomatique* are hostile to globalization. Bannon denounces "globalism and calls in pseudo-Derridean terms for the "deconstruction" of the administrative "deep state," all in the name of a toxic brew of white supremacy, racism, Islamophobia and right-wing libertarianism. The Marxist Third-Worldist economist Samir Amin, meanwhile, calls globalization "a euphemis for that forbidden word, imperialism."[11] *Le Monde Diplomatique*, in a similar vein, denounces globalization as a form of neo-liberal privatization and Americanization which spawns horrific inequalities and *la pensee unique*.

The apparent inconsistencies of approach are partially rooted in highly gendered oppositions. The Bannon-Trump hatred of the administrative state is hardly consistent, for example. While advancing the withering away of what Bourdieu calls the left "feminine" side of Leviathan, i.e. the nurturing side of government in the form of the Environmental Protections and the Department of Education (along with Planned Parenthood), it strongly favors the right hand of Leviathan, the hard, metallic, militaristic "masculine" side of Homeland Security, the Armed Forces, ICE deportations, rampant gun ownership, not to mention the hard-hearted downsizing power of corporations. The masculine disciplining of women's bodies through the banning of abortion goes hand in hand, ironically, with cutting all aid to the babies who actually get born into a society denuded of health care.[12] And needless to say, the withering of the "deep state" does not lead to a Communist society but rather to total capitalist hegemony and a free hand for financial capital.

As a result of these contradictions, many scholars refuse to regard the transnational as either a purely emancipatory concept or as an oppressive form of "universalism." The term is not an honorific, or a synonym for "progressive." Colonialism, Slavery, and Patriarchy were all thoroughly transnational, as were their political opposites—anti-colonialism, the anti-slavery movement, and feminism. Both corporate commercials, and radical music videos, can be "transnational." Most transnational scholars have eschewed a bipolar approach that would either applaud the transnational with unequivocal enthusiasm or condemn it with uncompromising disdain, preferring to examine the transnational as a productive knot of contradictions to be disentangled. The processes of globalization are clearly contradictory, entailing both oppressive and emancipatory effects. Within the corporate avant-gardism of TV and internet commercials, transnational allusions have become mass-media staples, as common and bland as white bread. The TV and internet ads for transnational corporations, in this sense, offer a transnationalist utopia of globally integrated cityscapes, a world without center or borders, conjured up in a hyperkinetic proliferation of deterritorialized simulacra. All their wildly dispersive centrifugal energies are ultimately disciplined, in most cases, by the centripetal force of the corporate brand.

We cannot simply applaud or decry the nation-state per se. Forgetting the nation-state's definitional tendency to exercise violence both toward otherized alien peoples and toward internal minorities, Westocentric historiographies of nationalism tend to pit the older, mature, civic, and supposedly inclusive forms of well-behaved Western nationalisms against the putatively young, irresponsible, and exclusivist forms of non-Western nationalisms. The "old" nationalisms are projected as benign, while the "new" nationalisms are seen as unprecedentedly violent.[13] Thus the Global North, along with China and Israel, have a natural right to have nuclear weapons, since it is assumed they would use the weapons "responsibly," even though the U.S. is the only nation to have actually used them, to devastating effect, and even though the U.S. and the U.S.S.R. came close to using them during the Cuban Missile Crisis, and even though Nixon and now Trump have played with the idea of devastating whole nations. (While individuals who threaten to kill other individuals are liable to criminal penalties, apparently heads of state who threaten to annihilate entire peoples are not).

The role of the state, meanwhile, is ultimately ambiguous. On the one hand, we might want to defend the welfare state against the neo-liberal privatization that would destroy it, or defend the nation-states of the Global South against the economic hegemony of the Global North. On the other, we might lament the role of the state's Weberian "monopoly on violence" in crushing indigenous peoples—as European and European-derived creole nation-states have done throughout the Americas—and in exploiting and marginalizing minorities, as has been the case not only, obviously, in the Global North but also, perhaps less obviously, in the Global South. (We need only think of Turkey's vexed relation to Armenians and Kurds, or Algeria's relation to Amazighs (popular known as "Berbers," or India's to the Dalit and to "scheduled tribes."))

18

TRANSNATIONAL CINEMA

As widely circulated cultural products, films have become a kind of privileged metonym for transnational processes generally, often figuring as iconic objects within debates about transnationalism and globalization. In cinema studies, the move toward the "transnational" first took the form of serious reservations about the long taken-for-granted centrality of the national—for example the long-standing dominance in cinema studies curricula of "national cinemas"—which led to proposals for altered terminologies. Globalization clearly played a role in these interrogations of the national by dissolving borders for capital and commodities (but not for desperate migrants), by deregulating markets and easing tariffs, thus contributing to the dissolution of the national state as the primary unit of analysis. These shifts operated in tandem with theoretical "post" developments which shed doubt on any essentialist notions of a national spirit or reality. Stephen Crofts proposed the term *"nation-state* cinemas" instead of *"national* cinemas";[1] Andrew Higson argued for "post-national cinema";[2] while Willemen and Vitally preferred *"culturally* specific" to *"nationally* specific."[3]

A key event was the founding of the influential journal *Transnational Cinemas* by Armida de la Garza, Ruth Doughty, and Deborah Shaw in 2010, a journal which played a crucial role not only by publishing ambitious theoretical essays and scholarship on a wide array or topics but also by setting research agendas in the field. Since that time, transnational approaches have been applied to national, regional, ethnic, and diasporic cinemas around the world including Bollywood, Nordic Cinema, Nollywood, Latin American Cinema, European Cinema, Australian Cinema, Chinese Cinema, and Hong Kong Cinema, Tamil Cinema, to name just a few. While some analysts prefer a narrow definition of filmic transnational as referring only to "transnational coproductions," other analysts, such as Mette Hjort, speaks more broadly of a "plurality of cinematic transnationalisms, which vary widely in form and promote a wide range of artistic, cultural, social, economic and political values."[4] Hjort distinguishes "strong" from "weak" forms of transnationality; it is strong when it involves a number of levels at once (she cites Mehdi Charef's *La Fille de Keltoum*, 2001) and weak when it involves only a few levels. Hjort also contrasts "marked" and "unmarked" forms of transnationality; in the former case, the production calls attention to transnational elements in the film itself, whereas in the latter the transnational dimension requires research and analysis to be disinterred. Hjort also suggests criteria for discerning the political and aesthetic drift of the transnational in relation to specific films. The term "transnational" she points out, should not be seen as a compliment that bestows political virtue on the film, *unless* the film exhibits resistance to a homogenizing globalization and also demonstrates aesthetic-stylistic independence and innovation.[5] In some ways, her formulation constitutes a latter-day updating of earlier stridently left formulations about "third cinema" and "transcontinental cinema" as instantiating, in any part of the world, resistant forms of the convergence of the political and aesthetic avant-gardes.

Hjort offers a suggestive taxonomy of transnationalisms, including *"epiphanic" transnationalism*, which combines deep national belonging mingled with aspects of other national identities to reach transnational belonging; *"affinitive" transnationalism*, based on identificatory fellow-feeling with those "similar to us" suggesting shared values or experiences; *"milieu-building" transnationalism*, as a "small-nation response, for example by the Dogma group, to Hollywood-style domination; *"opportunistic" transnationalism*," i.e. a financially motivated production or promotion strategy; *"cosmopolitan transnationalism*," produced by well-travelled multicultural cosmopolitans like Euan Chan, a New York based filmmaker, born in mainland China, bred in Macao, educated in Hong Kong and the U.S., who makes films for the global Chinese-speaking audience; *"globalizing" transnationalism*, or a necessary strategy for producing big-budget films for a transnational audience; *"auteurist" transnationalism*, which occurs when a very personal director with an iconic national status—e.g. Antonioni, Kiarostami– embraces collaboration beyond national borders; "modernizing" transnationalism, where an already transnationalized film culture such as the South Korean filmically signifies its own processes of modernization; *"experimental" transnationalism*, where cross-border collaboration— Hjort gives the example of *The Five Obstructions*—is primarily motivated by aesthetic research.

One could easily amplify Hjort's definitionally open schema with proliferating categories based on authorship (individual vs. collective transnationalism), audience response (identificatory versus distant transnationalism), ethics (opportunistic vs. collegial transnationalism), religious affiliation (Islamic transnationalism, Evangelical transnationalism), political tendency (radical vs. neo-conservative transnationalism), aesthetic traits (baroque transnationalism), epochal designations (postmodern transnationalism) and so forth, all of which might potentially shed light on the subject.

Paul Julian Smith suggests the different processes by which films, especially global art films, become transnational: 1) some films are locally produced and oriented in the sense of making coded references to the "home" culture appreciated only by local audiences, yet participate in transnational genres and narratives that have wide appeal; 2) some "festival films" circulate and thus become transnational thanks to the production support and exhibition practices of international film festivals; and 3) some "prestige films" become transnational by adroitly combining the local and the global through dispersed production models and global distribution.[6]

Here we also have to consider the implications of the digital turn in terms of films "becoming transnational." Take, for example an experimental exercise like *Man with a Movie Camera: Global Remake*, a crowdsourced recreation of Vertov's paradigmatically reflexive silent 1928 film, in which Perry Bard broke down the Vertov film shot-by-shot and made a world-wide call for submission of new shots where participants would recreate or change the original shots in whatever manner they chose. The Global Remake code would then pull shots at random from a database of similar shots, ensuring a film which would never be exactly the same twice, presumably generating ever-shifting coefficients of transnationality in terms of pictures locales, participants, and so forth.

The issue of scale impacts the discussion by introducing spatialized terms and concepts such as "infranational," the "supranational," and the "paranational, designed to deal with agencies which are metaphorically bigger, smaller, or "in excess" of the nation. In a series of publications, Mette Hjort, speaks of "small cinema studies," proposing four criteria for the category: geographical scale, small population, a relatively small GDP, and a history of rule by others.[7] Since the nation is increasingly felt to be simultaneously too large and too small a unit to serve as a precise object of identification and analysis, Thomas Elsaesser argues, we might speak of "sub-state and supra-state allegiances."[8] Terms like the "minoritarian," the "diasporic," the "indigeneous," and the "exilic," similarly, are simultaneously broader and narrower than the national. While the terms sometimes refer to minorities "contained" within the nation-state, these same minorities in one country often form majorities elsewhere and therefore can be seen, depending on the lens adapted, as equally "transnational" or even "global."

Here, as we shall see, the growing movement of "indigenous media," now found on every continent, comes to mind. As with cinematic lenses, methodological lenses shape what we see and how we see it; they bring some objects into focus while blurring or obscuring others. Many nations form "multinational states," with complex overlays of majorities and minorities. India and Indian Cinema are not only Hindi but also Tamil and Punjabi; Belgian cinema can be Flemish-speaking or French-speaking; Canadian cinema is both Quebecois and Anglo, and so forth. These conflicts sometimes explode (even in relation to the Oscar ceremonies) in relation contested national terrains. Do Palestinians with Israeli citizenship like Elia Suleiman and Mohammed Bakri make "Israeli films" or "Palestinian films?" That question is ultimately inseparable from a fundamental political question: is Israel a "Jewish state" or "the state of all its citizens?"

Rather than define the transnational as a delimited historical stage, or as a coherent set of aesthetic traits forming an artistic "school," one can see it more productively as an open-ended and multidimensional critical/methodological grid with historical, aesthetic, political, and cultural dimensions. Elizabeth Ezra and Terry Rowden define the transnational as a "conceptual tool" that "recognizes both the forces that generated the decline of national sovereignty in the wake of globalization, on the one hand, and the counter-hegemonic responses to those forces, on the other.[9] A transnational prism exposes the ways that film and media studies had quietly, almost unknowingly, enshrined the nation-state as the only valid form of social and political organization, while paying insufficient attention to the subnational, supranational, and paranational practices and perspectives that tended to fall into the cracks and fissures between nation and state. At its best, a transnational methodology can open up an entry point for all those films and movements and directors who transgress the rules both of canonical decorum and of national allegiance, creating a space for new subversive movements and *poets maudits*, as well as for those, such as indigenous peoples, who had long been denied entry into the charmed circle of "legitimate" cinema.

Thus the word "transnational" hosts diverse ideological tendencies and directionalities. One can distinguish between its centripetal, monologizing tendencies as opposed to the centrifugal, dialogizing tendencies as coexisting cross-currents within the transnational. In what has become a standard move in the wake of adjectival modifiers for terms like post-modernism, variously qualified as "top-down or bottom-up," analysts now contrast regresssive "top-down" forms with progressive "bottom-up" forms of transnationalism. John Hess and Patricia Zimmerman, for example, contrast a lamentable "*corporatist* transnationalism" with a laudable "*adversarial* transnationalism."[10] Will Higbee and Song Hwee Lim, for their part, add their own prophylactic qualifier to endorse "*critical* transnationalism."[11] Building on while critiquing Deleuze and Guattari, Françoise Lionnet and Shu-Mei Shih speak of "*minor* transnationalism,"[12] while Africa-oriented scholars speak of "*Afro*-transnationalism."

Many critics have warned against any premature leap from the national to the transnational that ignores the pivotal adjudicating role of nation-states. The nation-state remains a crucial actor and transmitter and mediator within the framework of globalization. Although the U.S. for example, does not have a state-supported cinema, nonetheless various levels of American government—municipal, state, and federal—support the cinema in multifarious ways. In Latin America, Nestor Garcia Canclini argues, the state plays a crucial role as the locus of public interest capable of preventing subordination by the media to market forces.[13] More generally, as Shohini Chaudhuri points out, a nation-state's involvement in cinema is often pivotal in creating the conditions that enable film production. This involvement can take many forms: state investment through subsidies; state protection through quotas or tariffs; state encouragement through incentive laws; or state inducements through festivals and prizes, and state surveillance through censorship.[14] As Randal Johnson has pointed out, "The most successful periods in the histories of Mexican, Argentinian, and Brazilian Cinema" were fueled by "enhanced state support."[15] In the context of Argentinian cinema, Joana Page speaks of a "strategic reassertion of the nation and a rearticulation of certain forms of nationalism in the context of the recent [2008] economic crisis."[16] Various cinema laws promulgated by the Argentine government, such as the *Lei de Cine* of 1994, she points out, helped sculpt out a space of exhibition for Argentinian cinema.

Jung-bong Choi chides what he calls "the academic exodus to the territory of the transnational," which he describes as a "rushed move, theoretically, methodologically, and epistemologically."[17] While acknowledging that the transnational can displace the "universalizing trope of the global," Choi prefers not to see the transnational against the national within a logic of supersession. Skeptical about any "congratulatory outlook" toward the transnational, as if it were "a messianic concept that will liberate us from the shackles of the legal, national, and even viciously universalizing global," Choi's own preference is to see the national and the transnational as "mutually parasitic" concepts, "tied, annexed and reciprocally kept hostage together," in relations of polyandrous connections, described in eroticized terms as "liaisons" and "flirtations." For Choi, the transnational forms "the intersection between the outward subnational and inward extra-national (not necessarily ""supra") forces [where] the national can thus be thought of as a switchboard operator, modulating the volume, velocity and valence of intersectional affairs."[18] The trick, then, is to avoid new binarisms in order to see both national and transnational as mutually invaginated, while also seeing localization and globalization as simultaneous and mutually constitutive processes sometimes summed up in the coinage "glocal."

Here an obvious yet absolutely crucial distinction asserts itself as a way to ward off a common misunderstanding. It is one thing to call for the transcendence of the nation-state, within an intellectual project, as a unit of analysis *in theory*, on the one hand, and a very different thing to naively assume that this theoretical-discursive gesture has actually enabled us to transcend *in practice* the role of the nation-state in political terms. I am clearly arguing the former, and not the latter.

19

THE COEFFICIENT OF TRANSNATIONALITY

Uneven in their applicability, terms such as "national" and "transnational" and "global" change their denotations and connotations in function of the scale, axes, and the grids of analysis or the chosen principles of pertinence. In the initial 2010 edition of the *Transnational Cinemas* journal, first Deborah Shaw and Armida de la Garza offered a schema consisting of fifteen categories and themes relevant to the transnational aspects of films: modes of production, distribution and exhibition; co-productions and collaborative networks; new technologies and changing patterns of consumption, and the like, related to the analysis of transnational cinema, ranging from modes of production, distribution and exhibition to ethics and postcolonial politics. (The schema was revised by Deborah Shaw in 2013.) What might be called the "coefficient" of transnationality varies widely depending on the axes under consideration. Cinema can be transnational by reason of its production (financing, personnel, locale, casting), or of its themes (immigration, exile, diaspora), or its typical genres and aesthetics. In an extreme case, a film might be transnational along all the axes (transnational in funding, locale, production personnel, casting, language, music, aesthetics, etc.), or transnational only along some axes (e.g., funding and casting), but not along others (e.g. music, crew, etc.). At times, we find links between such themes and the global economic system. The *verite* documentary *Mardi Gras: Made in China* (2000), similarly, disinters the subterranean connectivities between a globalized Chinese sweat shop (Tai Kuen), created in a Special Economic Zone in Fuzhou, and the millions of beads it produces thrown by Mardi Gras revelers in New Orleans.

In feature films, meanwhile, we sometimes find an aesthetic/narrative match, in feature fictions such as *Traffic* (2000) and the oft-cited *Babel* (2006) between the mobile interconnectivities implied by transnational themes, performers, and locations, as conveyed through interlaced Bordwellian "network narratives." One could distinguish between intra-national and intra-ethnic network narratives like the Argentinian *Relatos Selvajes* (Wild Tales, 2014) where all the networked tales have to do with white Argentinians, and intra-national but multi-ethnic network narratives like *Crash*, where most of the episodes revolve around racial tensions in Los Angeles. In his analysis of "*Babel*'s network narrative," Paul Kerr shows how the film's narrative bears a "structural homology" to the film's mode of production and the social relations of its production. Babel, he argues, is both *about and based on* border-crossings, with four story strands in four languages, and it becomes a vehicle for both an ensemble cast of unknowns and three international stars. Here crossing-borders are of the essence: the film endlessly cuts between Morocco, the U.S., the U.S.–Mexico border, and so forth. In terms of production, the film involved the Mexican production company Zeta films, the American Media Rights Capital. The American company Anonymous Content, the French Company Central Films, and the American Paramount Vantage.[1] As Deborah Shaw points out, the film ultimately privileges a North American perspective, in that the film is focalized by the white couple who suffer the consequences of missteps of people of color like the Moroccan boy who shoots the gun—the iconic glue that connects all the episodes—and the Mexican nanny who decides to cross the U.S.–Mexico border.[2]

The parameters outlined in a U.K. Film Council "cultural test" for Britishness, noted by Roy Stafford, could easily be reconfigured as a "transnational cultural test"; the parameters include cultural content (setting, lead characters, subject matter, language of dialogue); cultural contribution (British heritage, culture, and creativity); cultural hubs (studio or location shooting, music); and cultural practitioners (director, screenwriter, producer, composer, lead actors, cast, and crew). At the outset, it is hard to imagine that most of these items would be "purely British"—if such a thing even exists—and would turn up many transnational "impurities." In fact, the very origin-story of Englishness reveals "impurities" in that it conjoins two alien (German) tribes—the Saxons and the Angles, with an admixture of Jutes, Frisians, Franks, and a motley of Scandinavians. Thus the national test ironically points to its opposite—transculturality and transnationality within British nationality and cinema itself, only amplified in the wake of the massive multiculturalization of the U.K. in the postwar period as a form of colonial karma.

In her 2013 schema, Deborah Shaw usefully delineates fifteen categories of the transnational in relation to film: modes of production; distribution and exhibition; modes of narration; multiple locations; globalization as theme; exilic and diasporic filmmaking; cultural exchange; transnational influences; transnational criticism; transnational viewing; transnregion/transcommunity films; transnational stars; transnational directors; transnational ethics; transnational collaborative networks; and transnational films.[3]

The range of verifiability in the case of positing a coefficient of transnationality within such parameters can vary immensely. Along some axes, for example financing, casting, and technical crew, what I am calling the "coefficient of transnationality" is quite clear and even quantifiable in terms of money spent and persons contracted, while along other axes, such as the aesthetic, the generic, and the affective, the coefficient is more or less refractory to statistical proof.

The diverse axes of aesthetics are often non-synchronous with other parameters. The film *Woman on Top*, for example, concerns Isabella, a talented Brazilian chef (played by Spanish actress Penelope Cruz) who goes from Brazil to San Francisco to become the host of a live TV cooking show. The film combines an American director (Alan Poul), a Brazilian American screenwriter (Vea Blasi), a French cinematographer (Thierry Arbogast), along with transnational theme, transnational funding, and a multinational cast of American, Brazilian, and Spanish players, all relocated from one South American Bay with a Catholic name (All Saints Bay in Salvador, Bahia) into a North American Bay with a Catholic name (San [Saint] Francisco Bay). The film features salient aspects of a diasporic Afro-Brazilian culture, such as samba, *candomblé*, and Afro-Brazilian cuisine. In the film, the *orixa* Iemanja endows the protagonist with culinary gifts that enable her to leave her unfaithful husband to take care of her own life.

Despite its multiple layers of transnationality, one track in the film—the music track designed by Luis Bacalov—feels thoroughly and exclusively Brazilian in its mix of samba and MPB (Musica Popular Brasileira). But on another level, the assignation of national belonging depends on the analytical grid and the filmic track chosen. In this sense, the soundtrack of *Woman on Top* exhibits a paradoxical trait of Brazilian music—i.e. its own miscegenated transnationality, its alchemical, even anthropophagic, capacity to absorb virtually any musical current—tango, reggae, blues, country, calypso, jazz, rap—and make it recognizably "Brazilian." Not coincidentally, it was a Brazilian literary theorist—Roberto Schwarz—who criticized the chimerical search for a national essence through a process of "the national by subtraction," as if the national consisted in everything that remained once all the alien excrescences had been removed. The national, for Schwarz, is constituted by what is alien; or in Bakhtinian terms, the national exists in relation and in function of the transnational and vice-versa. In that vein, we would do well to move from "the national by substraction" to a (trans)national logic of ramifying additions, multiplications and algorithmic expansions.

Speaking more broadly, "national" directors are not necessarily "faithful" to their national music. Anglo-American popular music serves as a musical *lingua franca* in countless non-American films. The Turtles' "Happy Together" not only provides the title for a Wong Kar-Wai film, but has also been featured in myriad films from diverse countries. Indeed, Wong Kar-Wai's films meander between classical music to American pop to Chinese opera and Latin boleros, often sung by American singers like Nat King Cole.

For that matter, even the national identity of performers needs to be destabilized and de-essentialized even on a biographical level: Angelina Jolie is of Euro-American, Native American, German Slovak, Dutch, and French Canadian heritage; "American" actor Keanu Reeves was born in Lebanon and of English, Chinese, and Hawaian heritage; Cher is of Euro-American, Lebanese and Cherokee heritage and so forth. But when we move from biographical heritage to performative ethnicity and nationality, the picture becomes even more confused. Our impression of a player's nationality often depends on which film we have seen first, resulting in surprises such as: "I didn't know that Cate Blanchett was Australian." Apart from all the white players who performed in blackface (Al Jolsen), redface (Elvis Presley), yellowface (Marlon Brando) and brownface (Natalie Wood, Ben Affleck), we have the people of color cast as a wide array of substitutable "others"; Dolores del Rio as Samoan, Lupe Velez as Chinese, and so forth. As Ella Shohat and I pointed out in the second edition of *Unthinking Eurocentrism*, World Cinema, and especially American Cinema, is full of mutational fictions that point to the mutabilities of race in a structurally racist society. A quick taxonomy of the more striking figures and genres would include: 1) the racial *bindungsroman*, where whites blacken themselves to live, learn and communicate the reality of racism to skeptical whites (e.g. *Black Like Me*); 2) comic/ didactic switcheroos, where racial transformation triggers a pedagogical process for white racists (a rich white man in *Watermelon Man*, a racist Frenchwoman in *Agathe Clery*; 3) allegorical power reversals (*The White Man's Burden*); 4) thespian transformation (Robert Townsend as King Lear, Superman and "Rambro" in *Hollywood Shuffle*); 5) whiteface drag (Shawn and Marlon Wayans in *White Chicks*); 6) multiracial actors playing the same character (*I'm not There* and *Palindromes*); 7) morphing race (the racial kaleidoscope in Michael Jacksons "Black or White"); 8) posthumous transformation (Chris Rock turns white in *Coming Down to Earth*); 9) transracialized classics (Welles' "all-black Macbeth," *Carmen Jones, The Whiz*); and 10) transtextual/ transsexual adaptation (*Karmen Gei* as a Lesbianized and Africanized *Carmen*.

Then we have all the sketch-comic racial chameleons like Sasha Baron Cohen, Jordan Peele, and Keegan-Michael Key. Chapelle's "Racial Draft" sketch, for example, pokes fun at notions of ethnic essentialism by staging a "draft," as in an athletic league, for a multiracial audience, ethnically segmented into separate cheering sections, where the audience is asked to draft celebrities and politicians into a single "correct" racial team. Chapelle prefaces the sketch by insisting on the need to define people by a single race, in order to end his endless arguments with his Asian wife about "which part of Tiger Woods hits the ball so good." Although the draft supposed aims at clarity of racial definition, it actually reveals the impossibility of any such clarity. The Blacks vote to give Colin Powell and Condoleezza Rice to the whites (which suggests that politics can trump race); Tiger Woods rediscovers his blackness—"So long, fried rice; hello, fried chicken"—and mangles black slang (suggesting that food and language affect our perception of color); Lenny Kravitz joins the Jewish people (religion trumps race); the Wu Tang Clan come out as Asian (culture trumps race) and so forth. Ridiculing any stable and essential identity as chimerical, the sketch indirectly mocks the infamous "one-drop rule" that makes anyone even of the most partial African ancestry "black."

In terms of the locations of filmmaking, a metropolitan "urban studies" approach emphasizing cities rather than countries offers another way to bypass the nation-state, and to a lesser extent the Global North/South divide. For Johan Andersson and Lawrence Webb, a "global cities" approach allows us to decenter and reposition both Hollywood and European cinemas within a world map of economic and cultural flows and shifting Center-Periphery dynamics, where Lagos, Rio de

Janeiro, Hong Kong, Cairo, and Mumbai also enjoy pride of place.[4] The "global cities" move was partially inspired by Saskia Sassen's seminal intervention in her book *The Global City: New York, London, Tokyo*, which argued that the major financial center cities of the world had more common with each other than with the more provincial cities, often just miles away, within the same country.[5] In the mutually impacting dynamics of moving image media and the global city, we find "media capitals" scattered around the world. Building on the work of economist Michael Porter, Thomas Elsaesser, meanwhile, speaks of mediatic "cluster cities," where we find a critical mass of mediatic talent and technical expertise. Elsaesser also speaks of blandly modernist "generic cities" (Rem Koolhaas) which, à la Tati's *Playtime*, all resemble one another. Some cities, such as Paris, New York, and London, form hubs of synergistic clusters—mediatic, academic, cinematic, literary, and museological.

The question of location and locality in cinema, in such circumstances, becomes increasingly murky, scrambled, and unstable, whether in terms of transnational digital production techniques, where writing, filming, and editing can take place across space and time zones, or in the multiplication of locations in the films themselves, for example in the frenetic shaky-cam city-hopping of the Bourne series, as the digital turn de-realizes and pixillates urban space, severing "the indexical link to geographical space."[6] Even before the digital turn, there were urban "double" cities, as when the Italian neighborhood of Toronto stands in for New York's Little Italy in *Moonstruck* (1987). In some films we find an iconographic intermingling of cities reminiscent of the over-determinations of dreams, where various remembered cities, in oneiric versions of Kuleshov's "creative geography," merge and fuse. In *Blade Runner*, locations in Los Angeles become intermingled with those of Tokyo, while Los Angeles and Shanghai come together in *Her*, a trans-urban hook-up as implausible as that of the protagonist and his imaginary operating-system lover. As with most digital and globalized phenomena, we also find the opposite trend, i.e. of intense localization, as in the case of interactive virtual reality documentaries, where the spectator-participants vicariously lives in a 360-degree immersive experience of Syrian refugees, as in "the Syria Project."

Bakhtin's concept of the "chronotope" (etymologically, "time space") is also germane to transnational analysis. Building on Kant's ideas about the fundamental categories of cognition and on Einstein's theory of relativity and time as the fourth dimension of space, Bakhtin defines the chronotope as the intrinsic relationality of temporal and spatial relationships within artistic representation, where "time, as it were, thickens, takes on flesh, becomes artistically visible" and "space becomes charged and responsive to the movements of time, plot and history."[7] *Chronotopes* represent constellations of distinctive and spatial features within genres defined as "relatively stable types of utterances." These spatio-temporal structures correlate with the real world but are never equitable with it given their inevitable mediation through genre, medium, and authorial personality. Mediating between the historical and the artistic, they materialize time in space and provide fictional environments—and this is where films become political—where constellations of power become visible.

Building on Bakhtin, we might speak of a "transnational chronotope," which would simultaneously reference such cinematic dimensions as: (1) the transnational space/time of the *production* itself (for example the actual location and duration of the production); 2) the generative transnational social milieu or cluster (Elsaesser) from which the film emerged (varying from major mediatic centers like Hollywood and Silicon Valley, or a city packed with filmmaking talent to a tiny group of ardent filmmakers with little material support); 3) the artistic production of the transnational time/space of the diegesis of the actual film; 4), the space/time produced through mise-en-scène, editing, and art direction (aka production design) in molding a spectatorial sense of a fictive space/time; (5) the transnational spatio-temporalities evoked by the music track in terms of both lyrics, music, and musicalized noise; (6) the transnational space/time evoked through citation, posters, archival footage; (7) the transnational aesthetics embedded in the text's artistic procedures; 8) the embedded genres and aesthetic styles that characterize the film; 9) the use of composited digital locations to create a chrontopic simulacrum which is both completely fake and plausibly realistic; and finally, 10) the transnational spatio-temporalities implied by the theoretical grid itself. The most complete possible analysis would take all of these issues into account.

The advent of the digital and the "softwareization" of the media has on the one hand enabled powerful media actors to outsource the labor of filmmaking through globalized "time-shifting" and "location shifting." Hye Jean Chung speaks of the "media heterotopia" generated by transnational filmmaking.[8] More and more contemporary films use digitally created environments to create a "fluid sensation of movement across physical locations" in such a way as to embody "fantasies of a mobile existence acoss geographical, national, and ontological borders."[9] This production of affect works through a "labor-intensive process involving location shooting, editing, special effects, and computer generated animation." Hye Jean Chung examines the virtual experiences of physical mobility in the transnational spaces and "simulated cosmopolitanism" of three films: Tarsem Singh's *The Fall* (2006), Zhangke Jia's *The World* (Shijie, 2004), and Oshii's *Avalon* (2001). These uses of digital technologies, she argues, "facilitate, enable, and necessitate a global reconfiguration of labor in ways that dramatically differ from what came before." The concept of media heterotopia, she concludes, acknowledges new hybrid forms—"digital composites of multiple layers that contain material residues of globally dispersed production sites and laboring bodies"—and thus "reconnect the materiality of production spaces and laboring bodies with mediated onscreen environments and entities."[10]

20

TRANSNATIONAL RECEPTION, GENDER, AND AESTHETICS

I will now turn to the question of how cross-border "looking relations" (Jane Gaines), inform the transnational. What knowledge can be gleaned from the reciprocal interweavings of the national, the regional, and the transnational by studying what "passes" from one culture to another? Why are some genres easily appreciated and understood in some countries but not in others? Are some genres more "universal" in their appeal, or is their "universality" premised on the historical "accident" of Western hegemony and the prior dissemination of Western modes of storytelling? Are some themes, such as maternal love for children (biological or adoptive or symbolic) to be found in directors as different as D.W. Griffith and Walter Salles Jr—and some genres—e.g. melodrama—intrinsically more transnational in their appeal? Are comedies more limited in their appeal due to their dependency on language and wordplay? Or are all genres—e.g. Yoruba theater films—potentially "universalizable"—once they are supported and disseminated by powerful media institutions and circulation networks? And what about transcultural cultural values such as religion? Are religiously themed films—e.g., *The Message* or *The Passion of the Christ* or even Huston's *The Bible*—transnational because they revolve around the three "religions of the book," arguably transnational virtually by definition due to the religions' wide dissemination and their claim to spiritual universality?

Perspectives on the transnational are inevitably impacted, although not in a static or mechanical way, by spectatorial experiences, identities, identifications, and affiliations. Which aspect of identity becomes paramount in specific circumstances? How do our regions of origin, our political affiliations, and our class, gender, race, ethnicity, religion, and sexuality impact our view of the transnational and of transnational media studies? Transnational analysis has much to learn from Crenshaw's already mentioned concept of intersectionality—or one might say "*trans-sectionality*"—i.e the ways in which the various axes of social stratification—class, gender, race, sexuality and so forth are interconnected and mutually impacting. Indeed, the Crenshaw mantra could easily be tweaked to make room for other axes of stratification such as religion, age, region, and language.

The study of all these axes, and their intersectionalities, usually discussed in relation to single nations, can productively be enriched and transnationalized through the study of *transnational* and *transectional* modalities of racism, sexism, homophobia and so forth. These issues cannot be studied in depth within a single national context: colonialism and anti-colonialism, slavery and anti-slavery, sexism and feminism, homophobia and LBGTQ rights, are all transnational phenomena, albeit with regional and national nuances and inflections. Some analysts of contemporary politics have noted a transnational "white backlash," mistakenly called "populist" but more accurately called "nativist" or "white supremacist," or simply "racist," reflected not only in the rise of Trump in the U.S., Marine le Pen in France, Brexit in the UK, Neo-Nazism in Poland and Hungary and so forth, but even in the countries of the Global South, for example in Temer's replacement of Lula and Djilma's multi-colored Cabinet with the all-white male Cabinet of Temer. This world-wide turn to the right" can be seen as a broad counter-move to the liberatory resistance movements of people of color and the "browning" of the West. Thus it is illuminating to see issues of racial representation and stratification through a transnational prism, for example through comparative studies of white-dominant racial formations, where one finds variations on a racist theme, but with national nuances.[1]

The "mantra" of social stratifications, and the relations between them, is configured differently as our analysis moves from country to country and minority to minority, requiring constant recalibrations of the transactional mantra of oppression and resistance. A comparative truism has it that in Brazil, "class hides race," while in the U.S. race hides class, although perhaps in different proportions. In reality, of course, the social and the racial both mesh and reinforce each other in both contexts.[2] In the Middle East, religion (Islam, Judaism, Christianity, Buddhism, Bahai, etc.) and sect (Shia, Sunni) often trumps both race and class, without the latter categories ever losing their pertinence. And in relation to Europe, Franco-Algerian sociologist Nacira Soulimas-Guenif speaks of the "racialization" of Islam in contemporary France. Liberation movements are often both transnational and transectional. Multicultural feminism, for its part, built in political terms on the activist achievements of the anti-colonial movement, the Civil Rights Movement, the Gay Liberation movements, the international UN-sponsored feminist conferences beginning in the 1970s, and in theoretical terms on postmodernism, postcolonialism, and "border theory," as well as on the academic critiques of the Eurocentric premises of Western feminism by minoritarian, postcolonial, transnational scholars such as Gloria Anzaldua, Chandra Talpade Mohanty, Ella Shohat, and Jacquie Alexander.

We know there is a *national* emotion and affect, whether in its chauvinistic, militaristic form, or its reactive, anti-colonial national independence form. But can one speak of a *transnational* or *minoritarian* emotion and affect? The world-wide dissemination of U.S. minority culture, for example, forms a kind of positive corollatoral-effect of what is commonly seen as negative—the hegemony of American mass and popular culture generally. At times, the dissemination of U.S.-minoritarian cultures has inspired what might be called "homological affinities" or paraphrasing Raymond Williams again, "isomorphic structures of feeling" whereby minorities identify with other minorities in other continents due to affinities of situation; thus one stigmatized group in one country sees itself as mirrored within the sufferings of another group in a different country. Isomorphic structures of oppression and identification provoke affective bonds and link similar movements across borders. The U.S. Black Panther movement in the U.S. inspired cognate movements in countries as diverse as the Dalit in India, the Aborigines in Australia, the Catholics in Ireland, Blacks in England, Arab Jews in Israel, and North African immigrants in France. As a filmic corollary, Black Cinema in the U.S., similarly, inspired film movements around the world. Giving voice to the aspirations and grievances of a minoritized community victimized by job discrimination, police harassment, and Islamophobic prejudice, the so-called Beur/banlieu filmmakers of France like Abdellatif Kechiche, Rachid Bouhcareb, Karim Dridi, and Yamina Benguigi, for example, explicitly cite black American filmmakers like Spike Lee and Julie Dash as examples of what is possible, as do indigenous filmmakers in Australia. Parallel structures of oppression and resistance give voice to the logic of: "If they can do it there, we can do it here."[3]

In sum, the movement of ideas and activism has always been multi-directional; minority activists in the West were themselves inspired by African independence movements, as African Indepedence movements were inspired by Afro-diasporic activists. In aesthetic terms, African art inspired the surrealists; surrealism inspired Caribbean artists like Aime Cesaire, while Cesaire himself was inspired by the Harlem Renaissance, which was in turn inspired by dreams of Africa, and so forth around the Black Atlantic. Cross-border identifications and affiliations do not take place in a historical vacuum; they are embedded in layered histories of the crisscrossed identifications between African independence movements and Afro-diasporic liberation movements. Within the transnational circulation of resistance culture, the 1983 *Marche des Beurs* in Paris by the children of North African immigrants, for example, was explicitly modeled on the Martin Luther King march for justice in Washington in 1963, but then the King march too was embedded in a broader transnational trend, in that King himself modeled his protests on the mass protests against British colonialism led by Mahatma Gandhi.

We find a didactic treatment of the relationship between Gandhi and King in a surprising place—the genre of "epic rap battles." Within the World Literature tradition, "epic" evokes works like *The Iliad, The Odyssey*, and the *Aeneid*, and suggests a poem, of a certain magnitude, about a national culture hero. Here, "epic" simply means "great," and rap refers to Afro-inflected percussive conversation as musical form. The specific subgenre is a YouTube series created by Peter Shuckoff (aka Nice Peter) and Lloyd Alquist, which has millions of subscribers and consists of verbal combat between mismatch historical and pop-culture figures such as

Beethoven and Justin Bieber, Einstein and Stephen Hawking and so forth. The irreverent humor of one particular "epic battle," performed by Key and Peele, easily seeable on YouTube, has a didactic postcolonial and critical race dimension in that it teaches contemporary young people about Gandhi's struggle against British colonialism and Martin Luther King's battle against U.S. American racism.

The split-screen setting for each figure is itself richly informative. Gandhi performs against an austere amber-colored backdrop of Indian rural poverty, while MLK appears against a background of mountaintops—recalling "I have been to the mountain top" alongside street scenes of the Civil Rights marches of the time. The images are in black and white, appropriate to a struggle which was very much about the relations between Black and White. The mountain imagery traces back historically, of course, to the biblical Mount Sinai from which Moses looked in the direction of Canaan as "promised land," all posited allegorically to analogize the black struggle to achieve the constitutionally promised land of freedom. Gandhi is dressed in austere clothing reminiscent of what Gandhi actually wore, while MLK and the Civil Rights protestors are dressed in respectable suits that proclaim "I am a man" and I deserve my human rights. While Gandhi's dress betokens willful austerity and poverty; King's evokes middle-class respectability. In film-stylistic terms, the MLK imagery is reminiscent of the TV reportage of the 1960s, while the Gandhi imagery evokes both the realism of the New Indian Cinema and the stylization of the classical Hindu mythologicals. Here Gandhi "spits yoga fire" in a manner that recalls the mythologicals.

While Gandhi's struggle concerned external colonialism, of India by Britain, King's struggle concerned internal colonialism of a nation-state toward its own citizens. The "battle" is purely metaphoric, since the idea of a bitter contest between two heroes of passive resistance is as improbable as it is anachronic, given that the two figures were not contemporaneous, that the latter figure admired the former as a model of resistance, and that both men were noted for their abnegation and modesty, not for their narcissistic braggadocio. The lyrics are replete with information about the caste system, the Dalit (Untouchables), and popular films set in India. Gandhi speaks first: "I fought the caste system/but you still cannot touch this/Slumdog skillionaire/First Name Messiah/Rap so hot I spit yoga fire/Everything you preach/I said it first/You should just jot down these words/plagiarize my whole verse/Leave your thoughts on the door/like the real Martin Luther." The lyrics here refer to the leader of another "protest-ant" rebellion, that of Martin Luther against the hierarchical ceremonies and practices of the Catholic Church, thus creating a transhistorical fusion of diverse historical struggles. And although the struggles of Gandhi and Martin Luther King were not identical, they were clearly connected in that the situation of Blacks was also the product of British colonialism and the slave trade. It was the colonial powers who practiced enslavement, and both colonialism and discrimination were racist, while the caste system was a form of segregation like that suffered by Blacks.

Within this example of Hip-Hop didacticism, King's answers are rich in historical resonance. The word "overcome" in King's challenge that "you will not overcome this Junior" evokes the protest anthem "We Shall Overcome" but here rendered as an absurd individualist combat. The line "No shoes, no shirt, but I'm still gonna serve ya" refers to Gandhi's poor dress and modesty and desire to serve the people but here modulates its meaning to "win against you." The song's King admires the way that "broke the British Power," but his only "dream" is that "one day"—the words conjure up King's famous 1963 speech on the Washington Mall—Gandhi would "take a shower." In tones of rap braggadocio totally alien to the historical prototype, the video's King brags that. "I've got so much street cred they write my name on the signs" and "I'd ring you for tech support, but I got a no bell Prize," allusions both to the massive number of street signs named after King and to the innumerable South Asians working in "tech support" both in the diaspora and in the "Call Centers" of India, symptoms of the globalizing practice of outsourcing where Indians survive by learning American accents as low-age workers for communications companies.

The intellectual-discursive formation called "transnational feminism" first elaborated by such scholars as Caren Kaplan, Inderpal Grewal and extended into the realm of film by Alison Butler, Trin T. Minh-ha, Ella Shohat, Katarzyna Marciniak, Kathleen McHugh, Sophie Mayer, and many others. The Marciniak, Aniko Inre and Aine O'Healy's edited volume *Transnational Feminism in Film and Media* stresses that the relevance of transnational feminism goes far beyond a corpus of transnational films per se; rather, it reminds is that "transnational processes are inherently gendered, sexualized, and racialized."[4] The collection advances the discussion of transnational media by stressing the movement of gendered bodies not only across national borders but also across disciplinary divides, indeed across borders of all kinds, across and within nations, borders of disparate wealth, discrepant cultural capital, and racialized and gendered labor relations.[5]

In *Women's Cinema, World Cinema*, Patricia White inquires into the ways that women filmmakers have shaped novel transnational formations of film culture, challenging "dominant conceptualizations of cinema organized around national movements, waves, and auteurs," movements which misrecognize the import of women filmmakers' participation.[6] Building on Lucia Nagib's conceptualizations, White speaks of the "gendering" of World Cinema, and, in a remediated filmic version of "Sisterhood is Powerful," of "sororal cinema."[7] (Nadine Labaki's 2007 beauty parlor film *Caramel*, in this sense, might be seen as the female correlative of Spike Lee's fraternal barbershops). Though "still drastically underrepresented, "White notes, "women directors are increasingly coming into view within the circulation of world cinema."[8] In this sense, we can resist a discourse of loss which proclaims the end of the revolutionary film movements of the 1960s, forgetting that those movements were almost invariably led by heterosexual men, with barely a woman in sight. The French New Wave, and Brazil's Cinema Novo, were virtually all-male movements with the exception of Agnes Varda in France, and Elena Solberg in Brazil, but now there are scores of women directors in both countries— in France, Catherine Breillart, Claire Denis, Celine Sciamma in France, and in Brazil, Lucia Murat, Suzana Amaral, Eunice Gutmann, Lais Bodansky, Tizuka

Yamasaki, Sandra Kogut, Helena Solberg, Katia Lund, Sandra Werneck, and Tata Amaral and many others. Internationally, we find internationally recognized directors such as Li Yu, Zhao Wei and Sylvia Chang in China; Nadine Labaki and Maryanne Zehil in Lebanon; Samira Makmalbaf and Shirin Neshat in Iran; Iciar Bolain and Gracia Querejeta in Spain; Lucretia Martel in Argentina; Miwa Nishikawa and Yuki Tanada in Japan and so forth. Hollywood, especially in terms of Blockbusters, lags far beyond many countries in terms of gender equality.

Some feminist film scholars have linked the Deleuze-Guattari concept of the "minor" to the transnational in productive ways. In *Women's Cinema: The Contested Screen*, Alison Butler argues that women's cinema is better seen as "minor" rather than "oppositional," since it is not "at home" in "any of the host of cinematic or national discourses it inhabits, but ... is always an inflected mode, incorporating, reworking and contesting the conventions of established traditions ..."[9] While it is essential to focus on the contribution of feminist transnational "*autrices*," a focus on major feature films has the unfortunate side-effect of discriminating against "minor" forms and minoritized subjects, if only because it is only the global power elite that enjoys access to the financial power that undergirds big-budget features films and their marketing campaigns.

Transnational reception can also operate in less progressive ways, for example through ethnocentric misrecognition and "misprisons," as when Western spectators might "westernize" their apprehension of *anime*, delinking it from "Japaneseness." Some Lebanese militias in the 1980s, similarly, identified with the macho bravado of Stallone's Rambo, if not always with his right-wing imperialist politics. The reading was "resistant," but not in the progressive way envisioned within Raymond William's schema of emergent, dominant, residual, and archaic cultural practices, or in Stuart Hall's theory of "dominant," "resistant" and "negotiated" readings. In a different way, a kind of inadvertent transnational pedagogy informs spectatorship in major cosmopolitan capitals around the world. In some cases differentiated spectatorship results in an awareness of differentiated spectatorship and asymmetrical forms of knowledge, for example when members of a dominant group sees films representing diverse nations and cultures with an audience partially drawn from the nations or cultures portrayed on screen. When raucous laughter from the cultural "insiders" explodes in the theater, the cultural "outsiders" become aware that they have missed a joke or a reference, since the more culturally knowledgeable members of the audience are laughing hysterically at something that has left the "outsiders" cold and clueless. In such cases, the "home-team" spectators become "depayse" and "provincialized," made aware of the cognitive limitations of their own cultural repertoires.

One dimension of film that is almost inescapably transnational is aesthetics. Long before the advent of the cinema, artistic movements like the baroque, the romantic, and the modernist, were rarely limited to a single national location and were thus inescapably transnational. A visit to virtually any modern art museum or film festival, similarly, would suggest that the arts are fundamentally cross-border phenomena. "Transgenres" such as comedy or melodrama, in the same vein, have no clear national provenance. The seminal ingredients of melodrama can be found in Greek tragedy, in Hindi theater, in French melodrama, in Hollywood "weepies," in Latin American *telenovelas*, and Turkish *arabesk*. Long studied largely in relation to European and American cinema, melodrama has recently been found germane to Indian, Chinese, and Japanese films, applicable to filmmakers such as Arnaldo Jabor in Brazil, Douglas Sirk and James Cameron in the U.S., Almadovar in Spain, Ozu in Japan, Raj Kapoor and Udayan Prasad in India, Zhang Yimou in China, Fassbinder in Germany, and Nadine Labaki in Lebanon. Architecture, music, and cuisine, similarly, do not respect borders. While artists might carry nationally stamped passports, their art is virtually certain to be "in excess" of the national. While the production and consumption of the arts are inevitably shaped by national infrastructures and laws, the art itself, at least in stylistic terms, is almost invariably transnational.

The cinema was born transnational both in production and in aesthetics. Before World War I and the rise of Hollywood hegemony, cinemas in many countries mingled German, French, Swedish, Italian, British and American influences. The earliest silent films adopted novels and plays from many countries. Italian immigrants in Brazil, during the silent period, adopted American novels like *Uncle Tom's Cabin*, a film that resonated with the memory of Brazilian slavery. After the advent of sound, cinemas in the world continues to be influenced by transnational currents; a Brazilian feature, Humberto Mauro's *Ganga Bruta*, in 1933, reflected transnational aesthetic trends, betraying the influence of Hollywood-style continuity editing, Soviet montage, German Expressionist chiarascuro, and French Impressionist soft-focus. Dominant commercial American cinema, similarly, absorbed the montage techniques of the Soviets (usually shorn of their communist agenda), the artistic protocols (especially of lighting and staging) of German expressionism and *chiaroscuro*, the literary ambitions of the French *film d'art*, and the historical grandiosity of Italian epic extravaganzas.[10]

Nor can transnational aesthetic exchange be neatly aligned with political and economic relationships; in this sense, aesthetics enjoys what Althusserian theory used to call "relative autonomy." The fact that China has become Brazil's second greatest trading partner does not mean that Brazilian cinema has suddenly been inundated by Chinese films or been impacted by "Chinese aesthetics." The potentially transnational aesthetic character of film texts becomes especially apparent in the case of music tracks. Nanni Moretti's *Caro Diario*, for example, is a Franco-Italian production, largely Italian in language, casting, and theme, yet the film's soundtrack superimposes African music on Italian scenes in such a way as to "Africanize" the Italian cityscapes and landscapes through a kind of "transnational-musicality-effect." The social tensions between different forms and styles of music—going back to the patriotic singing of the Marseillaise in *Casablanca* up to the "battle of the boomboxes" in *Do the Right Thing*—can also echo larger sociopolitical tensions. The vibrant Raï music of Cheb Khaled and Cheb Mami in Zemouri's *100% Arabica*, "Arabizes" iconic Parisian landmarks such as Place de la Concorde, in what amounts to an acoustic take-over, a "Maghebianization," as it were, of the urban Center by the popular culture of the subalternized Periphery.

The rolling thunder of the various "New Waves" that stormed across Europe and the Global South—Italian Neo-Realism, the French *Nouvelle Vague*, Brazilian *Cinema Novo*, *Neuer Deutcsher Film*, *Nuevo Cine Latino American*, New Indian Cinema etc.—bought a new kind of transnational textuality to the fore by continually drawing on one another. Glauber Rocha coined the term "*Sur-Realismo*"—a play on Surrealism and the Spanish word for South (*Sur*)—as part of his call for a avant-garde-inflected cinema worthy of the Global South. In fact, Glauber Rocha himself practiced *Sur-Realismo* in films like *Terra em Transe* and *Antonio das Mortes*. A transnational aesthetic analysis of a Cinema Novo film like Glauber Rocha's *Terra em Transe* (1966), to take a signal, vulcanic example, in this sense, would have to take into account the following potpourri of elements: the film's native Brazilian literary influences, for example the abolitionist poet Castro Alves, whose famous line "The Plaza belongs to the People" is cited; the contemporaneous poet Mario Faustino, quoted in the film's epigraph ("So much violence, and so much tenderness"); along with Oswald de Andrade and all the Brazilian modernists; Brazilian musical influences such as the composer Carlos Gomes, the "Brazilian Verdi," whose "O Guarani" is featured on the soundtrack; along with morsels from symphonies by Villa-Lobos and the songs of popular composers and the culture of samba and candomblé.

All these influences in the film exist alongside various transnational filmmakers, dramatists, and pictorial artists, including Glauber's explicitly honored "gurus" representing four national cultures (the German Brecht, whose influence appears throughout, for example in the film's anti-veristic stylizations; the English Shakespeare, present in Rocha's Elizabethan option to represent a modern *coup d'état* in the form of a Shakespearean physical/spiritual wrestle over a quite literal crown; the Russian Eisenstein, with thinly veiled allusions to the "Odessa Steps" and to Dr. Smirnov and the rotten meat of *Potemkin*; and the American Orson Welles, with allusions to the mise-en-scène of the soliloquies in Welles' Shakespeare films). This all goes without mentioning the myriad European literary influences on the film (such as Rocha's respectful invocation in interviews of Lautréamont's "aesthetics of vomit"). Indeed, Rocha thought of entitling the film "Maldorado" in homage not only to "Eldorado" but also to Lautréamont's *Les Chants de Maldoror*—along with countless filmic debts and homages to Pasolini, Godard, Visconti, to Jean Rouch and *cinema verite*, and techniques emulating Godardian jump cuts and Resnais-like *faux raccords*. (Even this rather lengthy list hardly begins to register all the influences, allusions, and citations in the film.)

The issue of transnational aesthetics comes up in a different way in the case of transnational film remakes, the subject of an anthology—*Transnational Film Remakes*—edited by Iain Robert Smith and Constantine Verevis.[11] The problematics here are not so different from the already discussed issue of transnational film adaptations of novels, where novels from one country are remediated and indigenized by filmmakers from another country. What of the national "passes" in such cases. The editors bring up the case of Paramount Pictures casting Scarlett Johannson in the lead role of the science-fiction film *Ghost in the Shell* (2017). A

Hollywood remake of a 1995 Japanese anime (and manga), the film triggered charges of infidelity to the cultural spirit of the original. Comic book writer Jon Tsuei argued that the source text should be understood as "inherently a Japanese story, not a universal one."[12] It is impossible to westernize, he argues, what is basically a non-Western story. In short, East and West, never the twain shall meet in a transnational remake. But pointing to innumerable examples of transnational remakes while lamenting the Hollywoodcentrism of the scholarship, the editors rebut any essentialist approach by pointing out that *Ghost in the Shell* is "a multivalent cultural text that incorporates numerous cross-cultural influences from around the world."[13] To paraphrase Bakhtin once again, all nations are transnations. Rather than a bidirectional traffic—Hollywood remakes European and Asian originals while Europe and Asia remake Hollywood, the editors point to more complex and multi-directional configurations such as a triadic exchange between Hong Kong, Bollywood, and Hollywood in Sanjay Gupta's *Kaante* (2002), a recreation of Tarantino's *Reservoir Dogs* (1992) which was itself an (uncredited) remake of Ringo Lam's *City on Fire* (1987)[14] In this sense, a transtextual and transnational approach, as opposed to a fidelity and cultural essentialist approach, dismantles the notion of purity of origin in favor of a view that sees single texts as pointing backward, forward, and sideways, in a dialogical profusion of texts and genres of diverse provenance.

21

TRANSNATIONAL FILM SCHOOLS AND PEDAGOGY

Recent years have seen an explosion of books on film festivals in their various dimensions, whether based on national rubrics (Chinese, Australian, and Greek Film Festivals) or municipal rubrics (Cannes, Venice, Locarno, New York, Toronto), or genre (Horror Film Festivals), or identity categories (Queer Film Festivals), or corollary practices (Activism and Film Festivals). Some scholars speak of the phenomenon of "festival films," which make their way around various festivals around the world without necessarily being released in the director's "home" country. Although it is difficult to generalize, festival films tend to be art films by auteurs or soon-to-become auteurs, characterized by non-studio production, relatively low-budget production, and a mix of local and "universal" themes. I will not linger on the subject of festivals, since the field has already been thoroughly addressed by scholars such as Dina Iordanova, Marijke de Valck, Richard Porton, Cindy Hing-Yuk Wong, Chris Berry, Ruby Cheung, Leshu Torchin, Luke Robinson, Liz Czach, Thomas Elsaesser, Azadeh Farahmand, Julian Stringer, and Amalia Cordova, to name just a few of the scholars who form part of this burgeoning field.

At the same time, a subfield of transnational cinema and media studies has focused attention on a hitherto neglected facet of the transnational—the crucial role of film schools and media training workshops. Hardly a novel phenomenon, transnational film schools existed before being named as such. A number of key film movements of the twentieth century emerged out of film schools, beginning with the movement closely associated with what has usually been seen as the first film school, to wit the revolutionary Soviet montage cinema linked to the Russian State University of Cinematography in Moscow (VGIK) founded in 1919, where figures like Kuleshov and Eisenstein taught. (Vladimir Gardin famously asserted that "There is no Soviet Cinema without VGIK.")

Subsequently, other school-connected film movements followed the pathway opened up by VGIK. The Italian Neo-Realist movement in the late 1940s, for example, was closely linked to *Il Centro Sperimentale di Cinematografia* in Rome. Founded in 1953 in the wake of the Chinese revolution led by Mao Tse Tung, the Beijing Film School (later Beijing Film Academy) was also largely modelled on the VGIK model. Xie Fei, longtime administrator of the Beijing Academy, reports that the faculty staffing was transnational in its inclusion of professors from the Socialist Bloc countries, as was the programming of films for the students. Over a four-year period in the 1980s, he reports that 45.5% of the films screened were from mainland China; 14.7% were from the U.S.; 23.4% from the U.S.S.R., with 26.2% from other nations.[1] Film schools can also be transnational in terms of the future directors who attended them. In the 1960s, the Senegalese director Sembene studied filmmaking in the U.S.S.R.; the Mozambican (later Brazilian) Ruy Guerra studied at IDHEC in Paris; and a host of Latin American filmmakers—Fernando Birri from Argentina, Alea from Cuba and Triguerinho Neto from Brazil—studied at the Centro Sperimentale in Rome. More recently, Apichatpong Weerasethakul studied at the Art Institute of Chicago. In 1986, the Cuban-government founded *La Escuela Internacional de Cine y Television* in San Antonio de los Banos, attended initially by selected students from all over the Third World, and subsequently opened up to applicants from the world in general. The students were advised by a transnational group of prestigious teachers; the Colombian writer Gabriel Garcia Marquez, Cuban theoreticians/filmmakers Julio García Espinosa and Tomás Gutiérrez Alea, Argentinean poet and filmmaker Fernando Birri, the Frenchman Pascal Aubier, along with Brazilian filmmakers Orlando Senna and Sergio Muniz.

Filmmakers themselves have often been less than enthusiastic about film schools. Many of the New Wave movements anathemized the existing film schools. With Oedipally tinged outrage, the French New Wave directors excoriated the rigid hierarchies and technicist approach of the film training offered by the official IDHEC film school (now FEMIS (*Ecole Nationale Superieure des Metiers de l'Image et du Son*)), just as they criticized the stuffy studio style, linked to the official film schools, of *la tradition de la qualite*. When Claude Chabrol would provocatively tell aspiring young filmmakers that they could learn everything they needed to know about film technique in eight hours, he was subtly undercutting the prestige and pedagogy of the official film schools. Godard's professed goal in the early 1960s of bypassing the rules and *bienseances* of "correct filmmaking" and "going back to zero," similarly, was also an indirect slap at the established schools of filmmaking.

The various film schools reflect a wide variety of situations and relations to governments and universities and to the concept of the transnational. Some schools, such as New York University's Tisch School of the Arts, or the British Film School in London, are transnational less due to explicit vocation than intention by virtue of their cosmopolitan students and location in highly international world cities. Others have been closely linked to national industries. The National Danish Film School, during its half-century of existence, for instance, has been an essential force within Danish cinema, the catalyst for Dogma 95, for internationally acclaimed Danish TV shows, and for the recent revitalization of Danish documentary. Since many European film schools depend on government funding, they are regulated by their national education departments, the exception here being the French FEMIS, which works under the auspices of the Department of Culture. The International Association of Film and Television Schools (CILECT), for its part, have called for more international partnerships between institutions and across its five constituent regions: Africa/Asia/Pacific, Europe, Ibero-America, and North America.[2]

Two recent books shed welcome light on the subject of transational film schools. Mette Hjort's two-part anthology *The Education of the Filmmaker* (2013) brings together essays advancing a global perspective on the issue of innovative film training. Duncan Petrie and Rod Stoneman's *Educating Filmmakers: Past, Present and Future* (2014), meanwhile, explores the development of film training institutions in Europe and the United States. The authors identify three broad global phases in film school development: the first two phases—the interwar years and the post-World War Two period—retain a clear national focus, initially within the contexts of Soviet Russia and Fascist Italy. The third phase begins in 1989 with the end of the Cold War and the globalized triumph of neoliberalism.

While film schools historically emphasized the broad humanist cultivation of the filmmaker as artist, as intellectual, and (potentially) as activist, in recent decades many film schools have moved toward a more narrow professionalizing approach that fosters the development of employable industry-friendly skills, marketing, business plans, and mastery of "the pitch," within a social rhetoric emphasizing "content" rather than "films." These options form indices and symptoms, some would argue, of the neo-liberal global commodification of film culture. Rather than merely constitute preparatory schools for the established industries, film schools might ideally be conceived as critical spaces of freedom where aesthetic experimentation and theoretical research might thrive. As a formal statement by CILECT ("The International Association of Film and Television Schools") puts it, film schools should be "a welcome *lieu* to debate how filmmakers, schools, scholars, and students, situated in different parts of a violent, conflicted world, might contribute to turn audiovisual landscapes into dense environments for creative experimentation of new paradigms of 'how to live together.'"[3] If students are unable to experiment or take risks in film school, one suspects, they will find it even more difficult to be aesthetically daring in the high-presssure world of commercial production. At the turn of the 21st century, even before the full impact of the digital revolution, producer-director-theorist James Schamus warned against economic censorship and the impact of corporate hegemony on creative expression: "… we may soon live in a world where we are free to say anything, but where the cost of reaching out to anyone who can afford to hear us will be beyond prohibitive."[4] Even the supposedly iconoclastic American "indie" films, Justin Wyatt has noted, are usually located in "the safe domain of dominant ideological and commercial practice."[5]

In her thoroughly researched and insightful look into transnational film schools, scholar Zoe Graham, defines some key properties common, in varying degrees, to transnational training institutions: a multi-country focus; flexible practices, and a border-crossing pedagogy. Graham traces the social, historical, economic, ethical and aesthetic dimensions of film schools within an emergent discourse on transnational media pedagogy. Her particular focus is on the *Ateliers Varan*—based in Paris but with branches worldwide—which is at once a film school and non-governmental organization founded by anthropologist/filmmaker Jean Rouch in the newly independent Republic of Mozambique in 1978. Over decades, the *Ateliers Varan* have spawned a global network of grassroots film training workshops. Graham's analysis of the Atelier's institutional history brings into conversation two tutelary figures who created generative discourses—the founder Jean Rouch, with his "shared anthropology" and Paulo Freire, with his vision of critical pedagogy, developed in his highly influential *Pedagogy of the Oppressed* (1970). By bringing a Freire-inspired pedagogical lens to the analysis of transnational cinema, Graham multiplies connectivities across disciplines and links film theory to social activism. Her work uses the transnational as an "analytical prism" to be applied retroactively to a neglected aspect of cinema history that has been shaped by transnational energies and histories in ways not visible to scholars deploying a purely national lens.

Graham's case-study teases out the ethical pedagogies animating some transnational film schools like Atelier Varan and the trans-disciplinary theoretical potentialities of this "becoming" phase of filmmaking. By focusing on different locations within the Ateliers Varan network, she offers a "polyperspectival" understanding of one form of transnational film pedagogy, but one appropriated and indigenized in different global sites. A transnational frame also reveals collaborations and exchanges between various filmmakers and movements, which may have been overlooked due to "nation-state" thinking. Graham points to new transnational educational paradigms that are re-shaping the landscape of global film training—from the global network university, at one end of the spectrum, to peripatetic training initiatives at film festivals and NGO-run, community-based media workshops (such as "Nos de Cinema" in Rio de Janeiro) at the other. At their best, Graham argues, transnational film schools and film workshops privilege "pedagogies of possibility" rather than target global audiovisual consumers. Such initiatives are aimed at developing new audiovisual archives to preserve local memories, fostering the development of young filmmakers; at sharing technological skills with local populations in a democratizing gesture and at generating supportive and productive transnational communities of interest and exchange.

Contemporary film pedagogy, whether designed for prospective filmmakers or for students in general, has to take on board not only television but also a world in which students are "digital natives" at ease with smart phones, mobile apps, computers, Internet games, Augmented Reality, Web Cams, Skype, Google Earth, Vimeo, and so forth. Yet due to the "digital divide," a substantial proportion of the world's population lacks access to the Internet. The danger is that the "digital natives" might become complacent, provincial, elitist, and "presentist," that they might fetishize technology and forget the multiple pasts—technological, social, aesthetic—that shaped this new moment. The ideal, to my mind, is to constantly place in relation past and present, and theory and practice, to link Vertov to Bruce

Conner, the Situationists to Remix Culture, Godard, Kluge, and Santiago Alvarez to the mashup and so forth.

The invaluable collection *Teaching Transnational Pedagogy*, edited by Katarzyna Marciniak and Bruce Bennett, takes on this issue and many others. The editors begin by lamenting the masculinist portrayal of teaching as a stereotypically soft, nurturing "feminine" profession.[6] Both hailing and embodying the upsurge in academic interest in film pedagogy, a wide spectrum of scholars draws on their experience in teaching transnational cinema, with an eye to deprovincializing their students (and themselves) through a shared experience of screening and analyzing transnational films. In a latter-day digitally enabled update of what in the 1970s was called "consciousness raising," the contributors emphasize pedagogy as a form of praxis, again with Paulo Freire's *Pedagogy of the Oppressed* as a major reference. In her essay, Mette Hjort draws on her decade of experience teaching in Hong Kong to propose what she calls a "performative model of transnational film pedagogy," part of a "participatory transnationalism" which "links scholarship as advocacy to actual practice."[7] In a variation on Marx's exhortation to go beyond understanding the world to actually changing it, Hjort suggests that the point is to "*do* transnationalism" rather than merely reflect upon it. To that end, she proposes "a project-based and values-driven development of wired networks spanning local and nonlocal contexts." The practical realization involves the students working in groups to produce short "vodcasts" designed to "premiere" transnationally through a connected Net-based classroom. The experience, in her view, actually "transnationalizes" students, hopefully leading to other forms of transnational connectivities and activisms.

Teaching Transnational Pedagogy is rich in suggestively didactic concepts such as the "pedagogy of discomfort" (Aine O'Healy/Megan Boler), the "pedagogy of humility," (Alex Lykidis) and the "Pedagogy of the Practical" (Bhaskar Sarkar). The essays proliferate in concrete suggestions for on-line teaching. Matthew Holtmeier and Chelsea Wessels, for example, recommend breaking classes up into groups while producing a "wikispace" document that can be viewed and edited collectively. Reflecting on their experience teaching "World and Transnational Cinema," Ruth Doughty and Deborah Shaw suggest that the only realistic goal is less a Faustian impulse to "cover the world" than the Socratic (maieutic) goal of "midwifing" concepts by revealing the cognitive poverty of conventional mainstream cinema. David Martin Jones, for his part, discusses the role of film-philosophy as a pedagogical resource communicating the ways films reflect and refract a transnational gaze which embodies the mutual regard of cultures.

The innovative narrative forms exemplified by serialized TV series like *The Wire*, *Orange is the New Black*, and *Atlanta*, also open up new didactic possibilities. In these series, every episode forms part of an ongoing chain of events that the viewer, in a kind of narrative addiction or hermeneutic dependency, needs to know in order to understand what's happening, (The structural principle of many TV series might be summed up as a kind of tantric narratology of *catharsis interuptus*). What do we know about the transnational circulation and impact of such programs and series? What was the transnational impact of Ellen's coming out in episode 23 of Season Four of *Ellen*? What happens when Latin Americans or Africans for example watch series like *The Wire* where disillusioned cops come to realize that the real criminals are not in the streets but in the suites, and where spectators become acutely aware of parallel situations of corruption in their home countries? How do audiences in the Middle East receive *Homeland*? (We know, for example, that some mischievous film-workers, during the shooting of some of the episodes set in the Middle East wrote graffiti in Arabic to the effect that "*Homeland* is racist.")

TV pedagogy can also take ludic form. In the context of deep time, Bakhtin spoke of Dionysian rites and Medieval carnival as "the second life" of the people, an alternative world of parody, play, irreverence toward established power, and collective *jouissance*. In *Homo Ludens*. Dutch theorist Johan Huizinga posits three conditions for successful play, that it be: 1) voluntary; 2) suspend real-world rules for invented constraints; and 3) take place in a special, separate space and time. Roger Caillois, for his part, builds on Huizinga to posit six basic requisites for play that it be: 1) voluntary; 2) separate; 3) not totally pre-determined; 4) non-productive; 5) governed by its own rules; and 6) involve make-believe.

In her essay "Politics of Narrative," Sylke Rene Meyer, professor of screenwriting and dramaturgy at the International Film School in Cologne Germany, cites both Huizinga and Caillois to foreground the pedagogical potential of Internet games and interactive storytelling, where the user, unlike the classical passive couch potato, actively co-creates a non-linear story with no pre-determined end. She concludes her essay with an exhortation: "The 21st century film school will have to educate students to create stories that help and empower informed citizens to create pathways through the information jungle." She recommends turning serialized storytelling and interactive games into cyberdrama, where "the heterotopian and utopian laws of everyday life apply, but just as Hamlet makes decisions, the user will make decisions." The user of a game based on *The Wire*, she suggests, perhaps too hopefully, might be "empowered to end the racist genocide."[8]

Jane McGonigal, meanwhile, in *Reality is Broken: Why Games Make Us Better and How They can Change the World*, makes even broader, more utopian/dystopian claims for the salutary effects of gaming. In a more consumerist version of the Jameson and Dyer emphasis on the utopian dimensions of popular and mass-culture, McGonigal argues that the ideal worlds of games can make gamers feel that reality is broken and therefore in need of mending. (We are reminded of Bunuel's in some ways opposite embrace of Engel's idea that the artist describes real social relationships with the purpose of destroying the conventional ideas about those relationships, and that his films "repeat, over and over again, in case anyone forgets it or believes the contrary, that we do not live in the best of all possible worlds.")[9] In this sense, gamers presumably become dissatisfied with the actually existing world and begin to want to change it. But those repeat-viewer fans of the film *Avatar* who could not bear to return to a non-Avatar world did not probably turn toward activism. Just as occurred in the pre-digital literary world of Emma

Bovarysme, art-based disenchantment with the real world can lead to suicide as well as activism. In any case, McGonigal argues, more convincingly, that gaming fulfills genuine human needs for purposeful escape, for rehearsals for a changed world. But the activism in the book is largely therapeutic, in that she foresees games that reduce stress, treat depression, help the elderly feel engaged, and "raise rates of democratic participation."[10] The real question is whether it would be possible to use game to "game the system," in a truly subversive manner.

22

MINOR CINEMA, THE INDIGENE, AND THE STATE

What is lacking in binary models of hegemony and resistance, as Françoise Lionnet and Shu-Mei Shih point out in *Minor Transnationalism*, is a more nuanced spectrum reflecting "the creative interventions that networks of minoritized cultures produce within and across borders [and the] micropractices of transnationality in their multiple, paradoxical, and even irreverent relations with the economic transnationalism of contemporary empires."[1] Playing on the diverse resonances of the word "minor" (child, ethnic minority, minor key, less important) Deleuze and Guattari use the term to refer to literature written in a minoritized language (for example the Jewish literature of Warsaw and Prague) bearing a historically fraught relation to a dominant language. "Minor literature" for the authors is that of writers who live in a language not their own, with an oblique and eccentric relation to the major, dominant language. Minor transnational cinema, in the Deleuze-Guattari sense, would be not only that cinema made by minoritized people, but also films made in "minor" genres, in a minor, dissident key, or in "minor" genres and formats, or engaging minor, disreputable emotions, with a fraught and often combative relation to the dominant film discourses and language.

Of course, "minor" and "major" are relational and conjunctural terms; their valence shifts depending on historical moment and social context. In linguistic terms, Arabic is major in the Middle East but minor in the U.S. or the U.K.; Yoruba is major in Nigeria but minor in Brazil and so forth. "Minor" countries can also be relatively "major" producers of cinema through disproportionate production. A nation without a nation-state such as Palestine has produced scores of filmmakers and films, in a manner out-of-synch with their relatively small demographic numbers. The world of World Cinema, in this sense, might need to create the equivalent of the actually existing "World Cup for Unrecognized Nations," or in comparison with the world of art, an impressionist-like "salon des films (et des nations) refuses."

Palestinian cinema, representing a nation of 10 million souls, many of them dispersed around the world, is perforce transnational in that it is not the product of an industry "on the ground." Palestine represents a partially extraterritorial people in search of "territorialization." (When asked where Palestine was, Palestinian filmmaker Leila Sansour replied "wherever I am.")[2] The situation of Palestinian cinema is transnational, first of all in relation to Israel, the nation-state that "hosts" and besieges them, and second in relation to its own diasporas, and thirdly in its search for transnational sources of funding and legitimacy.

We find an extraordinary artistic-performative exposition of what it means to be an "unrecognized nation" in the films and installations of Palestinian artist/filmmaker Larissa Sansour. Most of her films ponder the difference between literally closed and virtually open spaces. Her short Kubrick-pastiche clip *A Space Exodus* (2009) shows the director herself in a white spacesuit, planting a Palestinian flag on the moon as she declares: "A small step for Palestine, a great leap for mankind," all set against the sonorous background of an Arabized version of "The Blue Danube." In a situation where Palestinians are increasingly corralled into open-air prisons, progressively rendered more and more homeless and exiled from their indigenous land commons, Sansour explores the magical space of science fiction to launch a fantasy homeland on the moon. All of Sansour's films play with the local and the global; as Palestine shrinks on the ground, it expands in cinematic space. Given the relentless state-mandated enclosure of Palestinian land, as a disaster-fatigued world looks on with weary and too often useless compassion, Sansour plays with a utopian space and time in a Palestinian "nowhere." Since actually existing Palestine is in crisis, her work carves out an imaginary "out-of-this-world" place for Palestine: You-Tube as homeland.

In her 2013 short *Nation Estate*, Sansour appropriates science fiction and slick CGI effects to depict Palestine as a gigantic high-rise residence designed to "contain," in both the physical and the ideological senses of that word, the entire Palestinian population. After undergoing a surveillance retina scan, a pregnant woman (Sansour) enters a glossy metallic lobby, graced with a giant Palestinian flag, where a promotional poster reads: "Nation Estate: Living the High Life." The film hints both at the necessity of a Palestinian nation-state and at its apparent impossibility in a situation where it can only be realized through the magic of CGI-generated fantasy. The film's title puns on the nation-state as a political category—precisely that which Palestinians lack—and an "estate" in the sense of a residence, while slyly alluding as well, perhaps, to the French "three estates" of the *ancien-regime*. The elevator's various stops open onto picturesque simulacra representing Palestinian cities: Hebron, Bethlehem, Ramallah. A keycard in the form of a Palestinian flag grants her access to an elegant flat where she waters an artificial tree growing out of the floor, while the push of a button calls up the simulacral image of Jerusalem. In sum, Sansour draws on science fiction, real estate commercials, and corporate advertising to posit an antiseptic utopian/dystopian solution for the "Palestinian problem."

As the ever-promised mirage of a "two-state solution" seems to vanish into thin air, becoming ever harder to imagine, the artistic imagination conjures up surreal "solutions" for an absurd situation. As occurs in Emile Habibi's novel *The Pessoptimist*, absurdity becomes a paradoxically persuasive form of realism. If Sansour's first film catapulted Palestine, in the body of the director, into outer space, and the second film compressed all of Palestine into the interiors of a single high-rise building, a later film—*In the Future they Ate from the Finest Porcelain* (2015)—projects artifacts from the Palestinian past into the future. The title's mixed grammatical tenses—"In the future they *ate*—scramble temporality by mingling past, present and future in an impossibly palimpsestic space-time. Addressing the politics of archeology as instrumentalized as proof of longstanding Jewish presence, the film has a resistant group of Palestinians on the brink of the apocalypse bury keffiya-decorated porcelain in hopes of a discovery by future archeologists who might unearth the proofs of Palestinian claims to the vanished lands.

It is noteworthy that another Palestinian filmmaker, Elia Suleiman, similarly develops a Middle Eastern version of "magic realism," sometimes said by literary critics to be the default mode of postcolonial aesthetics, especially but not exclusively in Latin America. Suleiman thus injects into the stylized yet ultimately realist narratives of his films moments of self-flauntingly magical solutions for the intractable challenges set up by the occupation. In *Divine Intervention*, for example, the director endows a tossed apricot pit with the power to blow up Israeli tanks, a pink balloon (adorned with Yassir Arafat's face) with the ability to fly over checkpoints, and a Palestinian woman with the martial skills of a Ninja.

Palestinians can on one level be seen as an indigenous people circumscribed by an anomalous form of settler colonialism—anomalous in the sense of Zionism's status as a colonialism without a metropole—a group that has been compared, and compares itself, to native Americans.[3] It is in this contexts that we can address the longstanding critique addressed to the nation-state by indigenous peoples. The term refers to those variously called "first peoples" or "fourth world," i.e., those still-residing descendants of the original inhabitants of communally held lands subsequently taken over by or circumscribed by European conquest (e.g. Aboriginal in Australia, Maori in New Zealand, Dine and Sioux in the United States, Kayapo in Brazil) who have been violently disenfranchised within the various nation-states whose hegemony they suffer, including within the "third world." (Estimates of their numbers range from 250 to 600 million, forming what Viveiros de Castro and Deborah Danowski oxymoronically call the "gigantesque minority" of the world's peoples.)[4] "Indigenism," meanwhile, refers to those international movements that aspire to "promote and protect the rights of the world's 'first peoples'" from what is estimated as the "four thousand distinct societies, strongly attached to regions that were recently, and in some cases still are ... the world's last 'wild places'."[5] Despite their limited power, indigenous peoples have become important political actors and strategists on the international scene, becoming a major form of resistance. But unlike many anti-colonial and anti-racist movements, their goal is less equality and inclusion than sovereignty and the recognition of distinctive collective rights.

Indigenous cultural and political thought, as reflected in the writings of figures like Vine Deloria, Jodi Byrd, Audra Simpson, Sandy Grande in the United States,

Davi Kapowama Yanomami in Brazil/Venezuela, Ailton Krenak in Brazil, and Linda Tuhiwai Smith in New Zealand, among many others, point to some of the theoretical/cultural limitations of western radicalism and even of some versions of postcolonial theory. Many intellectual projects that seem very radical from a Westocentric perspective seem more problematically ethnocentric from an indigenous perspective. Indigenous peoples bear an ambiguous and ambivalent relation to the very concept of the transnational. On the one hand, they have been "transnationalized from above" by settler colonialism, but on the other they have responded with their own pro-Indian "transnationalism from below." When a transnational corporation devastates the Amazonian forest or creates a hydroelectric dam which floods native villages, it clearly constitutes a case of transnationalism from above. But when native peoples appeal to NGOs or secure international funding for their films, or use the Internet to introduce themselves to the world and advance their interests, or form coalitions with other native peoples, or decorate James Cameron with war paint as part of their resistance struggle against the Belo Monte dam, they are clearly practicing "transnationalism from below." When Palestinian activists, representing another indigenous people, similarly, paint themselves blue to appropriate the mass-mediated image of the oppressed Navi of *Avatar*, they too practice an indigenous form of "detournement" or "transnationalism from below."

While the transnational is often cast as a progressive move beyond the hegemony of nation-state paradigms, the *indigenous critique* of the nation-state takes place both "below" and "above" and "beyond" the default mode of the national. Its critique of the nation-state is much longer, deeper, and more radical than other critiques, for a number of reasons:

1. many indigenous communities came into existence *before* the emergence of modern nation-states;
2. the dispossession of indigenous communities was partially *the product of* expansionism by nation-states;
3. the symbolic national identity of colonial-settler states in the Americas (and elsewhere) was constituted *in relation to* the "Indian" and the "aborigine" whether as the enemy to be massacred and displaced, or as the recuperated symbol of national difference from Europe (as imaged, for example by the Iroquois Eagle clutching thirteen arrows on the U.S. dollar as a symbol of the then thirteen states);
4. many small-scale consensus native societies have actively *rejected* the very concept of the nation-state, not because they could not achieve it, but because they did not want it, particularly objecting to the idea of coercion and the "state monopoly on violence";
5. the present-day boundaries of many indigenous communities actually *exceed* the borders of nation-states (e.g. the Yanomami in Brazil and Venezuela; the Mohawks in the U.S. and Canada; the Guarani in Brazil and Paraguay, etc.); and
6. some indigenous peoples are "transnational" not in the classical sense of forming nation-states but rather in the sense of constituting indigenous

"nations without states" of the kind celebrated by anarchist anthropologist Pierre Clastres;
7. many indigenous peoples, due to multiple dislocations, no longer live only on their original land base but are dispersed regionally and transnationally, the case of the Xavante in Brazil and the Cherokees and Seminoles in the U.S.;
8. indigenous peoples and their social systems have a close relation to radical currents in the West critical of bourgeois nation-states, which is why they were admired by Marxists for their valorization of the communal ownership of land, and by anarchists for their rejection of coercive authoritarianism;
9. while western Republics are founded on the Lockean triad of "life, liberty, and property," many indigenous communities are founded on a triad of life, liberty, and the Commons.

Indigenous peoples are often less invested in "inclusion" within a national polity than in tribal and pan-indigenous sovereignty, although they sometimes argue for "both/and." Indigenous filmmaking plays a role within this project by calling attention to the need to control the means of representation to achieve as what scholar Robert Warrior (Osage) calls "intellectual sovereignty," what visual artist and scholar Jolene Rickard (Tuscarora) calls "visual sovereignty," and what Randolph Lewis calls a "cinema of sovereignty," defined as the ability for a group of people to depict themselves with their own ambitions at heart."[6] (We will return to indigenous media in a later section.)

The indigenous movement also has some sharp questions to address to postcolonial theory as well. Despite the postcolonial project's in many ways radically progressive character, from the standpoint of indigenous critique many postcolonial topoi seem questionable and even suspect. First, indigenous thinkers often see their situation as *colonial* rather than postcolonial, or as simultaneously colonial, postcolonial, and paracolonial. Second, while postcolonial theory celebrates a cosmopolitan "travelling theory," indigenous discourse often valorizes a *rooted* rather than a cosmopolitan existence. Third, while a poststructuralist-inflected postcolonial critique questions any "originary" ideas and any nostalgia for lost origins, native groups often seek to recover and restore originary customs, rituals, and language as a matter of sheer survival in the contemporary world, without which they would disappear as members of a specific cultural world. Fourth, while postcolonial theory revels in the "blurring of borders," indigenous communities often seek to *affirm* borders by demarcating land against encroaching squatters, miners, corporations, and nation-states. Rather than "deterritorialization," those who have been made strangers on their own land literally seek "reterritorialization" in the form of the recovery of ancestral land. Fifth, while postcolonial theory highlights the inventedness of nations and "denaturalizes the natural," indigenous thinkers have insisted on actually existing nations and on the love of a land regarded as "sacred," a leitmotif to be found in relation to both the Standing Rock pipeline protests and the Belo Monte hydroelectric dam protests. In ecological terms, what Eduardo Viveiros de Castro calls "indigenous multinaturalism" challenges not only the rhetorical antinaturalism of the "posts," but also what might be called the primordial othering which separated nature from culture, animals from human beings. For the Amazonian indigenes, de Castro points out, all beings have a human dimensions, including animals and plants: if for westerners all beings were animal but some became human, for the indigenes, "we" all began as human, but some became animals.

The postcolonial privileging of "hybridity" is especially fraught for indigenous peoples. On the one hand, indigenous nations have always been hybrid among themselves, in that all around the Americas they were trading with, borrowing from, befriending and fighting with one another long before Columbus, a process only accelerated and complicated by the Conquest and the Columbian Exchange. In Brazil, the first *indio technizado* was Essomericq, a Carijo Indian sent to France by his group and by their French allies in order to study munitions, the cutting-edge high-tech field of its time. On the other hand, "hybridity" has often been weaponized to disempower indigenous peoples of mixed heritage or of syncretic lifestyles, dismissed as not "real Indians" deserving of rights, simply because they wear jeans, or use laptops, or because, as Donald Trump said derisively about his indigenous adversaries concerning land rights and gambling, "they don't look like real Indians." We will return to indigenous issues when we speak later of "indigenous media."

23

THE RISE OF THE "WOODS"

From Hollywood to Nollywood via Bollywood

The equivalent of Eurocentrism in film is Hollywoodcentrism, perhaps summed up in "there-is-no-alternative" style affirmations such as Bordwell's claim that "No absolute, pure alternative to Hollywood exists."[1] Or, as Bordwell claimed in 1985, in order to go beyond Hollywood one must first go "through it."[2] Although these claims have a strong grain of truth, in other ways they seem questionable, since a scholar would have to know all of the world's cinema to make such a claim—and a scholar like Bordwell (not to mention Kristin Thompson or Dudley Andrew) certainly come as close as anyone can to having such knowledge—but even if were true it would apply largely to mainstream industrial fiction film-based industry and not to the wide world of filmmaking in the broad sense. In this sense, Feature-centrism is as much a problem as Hollywoodcentrism in excluding short films, virtual no-budget films and so forth. But even within the domain of the feature film, the relation to Hollywood is not simple. In 1993, Stephen Crofts posited a wide gamut of attitudes and international relations to Hollywood, ranging from those industries or filmmakers which tried to ignore it or critique it to those who tried to beat Hollywood at its own game.[3] The Bordwell claim would have to be supplemented, moreover, by the stipulation that Hollywood itself is "impure," thoroughly infiltrated and even dependent on its alien "others." Thus one could equally well say Hollywood never had the alternative of not drawing on alien traditions. In any case, it remains true that the majority cinemas of the Global South are rarely featured in the Cineplexes of the Global North. While the Global South is inundated with North American films and TV series, the Global North (and especially Anglo-America) receives little of the vast cultural production of the Global South, and the little it does see is mediated by transnational corporations. Needless to say, there are innumerable exceptions in the form of cultural centers, art film venues, and institutions like the Forum des Images in Paris.) Historically, the thousands of films from what was once called the Third World (now Global

South) rarely circulated *beyond* their national borders, and sometimes did not even circulate *within* their own national borders. The thousands of films produced by the most prolific industry in the world—the Indian film industry—were totally ignored or summarily dismissed in the West as trash until recently, with the mania for Bollywood films and the emergence of voluminous scholarship on the subject.

Abbas Kiarostami once said "Hollywood is more powerful than military might and creates more problems."[4] Wim Wenders put it differently in the mouth of a character in *Im Lauf der Zeit* (Kings of the Road, 1976): "The Yanks have colonized our subconscious." Yet despite Hollywood's and the Global North's domination of the world market, which began during and after the First World War and which gained strength subsequently, and despite the fact that Hollywood devours the lion's share of film profits, much has changed. The vast majority of films are being made in the Global South. The two largest producers of feature films are now India and Nigeria, followed by Hollywood in third place. In *Global Bollywood*, Anandam P. Kavoori and Aswin Punathambekar point to what has become the almost ubiquitous presence of Bollywood in the world:

> Aiswarya Rai made it to the cover of *Time* magazine, and even taught Oprah Winfrey and her viewers to wear saris. The Simpsons ended their trip to India with a dance set to a Hindi film song; Bollywood films sold more tickets in the United Kingdom than English-language films ... Bollywood stars, no longer obliged to entertain the mafia, partied at Cannes instead [and] Shekhar Kapur, acclaimed director of *Elizabeth* and *Bandit Queen*, declared that Bollywood would define and dominate global entertainment in the twenty-first century.[5]

Ashish Rajadhyaksha, in a similar vein, claims that Indian cinema itself has been "Bollywoodized."[6] Speaking more generally, recent decades have seen the cinematic "Rise of the Rest," including even in terms of the Oscars, where over the past two decades a majority of the Best Director Academy Awards have gone to non-Americans. China, Korea, Hong Kong, Iran, Turkey, Pakistan, Indonesia, Bengladesh, Egypt, Brazil, Mexico, and Argentina are all now major producers of film. Deshpande and Mazaj cite evidence from trade journals that show many homegrown industries outperforming Hollywood fare in countries as diverse as India, South Korea, China, Japan, Mexico, and Argentina.[7] At its peak, Nigeria has produced some 2,600 straight-to-video films per year.[8] Yet Hollywood remains the leader in revenue, and its Oscars "alienate" the world by relegating the majority world film production to the literally alienating category of "foreign film," a verbal shifter which refers to any film which is felt as foreign by any spectator in the world.

At the same time, no clear border separates Hollywood from the World. Rather than the single "culture industry" of Frankfurt School Theory, some analysts prefer to speak in the plural of a highly differentiated spectrum of "cultural industries." In *Global Cultural Industry*, Lash and Lucy question the adequacy of "culture industry" theory à la Horkheimer and Adorno in the age of Globalization: the classical cultural industry, rather than disappearing, has given way to media convergence and impure admixtures of the global with the classical or "national" cultural industry."[9] The World has long been in Hollywood and Hollywood has long been in the World. In the wake of the early successes of Hollywood studios, its industrial model spread world-wide. Long before the emergence of the Bollywoods, Nollywoods, and Tollywoods, there was Cinedia in Rio de Janeiro, Elphinstone Biograph in Calcutta; Taikatsu in Japan, and Studio Misr (dubbed "Hollywood on the Nile") in Cairo.

Contemporary Hollywood is also *in* the world in the sense of searching for cheap labor and exotic locations, with many of its films made partially or totally in the Global South. Here we can mention films like *Blood Diamond* (2006) shot in South Africa and Mozambique, *Babel* (2005) shot in Morocco, Japan, and Mexico, *The Constant Gardener* (2005) shot in Kenya, *Life of Pi* (2012) shot in India, *Mad Max* (2015) shot in Namibia, and *Beasts of No Nation* (2015) shot in Ghana. Hollywood's audience is transnational, in that for decades international rentals of Hollywood films have exceeded domestic rentals. And in narrative terms, Hollywood remakes acclaimed Asian horror films like *Dark Water* (2005) and *The Grudge* (2004), while Bollywood remakes Hollywood films (Ghajini, 2005, Zinda 2006) and so forth.

Courtney Brannon Donoghue, meanwhile, points to the move by some Hollywood conglomerates toward strategies of "flexible localization for the Global Film Market."[10] Thus we find Columbia Films' *Producciones Espanolas* based in Madrid, During an early phase, Sony Pictures Entertainment established Local Language Productions (LLPs) in key markets in Asia, Latin America and Europe, and more specifically in Hong Kong, Brazil, and Germany, leading for example "Sony do Brasil" and the Hong Kong-based production company Columbia Pictures Film Production Asia. Sony do Brazil produced local-language productions such as Carlos Diegues' *Tieta do Agreste* in 1996 and Bruno Barreto's *Four Days in September* in 1997. But these localized Hollywoodeanizations were not ultimately so successful, and Donoghue notes that Sony's history of local-language productions revealed "the adoption of slippery globalization discourses, messy strategies of localization, and contradictory corporate relations that characterize contemporary media industries and continue to challenge local coproduction efforts."[11]

Conversely, the World is in Hollywood, and this in multiple senses. Hollywood has long been a magnet for international talent, going back to immigrant pioneers like Carl Laemmle, Ernst Lubitsch, Rouben Mamoulien, followed by the exiles like Fritz Lang, Bill Wilder, and later by an international group including Ang Lee, John Woo, Jose Padilha, and the award-winning *tres amigos* from Mexico (Alejandro Gonzales Iñárritu, Guillhermo del Toro, and Alfonso Cuaron). The World is also in Hollywood in that its industry is based in an "immigrant country," resulting in a need to satisfy an audience whose origins could be traced to Europe, Africa, Asia and many other parts of the world continents. Echoing the common critique of Systems Theory but on another register, Eleftheria Thanouli points out that a unidrectional Core-Periphery model neglects not only the peripheral and the minor, but also the minor in Hollywood itself, in that Hollywood had to please an amalgamated immigrant population originating from widely differing cultures. At the same time, she argues for the existence of a "new global vernacular" where the aesthetic influences are multi-directional and not dependant on Hollywood. Citing *Pulp Fiction, City of God, Chungking Express*, and *Amelie*, she describes an aesthetic characterized by multiple protagonists, interwoven plot lines, digressive structures, and spasmodic montage.[12]

A basic ambivalence haunts all the "Wood" coinages, in the sense that they imply attraction and repulsion, intimacy and distance; the suffix itself places the "Wood" movement within the Hollywood paradigm, while also relaying a feeling of rivalry and supersession. The momentous phenomenon called Nollywood, for its part, took many observers by surprise but it should not have, given the cultural strengths and specific conditions of its home country of Nigeria. Along with its well-known drawbacks—deficient infrastructure, widespread corruption, political instability, Boko Haram terrorism, ethnic tensions, and a lack of movie theaters, Nigeria also has signal advantages: a wealth of material resources, a vibrant multi-culturality, high technical awareness (for example a 30% smart phone usage) and a well-educated population. In academic terms, as of 2017, the NCU (National University Commission) reports that Nigeria has 40 Federal Universities, 44 State Universities, and 68 accredited private universities. Nollywood, which is of course not the totality of Nigerian cinema, has by now become a major trend in cinema and one of the most prolific producers of feature films. Nollywood makes roughly three times as many features as Hollywood, but gains only roughly 1/40th of the profit.

This is not the place to discuss a complex movement that has already been well addressed by scholars such as Manthia Diawara, Awam Ampke, Karin Barber, Jonathon Haynes, Onookome Okome, Kenneth W. Harrow, Jean-Paul Colleyn, Jeffrey Geiger and others—except to say that it clearly calls for altered categories of analysis.[13] All of our three key terms—World, Transnational, Global—are both relevant to and inadequate to Nollywood. The usual left esthetic-political categories are also inadequate. Neither critical race theory, nor political auteurism, nor anti-colonial critique are quite sufficient to the task. Up through the 1990s, the African films most seen in the West were drawn from the Francophone corpus and films such as *Xala* and *Emitai* and *Chronicle of the Years of Embers*, films which often had an anti-colonial thrust, conveyed in stories with clear national-allegorical overtones. While the Francophone films, at least in the early phase, often foregrounded colonialism, in the Nollywood films the postcolonial situation forms only a distant backdrop. The situations portrayed in films such as Kingsley Ogoro's *Osuofia in London* are less *anti*-colonial or even *post*-colonial than *para*-colonial. The idea that the contemporary world was shaped by colonialism is simply assumed rather than foregrounded or dissected by the films.

Despite exceptions such as Jet Amata's films about slavery such as *The Amazing Grace* (2008) or the same director's film about oil-corporations in Nigeria (*Black

Gold: the Struggle for the Niger Delta), the films generally are political not in stressing grand historical themes or expressing political outrage but rather in addressing immediate topical concerns such as HIV Aids or political corruption. Nor can most of the films be called "national-allegorical," first because they are usually not allegorical at all, and secondly because they are simultaneously *infranational* (ethnic, regional, Yoruba, Igbo, Hausa), *national* (Nigerian), *diasporic*, and thus *supra-national*. The Nollywood films, or more accurately video-films, offer a strong contrast with the Francophone films on virtually every level. Rather than see the Francophone auteurs as models, the Nollywood directors have often dismissed the Francophone films as "embassy films," more appealing to international festival filmgoers than to African audiences. If the auteur reigns supreme in the Francophone cinema, as Manthia Diawara points out, it is stars and distributors who reign as sovereigns in Nollywood,[14]

Clear differences separate the two groups in terms of the forms and methods of production. While most of the Francophone films were financed at least in part by a France—the former literal metropole of the colonies, and the figurative metropole of film theory—invested in forming a pantheon of directors from the former French colonies, the Nollywood industry is African-owned and privately financed. While the Francophone films were largely made on celluloid, the Nollywood films are largely made in digital or video, edited on computers and copied onto cassettes and disks. While the Francophone films were seen in theaters at Festivals both in Francophone Africa and abroad, the Nollywood films are seen on VHS, VCD, and DVD and in extremely varied venues including in churches, stores, public parks as well as on-line or on TV at home. While the Francophone films were popular with Western festival audiences but rarely seen by Africans; the Nollywood films offered the converse phenomenon; popular among Africans, they were rarely seen at Western festivals. And while the Francophone films coveted the status of auteurist High Art, the Nollywood films have largely been genre films. Among other genres, Jonathon Haynes mentions: Family Films, Cultural Epic films, Crime Films, Vigilante Films, Religious Films, Village Films, Political Films, Melodoramas, Diaspora Films, and Campus films. Jonathon Haynes points to a kind of bourgeoisification of African cinema in films and TV series portraying: "yuppie women sharing a flat have contrasting personalities, romantic lives and different professions, all of them fashionable and many of typical of Saskia Sassen's global city of outsourced professionals."[15] What has been called the New Nollywood has also produced polished big-budget adaptations of novels meant for an upscale transnational audience, such as Biyi Bandele's 2013 adaptation of Chimananda Ngozi Adichie's celebrated novel *Half of a Yellow Sun*. Transational in funding (Nigerian and British), casting (African and European) and theme, the film concerns the Biafran Independence movement and the Civil War which raged from 1967 to 1970.

Nollywood is now itself thoroughly transnational and diasporic, linked to Nigerian immigrant communities in the U.S., the U.K., Europe, and to other parts of Africa, including in the form of co-productions with other African countries like

Tanzania, with films like *She's My Sister* (2007). Many of the films, such as Tony Abulu's *Crazy like a Fox*, are set in the United States, Britain, or in Western Europe. Although they display transnational themes, as Jonathon Haynes points out, they "show a lack of interest in the foreign as such.[16] Although the films set in the U.S. often foreground what Haynes calls "alienation/hardship" in sequences of the kind that in standard immigration films would have usually formed a prelude to hard-won success, they do not necessarily buy into any exceptionalist American Dream narrative. In fact, in historical terms, the downside of success as immigrants in America is its devastating emigrant corollary—the tragic brain-drain out of Africa itself. In these films, the U.S. is thus less an ultimate telos than one possible terminus, often a temporary one, in a broader search for survival or success or merely exilic relief from economic scarcity or political oppression. And since African intellectuals and artists would tend to see slavery as a transnational undertaking, they rarely directly ponder the ironies of the fact that Africans—the so-called neo-African Americas—are immigrating to the homelands of slavery and segregation (in the U.S.) or of colonial rule (in the U.K.).

Nollywood, despite its name, is not really modelled on Hollywood, and to the extent it is so modelled it has to do with a preference for popular genres, the marketing of glamour, and the promotion of stars. But the Nollywood system is not modeled on Hollywood in terms of production methods and modes of distribution. Rather, it is based on cheap and quick productions aimed at a rapid return on investments, especially since the films are very likely to be pirated fairly early on. Alessandro Jedlowski speaks of "rhizomatic" production arrangements, and attributes the Nollywood Video-boom to two key factors: "the informality of the Nigerian economy and the adoption of digital technologies."[17] As perhaps the first major film industry to be founded *after* the advent of the Internet, Nollywood is a "digitally native" cinema. At the same time, as Haynes points out, the films are massively influenced by television, watched on television, and aesthetically tailored for the small screen.[18]

In thematic terms, meanwhile, many of the films are concerned above all with what Manthia Diawara describes as "physical and psychological mobility in the face of current dislocation and Afro-pessimism.[19] Nollywood offers a version of what John and Jean Comaroff call "Afromodernity," which is less a "response to European modernity, or a creature derived from it" than a sui generis entity that is "actively forged … from endogenous and exogenous elements of a variety of sorts."[20] Brian Larkin, meanwhile, points to the virtual impossibility of imitating Hollywood "production values," in a context where "cheap tape recorders, old televisions, blurred videos [result in a situation of] the copy of a copy of a copy [as] the material distortions endemic to the reproduction of media goods in situations of poverty and illegality."[21] Since the everyday experience of a Hollywood film is a degraded and muddy copy of a copy, reminiscent of Hito Steyerl's "poor image" then the advantages posed by superior equipment and production processes are devalued."[22]

Unlike minoritarian films in the U.S., and elsewhere, the Nollywood films are also not terribly concerned with presenting a "positive image" of Africa and

Africans; rather, they present Africans in all their dappled heterogeneity, "warts and all," as people who are sometimes magnanimous and generous, and sometimes petty and cruel, a people capable both of nobility and of 419 fraud schemes, bigamy, and green-card marriages. (In short, Africans—surprise!—resemble people everywhere.) But this lack of concern with beatific positivity in a way signals a boundless self-confidence, suggesting the limitations of a "positive image/negative stereotype" approach which can be overly protective, somehow traumatized by an internalized Western gaze. The 1950s–1960s strategy of creating such heroic "raisin-in-the-rice" black characters placed a different kind of "burden of race"— the burden of a humanly impossible perfection. Perhaps because Africa is a continent secure in its Africanness—the tiger does not doubt its tigritude, as Wole Soyinke suggested—and because European imperialism reached less deeply into the heartland and psyche of Africa, the films avoid the Sidney Poitier syndrome of a defensive, prophylactic, and ultimately unattainable idealization.[23]

Ironically, dominant ethnicities and nations and ethnicities seem to worry less about their image. Hollywood constantly produces negative images of white Americans as prostitutes, drug addicts, freaks, and mass-murderers, without worrying about the damage to the image and psyche of the dominant group. Mafia-themed films and TV series are not concerned with promoting a "positive image" of Italian-American gangsters. Contemporary American "reality shows" do not mind showing white housewives as materialist, vulgar, catty, spoiled, and foul-mouthed. Inside the stage coach (or now gated community) of white privilege and hegemony, as Tom Engelhardt pointed out long ago in relation to the frontier Western, it matters little if the white characters are drunks, cowards, and snake-oil salesmen; what is important is that the civilizing "us" remain always definitionally superior to the war-whooping savages raining down arrows on the wagon, and even more important that "we" remain the focal point of identification.[24]

In political terms, as Haynes points out, Nollywood films do not occupy a single position; rather, they form a constellation of discourses; "they are knowing about their society, sometimes angry, sometimes complicit."[25] On the one hand, the films often promote consumerism, and on the other, they express moral outrage at corruption and the abuse of power. Although the Nollywood films have been accused of producing a new kind of "Tarzanism," critics such as Diawara argue that Nollywood should be saluted for telling African stories that everyone can identify with."[26] On some level their very technical imperfections remind us of Third Cinema calls for an "imperfect cinema" and an "aesthetics of garbage" that eschewed Hollywood production values, but here everything is done in a different and less militant spirit. While usually not explicitly anti-colonial or even critically postcolonial, the films at least have the virtue of resonating with the desires and curiosities of African and Afro-diasporic audiences. "By stealing from Hollywood the star system, the dress style, the music, by remaking Western genre films, and by appropriating the digital video camera as an African storytelling instrument," Nollywood is, as Diawara puts it, "a copy of a copy that has become original through the embrace of its spectators."[27]

24
GLOBALIZATION, POLITICAL ECONOMY, AND THE MEDIA

The final major keyword in this book's analytical arsenal is "global," already familiar from our discussions of globalization. Some film analysts such as Roy Stafford speak of "global film," and others speak of the "global art film." The title of an important volume co-edited by Rosalind Galt and Karl Schoonover, for example, is *Global Art Cinema*.[1] For Roy Stafford, the term serves purposes similar to those served by "transnational" and "World," In general, the word "global" is less likely to appear in studies of film than in the context of television and media studies. In television studies, for example, a major area of study is the "global" phenomenon of the soap opera/telenovelas found in countries as diverse as Brazil, Mexico, Lebanon, Turkey, and India, and often exported widely beyond their "home" countries. The term "global" is also less used in relation to World Literature and World Cinema, although "global" is occasionally wheeled in as a synonym for "world"; Damrosch, for example, uses both words in combination by referring to "global world literature."

In his very comprehensive *The Global Film Book*, Stafford cites *Life of Pi* as an example of globality in that it adapts a Canadian novel by a novelist (Yann Martel) born in Spain to Quebecois parents, and is directed by a Taiwanese director trained in the U.S. who has made films in the U.K., China, and Taiwan, while deploying a Canadian composer, a Chilean cinematographer, and Indian and British actors, all as part of a Hollywood movie.[2] Stafford also emphasizes new modes of distribution, such as "tentpole releases" where films are released more or less simultaneously across thousands of screens worldwide, and where major Indian distributors release big-budget Hindi and Tamil films in 18 territories on the same day.[3] Stafford also points out that filmmakers like Mira Nair, Deepa Mehta, and Shirin Neshat make films about their birth-cultures from a North American base.

In the literary field, meanwhile, Adam Kirsch speaks of the "global novel," as exemplified by Orhan Pauk's *Snow*, Haruki Murakami's *1Q84*, Roberto Bolano's

2666, Ngozi Adichie's *Americanah*; Mohsin's *The Reluctant Fundamentalist*; Margaret Atwood's *Oryx*; and Michael Houellebecq's *The Possibility of an Island*.[4] Much as the "World" evokes capitalized Germanic abstraction and a fully constituted object, the word "global" calls up another constituted object, i.e. the "globe." We are reminded of the spinning-globe logos of Hollywood studios like Universal and RKO, later picked up by TV World News programs which broadcast the idea of a Herculean globe-grabbing imperial mission. Whereas "World" à la Damrosch evokes a comprehensible organic whole, the graspable totality of a corpus, "global" evokes a mobile profusion of intersectional processes and trends. "Global media" evokes a wide spectrum of communication media ranging from print journalism to radio, television, and the Internet. The cinema is sometimes included in that media spectrum and sometimes positioned as if apart from the media in general, as when academic departments name themselves departments of "film *and* media studies." In most cases, global media studies tends not to perform textual or intertextual analyses; in fact, it tends not to plumb the depths of texts at all, preferring instead to develop verifiable, indeed quantifiable, hypotheses and generalizations about perceptible trends. Unlike World Literature and World Cinema, global media studies is less preoccupied with qualitative evaluation than with data-based quantitative analysis.

Each of our key terms implies a distinct temporal scope. Since World Literature revolves around a corpus of written texts, it is logically circumscribed by the limits of written history and literature and the availability of writing. The "global," in contrast, implies relative contemporaneity in a globalized setting. One might argue, again, about exactly when that globalization began. In his essay "Periodizing Globalization: Histories of Globalization," Jan Nederveen Pieterse contests the common view of globalization as recent by citing its many antecedents. Moving backward in time *Memento*-style from neo-liberal globalization (in his analysis, from 1980 to 2000) to capitalist modernity to Columbus, back to European capitalism to the 13th century as traced by Braudel, to the Greco-Roman Empires. These alternative periodizations, for Pieterse, "break the spell of Eurocentrism."[5] The key dates, Pieterse explains, also vary with the disciplines invoked, the unit of analysis chosen, and the questions being asked. In a suggestive but probably unverifiable claim, Pieterse hypothesizes that disciplines like Economics, Political Science, Cultural Studies and Communication Studies operate in a short time-frame that begins in 1970; that sociology offers a medium time-frame going back to a modernity starting around 1800; that political economy goes three centuries farther back to 1500 and the world market; while history, anthropology, and archeology pursue a much longer *durée* reaching as far back as 3000 BC.

Pieterse distinguishes between an early wave of "global*ization* studies" and a later wave of "global studies." While "globalization studies" has a constituted object of study—globalization itself– "global studies" is dedicated to creating *new* "domains, approaches, or subjects and sensibilities that did not exist or were not recognized at the time when the disciplines took shape, largely in the 19th century."[6] These new objects form the purview of the various transdisciplinary "studies": border studies, queer studies, feminist studies, critical law studies, critical race studies, migration studies, and all their combinatory parameters (e.g. the "minor cosmopolitanisms" program at the University of Potsdam). Although these "studies" programs are still "on probation" in the eyes of some elders from the academic establishment and sometimes dismissed as dilettante fads, they also form the key locus of emerging energies, concepts, and novel interfaces across disciplines, communities, and discourses. For Pieterse, these trends range across a transdisciplinary spectrum and are more likely to be more multicentric, polyperspectival, and multi-scalar—and I would add more intersectional—in outlook than the traditional disciplines. At the same time, Pieterse is cognizant of the challenges and pitfalls within these broadly conceived "studies" in that they might end up encouraging ahistorical analyses, simplistic assumptions, sweeping generalizations, and linear thinking.

A key question confronting Global Studies is which schools of economic theory—Marxism, Keynesianism, Take-off Theory, Systems Theory—can best illuminate global media and globalization. Many critics argue that financial globalization leads to an atmosphere of constant crisis due to its creation of bubbles—the Internet bubble of 2000, or the housing "suprime" bubble of 2008—arising from the gambler-like addiction to speculation and quick profits for too-big-to-fail banks and corporations that sit on their money rather than hand it over to workers. The promised "trickle-down" is endlessly deferred as workers are downsized and Uberized, as pensions dwindle or disappear, and as everyone is thrown on the tender mercies of the market in an era of shredded safety nets, most notably in the U.S., but also in weakened welfare states even in Western Europe.

A political economy approach stresses the corporate domination of the media, the commodification of media forms, the role of government support and interventions, and the exercise of economic and social power. While classical Marxism stressed economy over culture, infrastructure over superstructure, post-Marxism tends to stress the mutual imbrication and interaction of culture and economy; as French Culture Minister Jack Lang put it in a memorable phrase: "*Economie et Culture: meme combat.*" For a left rooted in systems theory and political economy or in Frankfurt School Critical Theory, the word "transnational" is likely to evoke a late stage of capitalism and its corollaries such as transnational corporations and financial capitalism. The move to transnational production, a leftist film scholar might point out, meanwhile, operates in tandem with "competiveness" (aka the "race to the bottom") in terms of the search for cheap labor, embodied in differential pay scales for Westerns and non-Westerners, even in putatively anticolonial films like *Gandhi*, a financial unevenness critically foregrounded in relation to Spanish filmmakers and Bolivian Quechua workers in Iciar Bolain's *Even the Rain*.

In the long view, the political economy-based analyses of Globalization and Global culture build not only on Marx but also on the work of Braudel and the Annales School idea of a world economy as well as on later dependency/world-systems theory, which posits, as we have seen, an empowered Western "Core" and a disempowered non-Western "Periphery. Political economy, in the long run, must be understood, again, in relation to the "long 1492," which, as we saw earlier, was a foundational event for what later came to be called "globalization." Deborah Danowski and Eduardo Viveiros de Castro, put it with brutal clarity:

> The genocide of Amerindian peoples—for them the end of the world—was for Europeans the beginning of the modern world: without the dispossession of America, Europe would have been nothing more than the very back of the backyard of Eurasia, the continent which sheltered, during the so-called "Middle Ages," civilizations such as Byzantium, China, India, the Arab World, which were immensely richer than European civilization). Without the plundering of the Americas, there would be no capitalism, nor, later, the industrial revolution, nor even, perhaps, the Anthropocene.[7]

Peter Linebaugh, meanwhile. articulates the link between the plundering of the Americas and the contemporary attempts to restore the commons. The April 2010 publication of "the Universal Declaration of the Rights of Mother Earth by the World People's Conference on Climate Change" was issued from Cochabamba, Bolivia, the site, as we saw with *Even the Rain*, of the dramatic defeat of attempts to privatize water by the Aymara and Quechua peoples, those:

> … whose labors at the silver mountain of Potosi produced the silver of the monetary system at the birth of capitalism, basically turning the mountain of silver into a monumental genocidal coffin. What was ripped out of the earth became fetishized tokens organizing the global division of labor and the exploitation and oppression of people. People with such a history know what it means to declare 'we are all part of Mother Earth, an indivisible, living community of interrelated and interdependent beings with a common destiny.'[8]

The question of intellectual property rights provides a vivid example of the historical "morphing" that takes us from Columbus and the Conquest to the CEO-captains of contemporary corporations and media conglomerates. The word "patents," for example, referred in 16th-century Europe to the official royal letters (*litterae patents*) by which sovereigns conferred privileges, rights, and land titles on various members of the nobility, for example, the *capitanias* in Brazil granted by the Portuguese king. In the "Age of Discovery," these "letters" became associated with the literal conquest of territory; five hundred years later, they are associated with transnational corporations' updated version of the conquest of economic rights in the Global South, where forest biodiversity becomes much linked to the cultural knowledges of indigenous peoples as an object of transnational commercial desire. As Djelal Kadir points out, the letter authorizing Columbus's conquests, conceded on April 17, 1492, by Fernando and Isabel was "the literal prototype," the paradigm, the *locus classicus* of its genre. Columbus possessed, as it were, the "patent of patents and the license to appropriate the land and material wealth of the New World."[9] Five centuries after the Conquest, the World Trade Organization rules concerning copyrights constitute reformatted, secular versions of the papal bulls and regal edicts that legalized the liquidation of the indigenous commons. For Vandana Shiva, "The "freedom of action which transnational corporations demand today is the same freedom of action that European colonies demanded, after 1492, as a natural right over the territory and riches of non-European people."[10] Indeed, the proprietary ideology and actions of the economic globalizers in the name of "intellectual property rights" can be seen as a kind of enclosure or profitable "locking in" of all the technological and material advantages that accrued over centuries to the latter-day heirs of the conquerors of the "New World."

Over the centuries, natural resources materials thought to be an integral part of the natural "commons" have been "poached on" by corporations. Since corporations can package H2O in fancy bottles, decorated with simulacra evoking the natural sublime, and sell it at exorbitant prices and to great environmental cost, a number of multinational corporations are eager to privatize the world's water supply. As Peter Linebaugh argues in *The Magna Carta Manifesto*, the key profit-generating material has changed over time: the "Oil" of the 17th century was Wood (e.g. Brazil-wood or "pau Brasil" sent to France), the Oil of the 20th century was Oil itself. and the Oil of the 21st century might become Water. As Sean Cubitt points out, the "commodification of water has become a major biopolitical tool in enforcing the regime of the corporate cyborg."[11] Struggles over the aquatic commons are taking place around the world. Alan Snitow and Deborah Kaufman's film *Thirst* (2003), in this sense, follows the struggles over privatization in three sites—India's Rajasthan desert area; Stockton, California; and Cochabamba, Bolivia—where the communities try, with diverse degrees of success, to reverse the privatization of their formerly public water systems. At the premiere screening of the film, the directors blind-tested spectators to rank three kinds of unlabeled water, two of them name brands and one the local New York tap water (popularly known to the literati as *L'Eau Bloombergien*"). Without the usual packaging and sublime imagery, the majority of the guests chose the tap water as superior!

The ways that contemporary globalization was shaped by 1492 and the proto-globalization of the Conquest is the subject of Iciar Bollain's feature film *Even the Rain* (2010). On one level, the film demonstrates the relevance of our key terms in the sense that the film qualifies simultaneously as: 1) "World Cinema" in terms of its authorial character, known actors, and art film status, and qualifies as 2) "global" insofar as its very theme is globalization, and qualifies as 3) "transnational," finally, not only in terms of its transnational funding, its transnational filmmaking team, its translingualism (Spanish, English, Quechua) and its multiple diegetic locations; and finally, as an example of Hjort's "strongly marked transnational," it is at the same time a reflexive examination of the aporias of globalization and transnationality itself. On another level, then, the film addresses the issue of managing the commons for individual and collective benefit, and in this case the literal aquatic commons linked to the basic human/animal need for water to survive.

Bringing the 16th-century debates about Columbus and the Conquista into the present, the film accompanies a Spanish crew in Bolivia as they shoot what they see as a highly critical anti-colonialist film about Columbus' first voyage, one that will underscore Spanish exploitation and indigenous rebellion. The film connects past and present through a local activist named Daniel, who plays the role of the Taino rebel leader Hatuey in the film-within-the-film, but who in "real life" leads demonstrations against the corporations that would privatize everything, "even the rain." By counterpointing the two historical moments, 1) that of Columbus and the Conquest, and 2) that of the "Water Wars in Bolivia," the film stresses their transhistorical circularities of extractive oppression. Columbus' dispossession of the Tainos is juxtaposed with the multinationals' exploitation of the Quechua. While the conquistadores lusted after gold; contemporary multinational corporations crave water; only the material to be extracted from the natural commons has changed.

Even the Rain relationalizes a tripartite exploitation: the Conquistadores' lust for gold, the multinationals' thirst for raw materials, and, to a lesser degree, the "progressive" filmmakers' need for a globalized cheap labor as part of a "race to the bottom," in both senses of the word "race." One sequence exposes the cynical premises of the racialized division of global labor. Speaking on his cellphone, the producer gleefully reports to the American "money people" that in financial terms the production is doing "fucking great," since the local technicians and extras are content with just a few dollars a day. He is taken aback to discover that Daniel/Hatuey has overheard and understood the conversation thanks to the English he learned while working as a construction worker in California. Sarcastically echoing the producer's own words, Daniel tells him: "Fucking great, man … I know this story [of exploitation]," and walks off the set. The producer profits from globalization, but he must also confront Bolivian workers/extras whose global diasporization has equipped them with the cultural/ linguistic capital needed to critically resist globalization. Within globalization, we find alter-globalization, and within transnational corporations, we find transnational activism.

While classical Marxism is anticapitalist yet ultimately productivist, the Andean movements portrayed in *Even the Rain* are often more radically anticapitalist in their assertion that the commons of "mother earth" should not be commodified. The culturally instilled refusal of commodification was one force-idea that helped energize the Bolivian movement and enabled it to prevent the privatization of water, as the first indigenous president, Evo Morales, proclaimed that water must be free and cannot be run by private business. Activists speak of communal forms of politics and of what Arturo Escobar calls "the political activation of relational ontologies." In Escobar's account, the activists call for (1) substantive rather than formal democracy, (2) "biocentric" sustainable development, and (3) interculturality in polyethnic societies. The goal is to move beyond capitalism, liberalism, statism, monoculturalism, productivism, Puritanism, and the ideology of "growth."[12]

In the realm of mass culture, the mediatic corollary of Dependency Theory was the concept of "media imperialism" advanced by figures like Ariel Dorfman, Armand Mattelart, and Herbert Schiller, who argued that the negative dialectics of Northern wealth shaping Southern poverty also held true in the domain of the media. Media imperialism scholars focused attention on infrastructures, structures of ownership, and regulation as fostering unequal power relations in the realm of the media and mass culture, which tended to favor the mediatic giants of the Global North. The U.S. and Western Europe, in this view, were hegemonic in the spheres of film production/distribution, television, advertising, news journalism and so forth. In the 1980s and 1990s, however, scholars on the left called for a more subtle analysis which allowed for the contradictory effects of globalization. An emphasis on "cultural imperialism," as Toby Miller and Marwan Kraidy point out, gave way to a more nuanced "cultural globalization."[13]

In terms of Global Media Studies, the political economy approach developed by Toby Miller, Nitin Govil, John McMurria, Ting Wang, and Richard Maxwell in their indispensable *Global Hollywood 2* focuses on a global economy massively shaped by a globalization which links productivity, exploitation, and social control while advancing and carrying out the "new international division of cultural labor."[14] Emphasizing political economy and cultural policy, the authors emphasize the global infrastructure of Hollywood hegemony which operates through corporate and state domination and the U.S. government's role in capital accumulation within the film industry. Although they express a desire to interrelate structures of the economy with structures of meaning, they emphasize the former, perhaps as a corrective to what they see as the dominant textualist trend within "screen studies."

Veering sharply away from the cultural studies emphasis on consumption, and away from what the authors somewhat overstatedly see as cinema studies' exclusive preoccupation with texts, the authors stress the stubbornly intractable realities of production and distribution. The global cinematic system, the authors point out, is indeed on some levels a zero-sum game; Hollywood's gains *are* in fact the world's losses, especially in terms of the unequal allotment of physical space and screens in the world's cineplexes and movie-theaters. The authors demonstrate what has become a truism among media intellectuals in many nations of the Global South, to wit that the problem lies less in production—films are in fact being produced in quantity—than in distribution and exhibition, since the produced films are not shown, or shown only briefly, or shown but not on television. With bleakly irrefutable statistics at the ready, the authors point out that Hollywood gobbles up almost the quas-totality of global box office, that the U.S market is generally closed to non-American films, that the European share has declined precipitously, and that U.S. companies own a large proportion of the films seen around the world and the cineplexes where the films are screened.

Unlike most analysts of the cinema, the authors also address the impact of global corporate control on the environment, as well as on actually existing workers such as secretaries, janitors, accountants, drivers, and editors. As for the geo-politics of globalization, they take Henry Kissinger at his word when he claimed that globalization is just "another name for the dominant role of the United States."[15] Despite the "irrational exuberance" (Greenspan) about the democratizing potentialities of the Internet, meanwhile, the digital era has not destroyed Western hegemony in the cinema, since Hollywood retains its tentacular grip on mediatic exchange and discourse. One telling index of this global Americanization is that even Global South Airlines tend to program Hollywood blockbusters, dramas, and comedies as their idea of "universal fare," despite having the most multi-colored and multi-faith "captive audience" one can imagine.[16] Another index is the ethno-provinciality of American cable television; while French cable offers a wide array of international cinema offerings, U.S. cable TV offers an endless diet of the usual conventional American cinematic fare, with rarely a Global South, or even a European auteur film, in sight.

At the same time, the authors deconstruct the tarnished myths of Hollywood and American "superiority." Hollywood's global recognition as a brand, they point out, may have derived less from "American ingenuity" or hard-wired "universal appeal"—fantasies once championed *ad nauseam* by industry lobbyists such as the late Jack Valenti—than a result of unfair business practices, now amplified by the WTO and its anti-democratic policies. A political economy approach to Global Hollywood uncovers ways that private industry benefits from public support and monies, so that the "free market" comes to signify a highly protected North American "home market." Unfortunately, *Global Hollywood 2* paints a rather caricatural portrait of a supposedly apolitical "screen studies," a view which ignores the accomplishments of an ambiguously progressive field, or more accurately, fields, in calling attention to issues of race, class, gender, sexuality, and empire, as well as opening up the canon to Third World, Marxist, feminist, indigenous, and ecological films. On the other hand, the book does at least offer a salutary rebuff to a politically acquiescent textualism and a romantic auteurism, and a strong reminder that cultural studies and screen studies, at the risk of political irrelevance, need to address not only aesthetics and consumption but also industrial production, political economy, and cultural policy.[17]

In economic terms, the new "majors" are no longer Hollywood studios per se but rather the Big Tech corporations that both collaborate with and compete with Hollywood. Netflix, for example, strengthens Hollywood by paying it billions of dollars for the rights to stream its films and TV shows, but undermines it in other ways. With the decline of American economic power and the "rise of the Rest," the U.S., and "Hollywood" as its metonym, are no longer the unquestioned Hobbesian sovereigns that provoke awe, no longer the impregnable fortress of mediatic power. Even the corporate world has become more diversified and multi-centered. Between 1990 and 2010, the proportion of the 500 largest corporations from the Global South went from 5% to 17% and might reach 45% by 2025.[18] At the same time, one finds corporations like Amazon that distribute (and sometimes produce) both films and books. Amazon, Netflix, Hulu and iTunes can acquire film projects from producers and exhibit them outside the usual chains of movie theaters. Netflix, for example, has paid Hollywood billions of dollars for the rights to stream its films and TV shows, but competes with it in other ways. With the 2017 Oscar nominations, Amazon became the first streaming service to earn an Academy Award nomination for Best Picture.

A June 2, 2016 *New York Times* article called attention to the global panic provoked by the burgeoning power of the "Frightful Five," i.e. the American new-technology companies (Apple, Amazon, Facebook, Microsoft, and Alphabet) that are slouching toward global hegemony in ways that potentially transform the audio-visual media and the experience of cinema. Thus Facebook co-opts the news media (and allows an invasion of Russian bots); You-Tube and Netflix take over television and film production and distribution; while devices like the smartphone, controlled by Apple and Google, become major platforms for entertainment. The tensions between traditional forms of exhibition and the new video-on-demand streaming model came to a head at the 70th annual Cannes Film Festival in 2017, when Netflix, which now invests billions of dollars in film production, decided that two of their productions in the competition, the South Korean film *Okja*, and the U.S.-American film *The Meyerowitz Stories*, would be launched on their platform and not through the classical movie theater route. (Swimming against the current, Sofia Coppola and Christopher Nolan declared their allegiance to classical forms of exhibition.) As a consequence, the Festival Committee devised a new rule—that films chosen for the competition would have to be first screened in the traditional theatrical manner of exhibition.

Even with the decline of American economic power and the "rise of the Rest," U.S. hegemony and that of neo-liberal ideologies persist. In France, China, India and in much of the world, the Americanness of these media conglomerates is seen as a source of fear rather than comfort. To rephrase the old adage one might make the warning "beware of transnational corporations bearing gifts." In this analogy, the gift bearers are the Global Greeks of the North, and the Trojans the Turks of the Global South, whose "free" offerings are means of seductive entrapment. In an oft-repeated pattern, the radical hopes catalyzed by new technologies initially praised as egalitarian and decentralized give way to financial concentration and the undermining of Net Neutrality, leading to disenchantment and ideological "buyer's remorse."

25

AQUATIC TROPOLOGIES

Over the last few decades, as we noted earlier, cultural studies and media studies have been "flooded," by aquatic metaphors. Globalization, for example, is sometimes seen as a calm and beneficent rippling sea of progressive movement, and at other times as an overwhelming tsunami, a "juggernaut, a force, a process, as asymptote" with unpredictable effects.[1] In some cases these aquatic metaphors come from the very summits of geo-political power. In his 2017 speech at the Davos World Economic Forum, Chinese president (for life) Xi Jinping compared the global economy to a "vast and inescapable Ocean," in which China had the "courage to swim," while those "afraid to brace the storm" would "sooner or later get drowned." Despite "whirlpools and choppy waves," China's strategic choice, he added, was to "learn to swim" and not cut off "the flow of capital."

In media discourse, the special fondness for metaphors of "flow" has roots in the ancient past of "deep time." For John Durham Peters, the ocean can be seen as "the medium of all media, the fountain from which all life on earth emerged."[2] The ocean even has its artists. Vilem Flusser saw vampire squids as self-destructively orgiastic Georges Bataille-like artists whose polymorphous perversity led to their eating themselves and each other.[3] Squids' artistic equipment consists of squirting and shaping liquid clouds of ink, a ready point of identification, Peters adds mischievously, for writer-theorists.[4] In media studies, aquatic tropes emerged in relation to electronic media, in relation to the flow of electricity through wires. Media and literary critic Raymond Williams proposed the concept of "flow" already in the early 1970s to refer to the streams of televisual content over the course of the viewing day, thus switching attention from discrete individual texts and particular programs to flow as "the defining characteristic of broadcasting, simultaneously as a technology and as a cultural form."[5] Henry Jenkins, decades later, speaks of the "flow" of content across multiple media platforms, the cooperation between multiple media industries, and the migratory behavior of media audiences ..."[6] Other analysts expanded the trope to apply to the globalized world in general, with its cross-border flows of energy, raw materials, labor, money, and information. Arjun Appadurai's 1990 essay "Disjuncture and Difference in the Global Economy," meanwhile, offered an elaborate theory of the mediation of global flows as channeled through ethnoscapes, financescapes, mediascapes, ideoscapes, and technoscapes, concepts which became enormously influential in a wide range of fields. In contrast with the "Worlds" of the World Arts, which evoke the artistic poesis of "worlding" that fabricates imaginary worlds, and the stabilization of literature and cinema into a relatively stable canon of works, "flow" evokes incessant process, change, and adaptation.

Everyday netizens employ aquatic tropologies when they speak of "internauts" who "surf the net" and ride on "digital waves" while "navigating" floods of information and using "immersive media." in UNESCO fora, meanwhile, the Global North globalizers speak of the "free *flow* of information," while representatives of the Global South argued that "free flow" was actually not free and that "free trade" automatically favored the Global North. The globalized world of commerce, for its part, depends on the "flow" of credit. Neo-liberal rhetoric defends "trickle-down" (or for its critics "tinkle-down") economics and a supply side economics that will "lift all boats," or for the critics "float all yachts." For Ulf Hannerz, flow metaphors have become a transdisciplinary norm, a "way of referring to things not staying in their places, to mobility and expansion of many kinds, to globalization along many dimensions."[7] When applied to global media, flow metaphors have been criticized as covertly regressive in eliding the nation-state and corporate dams, blockages, and floodgates that regulate the flow of people and cultural products. Discernable patterns of domination and impact the "fluidities" even of a multipolar world; the same hegemony that unifies the world through global networks of circulation of cultural goods and information also distributes those circulating goods according to hierarchal structures of power, even if those structures are disguised and dispersed. Liquid metaphors, in this sense, subtly idealize the fluid yet destructive practices of financial capitalism while prematurely assuming the end of the nation-state as a key agent in the regulation of flow.

"Flow" per se, then, is not necessarily progressive; Wall Street bankers also speak of "capital flows" and "liquid assets." Wall Street's critics, meanwhile, call up the monsters of the Deep, calling financial capital a "Vampire Squid." As an answer to neo-liberal metaphorics, Kathleen Newman injects Mary Louise Pratt's notion of "contact zones" into the discourse of transnational media exchange—a concept designating geographical and ethnographic spaces of cultural encounter—and made a suggestive call for film studies, asking:

> What would happen if we were to consider the geopolitical scales of cinematic exchange to operate as contact zones? What, for film studies as a discipline, would be these points of contact or interaction that occur simultaneously on multiple scales?[8]

The key questions about flow, in this sense, have to do with volume, directionality, and power differentials. Cultural flows, as Inderpal Grewal and Caren Kaplan suggest, are designed to move from the West to the Rest."[9] In terms of volume, flow can come in drips and drops or in the form of a flood or tsunami. Flow metaphors risk downplaying the unevenness and differential velocities of flow, evidenced in the stark contrast between the easy flows of currency as opposed to the blocked passages encountered by bodies of color in the form of refugees, migrants, and undocumented workers. By failing to distinguish between kinds of flow, the flow metaphor sometimes naturalizes certain hegemonic forces within capitalist globalization. Walter Benjamin, interestingly, anticipated this concern with scales and direction of flow decades earlier through a metaphorics of flows inflected by power differentials in his trope of river "power stations." "Intellectual currents," he noted, "can generate a sufficient head of water for the critic to install his power station on them." In the case of Surrealism, for Benjamin, the "gradient," was produced by the "difference in intellectual level between France and Germany."[10]

Another aquatic trope explores the historical reality and the concept of piracy. In *Shadow Economies of Cinema*, Ramon Labato identifies six conceptualizations of piracy, ranging from the sinister to the positive: 1) the MPAA view of piracy as unambiguously as a form of theft; 2) the informal free enterprise view of video equipment vendors who see piracy as enabling a horizontal economy which benefits, for example, the manufacturer/vendors of Nigeria; 3) the anti-corporate view of privacy as an issue of free speech in the support of the fair-use creativity of scholars, you-tubers, film critics, and media-makers; 4) a pro-authorship position that favors the use of public domain materials for the ends of art and that wants to have creators have a fair share of profits; 5) the anti-Hollywoodean view that favors the resistance of the digital creative commons over against corporate abuse of copyright; and 6) an anarchist view that echoes Proudhon's radical claim that "property is theft"; and 7) the view that favors "pirate modernity" that creates alternative routes of knowledge and productivity.[11]

Shekhar Seshpande and Meta Mazaj note the positive impact of piracy on artistic creation in that piracy is "an act of dissemination and desire" that has enabled filmmakers to be inspired by "films of world cinema that were accessible only through pirate channels."[12] Alongside such analysts, Bhaskar Sarkar has applauded piracy as a metaphor for water-borne mischief, in a version of the "piratical" which challenges "hegemonic sovereignties and binding legalities."[13] The *littorum*, the confusion of land and sea becomes for Sarkar the site of "fluid connections, risky undertakings, and deracinated communities." Sarkar reconfigures a practice regarded by Hollywood studios and its lawyers as illicit and a venal sin against intellectual property– to wit media piracy—as a positive antidote to the rise of massive media conglomerates and the global standardization of platforms and formats. Reminding us of the progressive role of "pirated" publications in the dissemination of revolutionary ideas during the Enlightenment, Sarkar proposes a "pedagogy of the piratical" that calls for Barbary pirate-like raids on the open seas of film distribution and exhibition. Of course, the politics of piracy depend on who is committing the piracy, whether one has in mind Sir Francis Drake, the Somali pirates, impoverished cinephiles, "content" creators who risk losing royalties, or Hollywood moguls trying to "enclose" and patent the cultural commons in the name of profit. Sarkar calls for rebooting, rewiring, recycling, remediating, and rerouting—here we find echoes of Situationist "detournement" or the highjacking of media products in ways that thwart official and corporate goals of opportunistic censorship and maximum profit. (In a delicious irony, in May 2017 *Pirates of the Caribbean* was itself pirated!)[14]

Transnational cinema, Bhaskar argues, cannot be studied in isolation from "protocol-circumventing devices, chat-room trolls and 149 scammers, micro SD cards loaded with stolen media and rambunctious video films made in the hinterlands of India."[15] In this funky basement form of "transnationalism from below" we find "VCDs of Greek art films subtitled in Russian, dubbed in Mandarin, and sold at the back of a Beijing store." For Sarkar, the prevalence of piracy in the Global South derives not from the thieving propensity of dark-skinned "natives" but simply from the brute economic fact of differential cost between Global North and Global South; in comparative terms, a DVD of a Hollywood Blockbuster costs the equivalent of $663. It is in this context that Sarkar scores the hypocrisies of some left defenders of the digital commons such as Lawrence Lessig who draw a quasi-colonial binary between good "respectable" Western-style forms of piracy with its creative modalities of collage and remix, versus the disreputable "bad" forms of piracy, seen as the outright theft of intellectual property. It is no accident, Sarkar points out, that the good creative kinds of piracy, for Lessig, are those practiced by the privileged digerati of the Global North, while the bad non-creative "colonial mimicry" kinds are those practiced by the relatively impoverished netizens of the Global South.

The metaphorics of the directionality of flow have everything to do with the unequal relations between the North and the South. Do power and ideas flow from the empowered nations to the periphery, or are there reverse or even contradictory currents like those of the Bhosphorus? It is because of the multidirectional and contradictory nature of flows that analysts speak of "contradictory currents" and "counter-flows." In the televisual realm, the North-South flows are being partially rerouted and at times even reversed. Mexico (Televisa) and Brazil (Globo) have become leading exporters of television drama. Many telenovelas mix national stories—e.g. the Brazilian *O Clone* counterpointed scenes and characters in Brazil and Morocco, while *Caminho das Indias* (2009), in a kind of BRICS romance involving the five "emerging economies" of Brazil, Russia, India, China, and South Africa, develops a melodramatic cross-border relationship involving Raj, an Indian executive who falls in love with a Brazilian woman, and a young middle-class woman who has a relationship with a well-educated Dalit, in an India which seems to be exclusively Hindu. Meanwhile, Indian, Japanese, Philippine and Taiwanese film producers now compete with Disney. Giving voice to the challenges to the somewhat binaristic and defeatist "media imperialism" thesis, Joseph Straubhaar in a 1991 article saw "counter-flows" as a challenge both to Dependency Theory and its corollary the Media Imperialism thesis.[16] Within this more optimistic perspective, he argues that when given a choice Global South audiences, for linguistic and cultural reasons, actually *prefer* the local product, thus giving rise to counter-hegemonic currents.

In a later book, *World Television: From Global to Local* (2007)—the subtitle reverses the usually assumed trajectory of "from local to global"—Straubhaar suggested that local, regional, national and transnational instances are all impacted in complex and contradictory ways by transnational media flows. Audiences everywhere, in this view, prefer TV programs that are "most directly relevant to them in cultural and linguistic terms."[17] Roland Robertson, for his part, speaks of "glocalization" as the capacity to "absorb and localize foreign influences into domestically created products."[18] One might also speak of "South-South counterflows, as when Turkey, longstanding importer of Latin American telenovelas, begins to export its telenovelas not only to the Arab Middle East but also to Latin America.[19]

In his essay on "Corporate Transnationalism," Juan Pinon, meanwhile, delineates the contradictions involved in the multidirectional traffic of mass-mediated cultural flows in the Americas. He describes the Latin American broadcasting landscape as an "increasingly complex and multilayered transnational industrial space, characterized by regional counterflows from competing national, regional, and global media corporations deploying a variety of strategies to produce and distribute appealing programming to audiences in several domestic markets."[20] In terms of media circulation, Arlene Davila, in a similar vein, laments the nation-centric tendency on the part of traditional media scholars to arbitrarily split off Latin America from Latino media industries, in ways that "downplay the intricate connections between Latino and Latin American media at the level of production, circulation, and consumption."[21] Davila finds evidence of this failure to connect in the scarcity of analyses of cultural production in Miami, notwithstanding the key role played by Cuban Americans and other Latin Americans in the development of transnational Spanish-language media and the rising role of Miami as a "Latin Hollywood."

Moving from the aquatic to the gaseous, it is striking that some of the metaphors mobilized to convey the effects of digitalized globality obscure its materiality. In a succinct summary of the ambiguous politics of the digital, Siegfried Zielinski suggests that the word "digital" has become endowed with magical powers:

> The digital became analogous to the alchemists' formula for gold ... endowed with infinite powers of transformation. All things digital promised to those who already possessed wealth and power more of the same and, to those who possessed nothing, that they could share in this unbloody revolution without getting their hands dirty.[22]

The "Cloud" plays into the myth of immateriality, which John Durham Peters points out that the sky, contrary to its reputation, "is full of media and has been for a long time, though modern astronomy and space exploration have filled the sky vertiginously with staggering new things from space stations to dark matter."[23]

The rhetoric of "the Cloud" as an infinite space of digital storage sometimes becomes mystificatory. The cloud metaphor, writes John Dunham Peters, "has been a smashing success for the information technology business, and fluffy, benign cumulous clouds are now the standard iconography of digital storage."[24] The cloud trope would seem to relay a beatific Platonic Ideal, far from Plato's dark and stony Cave, a soft and fuzzy aggregation of fleece, imagined as unmoored from any earth-bound materiality. The Cloud, for Peters, evokes the "ancient idea of a heavenly record containing everything ever done or said."[25] But a historical cloud hangs over the Cloud. The rhetoric of a global Internet connecting communities and transcending national borders, Tung-Hui Hu points out, actually emerges from a 19th-century imperial vision, in that the immediate predecessor of the Cloud's fiber-optic backbone was the system of submarine cables designed to bind together British colonial territories in the Pacific, part of the connectivities of the British Empire.[26]

The metallic cables of the Net, like the discarded chains of the Middle Passage, are literally and figuratively buried deep both under the surface of the Sea and in a kind of Political Unconscious. Just as the slave trade relied on the high-tech modernity of slave ships and sugar mills, and just as imperialism, and the dissemination of cinema, depended on networks of shipping lanes, railroads, factories, electric wires, and forced labor, so the digital depends on the racialized division of global labor—for example Apple products made in Chinese sweatshops—and on the very material infrastructure of the Internet, embedded in the nitty-gritty of wires, switches, and routers. Here we find a truly elemental form of globality. Computer chips, for example, are rooted in geophysics, composed of myriad material elements dug up from the bowels of the earth, hidden under nationally defined territories.

The frantic race between our ability to create data and our ability to store and manage that data has been extremely anxiogenic. According to Jennifer Holt and Patrick Vondereau, the energy needs of the "Cloud" are astronomical: "a single data center can require more power than a medium-sized town."[27] If the Cloud were a country, according to a Greenpeace Report, it would have the fifth largest electricity demand in the world.[28] In *Greening the Media*, Richard Maxwell and Toby Miller detail the huge resource demands and environmental footprint of the global media economy generally, reporting that as of 2007 media technologies were responsible for between 2.5% and 3% of the world's greenhouse gas emissions.[29] The emerging field of "Critical Studies of Media Infrastructures," in this sense, addresses the transnational traffic of electronic media across various parts of the planet. The focus of what Lisa Parks and Nicole Starosielski call "Signal Traffic," marks a "critical shift away from the analysis of screened content alone toward an understanding of how content moves through the world and how this movement affects content's form."[30] The two scholars remind us of the materiality of the infrastructures of media production and distribution in the form of google data centers, undersea cables, and power grids that "distribute the signals that become entertainment, whether they exist under the sea, across lands, or 'in the cloud.'"

26

TECHNOLOGIES OF INTERMEDIAL FLOW

Many of the most powerful "flow metaphors" within present-day mass-mediated contemporary culture arise from pervasive digitalization. The digital economy, for Kevin Kelly, "runs on the river of freely flowing copies."[1] The Internet "bathes" us in streams of notifications and updates. The "Cloud" is formed by the union of a "zillion streams of information intermingling, flowing into each other."[2] Kelly speaks of the "four stages of flowing," moving from 1) fixed and rare; to 2) free and ubiquitous; and 3) flowing and sharing; and 4) opening and becoming, all as ways to shape new things "out of ceaseless change and shape-shifting processes."[3]

The recourse to the aquatic metaphor of "streaming" signals a major shift in technology, film exhibition, and media circulation that forms part of the pervasive digitalization of everyday life and culture. The digital era obviously brings us immense gains; indeed, most of us would feel absolutely bereft if deprived of our beloved apps and devices. (The phrase "if left to our own devices" does not usually have a happy ending.) But along with a cornucopia of goodies, the digital epoch brings horrifying glimpses of a future of irretrievable losses, with privacy and democracy drowned in the icy waters of Big Tech corporate abuse and the politics of bots à la Cambridge Analytica. Thus digital "progress" simultaneously disseminates and "disappears" media. In purely cinematic terms, streaming brings benefits in terms of distribution and exhibition, not to mention audio-visual pedagogy, but streaming might also very well trigger the final demise of 35 mm film, DVDs, and even Cable Television in a kind of death by "bitification."[4] Technological obsolescence, no longer generational, has become virtually instantaneous, a matter of weeks rather than years or decades. Just as thousands of nitrate films were lost to studio fires in an earlier period, thousands of films might be relegated to the digital equivalent of the proverbial "dustbin of history." In metaphorical terms, streaming facilitates reception of film and media "content" but also threatens to "flood the market" with corporate products and to "drown out" the endangered species of alternative media. Expanding at lightning speed, with thousands of photos, ads, emails, posts, and videos introduced every second, the Internet and streaming introduce a Heraclitan flux whereby the spectator can never step into the same format or mediatic river twice, or for that matter, even once.

Every change generates more change, where change is injected into the technology itself, changing even change itself, or as Kelly puts it, changing "how other things change, and changing itself, is mutating and growing."[5] On the bright side, digital storage and new delivery media such as streaming have expanded the platforms and formats for seeing films, integrating film spectatorship into the everyday lives of millions and perhaps billions of people. While the French New Wave directors became aware of the history of World Cinema thanks to screenings at the Cinemateque française, young, aspiring directors now have access to an incomparably more capacious cinemateque in the form of an extremely vast achive of films and other audio-visual materials available through the Internet, enabling what Elsaesser calls "cinephilia Take 2" or what one might call streaming cinephilia, or laptop cinephilia, or even smartphone cinephilia.

Another cluster of questions, in this sense, has to do with the relevance of and impact of the new media and digital technologies on terms and academic formations like World, Transnational, and Global. In the present moment, the protocols of film spectatorship, for example, have changed dramatically; most spectators now screen media on their computers and mobile devices, rather than attend scheduled screenings at movie theaters or wait for programmed televised broadcasts of episodes. As movie theaters all over the world have been turned into churches, warehouses, and parking lots, or been given over to streamed opera and boxing matches, the emergence of multimedia and multiplatform spectatorship has led to the programmed obsolescence of the cinema as a collective social experience, and what Garcia-Canclini has called "a radical change in the relations between cinema and public life."[6] With multi-site multi-screen spectatorship and the ubiquitous smartphone, we are far from the dark "Plato's Cave" of 1970s film theory; now, rather than dwell spellbound in the darkness of a cinematic cave, we now see the cave from outside, often in lighted areas, far from the world of the domineering apparatus of 1970s film theory, premised as it was on the sealed-off environment of theatrical exhibition.

Meanwhile, "social networking," according to Linda Hutcheon, "has altered forever the communication landscape."[7] The very meaning of the filmgoing experience as a gregarious experience has been dramatically altered. Gone are the days when the release of a film like *Hour of the Furnaces* was an eagerly anticipated political event, when merely seeing the film, then banned, was an engaged political act which might lead to jail or torture. In fact, gone are the days of a ritualized desire to see films in movie theaters, with the possible exception of 3D and blockbuster films, where a visceral experience is sought. As Dale Hudson and Patrica Zimmerman point out, films such as *Cinema Paradiso* (Giuseppe Tornatore, Italy/France, 1988), *Bye-bye Africa* (Mahamat-Saleh Haroun, Chad/France, 1999) and *Good-bye Dragon Inn* (Ming-liang Tsai, Taiwan, 2003), "express how almost-empty cinemas have themselves become objects of mourning and melancholia due to their imminent closure or conversion to venues for encounters and pleasures other than the cinematic."[8]

Films are now less likely to be seen in theaters than they are to be downloaded or streamed. Rather us "going to the movies," now the movies "come to us." Raymond Bellour's "unattainable text" of the 1970s, at a time when films were screened frame-by-frame on clunky Steenbeck editing tables, has given way to 24/7 availability, to the "stoppable" and the "downloadable text" and "spreadable media" (Jenkins) under the premise that "If it doesn't spread, it's dead." Now we can retroactively "binge watch" entire seasons of TV series in one fell swoop. Now prestigious film scholars like David Bordwell and Kristen Thompson have blogs, and recent Ph.Ds. in film studies are practicing "videographic criticism." Rather than be vetted by well-known film critics, films come recommended via TV News box office reports—TV film reviews are no longer part of Arts Reviews but of Business News—or the algorhythms of personal taste and automated suggestions based on previous viewing practices. Vertov's derisive metaphor of an addictive "cine-opium" in the 1920s has turned into the actually existing phenomenon of Internet addition, and its social corollary of detox camps for cyber-addicted children. Meanwhile, the word "revolution" seems to have disappeared from the left lexicon to form part of the corporate encyclopedia; it is now reserved for TV commercials advertising products or for technological advances. Even real-life actually existing in the street (near) revolutions like that in Tahrir Square in Cairo are credited not to activists but to the new technologies and therefore dubbed "Twitter Revolutions."

On the other hand, the digital has clearly democratized filmmaking, at least for the tech-savvy children of the world's middle classes. According to Nicolas Bourriaud, we are now in an artistic era of postproduction: an era of the proliferation of viewing screens, new communication technologies (iPhones, Twitter, Instagram), and digital distribution (file sharing, downloading, streaming).[9] Costas Constandinides speaks of the translation of texts and characters from a preexisting medium (verbal or filmic) into a digital medium, generating a "multiplicity of texts that function across collaborative media," resulting in "franchise adaptations" and the "franchise multitext."[10] Since virtually anyone with a digital camera or smartphone and a laptop and software like iMovie o Adobe Premiere can shoot and edit films, low-cost and light equipment can enable the tech-savvy members of marginalized populations to make films. While the "digital divide" exists both within and between societies, it is nonetheless true that H-D quality films can be shot on iPhones, and Final Cut Pro X has been used to edit Oscar-winning films. Thus feature films can be made without tremendous financial resources or studio backing and yet reach a very wide audience. With a miniscule budget, a digital camera, Kickstarter funding, and a software program like Final Cut—an "idea in the head and a smartphone in hand," to update Glauber Rocha's coinage "an idea in the head and camera in the hand"—an aspiring filmmaker can make a film and send it out through web-networks to a transnational audience. As inexpensive tools have created a situations where millions of people are making billions of videos and uploading them to YouTube, in an era where "the ease of making video approaches the ease of writing,."[11]

If the surrealists in the 1920s and 1930s dreamed of "everyone an artist" and Roland Barthes spoke in the 1960s of the "death of the author" midwifing the "birth of the reader," the Internet has given birth to the "prosumer" (a term coined by Toffler in 1980) a hybrid of producer and consumer, and the "produser," a hybrid of producer and user. Within what Henry Jenkins calls "participatory culture," the public no longer simply consumes "preconstructed messages … [rather, they become] people who are shaping, sharing, reframing, and remixing media content in ways which not have been previously imagined."[12] The dreams of 1960s figures like Solanas and Getino in Latin America, or Chris Marker in France, who advanced the idea of universal training in filmmaking, have become a reality in French high schools, albeit without any concomitant social militancy. The utopian proposals of the *Etats Generaux du Cinema* in 1968 such as universal initiation into the trade-secrets of filmmaking—have been partially realized, but not in a way that the radicals imagined.[13] Today, *nous sommes tous des cineastes*, yet the domination of powerful media corporations, and the sheer volume of product, makes it difficult to get large numbers of people to actually see many of the films made in the newly democratized environment. The point now would be to become prosumers, active participants, in the production of our collective social life in the social commons.

The animated 2008 Internet feature *Sita Sings the Blues* takes great artistic advantage of these new possibilities to communicate with a very large audience. Written, directed, produced, and animated by American artist Nina Paley with the help of a computer in her Chicago apartment, the film constitutes a kind of low-budget digital blockbuster, an epic film created not with millions of dollars and a cast of thousands but only with 2D computer graphics and flash animation. *Sita* counterpoints a feminist version of a *Ramayana* story, concerning the relationship between the entitled and demanding Prince Rama and the endlessly patient and devoted Sita, with the story of the artist's breakup with her husband, in such a way as to link Sita and the author as two women tormented by the slings and arrows of male insensitivity. The two stories are then interwoven with a third "series"—the 1920s public domain recordings of the jazzistic scorned-love crooning of Annette Hanshaw—acted out and "sung" (in the manner of Bollywood "playback" singing) by a simulacral Sita, visually presented, thanks to vector graphic animation, as a reincarnation of Betty Boop.

This already layered and multitemporal construction is then interspersed with amicably impromptu voice-over commentaries about the *Ramayana* by three Indian friends of the author, incarnated on screen as silhouetted shadow puppets who debate the validity of different versions of the story. Episodes with dialogue are enacted through painted figures of the characters in profile in a manner resembling the 18th-century tradition of *Rajput* brush painting, a tradition historically associated with illuminated manuscripts telling epic stories such as the *Ramayana*. The syncretic dialogue shifts temporal and stylistic registers by mixing the noble epic stylistic register with vulgar colloquialisms such as "Your ass is grass." The deliberate lack of composition in depth reminds us of the modernity of the traditional, in that modernist painting, like art in the Rajput tradition, also eschewed the depth of field of Renaissance perspective in favor of flatness and de Cirico-style contradictory perspectives.

27

GLOBALIZATION

The mediatic resistance

The digital era's eclipse of analog media necessitates a revised conceptualization of the definition of "film." The category "World Cinema" subtly privileges the auteur and the fiction feature film as the ontological quintessence of the "real film," while seeing the documentary, the short film, and video and digital productions as subordinate and inferior forms below the threshold of legitimate art. In the present media environment, however, we can see all audio-visual moving image materials as potentially "films." The digital era obliges us to rethink not only what constitutes a "film" but also what constitutes "progressive political film." Rather than look back nostalgically to the classic revolutionary films like *Potemkin* in the 1920s, or to "tricontinentalist" films like *La Hora de los Hornos* and *The Battle of Algiers* in the 1960s, the "political film" today might evoke the camcorder activism of videos capturing police abuse, or a fake-corporate "Yes Men" intervention on BBC World News, or a Colbert monologue or a filmlet like "Mitt the Ripper" mocking Romney's claim that "corporations are people," or a music video like Racionais MC's "Diary of a Prisoner," or a John Oliver sketch on Net Neutrality, or an immersive documentary in the style of the "Syria project" or a politicized virtual game like GetGitmo," all as valid expressive variations on the theme of the contemporary "political film."

In *Postmodernism, or, The Cultural Logic of Late Capitalism*, Fredric Jameson argues that given the difficulty of subjects to grasp social totality or to organize past and present into a coherent whole, cultural productions are likely to be composed of "heaps of fragments" marked by "the randomly heterogeneous and fragmentary and the aleatory."[1] The "ideologeme of elegance and glossiness," James argues elsewhere, has its dialectical "opposite number in sleaze, trash, and garbage art of all kinds."[2] Jameson's words aptly define the globalized aesthetic of a Brazilian genre of "garbage films," most notably Jorge Furtado's collage essay-film *Isle of Flowers* (1990), as a film which takes emergent globalization as its (unnamed) subject. The essay-film, it would seem, has a special affinity with transnational themes. Described by its author as a "letter to a Martian ignorant about the earth and its social systems," Furtado's 15-minute short exploits Monty Python-style animation, archival footage, and parodic-reflexive documentary techniques to indict the global distribution of food and wealth in the world. In fact, the film, which signals its theme through the image of a revolving globe, can be seen as one of the first films to denounce the social violence of the then widely touted phenomenon of globalization, and also as a precursor of the neo-archival films of the 21st century.

The film condenses in its 15 minutes of duration a non-Eurocentric history of human civilization, emphasizing industrial capitalism's profligate production of waste. The film's protagonist is an allegorical tomato—planted, harvested, exchanged, refused, and then dumped—which makes its way from a Nisei farmer, to a Porto Alegre supermarket, to a bourgeois home, to its final destination—the titular Isle of Flowers. The structure of *Isle of Flowers* is rhizomatic in the Deleuze/Guattari sense in that it develops through a series of lateral associative moves rather like a plant that grows horizontally, sending out shoots. An aleatory technique superimposes an arbitrary yet orderly structure on apparently random materials, revolving around definitions of basic terms like "money," "water," "island" and "human being." The first inkling that the film is not merely farcical comes when the word "progress" segues to the image of an atomic mushroom cloud. Modeled as a parody of TV educational programs for children, the film charts the history of capitalist exploitation in relation to human sustenance. A landowner, who by definition is a person who has enclosed the commons, allows the famished poor exactly ten minutes to scrounge for food inside a fenced-in organic refuse pile. In this social anatomy of garbage, the truth of a society is revealed through its detritus. In what might be called, riffing on both Brecht and Bordwell, the "*socially* causal network narrative," the urban bourgeois family is linked to the rural poor via the sausage, the pig, and the tomato within a web created by the center-periphery system. Showing the seamy underside of globalization, the film exposes the transnational capitalist system as generating a world of wasteful immiseration. A social anatomy of garbage reveals the hidden face of a global system that was then being idealized through the euphoric nostrums of "globalization."

The Marxist critique of globalization sees it as indissociable from neo-liberal hegemony and *la pensee unique*—which argues that formal democracy plus capitalism and "intellectual property rights" have become universal norms, thus moving us all toward a putatively glorious "end of history." (Here we find the upside-down version of the Marxist vision of an inexorable advance toward socialism.) Countless films from the Global South have critiqued globalization. To take just one signal example, in Abderrahmane Sissako's *Bamako* (2006), the director returns to his family home in Bamako to put globalization literally on trial. The home's large courtyard become the setting for a people's court from the Global South, where the World Bank and the IMF are formally charged with "underdeveloping Africa," as Walter Rodney put it in a title, and stealing its resources. Not lacking in humor, the film has the family watch a mock spaghetti Western featuring the

Palestinian director Elie Suleiman and African American actor Danny Glover. (Glover is also featured in Manthia Diawara's earlier and in some ways similar *Bamako Sigi-Kan*.)

Any number of major fiction features, *La Promesse, The Constant Gardener, Dirty Pretty Things, The Insider*, critique globalization and corporate abuse. The films of Jean-Marc Moutout explore these social dilemmas of globalization as experienced from within the intestines of the corporate world. The symptomatically titled *Violence des Echanges en Milieu Tempere* (2003), for example, exposes the soft-spoken sadism of corporate downsizing, where a young employee, through a kind of hardening of the moral arteries, gradually aligns himself with management by coldly firing those whom he knows very well do not deserve to be fired. Costa-Gavras *Le Couperet* (the Axe, 2005), an adaptation of a Donald Westlake novel, meanwhile, both exemplifies transnational filmmaking—a Greek director working with French, Belgian, and Spanish funding—and denounces the abuses of trannational corporations. The film offers a kind of revenge plot for downsized employees like its anti-hero Bruno Davert, who resolves to systematically eliminate all the male rivals for a coveted position in a corporation. Laying bare the Ayn Rand-style Social Darwinism typical of right-wing American ideology, the film plots out what the film's trailer calls the "irresistable ascent of a social serial killer." Stuart Townsend's *Battle in Seattle* (2007), meanwhile, picks up on the cues left four decades before by Haskell Wexler's *Medium Cool* (1968) by mixing real-time events with staged scenes featuring actors such as Woody Harelson, Andre Benjamin, Ray Liotta, and Charlize Theron, to offer a sympathetic portrayal of an early explosion of anti-globalization activism.

A number of films and remixes—*Everything is a Remix, Copyright Criminals, Good Copy Bad Copy, Steal This Film, Rip: A Remix Manifesto, Sonic Outlaws*, and *This Film is not yet Rated*—denounce the corporate enclosure of art and social life in general through the abuse of intellectual copyright. Innumerable radical documentaries also offer acid critiques of globalization. *The Corporation, The Shock Doctrine, Big Bucks, Big Pharma, Capitalism: A Love Story, Profit and Nothing Else, The Globalization Tapes, Outsource This, When Corporations Rule the World, Inside Job, All for One, The Hidden Face of Globalization, Controlling Interest, Global Village or Global Pillage?* and *Le Profit et Rien d'Autre* offer frontal attacks on the globalized capitalist order.[3] *The Corporation* (2004) is structured around a literalization of the neo-liberal metaphor of "corporate personhood." If corporations are people, the film argues, those "people" have a psychopathic personality; they knowingly cause harm, show callous disregard for others, and are incapable of empathy and of sustaining human relationships. Michael Winterbottom and Matt Whitcross's *The Shock Doctrine*, meanwhile, superimposes a Naomi Klein lecture about the unholy alliance of shock-and-awe militarism with shock-and-awe neo-liberal economics on archival footage of literal shock treatments, in order to denounce the free-market fundamentalism hawked by Milton Friedman and his latter-day disciples. The Quebecois film *Encerclement* (2008), finally, enlists Noam Chomsky, Ignacio Ramonet, and Susan George in a didactic critique of globalization and neo-liberal ideology. Steve

McQueen's short film *Gravesend* (2007), not unlike Conrad's *Heart of Darkness*, connects England and the Congo through the new ivory—coltan—the mineral used in most cell phones and computers. In an abstract, poetic style, McQueen intercuts images from a shiny antiseptic British cellphone factory with the dark satanic mines of Congo mineral extraction. Joshua Oppenheimer's *The Globalization Tapes* (2003), finally, contrasts the harsh realities lived by Indonesian workers with the euphoric nostrums of neo-liberal globalization.

Switching genres, three satirical films—*The Yes Men* (2003), *The Yes Men Fix the World* (2014) and *The Yes Men are Revolting* (2015)—depict the pranks of the anti-corporate "Yes Men"—the activist team and its network of supporters created by Andy Bichlbaum and Mike Bonanno—which impersonate the human avatars of corporations in the form of fictitious spokesmen for McDonalds and Dow Chemical as part of another World—that of the World Trade Organization (WTO). Carrying subversion to dizzying and legally risky heights the Yes Men create fake-corporate websites, and thus get themselves invited to appear in the media as CEOs, thus "infiltrating" what Rancière calls "the networks of domination."[4] The artists send imposter-delegates to make outrageous (and even murderous) "modest proposals" at World Trade Organization meetings, proposals that like Swift's, are sometimes taken seriously by the "suits." One proposal consists of special surveillance equipment, a kind of giant wearable phallic panopticon, which allows CEOs to observe their globalized workers while pursuing leisure activities like jogging. No idea, no matter how inhumane or repellant—for example Big Macs made out of recycled human feces, or foul-smelling candles purportedly made from decaying human flesh (actually animal flesh)—struck the business people as out-of-bounds, as long as a profit was in the offing.

In a Swiftian spoof on lifeboat survivalism and corporate individualism, the Yes Men modeled a bizarre hilarious-looking inflatable "Survivaball" designed as a self-contained personal living system for the post-apocalyptic businessman trying to survive the devastating effects of global warming. Many in the audience were intrigued, rather than horrified, at the idea. Their "vivoleum project," meanwhile, promised to keep fuel flowing by transforming the millions of people who would die from oil-based calamities into crude. In a more notorious case, the corporate mimic Bichlbaum appeared on a BBC news program as Jude "Finisterra" (etymologically an apocalyptic "end of the earth")—invited as official representatives of Dow Chemical—to announce that the corporation, notorious for its vigorous efforts to avoid compensating its victims, had decided to fully compensate the victims of the poisonous explosion at the (formerly Union Carboide-owned) gas plant in Bhopal, India. The result was to spark a dramatic downturn in the value of Dow Stocks and call attention to a calamity that the corporation had hoped the world would forget.

Among the many films that portray the bleeding border between Mexico and the U.S. (worsened most recently by the Trump-inspired ripping of children from their parents)—*El Norte* (1983), *Mi Familia* (1995), *Lone Star* (1996) *Under the Same Moon* (2007), *Una Vida Mejor* (2008), *Sin Nombre* (2009), Alex Rivera's *Sleep Dealer*

(2008) is one of the most experimental and radical. An example of Global South cyberpunk science fiction, the film portrays a Swiftian solution to the labor problem for Agribusiness through the cyber-outsourcing of latino Labor thanks to *cyber-braceros*, remotely controlled labor-robots. After the construction of a wall along the bored, this computerized dystopian version of the American corporate Dream has all of the work usually performed by undocumented workers replaced by cyber-laborers, without those annoying actually existing flesh-and-blood Mexican workers. Archival clips from Hollywood and Mexican films underscore the role of the media in advancing such projects.

A book whose title echoes and remixes the famous aphorism of Malcolm X—*By Any Media Necessary*—calls attention to a central aporia of contemporary social life, i.e. the experience of dysfunctional and unequal liberal democracy and Darwinian capitalism, on the one hand, and of an expansion of communicational and organizational resources available to everyday people on the other, calling, in the end, for more activist forms of participatory culture which go beyond reactive "culture jamming." Rather than look for radical critiques of globalization in feature films, we might do better to surf the Internet for radical critique. The Web Series project "We the Economy," for example, offers 20 short films about the economy by leftist directors such as Barbara Kopple, James Schamus, Morgan Spurlock, and Steve James, all available free across cable, mobile, and video-on-demand (VOD) services. The purpose of the series is to use any audio-visual means necessary—including the pop didacticism of animation, collage, puppets—to cut through the mystifying jargon of mainstream neo-liberal economics. While Cable News abandons "the economy" rubric in favor of a pro-corporate "Business News" or an individualistic "Your Money" rubric—addressing the telespectator as "citizens" but as "consumers" or "investors." "We the economy" stresses the collective dimension of economic relationalities, whether by highlighting the wealth abyss separating the 1% from the 99%, or by linking the tin embedded in our mobile phones to the exploitation that makes mobile phones possible.

While uneven and sometimes reformist in political terms, the more radical episodes deploy innovative strategies to cut through the murk of financial jargon like "credit default swaps," "deleveraging," and "quantitative easing." The series suggests that language matters: calling corporation "job exporters" rather than "job creators" carries a strong affective charge. Bob Balaban's segment, "Globalization: Who Cares? You Do," finally, features actress Sussie Essman from "Curb Your Enthusiasm" in a critical vignette alongside biting commentary by Joseph Stiglitz and Jagdish Bhagwati. A James Schamus episode explores the essential irreality of money as fetish by showing that, although it is often assumed to be the ultimate ontological real—"you can bank on it"—money is actually little more than a figment of our collective indebted imagination. Those temple-like banks, Schamus explains, do not keep our money—they are legally obliged through the fractional reserve monetary system to have only 3% of their holdings actually "in" the bank, while they loan out our money at exorbitant rates. Furthermore, in a scam whose audacity beggars the imagination, the government prints money and gives it at virtually no interest to the banks, which then loans it, with interest, back to the government. The Adam McKay episode, meanwhile, follows three lollipop-loving cartoon alpacas (voiced by Amy Poehler, Maya Rudolph, and Sarah Silverman) whose adventures after graduation from "sweetness school" reveal the social damage done by class prejudice and income inequality. Two allegorical lemonade stands in the Ramin Bahrani episode illustrate the often sleazy ties between big business and government regulators.

28

TRANSOCEANIC CURRENTS

The red, black, and white Atlantic

Another eddy in the aquatic turn is the trend toward what is variously called Oceanic Studies, Delta Studies, Atlantic Studies, Black Atlantic Studies, and the like. The Atlantic Ocean, for example, has been a privileged object of study, adjectivally qualified through many grids—national (the "French" Atlantic), political-ideological (the "revolutionary" Atlantic), and cultural-religious (the "Sephardi Moorish" Atlantic).[1] Most strikingly, the Atlantic has been metaphorized through chromatic tropes with racial-ethnic connotations, most conspicuously as "Black" (Farris Thompson's "Black Atlantic Civilization" and Paul Gilroy's "Black Atlantic") but also as white, in the sense of a transnational Whiteness Studies critique of white supremacy.[2] Jigna Desai, meanwhile, has spoken of South Asian cinema in the "Brown Atlantic."[3] While in some ways arbitrary, these chromatic metaphors serve to shape new objects of study and units of analysis that bypass the nation-state.

Some transoceanic art works stress the sea as literally the site of mass-death in the wake of colonialism, slavery, and postcolonial migration. Manthia Diawara's *Opera of the World* (2017) superimposes music and words in order to simultaneously evoke the Homeric *Odyssey* and the contemporary tragic "Odyssey" of the migrants risking death in what has been called the "Black Mediterranean."[4] John Akomfrah's three-channel film-installation *Vertigo Sea* (2015), meanwhile, forms what one of the film's intertitles calls "oblique tales on the aquatic sublime." The film superimposes audio-clips from aquatically oriented literature—Olaudah Equiano's Life Narrative, Melville's *Moby Dick*, and Virginia Woolf's *To the Lighthouse*—on enchanting images of seascapes and marine life alternating with shackled black figures, slaughtered whales, and drowned migrants, revealing, à la Melville himself, the subaquatic affinities of the shipwrecks of history. Ethiopian director Dagwami Yimer's short animation film *Asmat* (Names, 2013), meanwhile, forms a sublimely minimalist tribute to the 268 people who lost their lives off the coast of Lampedusa on October 3 2013. Alternating between evocative animation and beautiful underwater footage, underscored by a woman's mournful song in Amharic, the film has the names of each of the victims—Selam (Peace), Tesfaye (My Hope) and so forth—float over the screen to remind us that the "bodies without names" that we see on the news were actually human beings who perished out of a desperate search for a life worth living.

On a more academic level, multi-faceted transnational comparisons within Atlantic Studies can deconstruct intercolonial narcissism—the penchant of imperialist nations to phantasize that their imperialism is somehow better than that of the others—and nation-state based exceptionalism in order to discern both commonalities and differences within the societies formed in the wake of colonialism and slavery.[5] Racial discrimination, for example, is often studied in relation to a single nation-state, yet much can be learned through a comparative study of the structural racisms and patterns of power that shapes most Black Atlantic societies. Such a relational and comparative approach might study the filmic representations and the ideological analyses of representations of racialized neighborhoods in the Black Atlantic—the favelas in Brazil—as portrayed in films like *City of God, Quase Irmaos, Elite Squad*—the inner cities of the U.S.—portrayed in *Do the Right Thing, Boyz in the Hood*, and *Straight outta Compton*—and the banlieux of France (*La Haine, Hexagone, 100% Arabica*). The racial oppression portrayed in the US-American and Brazilian films (and societies), embed, as it were, the legacy of slavery (and indirectly of colonialism), while the oppression portrayed in the French films (and in French society), embed the legacy of colonialism (and indirectly of extra-Hexagonal slavery). A 1994 rap song by Brazilian rapper "Rappa" offers a percussive evocation of the shared features of the same three national sites—the U.K., the U.S. and Brazil—figured in the films. The title "Brixton, the Bronx, and Baixada"—the last referring to Baixada Fluminense, a Rio site of numerous favelas. The rapper ask what the graffiti are saying, and the walls tell him of social oppression and but also of "black Beethovens." Yet poetry does not die but only transforms itself into moving hands and rhythms that beat out percussive stories in the form of jazz, samba, reggae, hip hop, whether from James Brown or Jorge Bem.

Within these family resemblances, there are commonalities in the three sites—police brutality, racial profiling, economic marginalization, disproportionate incarceration, hip hop cultures of resistance—and national nuances (the cushion of the welfare state and the greater saliency of religion in France, the tattered safety net and the proliferation of guns in both the U.S. and Brazil, and so forth). While the question of Islam is crucial in the French *banlieue* films—sociologists like Nacira Guenif-Soulimas speak of the "racialization of religion" in France—it barely registers as an issue in the American and Brazilian films.[6] A relational circum-Atlantic approach generates "mutual illumination" and "excess seeing" across cultural geographies to illuminate a kind of Afro-diasporic cultural commons. For example, it is revealing to place "in relation" three films by three black documentarians treating the subject of black televisual representation in three distinct Afro-diasporic situations—the United States, the United Kingdom, and Brazil: the Africa-American

Marlon Rigg's *Color Adjustment* in the U.S.; the Afro-British Isaac Julien's *Black and White in Color* in the U.K.; and the Afro-descended Joel Zito Araujo's *Negation of Brazil* in Brazil, all of which offer sophisticated analyses of TV representations of black people in, respectively, American, British, and Brazilian Television. Riggs offers a layered analysis that combines voice-over narration by Ruby Dee, clips from TV shows, interviews with white executives (Norman Lear), black performers (Esther Rolle, Diahann Carroll), and black public intellectuals (Herman Grey, Skip Gates), scrolled statistics, quotations from James Baldwin, and staged scenes telespectators watching TV on a historically sequenced series of TV monitors. Counterpointing the all-white suburban pastoral of *Leave it to Beaver*-style sitcoms with anti-black violence in the streets, the Riggs film constantly puts the representations to the test: "Is this positive." The "positive images" of the Bill Cosby Show, Skip Gates points out in his interview, did not ameliorate the social conditions of black people. (Recent revelations about Cosby illustrate the danger of over-investing in such idealized iconic figures.) In *Black and White in Color*, Isaac Julien uses similar techniques of juxtaposition, along with his signature technique of combining talking-head interviews with floating, constantly changing, quoted film backdrops, stitched together by a narrative voice-over (in this case by Stuart Hall). Joel Zito Araujo, for his part, emphasizes the same themes and techniques as Julien and Riggs but provides his own voice-over, reflecting on his experiences as a black tele-spectator hungry for screen images of black people. Black performers like Milton Goncalves and Ruth de Souza recount their travails in dealing with the stereotypes and paternalism of white-dominant media, in anecdotes strikingly similar to those of black artists in the U.S. and the U.K. What emerges from such a comparative transnational study is, once again, a paradoxical commonality of differences, nuanced variations on a common intersectional theme of white power and black resistance.

By casting a specific light on the subject at hand, Atlantic-chromatic metaphors bring into focus and visibility broad patterns, comparabilities, and family resemblances common to the entire Atlantic world, as it has been shaped negatively by genocide, the slave trade, by chattel slavery, and, at the same time, to some extent positively, through their corollaries of cultural syncretism and the indigenization and Africanization of world popular culture. The concept of Black Atlantic Cinema, in a similar way, calls attention to a broad spectrum of African and Afro-diasporic filmmakers in the Americas, Europe, and Africa, and to the thousands of mediatic treatments of large-scale Black Atlantic themes such as slavery, abolition, discrimination, and Afro-diasporic cultural expression.

The Atlantic World, including on its European shores, can also be productively seen as "Red" or better "indigenized" in something like the same sense that the Atlantic world is "Black." The two worlds share not only cognate form of colonial oppression, including in the form of racialized enslavement, but also a massive cultural presence and influence of both groups on the dominant group. The emergence into the European consciousness of indigenous peoples triggered an epistemological crisis and excitement that generated both the dystopian imagery of the nasty and brutish savage on the one hand, and the utopian imagery of an egalitarian life style markedly different from that of a rigidly hierarchical Europe on the other. Indigenous peoples, as Jodi Byrd points out, "have a presence in the Western imagination, in its fibre and texture, in its language, in its silences and shadows, its margins and intersections."[7] The trope of the indigenous Red Atlantic calls attention to such issues as the transnational depictions of native peoples by the invading settlers, as well as to the transnational indigenous resistance to colonization.

The figure of the "Indian" has a crucial, if in some ways oblique, relation to the World, the Transnational, and the Global. First, the so-called "Indian" has been a key figure both in World Literature and World Cinema, for example through Indianist literary classics and the hundreds of filmic adaptations of those classics. One thinks, for example, of the multitudinous adaptations of the hugely popular 19th-century Indianist novelists in various countries—James Fenimore Cooper in the U.S., Jose de Alencar in Brazil, François Rene de Chateaubriand in France, Karl May in Germany, and so forth. In the U.S. alone, the adaptations of *The Last of the Mohicans* go at least as far back as the 1912 silent version by James Cruze, on to a 1920s version, two 1930s versions, one 1940s version (*Last of the Redmen*, 1947), to a 1950s version (*The Iroquois Trail*, 1950), two 1960s versions, on to the 1992 version by Michael Mann starring Daniel Day-Lewis. In Germany, meanwhile, *Der Letzte de Mohikanes*, with Bela Lugosi as Chingachgook, formed the second part of the two-part *Lederstrumpf* film released in 1920. *Der Letzte Mohikaner* directed by Harald Reinl, meanwhile, was a 1965 West German/Italian/Spanish co-production whose story was set in the post American Civil War era. *Chingachgook die Grosse Schlange* (*Chingachgook the Great Serpent*), starring Gojko Mitic as Chingachgook, meanwhile, appeared in East Germany in 1967, and became popular throughout the Eastern Bloc.

Although the "Indians" have been endlessly featured in the literatures and cinemas of the world, Hollywood has loomed especially large for native Americans and indigenous people because, as Paul Chatt Smith puts it, Hollywood "defined our self-image" by telling the "entire planet how we live, look, scream, and kill."[8] In this vein, the frontier Western forms part of what Chickasaw scholar Jodi Byrd calls "the foundational paradigmatic Indianness that circulates within the narratives U.S empire tells itself."[9] Native Americans have never stopped contesting these master-narratives. Already in 1911, an issue of *Moving Picture World* reports a Native American delegation to President Taft protesting erroneous presentations of their culture and history and asking for a Congressional Investigation.[10] But the massive presence of the misnamed Indians, and more broadly of indigenous peoples, is a global phenomenon, albeit one which often goes unrecognized as such. "Indians" have been a ubiquitous presence in the cinemas of the Americas, appearing not only in U.S.-American and Canadian films but also in films from Mexico, Brazil, Chile, Ecuador, Colombia, Venezuela, and indeed in most Latin American countries. Yet while there have been many book-length studies of the representation and misrepresentation of the Native American in Hollywood films, I know of no comparative in-depth studies of the analogous representations in scores if not hundreds of Latin American films that treat the subject of the Indian.[11]

Atlantic-scale formulations have implications for our conceptualizations of the World, the Transnational, and the Global because they go beyond individual nation-states to embrace a larger world, defined, somewhat arbitrarily, by the limits of a chromatically defined body of water. Some scholars, such as Awam Amkpa and Gunja Sengupta, go even farther by "provincializing" even Atlantic Studies by mingling the scholarly waters of Black Atlantic Studies with those of Black Pacific studies, reconfigured as an even broader Transoceanic Black Studies.[12] Atlantic-inflected studies are of course by definition less broad than both the World and the Global, so once again "Transnational" suits the situation best. If one expands the notion of the "Indian" to include indigenous peoples generally, the relevance of the Indian to World Literature, World Cinema, Transnational Cinema and Global Media becomes ever clearer. Europeans, for example, as Christopher Frayling points out, have had a longstanding love affair with the "Indian" and with the Western genre. Some of the earliest American Westerns made more money in France than in the home market. In France, Gaston Méliès filmed a series of French Westerns featuring Indians between 1907 and 1913. In 1918–1919 a Winnebago Indian named James Young Deer made short Westerns for the Pathe Brothers in France. A half century later, inspired by the tremendous success of the German Indian films of the 1950s and 1960s, the spaghetti Westerns cooked up in Italy triggered a craze among film journalists to append culinary labels to Westerns from various countries, generating "Sauerkraut Westerns" (produced in West Germany); "Paella Westerns" (co-productions shot in Spain); "Camembert Westerns" (produced in Fontainebleau, France); "curry Westerns" (made in India); and "Chop Suey Westerns" (made in Hong Kong).

The Indian also appears with surprising frequency even in the work of European auteurs such as the arch-Auteur Jean-Luc Godard. We can now trace the changing role of the Indian figure in Godard's oeuvre thanks to Eyal Sivan's online interactive "Montage Interdit" web-site." The site arranges clips drawn from Godard's films under rubrics such as "Blacks," "Jews," "Indians," "Arabs," "Third World," etc. By scrutinizing the chronologically ordered clips, we can discern Godard's overall trajectory from apolitical right-wing anarchist, fond of Nouvelle Vague *clins d'oeil*, to theoretical practitioner of radical politics. The trajectory begins with Ana Karina, in *Une Femme est une Femme* (1961), as a cabaret performer costumed in Sioux Indian headdress—in short as a stereotype, a joke. Later, in *Bande a Part* (1964), the dialogue places Indians, alongside Jews and Blacks, within a paradigm of analogously oppressed peoples. *Weekend* (1968), meanwhile, has a long voice-over citation of Engels praising the egalitarian society of the Iroquois as examples of communalism, gender equality, and "primitive socialism."

In Godard's "Dziga-Vertov" period (1968–1972), the Indian of the Western becomes a synecdoche for Hollywood racism, which produces an "Indian" who is "juste une image" (just an image) rather than an "image juste" (an accurate image). The trajectory culminates in *Notre Musique* (2004) where Godard evokes a strong connection between Native American elders/activists—speaking in their own name—and a Palestinian poet, suggesting an alliance between two occupied peoples. The film features the literal presence of the late Palestinian poet Mamoud Darwish, the author of the poem "The Speech of the Red Indian," which spins an extended analogy between the situations and sensibilities of Palestinians and those of native Americans as those who "lived and flourished before the onslaught of English guns, French wine and influenza, living in harmony side by side" who "refuse to sign a bill of sale/that takes possession/of so much as one inch of my weed patch …" Thus Godard moves over the decades from displaying Ana Karina as a stereotypically sexy "squaw" in a nightclub, to an indictment of Hollywood's racist iconography, to a poetic evocation of a symbolic alliance between two "settled" and "unsettling" peoples besieged by settler-style colonialism, with the difference, in the Jewish/Israeli case, of an anomalous colonialism, one, again, without a metropole.[13]

29

GLOBAL INDIGENEITY AND THE TRANSNATIONAL GAZE

Although Indigenous peoples have been disenfranchised by the settler colonialism of the various nation-states whose hegemony they have had to suffer, including within the "Third World," they have been a ubiquitous presence in the cinema, although usually as objects of negative and positive stereotypes. In general, indigenous people have been represented by others; only recently have they begun to represent themselves in film and across the mediatic spectrum. As a Brazilian *indigenista* notes, indigenous people have functioned as a canvas upon which Brazilian official culture paints "with bold strokes" its own troubles and unresolved tensions.[1] Indians have been demonized in the Hollywood frontier Western, romanticized in German *Indianer* films, allegorized in Cinema Novo films, simultaneously paternalized and valorized in independent American cinema, and mystically exalted in Australian "outback" films. But the indigenous world is "filming back" with gusto. The burgeoning world-wide movement of "indigenous media" refers to the use of audio-visual technology (camcorders, VCRs, digital cameras) to foreground the stories, values, and perspective of indigenous peoples. Within "indigenous media," the producers are themselves the receivers, along with neighboring communities and, occasionally, distant cultural institutions or festivals such as the "Native American" or "indigenous nations" or "first nations" film festivals held in many parts of the world. For anthropologist Faye Ginsburg, indigenous media serve as self-conscious modes of cultural production, which uses media for "internal and external communication, for self-determination, and for resistance to outside cultural domination."[2]

In an uncannily prophetic song written in the mid-1970s, entitled "The Indian," composer-singer Caetano Veloso predicted the rise of a high-tech Indian who would come to redeem his oppressed people. The song's lyrics illustrate once again the convergence of multiple arts in a popular song which mingles references to literature (erudite and popular) to cinema and to philosophy, and all in musical form. The poem is not only written in the prophetic genre, but also turned out to be literally prophetic of an indigenous resurgence. Some of the lyrics of "O Indio" go as follows:

> From a shining colored star will descend an Indian
> From a star that spins with dazzling velocity
> A star that will lodge in the heart of America in an instant of clarity
> An Indian preserved in his full physical presence
> In solid, in gas, in atoms, words, soul, color, in gesture, in smell, in shadow, in light, in magnificent sound
> As a spot equidistant between the Atlantic and the Pacific
> The Indian will descend from a resplendent object ...

Encoding indigenous ideas about stars and astronomy, and specifically the idea that culture heroes transform themselves into constellations—an idea not unknown to the West—the Indian pictured in Caetano's song arrives in the guise of a visitor from another planet, in a spaceship reminiscent of Spielberg's *Encounters of a Third Kind*, a film that had recently enjoyed tremendous box-office success in Brazil. The song portrays a kind of Columbus "Discovery" in reverse, in terms that recall both native legends and blockbuster science fiction. But this time the "god who arrives from afar" is not European but indigenous. We are reminded of Lévi-Strauss's observation that when the Europeans encountered "Indians" they wondered if they were animals, while the native peoples, much more generously, wondered whether the Europeans were gods.

Scrambling various literary genres (prophecy, science fiction, Indianist poetry), the song at the same time resuscitates the prophetic Enlightenment topos, found in Abby Raynal and Diderot, of the "New World" avenger, the Indian rebel or black Spartacus who would come to avenge their suffering peoples. The reference to the "most advanced of technologies," meanwhile, subverts any kind of primitivist nostalgia for the "natural" Indian and echoes both 1) Oswald de Andrade's "*indio tecnizado*" and 2) contemporaneous manifestations of Brazilian Indians using technology to outwit the powerful, for example activist-politicians like Mario Juruna, who at the time always carried a tape-recorder, because "Brazilian politicians always lied to the Indians."

"O Indio"s *transnational* references draw on the taproot of indigenous culture, Brazilian literary and filmic Indianism, as well as the Modernist movement, with its exaltation of the festive indigenous life-style and communal ownership of land. At the same time, the song becomes trans-mediatic with its reference to Hollywood-style science fiction blockbusters.

> And the thing that I know he will say I do not know to say explicitly
> And what is to be revealed at that moment to the people
> Will surprise everyone by not being exotic

And by its power to have always remained hidden
When in fact it was obvious.

The film's refrain, which repeats the line: "He will come," imagines the redemptive figure of the Red Avenger in transcultural pop terms, as a multi-racial amalgam of postmodern culture heroes: first, Muhammad Ali, African-American boxer and war-resister who converted to Islam and whose transnational genealogy goes back to Africa, moving through an imposed European (slave) name (Cassius Clay) and finally to an Arabic/Islamic name; second, Peri, the pure romantic Indian Platonic lover from Alencar's Indianist novel *O Guarani*, valued for his passion but not for his role as the kind of "good Indian" collaborator beloved by whites; and third, Bruce Lee, an Asian master, with an Anglo-American name, of a millennial martial art.

The final reference in the chorus is to the Axé" (yoruba for energy or power of realization) of the *afoxé* (Africanized carnival percussion groups composed mainly of black people from Salvador, Bahia) and in particular to the group "Sons of Gandhi," founded by black dockers in 1948, a year after Indian independence, as a protest against racial discrimination and an homage to the pacifist Indian leader Mahatma Gandhi. With costumes modeled on those displayed by the Indian characters in a British film (*Gunga Dinn*), the music and practice of "Sons of Gandhi" constitute a sterling example of Afro-pop vernacular cosmopolitanism, in that the group was created by poorly educated black dockers who probably never travelled outside of Brazil or even outside of the state of Bahia, led by a man accoutered like Gandhi himself, in a performative gesture which revealed an intuitive sense of the transoceanic connectivities between Indian independence and black liberation.[3]

Indigenous media fits awkwardly into categories like World, Transnational, and Global, because it is simultaneously "in default" and "in excess" of such categories. The movement is transnational in the sense of making various cross-border connections, first of all, between (and across) indigenous nations themselves, whether in Brazil, in the U.S. or Canada, in Mexico and Peru, in Australia and New Zealand, or among the Sami people of Scandinavia and so forth, and secondly, in the sense of distributing their films to national and international audiences. Given that forms of indigenous media are emerging on virtually every continent, they can be seen as well through a broader grid as a widespread and thus "global" movement. Playing on the expression "Negritude," James Clifford speaks of "global *indigeneitude*" in order to call attention to indigenous culture as a world-wide phenomenon.[4] Although Indigenous media often takes non-feature forms, ranging from small-scale videos and Internet websites videos to cable-TV programs and documentaries, at this point indigenous filmmakers have also achieved "global indigeneitude" through feature films, many of them, such as the Native American *Smoke Signals* and the Inuit *Atanarjuat: The Fast Runner*, quite successful both in commercial and artistic terms. The makers of the latter film knitted together materials from the indigenous commons of Inuktitut narratives into an effective tale mean for Inuit and non-Inuit audiences. *Bran Nue Dae*, meanwhile, a kind of

School Daze set in the Australian outback, for example, directed by the Aboriginal filmmaker Rachel Perkins, was a box-office hit in Australia in 2009.

Some indigenous productions have reached large audiences through what might be called televisual indigeneity. In Australia, the seven-part, indigenous-directed series *First Australians* in 2008 offered an alternative to settler-colonial history, from pre-contact to the present. In the same year, the five-part "American Experience" PBS Series "We Shall Remain," featuring Native American directors like Chris Eyre (Cheyenne/ Arappaho), and Dustin Craig (Apache), explored key moments in Native American history. The Mayan people of Mexico, meanwhile, have produced a 21-episode *telenovela*, entitled *Baktun*, performed in Mayan by the residents of Tihosuco, Mexico. In 1999 indigenous Canadians created APTN, the Aboriginal People's Television Network (APTN), as the self-declared "first Aboriginal TV network with programming by, for, and about Aboriginal People."[5] Asserting "sitcom sovereignty," the APTN show *Mixed Blessings* indigenized the genre while spoofing lily white shows like the *Brady Bunch*.

A hallmark of some APTN productions is an irreverent humor that one finds in much of the indigenous world. A key figure in North America is the Oneida/ Mohawk/Cree stand-up comedian/activist Charlie Hill, who appeared on the Richard Pryor Show in 1997, and subsequently on the Johnny Carson, Jay Leno, and David Letterman shows. Charlie Hill would usually begin by acknowledging that white audiences might be surprised to see Native Americans doing stand-up since they assumed that "Indians didn't have a sense of humor." But then he adds, "We didn't think *you* were too funny either!" Charlie Hill was a master of embodying what Thomas King calls the "Inconvenient Indian" who uses humor and analogy to disarm the audience and make white people laugh at their own racism. He had a gift for explaining settler colonialism through didactic analogies, comparing settlers taking over the land to house guests who promise to just stay one night and then "stay till Thanksgiving." (Charlie Hill also did a bit on Roseanne, "Last Thursday in November," which involved a parody of the Thanksgiving celebrations where the Indians call the pilgrims "nuckleheads" but end up leading them in a native dance).[6]

One native Canadian comedy group is called "the 1491s," in a nod to the world before Columbus and colonialism, reminiscent of the Brazilian Modernist penchant for dating their manifestos "October 11, 1492, or the day before Columbus' landfall. The troupe writes, produces, performs, and uploads videos on their 1491s website and YouTube Channel. On their website we can read:

> The 1491s is a sketch comedy group, based in the wooded ghettoes of Minnesota and buffalo grass of Oklahoma. They are a gaggle of Indians chock full of cynicism and splashed with a good dose of indigenous satire … They were at Custer's Last Stand. They mooned Chris Columbus when he landed.

(The Brazilian Modernists, in a similar spirit, dated their manifestos Oct 11, the day before Columbus' landfall in a reference to the pre-Columbian utopia of the matriarchal Tupi society called Pindorama).

Native humor constantly riffs off American mainstream popular culture, often playing with names, with sports teams called the "Cleveland Caucasians" and the "Washington Rednecks," bands named "Red Zeppelin" and the remix group "A Tribe Called Red." On APTN "Threes Company" becomes "Crees Company." Drew Hayden Taylor, as half Ojibwe and half Caucasian, calls himself "Special Occasion." One episode of "Mixed Blessings" features a German-accented "more Indian-than-the-Indians" purist who berates the native Canadians for not having teepees and sweat lodges and not cooking caribou in a correct manner. At a dinner which becomes a contest in authenticity as imagined by a German Wannabee, he finally explodes in disgust: "In Germany, we have names for people like you. We call you 'Coca Cola Indians.'" Locking them into an allochronic prison, he declares: "You have been corrupted by the 20th and the 21st century. I think, no, I actually know, I am more Indian than all of you!" After he leaves, they all laugh uproariously. Such satirical vignettes point to the ethnocentric limits not only of "White Savior" films like *Dances with Wolves*, but also of what Harmut Lutz calls German "Indianthusiasm."

Although some filmmakers such as Chris Eyre, Zacharias Kunuk, and Rachel Perkins are talented directors with personal styles who could clearly qualify as "auteurs" and thus might seem to be eligible for World Cinema status, the "World Cinema" rubric does not work for indigenous media generally because the indigenous filmmaking community is usually less invested in claiming personal authorship than in developing what Foucault called "discursive practices" and what Faye Ginsburg calls "embedded aesthetics."[7] Within a kind of tribal auteurism, indigenous filmmakers often see themselves as primarily accountable to family and clan rather than to producers, sponsors, or non-native audiences. Indigenous (Inuit) filmmaker Zacharias Kunuk describes the collective storytelling practices that informed films like *Atanarjuat* and *The Journals of Knud Rasmussen*:

> The Inuit style of filmmaking takes lots of teamwork. We work horizontally, while the usual Hollywood film people work in a military style. Our entire team would talk about how to shoot a particular scene, from art directors to the sound man. We put the whole community to work. Costumes, props— we had a two-million dollar budget [for Atanarjuat] and 1 million stayed with the people of Igloolik.[8]

Unlike the French New Wave with its Oedipal *ressentiment* against "*le cinema de papa*," the indigenous filmmakers respect the transgenerational commons and gnosis and consciously seek the approval of the elders, who sometimes insist on certain communal norms, for example that the participants not interrupt each other in mid-speech, that the film not harm members of the community and so forth. In an era of massive individualism and corporate enclosure, indigenous media stresses that which is common, including land and cultural knowledge. Many of the elders see film as a way to preserve the traditional corpus of songs and stories drawn from the common narratological inheritance. Just as the indigenous natural world harbors much of the planet's biodiversity, the indigenous world could be said to harbor much of the world's cultural diversity. Since stories and legends constitute the lifeblood of the native community, one could reasonably speak of bio-narratological diversity.

Intensely local but potentially global, the filmic address of indigenous films can be multi-directional by addressing multiple tribal, national, and transnational publics. Kyra Landzelius speaks of "inreach" toward members of the native communities and "outreach" to external non-indigenous publics.[9] While the authorship is tribal and local, the funding can be local, national, and transnational. Some of the constituencies of address of the Brazilian Video in the Villages project, for example, include ever-widening circles, first addressed to the tribal group itself, then to distant tribal relatives, then to Brazilians in general, and then to distant indigenous peoples and to the outside world in general. Indigenous media as practiced in Native North America, the Amazon Basin, and in Australia and New Zealand, comprise an empowering vehicle for communities struggling against geographical displacement, economic deterioration, ecological devastation, and cultural annihilation. Although occasionally sponsored by liberal governments or international support groups, these efforts have been generally small-scale, low budget and locally based. They can be both intensely local and infra-national– for example rooted in a very concrete and delimited parcel of communally shared land—and intensely supra-national and global in their reaching out to other indigenous communities and to sympathetic ecolocially minded activists around the world. The motto of APTN (Aboriginal People's Television Network)—"Sharing our stories with all Canadians as well as viewers around the world"—encapsulates these multi-directional aspirations.

Unlike the peasantry for Marx, first peoples *are* now capable of representing themselves. In the Granada TV documentary *Kayapo: Out of the Forest* (1989), the Kayapo and other native Amazonian peoples stage a mass ritual performance to protest the planned construction of a hydroelectric dam that would flood their communities. Their leader Raoni, a genius at forest diplomacy and public relations, appears with the rock-star Sting in what turned out to be a successful attempt to capture international media attention and cancel the World Bank loan that would have financed the project. (Raoni also met with French Presidents François Mitterand and Jacques Chirac in his search for international support.) A decade before, Raoni had been the subject of a 1978 Franco-Brazilian film, entitled simply *Raoni*, where we see the Kayapo leader, in an unstaged scene, literally save the life of the French and Brazilian filmmakers when the Kayapo people want to kill the whites because of the invasion of their lands; Raoni wisely argues that the tribe spare the filmmakers since they carry their story to the wider world. Raoni's prediction came true shortly thereafter when the film, narrated by Marlon Brando, was nominated for an Oscar. Many decades later, native activists are opposing still another attempt to dam the Xingu River—the Belo Monte Dam—shrewdly taking advantage of the world-wide success of *Avatar* to enlist James Cameron into their cause and describing themselves as the Navi' of the Amazon.

Unlike World Cinema, indigenous media is a social-mediatic movement and not an assembly of directors aspiring to auteur status. One of the most prolific of the *indigenous-media* movements is Video in the Villages in Brazil, which since 1986 has been affirming indigenous cultural identity and supporting indigenous struggles to protect territorial and cultural patrimonies. Video in the Villages (VNA), a collective and an indigenous school of cinema that includes indigenous and non-indigenous filmmakers, has trained scores of native filmmakers and generated almost a hundred films representing some thirty-seven indigenous peoples of the Amazon, such as the Kayapo, the Xavante, the Ashaninka, Ikpeng, Guarani, Waiapi and the Kuikuro. It is no longer a question of filmmakers "giving back" but rather of "making with." Some Video nas Aldeias projects such as *Xina Bena* (New Era, 2006), *Prinop: My First Contact* (2007), and *De Volta a Terra Boa* (Back to the Good Land, 2008) repurpose the archive by using non-native footage to their own ends.

In Brazil, first contact did not end in the 16th century, or in the 20th; it continues in the present. The indigenous-made *Prinop: My First Contact*, tells the story of the first encounter from an indigenous point of view. An Ikpeng elder reminisces about the group's first contact with whites: "in the past, there were no white people ... Life was good without them. They didn't think about us and we didn't think about them. They were the ones who came looking for us." The older villagers reenact their memory of the first sight of the plane seeking them out—they describe a "noisy bird shitting packages"—before the film cuts to the same event as seen in a historical reverse shot—archival footage of the 1964 contact now from the point of view of whites, seen in a film by the Villas-Boas Brothers recording the encounter.

The VNA project, as Ivana Bentes points out, demonstrates the possibility of passing from an oral-communal culture to an audio-visual one, without necessarily passing through literacy and literate culture as the only legitimate form of knowledge.[10] Nonetheless, the use of video cameras by indigenous media-makers sometimes brushes up against a prejudicial backlash, the museological-mediatic equivalent of "salvage anthropology," i.e. the idea that "Indians" must remain "pure" and undefiled by technology, living allochronically in a time-out-of-time. Renato Rosaldo speaks of "imperialist nostalgia," an "elegiac mode of perception" by which people "mourn the passing of what they themselves have transformed."[11] The VNA project, in contrast, favors reflexive self-awareness though the image, a theme which animates many of the early VNA films such as *O Espirito da TV* (The Spirit of Television, 1990) where Waiapi elders articulate the benefits of seeing themselves on the screen, of preserving the image of the elders for posterity, of teaching the songs to young people, and of encountering the language and image of their close relatives in other communities. In *A Arca dos Zo'e* (1993) features a historically unprecedented encounter between distant relative tribes the Waiapi and the Zo'e; the two groups exchange gifts, examine body ornaments, and articulate their cultural differences. While one group finds nudity completely normal, the other moves from initial shock to final acceptance. Both groups realize that the nuances between indigenous tribes pale in importance when compared to the overweening alterity of the dominant white culture that threatens the land and community well-being. In a twist on Deleuzian formulations, Bentes calls this process the "becoming anthropological" of the Indians themselves, a performative instantiation of Rouch's celebrated "shared anthropology" but from the other side of the colonial divide.[12]

Another VNA project, the TV series *Indians on TV* (2000) shows Indians reacting with irritable amusement at the prejudices and stereotypes typical of mainstream Brazilian TV—for example those of the Globo telenovela *Uga Uga*. Some films incorporate archival footage from films by non-Indians while showing the tantalized fascination of the indigenous people upon seeing images of their ancestors at the time of first contact with the Rondon Commission in the 1920s. In *Das Criancas Ikpeng para o Mundo* (From the Ikpeng children to the World, 2002), Ikpeng children explain (initially for an audience of their Cuban peers) their everyday life, their family relations, and their games. A mischievous youngster explains that his younger sibling is not a human being but rather a battery-operated creature. Laughingly, he points to her bum as the hiding place that contains the battery. (We are reminded that the early European visitors to Brazil frequently spoke of the native love of laughter and mischief.) The many scenes in these films of children playing gleefully in rivers remind us not only of the ordinary happiness of children playing everywhere, but also serve as a token of the kind of communal happiness that many indigenous people, betrayed and saddened by white invasion and domination, have lost.

Still another VNA film, *The Master and the Divine* (2013), co-directed by Thiago da Costa and Divino Teserahu, brilliantly conveys the crossed transnational gazes—here Brazilian, American, German, Xavante—directed at the Indian. The title refers to the two characters whose relationship structures the film—the "Master" Father Adalbert Heide, an eccentric Silesian monk who for decades has been filming the story of his life with the Xavante Indians, and "Divine," a Xavante Indian literally named "Divino," a former altar-boy with Father Heide, and now a filmmaker and village leader. Doubly reflexive, *The Master and the Divine* is not only a reflexive film-about-filmmaking but also the registry of the fraught yet friendly dialogue between two filmmakers emerging from distinct cultures. Through criss-crossed "becomings," a white European "becomes Indian" (while retaining his Western "positional superiority") while a "red" Indian becomes "white" (while still remaining proudly Xavante). Presented on a German TV program as a white adventurer in the tropics, Heide is a self-declared "white Indian," a European, fluent in Xavante, who has "gone native" to the point of wearing a Xavante headress and being decorated with war paint. But this imagist self-fashioning did not emerge ex nihilo from Heide's immaculate brain, since the "white Indian," as we have seen, is a transnational figure found all around the Red Atlantic, including in Europe, a product of five centuries of genocide, racism, and romanticism, formed over centuries of literature and a long century of cinema.

The dialogue between the Master and Divino reveals an imagistic battle of two cultures and two aesthetics. In an inversion of stereotypes, it is the Indian who is high-tech—a latter-day incarnation of Oswald's "indio tecnizado." Divino mercilessly needles the priest about the snail-like pace of his computer and his lack of Final Cut Pro software. Equally ironically, it is the foreign priest who cultivates a "positive image" of the Xavante—although one steeped in primitivist images of the noble savage—while the native Divino has no qualms about showing negative Xavante behavior such as drunkenness and tribal conflicts. While Heide sweetens everything in an epic-romantic style underscored by Andean flutes and the theme song from the Indianer film *Winnetou*, Divino prefers a self-reflexive critical realism which foregrounds the tensions not only between the Xavante and the whites, but also among the Xavante themselves. While the priest prefers pastoral shots of canoes on pristine creeks, the supposedly nature-loving Indian prefers talking heads, especially those of elders like his father who can provide vital information about Xavante history. The older European filmmaker, in a regime of cinematic "tutelage," prefers to "protect" and clean up the image of the Xavante, betrays resentment toward the indigenous upstart who might terminate his imagistic monopoly.

On Brazilian television, even Indians get to "play Indian," as we see in an climactic sequence that shows Divino appearing on TV as a child responding to the call of blonde TV star Xuxa—dressed syncretically in the headdress of a Sioux warrior—singing "Vamos brincar de Indio" (Let's Play Indian). To the accompaniment of putative "Indian war cries," Xuxa leads the children in a happy song featuring fake Indian-speak lyrics:

> Let's play Indian, but without anyone to capture me!
> Come, join my tribe? I'm chief and you're my partner.
> Indian make noise. Indian have pride.
> Come paint your skin so the dance can begin ...

In a stagey show of *mauvaise foi*, Xuxa, like Heide but with even less reason to make the claim, Xuxa becomes the putative "white Indian" defender of Indian rights. In Hollywood-style Injun-speak," she sings "Indian need land." Ironically, she is better at playing Indian than the Indians themselves; she has to teach the Indians to "become Indian." As Xuxa drags the rather frightened-looking Xavante boys into her photogenic circle of fun, they look stiff and reluctant. With their body paint and spears, they become Hollywood-style "spearchuckers" in a film where they are the "extras" of history while she plays the literally leading and starring role. The sexualized icon of white beauty tries to teach them to be good little Indians, but they are not very good pupils, not really good at "becoming Indian," and in a kind of sullen opacity, refuse to perform her caricatural image of themselves.[13] At this point in the film, the non-indigenous co-director's voice over informs us that as a child he probably saw that Xuxa show, and that he probably sang along with "Let's Play Indian," blithely unaware of the its racist implications, yet now he is a collaborator/friend of Divino, a Euro-Brazilian who has been transformed by the indigenous knowledge of people like Divino.

While specifically about Brazil, some of Vincent Carelli's documentaries, such as *Corumbiara* (2009) and *Martirio* (2017) have global relevance, in that the indigenous genocide they describe has taken place, and is still taking place, across many parts of the globe. The Amazon, in particular, has been convulsed by an enormous movement of corporate enclosure. The former film, shot over two decades, traces Carelli's attempt to discover the truth about a massacre of Indians reported to have taken place in 1985. In the process he discovers not only evidence of the massacre, but also evidence of the efforts by landowners and politicians to erase all traces of the episode, and the lack of interest of the government into looking into the question, at the same time he questions himself as an *indigenista*. He meets members of previously uncontacted tribes, argues with the landowners who deny the reality of the massacre, and gets glimpses of the last remaining survivor of what must have been a massacre. Approaching the man's hut-fortress, they see an arrow, aimed at the filmmakers, protruding from an opening in the hut. At that moment, a doubt sets in and the filmmakers decide not to pursue an encounter with the lone remaining Indian, given his transparent desire not to be "contacted" even by sympathetic outsiders. The filmmakers applaud the resistance of the indigene to white dispossession, but they also respect his desire to retain his own "opacity" (Glissant)

Martirio, meanwhile, offers a searing account of a century of massacres and dispossession of indigenous people in Brazil. A veritable film-event, *Martirio* relates the perennial struggle of the Guarani-Kaiowá, a group of indigenous people in the Mato Grosso do Sul, fighting for the dispersed remainders of their forest commons, now threatened by Agribusiness and confiscation by the Brazilian State. Their weapons in this unequal contest are protests, performances, films, bows and arrows (and sometimes guns), and a combative form of spirituality. Filmed over the course of four decades, the film mingles indigenous people speaking in their own voice with shocking archival material used to narrate what amounts to a slow-motion genocide. The martyrdom involves a historical sequence of moments of dispossession: the devastating effects of the War of Paraguay in the 1860s; the "humanitarian" assimilationism of the Rondon Commission in the 19teens and 1920s; the expansionist incursions of the Vargas regime in the 1930s; the military dictatorship's attempt to "integrate the national territory" at the expense of the indigenous peoples themselves in the late 1960s and the 1970s; right on up to the present-day collaboration between corrupt politicians and powerful corporations.

Martirio was a sock to the gut to those Brazilians and non-Brazilians who would have liked to believe in the romantic myth of a cordial relationship between the Euro-Brazilian and the Indigene. In this film, both the "Indians" and their racist enemies speak for themselves. With painful lucidity, the Guarani-Kaiowá lament that "capitalism is killing us." Another indigenous (Krenak) representative says mockingly and poetically: "The markets wake up in a bad mood, and they decide to devour mountains." Brazilian parliamentarians, meanwhile, proudly display their tendentious ignorance. Audiences are confronted with the blatant racism of the "ruralistas"— large property owners complicit with Agri-business and the *latifundistas*. One ruralist

Senator, Katia Abreu, proudly reminds her admirers that they had already succeeded in getting rid of the landless movement, and then of the *Codigo Florestal* (the ecology-friendly law protecting the vegetation of indigenous land). All that remains, she concludes, is to get rid of the "Indian problem." The ruralists use all the classic colonialist arguments to disqualify those who call themselves Indians as not "real Indians" point out that some wear jeans and wield cameras, and after all there are "too few Indians occupying too much land."

The film deals a death blow to the sentimental Indianism of Brazilian elites lauding the glorious triad of Red, Black, and White living together in a mythical "racial democracy" à la Gilberto Freyre. For indigenous people, in Brazil as in most of the Americas, have been living a "state of exception," within which they are often reduced to "bare life" (Agamben) and subject to the acts of not-so-random violence to which the film bears vibrant witness. *Martirio* demonstrates that anthropology and solidarity, emotion and reason, art and indignation, can operate in concert. At a time when indigenous peoples are protesting injustice from Standing Rock to Belo Monte, from Alaska to Patagonia, *Martirio* has burning relevance.

For indigenous peoples the issues are less of inclusion and citizenship than simply of sovereignty and land. The issue of the "indigenous commons" comes to the foreground in Aboriginal Australian filmmaker Rachel Perkins' *One Night the Moon* (2001). Based on actual events that transpired in Australia in 1932, the film revolves around a young white child who goes missing in the outback. The father, out of racist arrogance and an exacerbated sense of private property, refuses the help of a savvy Aboriginal tracker. The father's arrogance and his ethnocentric dismissal of other forms of knowledge (subaltern gnosis) leads to the death of his own child, since it turns out that the tracker, through his intimate familiarity with the land, could have saved his daughter's life. Marcia Langton's definition of aboriginality as "a field of intersubjectivity ... that is remade over and over again in a process of dialogue, of imagination, or representation and interpretation" perfectly suits *One Night the Moon*.[14]

But what is most striking in aesthetic terms, in this Aboriginal musical, is the film's revisionist orchestration of two genres—the Western and the musical—to make a point about the commons in an almost literal sense. From the perspective of colonized people of color, both genres might well be seen as suspect examples of what Maori filmmaker/theorist Barry Barclay calls the "invaders' cinema" typical of hegemonic groups in colonial settler-states. The Hollywood musical appropriated and marginalized people of color, and the Western consecrated the dispossession of native peoples through the doctrine of Manifest Destiny. The Western, in its various forms, has served as an ideal medium for expressing both the genocidal thrust as well as the ethical dilemmas of colonial settler-states like the United States and Australia, often legitimating Western domination. The Hollywood musical, meanwhile, has choreographed this legitimation, as when the lyrics of the theme song of *Oklahoma!*—a state with an indigenous name, but ripped out of traditionally native territory—tell us that "We [whites] know we belong to the land/and the land we belong to is grand." The hybrid Western-musical *Calamity Jane*, where natives are called "painted varmits," has white settlers sing the glories of the Black Hills—the sacred lands of the Sioux—in terms of *white* ownership. Ironically, even these acts of lyrical appropriation borrow from Indian conceptions of "belonging to the land."

In both the U.S. and Australia, settlers butted up against indigenous peoples as part of what Glissant calls, in contrast with the "circular nomadism" of indigenous peoples, the "straight-arrow" nomadism of conquest."[15] In both countries, nation-states destroyed long-existing systems of communally held land in favor of Dawes Act deeds of private ownership. There is nothing that divides the Western world view from the indigenous world view as much as the conception of the common land as what Thomas King calls the "defining element of Aboriginal culture," that which "contains the languages, the stories, and the histories of a people [and] provides water, air, shelter, and food."[16] *One Night the Moon* tells the story of conquest through indigenous eyes, in ways that go far beyond other revisionist "white Indian" stories like *Little Big Man*, *Dances with Wolves*, and *Avatar*. The film hybridizes the Western with the musical, furthermore, by showcasing the Country-and-Western music popular not only in the American Southwest but also with the aboriginal people in the Australian interior. This technique reaches its paroxysm in an open-air production number wherein the song is alternately sung by the white settler and the Aboriginal tracker. The lyrics counterpose two views of the land, in an antiphony at once musical and socio-ideological. As they stride off in their opposite ways against the arid backdrop, the settler's refrain is "This land is mine" owing to the fact that he "signed a deed on the dotted line." The tracker's refrain, which answers the settler's, meanwhile, asserts a strong identification between the land and the tracker. It goes "This land is *me* … this land owns me," culminating in a claim of indigenous knowledge and of settler alienation from the land: "You only fear what you don't understand."

Voiced in direct mono-syllabic terms, the production numbers stage a discursive duel in the sun, an ideological standoff over competing views of the land– on the one hand, what Chadwick Allen calls "native indigeneity," or the Aboriginal collective view of the land as sacred and communally owned, and on the other hand "settler indigeneity," or the Western view of newly cultivated land as alienable private property.[17] The question evoked in the lyrics and realized in the setting was at the heart of the colonial doctrine of *terra nullius*, which decreed that the land, à la Lockean theory, did not rightfully belong to the indigenous people unless they had fenced it off and practiced sedentary agriculture. In the Lockean view, the land belongs to those who work it. Locke calls the acquisition of land through agricultural appropriation "enclosure"; "He by his labor does, as it were, enclose it from the commons."[18] To merit ownership, those who had lived on and cared for the land for millennia had to mix it with their labor in order to make it productive of commodities. The lyrics in the film mention all the requisite measures to justify possession: a fence, a deed, farming, bank payments, and the production of commodities ("make it pay"). The Lockean view anticipates the idea of the

Anthropocene in its assumption that human beings have irreversibly changed nature itself. What is ultimately a philosophical/ political/epistemic confrontation here takes the form of a subtly choreographed musical number staged as part of a Western-style genre and set against the backdrop of the very land where sovereignty is in dispute.

Any view that warns indigenous peoples to flee the media to avoid Western "contamination" denies them the indispensable tools of self-defense in the digital age. Undeterred by Promethean/Heideggerian pessimism, the children of recently contacted groups—allochronically designated "stone age tribes"—now use Facebook and post YouTube videos to introduce themselves to multiple publics. Many indigenous children, like middle class children around the world, now learn how to use computers before they learn to read and write and in formats that in some ways accord well with oral traditions. In South America, Mapuche and Aymara activists use the Internet, Facebook and YouTube to disseminate hip-hop protest songs, while in North America, Native Americans hold cyber-pow-wows sending "cyberspace smoke signals."[19] Meanwhile, the Internet connects both continents; as bilingual Purepecha speakers in Chicago are now in contact via the Internet with Aymaras in Bolivia, Yanomami in Venezuela, and Guarani in Paraguay. In the Amazon, "First Contact" is still occurring, but this time the "Indians" come armed not with bows and arrows but rather with books, computers, digital cameras, websites, blogs, and listserves.

30

THE MEDIA'S "DEEP TIME" AND THE PLANETARY COMMONS

In *Through Other Continents*, Wai Chee Dimock speaks of "deep time" to refer to a "set of longitudinal frames, at once projective and recessional, with input going both ways, and binding continents and millennia into many loops of relations, a densely interactive fabric."[1] "In a multidirectional temporality, "deep time" moves backward into the past but also leaps forward toward a *planetary* future. This planetary discourse is not completely new. In 1969, Erich Auerbach anticipated both the transnational and the planetary move when he said that "our philological home is the earth, it can no longer be the nation."[2] Given the global climate change crisis, it is perhaps no surprise that words like "planetary" and "ecology" have begun to proliferate in the texts of those who speak of World Literature.[3] Franco Moretti, for example, envisions literature as a "planetary system."[4] And Gayatri Spivak, in the wake both of Auerbach's exhortation and of the disciplinary crisis in Comparative Literature, has called for a "planetary" approach which enables us to "write the globe,"

Contemporary academic discourse resounds with echoes of this planetary crisis. A volume edited by Amy J. Elias and Christian Moraru, entitled *The Planetary Turn: Relationality and Geoaesthetic in the 21st Century*, argues that the planet itself has become a key framework for contemporary artists and intellectuals. In his essay "The Anthropocene: the Promise and Pitfalls of an Epochal Idea," Rob Nixon asks us to think about *Homo Sapiens* not merely as a historical but also as a geological actor, a "force of such magnitude that our impacts are being written into the fossil record … for the first time in history, a sentient species, our own, has shaken Earth's life systems with a profundity that paleontologist Anthony Barnosky has likened to an asteroid strike?"[5] In the "Climate of History," Depesh Chakravarty speaks of the transformation of our human species as biological agent into a geological force, "the only one endowed with consciousness of its own purposes."[6] Given the inexorable march of an ominous set of negative trends—global warming, the acidification of the oceans, the depletion of the ozone, and the loss of bio-diversity, it is as if World

Systems Theory needs now to be transformed into Earth Systems Theory. This planetary transformation dissolves the old binary of the local and the global, given that none of these phenomena can be seen as merely local, since every local gets absorbed into a planetary crisis. We are confronted, in a sense, with the final consequences of the Pyrrhic victories of Progress—the ruin of global civilization at the very moment of its uncontentested hegemony.

The division of Global North and South works to the advantage of the Global North even in apocalyptic times. Macarena Gomez-Barris points out that the very term "Anthropocene" would seem to blame all of humanity for ecological disaster rather than colonialism and industrial capitalism.[7] As Deborah Danowski and Eduardo Viveiros de Castro put it in *Ha Mundo por Vir? Ensaio sobre os Medos e os Fins* (Is there a World to Come? Essay on Fears and Ends, 2017): "In the case of the anthropocene ... the countries which contributed to global warming are the same countries which now enjoy greater security, even if only temporarily, due to their greater capacity to mitigate the disastrous economic effects of climate change on their own territories."[8] "Just as we were conquering the new frontier of space," they write, "we discovered that our earthly launching-pad was collapsing."[9] As a result, a tragic gap opens up between "our (scientific) capacity to imagine the end of the world and our (political) incapacity to imagine the end of capitalism."[10] It is in this context that the authors cite the indigenous critique of capitalism as engendering what Yanomami shaman/philosopher Davi Kopenawa calls the "fall of the sky." In an indigenous version of what Marxists call "commodity fetishism," Kopenawa blames the ecological catastrophe on the lamentable fact that "whites love only their merchandise."[11]

The crisis of the Anthropocene was foreshadowed, in a way, in the prophetic ending of Hitchcock's *The Birds* (1963), a film which heralded those whom Hitchcock called in the trailer "our good friends the birds," noting their "age-old relationship with man," who has "played a conspicuous part" in their "noble history." With acid irony and inappropriately saccharine background music, the Master of Suspense himself speculates about "how proud the birds must have felt to have their eggs stolen, their feathers plucked out for plumed hats." He speaks of the species which have "disappeared," but then clarifies that in fact they have been "killed off." We have "honored our feathered friends," the director reminds us, by "caging them, exhibiting them, hunting them, and making them the guests of honor at our Thanksgiving celebrations." The film's final point-of-view shots unknowingly instantiates Eduardo Viveiros de Castro's claim that for the Amazonian Indians a species represents a point-of-view, in the sense the film's finale encodes the perspective of four crows calmly observing the traumatized departure of the last by now superfluous human protagonists.

We find similar themes in Abel Ferrara's *4.44 Last Day on Earth* (2012) and Lars von Trier's *Melancholia* (2012). The former film has a couple make their wedding vows at the very moment of immanent apocalypse. The latter film counterpoints the dramas of the human world with all its contradictory beauty and pettiness with what Danowski and de Castro call the "austere ballet of the spheres" which triggers the "the event that ends all events" where no one survives to tell the tale.[12] As

Peter Szendy puts it: "The end of the world is the end of the film, and the end of the film is the end of the world."[13] The conjunction of the bluish planet Melancholia slouching toward earth and its earthlings, combined with a dark bass rumble and a chord transition from the prelude to Wagner's *Tristan & Isolde*—a locus classicus of the *liebestod* motif—together conjure up the boundless tragedy that would be the destruction of our planetary commons and the end of our collective species-being.

Another film that gives us a sense of a palimpsestic planetary time is Patricio Guzmán's *Nostalgia for the Light* (2010). The film's *discordia concors* meditates on the relationalities between three apparently discordant entities: 1) astronomers scanning the sky above; 2) archeologists exploring what lies beneath the earth below; and 3) indefatigable Chilean widows scratching the desert's surface in search of the bones of relatives murdered during the dictatorship. Although astronomers, archeologists, and widows would not on the surface seem to have much in common, the film reveals their subterranean affinities through different relations to "deep time." All three groups explore the past—the archeologists and the widows, obviously, but also the astronomers witnessing events that occurred light years earlier. Neil Shubin, in a different context, speaks of the "common roots of rocks, planets and people" in ways that evoke the sense of mystery that haunts the film: "The stars in the sky and the fossils in the ground are enduring beacons that signal [that] we are but a recent link in a network of connections as old as the heavens."[14]

Various traits of *Nostalgia for the Light*—the interweaving of themes, the passionate rationality of the voice-over, the digressive structure, the heterogeneous materials, the hybridization of documentary and fictional procedures—all signal the generic presence of an essay film. In a kind of "network narrative" version of the genre, all three narratives are linked to the Atacama Desert, a moisture-free place which allows unusual visibility for telescopes. The site's dryness also enables it to conserve the human and animal past as readable in untouched remains of fish, mollusks, Indian petroglyphs, and even mummified humans. The same lack of humidity that helps astronomers scrutinize the universe also helps archeologists and Chilean victims of the dictatorship trace the remainders of the past. The women scour the desert for calcium in the form of bones of their murdered relatives, while the astronomers look for calcium as a remnant of stars and the Big Bang. (One of the women, Vicky Saavedra, reports crying endlessly while clinging to the single relic—a foot—of her brother's material being). In a kind of astronomical sublime, the observer is overwhelmed by the unmasterable totality of an infinitely vast universe, as uncannily beautiful images of asteroids segue into extreme close-ups of asteroid-like bone fragments. A skull becomes a *paysage moral*. In a case of the microscopic-astronomical sublime, the closest of close-ups transition into the longest of long shots; we see the world in decaying bones, the universe in a grain of Atacama sand.

Nostalgia for the Light is *multi-chronotopic*, in Bakhtin's version of "deep time." Quite apart from the film's adherence to the Menippean three-plane schema (earth, sky, underworld) the film orchestrates multiple chronologies—the human life span, the life of species, the life of planets and galaxies, and the birth and death of a dictatorship—all emerging from a single topos. The Guzmán film also rhymes with Deleuze's reference in *The Time-Image* to sidereal time as "a system of relativity, where characters would not be so much human as planetary, and the accents not so much subjective as astronomical, in a plurality of worlds constituting the universe."[15] In Guzmán's archeology of the present, various lived temporalities converge with the buried histories of a desert that shelters ancient rock paintings, pre-Columbian mummies, dinosaur skeletons, the dead from saltpeter mines, Pinochet' victims, and the corpses of the first, aboriginal *desaparecidos*—the massacred indigenous people. Guzmán reminds us of the matter of memory, and the memory contained within matter itself, and that memories matter, and that those without memory have no future.

The stars, according to John Durham Peters, "remain singularly sublime and beautiful" while pondering "why a black field spangled with small lights of subtly varying colors and intensities should be so captivating remains an open question."[16] Dante ended all three parts of the Divina Comedia with the word *stelle* (stars). In the end, *Nostalgia for the Light* communicates a sense of politicized mysticism, a subdued tenderness for people and the universe, a Dantean wonder at the "love that moves the sun and the other stars." In David Martin-Jones' anthropocemic gloss, the film explores "the intertwining of human and planetary history via an encounter with the Earth's past."[17] The film heralds what risks becoming a final form of politics rooted in a galactic consciousness of species vulnerability, registering a proleptic nostalgia for our not-yet lost planet. In their lunatic search for the truth, the astronomer, the archeologist, the cineaste, and the widow, to borrow from Shakespeare, are "of imagination all compact." The filmmaker's eye, in a fine frenzy, "doth glance from heaven to earth, from earth to heaven," bodying forth the "forms of things unknown." As an intergalactic meditation on time and space, the film brings us back to the perennial conundrums of philosophy, where one asks with childlike wonder: "When did time begin? Where does space end? Why is there something rather than nothing? And what strange force makes us care?"

It is hard to imagine a Commons in an age of Enclosure, when it has become a truism that we find easier to imagine the end of the World than the end of Capitalism. We are now in the endgame of what Marx and Engels in the *Communist Manifesto* called the "subjection of nature's forces to man's machinery." As James Hansen writes, "… the continued exploitation of all fossil fuels on Earth threatens not only the other millions of species on the planet but also the survival of humanity itself …"[18] Franny Armstrong's drama-documentary-animation-essay film *The Age of Stupid* (2009), in a didactic and populist manner, links the digital commons to the planetary commons in its discussion of the threat of climate change. Highly innovative in its transnational funding, production, distribution, and theme, the film was also innovative its style and its mix of genres and formats. A kind of low-budget blockbuster, the film's methods form the polar opposite of the standard Hollywood protocols. Working in collaboration with NGOs and organizations such as Greenpeace, Move-On, and the performance group Yes-Men (who wore their satiric Model X7 "Survivaballs"), the filmmakers encouraged public involvement through an interactive website. In order to have full independence, the film was produced and financed independently through the crowdfunding model. The filmmakers also pioneered a new web-based form of film distribution called Indie Screenings, whereby anyone, anywhere, could publicly screen the film and keep whatever profits ensued. Rather than procure massive profits, the filmmakers multiplied free screenings to spread the word. Linked by satellite to scores of cinemas around the United Kingdom (and later around the U.S. and beyond) the premiere received the Guinness World Record for being the largest film premiere in history, for an estimated total of a million spectators, a feat rarely achieved by leftist documentaries not made by Michael Moore.

In aesthetic-narrative terms, the film borrows the very old literary frame- device of shipwreck narration, à la Ishmael in *Moby Dick*, by the sole survivor of a disaster, the one who remains to tell the story, with the difference that the shipwreck, in this case, is not of a single ship but of spaceship earth itself. The narrator, played by Pete Postlethwaite, lives in the post-apocalyptic world of a high-tech tower, a kind of dystopian commons, called The Global Archive. Pressing on the icons and rubrics on the computer screen, the Archive grants access to the intellectual-mediatic commons in the form of a vast repository of everything that has been written and filmed, which he probes for clues as to how the planet earth and its people somehow managed to commit collective suicide. In this sense, the narrator becomes a planetary *griot*, the keeper of the flame of memory, custodian of the surviving store of art, media, and knowledge.

After an evocation of the primordial beginnings of the universe—conveyed in minimalist fashion through the slow-motion stirring of milk in a glass—the opening animation reveals a planet devastated by climate change—Las Vegas swallowed up by the desert, Sydney in flames, the Alps transformed into a snowless desert, and the Taj Mahal consumed by vultures in a war-devastated India. Also innovative in narrative terms, the film transposes into a documentary format the interwoven stories of the "network narratives" (Bordwell) of films like Soderberg's *Traffic* (2000) and Iñárritu's *Amores Perros* (2000). Playing a futuristic restrospective Cassandra, the narrator marshals evidence for an indictment of the human shortsightededness that facilitated the apocalypse. In a transnational polyphony of voices, intermingled tableaux of individual characters (from seven countries) all search for solutions. Vignettes reveal an Alpine climber lamenting the disappearing snow, a Nigerian woman afflicted by the polluted water generated by corporate-owned oil projects, a windfarm developer fighting corporate lobbyists, and a literal-life saver in the wake of Katrina. The vignettes flesh out the portrayal of the endgame of the instrumentalization of the planet's resources exposed decades earlier in Adorno-Horkheimer's *Dialectic of Enlightenment*. In an ethic/aesthetic of global connectivity, the film rejects plot-centered network narratives in favor of a theme-centered "*causal network of events*" à la Brecht, and specifically what are emerging as central political issues of our time—the insidious synergies of private ownership, the dominance of fossil fuels, and the devastation of our common planet.

31

THE COMMONS AND THE GLOBALIZED CITIZEN

While classical Marxism is anticapitalist yet ultimately productivist, the indigenous movements as expressed in indigenous thought and media are often more radically anticapitalist in their assertion not only of their collective right to their ancestral communal land but also to their universalizing claim that "mother earth" should not be commodified. Not only were indigenous societies the most likely to have communally owned land—for example the *allyus* of Andean societies and the *ejidos* of Mexico—but they were also the major targets of land confiscation. This commodification of nature and the lust for privatization at times reaches absurd lengths. For example, what could be more "common "and more assumed to be owned "in common" than the milk that comes from a mother's breast? Yet the Trump administration, in league with the baby food corporations like Nestle, stunned World Health officials gathered in Geneva by opposing efforts to encourage breastfeeding in the Global South and discourage the misleading marketing of breast milk substitutes.[1]

In this realm too aquatic metaphors bubble up to the surface. The "liquidation" of the indigenous commons was performed, as it were, in the name of "liquidity." Quechua and the Amayra activists in Bolivia say that "politics should be like water—transparent, in constant movement, and *mui alegre*." The protestors at Standing Rock, similarly, proclaim that "water is sacred," a slogan that human beings, largely composed of water in any case, should readily understand. In the wake of indigenous activism and the UN declaration of indigenous rights, Ecuador and Bolivia have begun to inscribe indigenous rights and even the "right of Nature not to be harmed" into their constitutions. Andean struggles over the natural commons on one level reverberate with the various "Reclaim the Streets" and the "Occupy" struggles over the urban commons (including the right to conduct protests in public parks). Yet on another level, indigenous intellectuals/activists like Sandy Grandy offer an even more radical critique. While the Occupy Movement wanted to liberate Zucotti Park from private ownership, that "enclosure" by a single Euro-American, she reminds us, was made possible by an earlier "occupation"—that of indigenous land by Europeans.

In the wake of the global turn and the emergence into the public sphere of indigenous social thought, we find a search for longer and larger time schemes and even more inclusive spatial categories. Emily Apter speaks of "*terrestrial* humanism."[2] Ursula K. Heise, in the context of Ecocriticism, speaks of "*environmental* World Literature."[3] James Clifford speaks of "international *indigenism*."[4] Wai Chee Dimock, similarly, connects Native American culture to a "deep time" of the commons closer to the life of the human species than to the 500-year history of Europeans in the Americas. She cites Leslie Marmon Silko: "Five-hundred years is not a very long time. Because for 18,000 years there is evidence of the Pueblo people being in [their] land."[5] Dimock concludes her book by talking about "geological time." Watersheds and Mesolithic dwellers, she writes, "remind us just how recent the nation-state is, how small a part it plays in the recorded life of the species."[6] She calls up the example of the Native American Turtle Island as not only the name of the North American continent but also a "rallying call for a new environmental ethics, one that looks back to the kinship of humans and animals in indigenous cultures."[7]

One of the most succinct statements about the relevance of the commons to contemporary social life is found in a short book by Antonio Negri and Michael Hardt, entitled (a la Magritte) *This is not a Manifesto*—even though the book is manifestly precisely what it denies being—a manifesto.[8] All the popular revolts that began in 2009 in Iran and the spread to Tunisia. Cairo, Bahrain, Barcelona, Madison, New York and beyond, the authors note, form a transnational assemblage of insurgencies which shared, in however an inchoate manner, the idea of a commons, an animus against privatization and the hegemony of financial capitalism, and even, at their most radical, a rejection of private property. Within this synchronicity of protest, perhaps for the first time, demonstrators in both the Global North and the Global South seemed close to being on the same wavelength—the common enemy was financial capitalism, the matrix of global financial power of the 1% which dominated not only the U.S. but much of the world, for which Wall Street served as metaphor and metonym.[9]

The dominant model of financial capitalism, for Negri and Hardt, molds subjectivity to produce a certain kind of subordinated subject, which they classify as 1) the *indebted subject*; 2) the *mediatized subject*; 3) the *securitized subject*, and 4) the *represented subject*. Here I will focus on the two categories most relevant to our theme of global media—the indebted subject citizen as a kind of sub-citizen, and the mediated citizen. The new master/slave dialectic, it seems, is no longer just a Hegelian struggle between Master and Slave, or a Fanonian struggle between Colonizer and Colonized, or even just the old Marxist struggle between Capital and Labor, but also, importantly, between the globalized struggle of Creditor and Debtor, Representer and Represented, Code-writer and Code-written. The modern-day slavery of school debt, mortgage, and health insurance—are the "new normal" for the vast masses of the indebted. The enemy is not just the policeman in uniform, but also parlamentarians in Congress and creditors in suits snapping at the heels of students mired in debt, objects of foreclosure and health-related bankruptcies. In a similar vein, Andrew Ross points out in *Creditocracy: the Case for Debt Refusal* that indebtedness has become the precondition both for material improvements in the quality of life and even for a "bare life" existence.[10] Profit accumulation through the exploitation of debt is the figure in the carpet that threads together major forms of oppression in the neoliberal era. An intricate global web, Ross points out, connects apparently disparate phenomena such as colonialism and Third World debt, slavery and reparations, public debt and austerity policies, student debt and political corruption, colonial resource extraction and contemporary debt bondage, climate debt and the ecological crisis.

The idea of the contemporary subject/citizen as "mediatized," meanwhile, is also relevant to global and transnational media. Citing Deleuze, Hardt and Negri point out that self-empowerment "… is not enough, the people have to have something to say!" As racist populism encourages a false sense of empowerment as an answer to an equally false sense of resentment, mediatized subjects "rush toward their own servitude while fantasizing it as salvation." In the Internet era, the authors argue, the dominant corporate media "create obstacles to all emergent forms of democratic participation. The represented subject/citizen of classical democratic theory morphs into the consumer/spectator. Yet at its best the media, including a reconfigured social media—we can have no illusions after Cambridge Analytica and Facebook's aid to the Trump campaign—could foster collective self-production and provide a forum for experimentation in democratic and "multitudinous" governance. The commons, for the authors, exists in the hearts and minds of those who struggle to imagine and create new forms of social life. The concept of the commons and the common good becomes the key to egalitarian social organization.

The moral authority of the first peoples of America, according to Philip J. Deloria, derives "not from priority but from the ecological commons whose material memory was maintained by a spiritual notion, the sacred hoop. "Someday the United States," Deloria predicts, "will revise its constitution, its laws, in terms of human beings, instead of property."[11] For native peoples, the American revolution was a land grab. In a concise summary of what might be called a pro-indigenous and post Republican- Revolutionary discourse– "Republican" here in the sense of the transnational political commons, however compromised and incomplete, of the American, French, and Haitian revolutions—Hardt and Negri offer a succinct summary of their credo:

> … only a constituent principle based on the common can offer a real alternative. We hold these truths to be self-evident; that all persons are equal, that they acquire, through political struggle, certain inalienable rights, among them life, liberty, and the pursuit of happiness, along with free access to the Commons, equality in the distribution of wealth and in the sustainability of the

Commons. It is also evident that to assure such rights democratic governance must be instituted. Finally, it is self-evident that in the case that any form of government which becomes destructive to these ends, it is the right of the people to abolish that government and institute another, which will base itself on these principles and organize its power in the form which will best guarantee the security and happiness of the people."[12]

These formulations obviously riff on the American Declaration of Independence and the French "droits de l'homme" but with crucial amendments: In the tradition of revisionist feminist versions of the "Declaration of the Rights of Man[sic]" in the style of Olympe de Gouge's "Declaration of the Rights of Woman and the Female Citizen," penned in the wake of the French Revolution, Hardt and Negri remind us that all *persons*—not *men*—are created equal; that rights are achieved not through top-down declarations but only through *struggle*; that these rights include not only political rights but also *economic* rights in the form of equal distribution of wealth; and ecological rights to a sustainable commons.

With an alert eye to the possibilities of dialectical jiujitsu within a situation of globalized domination, Portuguese scholar Boaventura de Sousa Santos, an intellectual deeply familiar with the European, Latin American and North American academic scenes, points to five "fields" in which counterhegemonic globalization creates viable opportunities: (1) participatory democracy, (2) alternative systems of production, (3) multicultural justice and citizenship, (4) biodiversity and communitarian knowledge versus corporatized intellectual property rights, and (5) new working-class transnationalism. While provoking new forms of transnational racism, globalization can also create new conditions for the emergence of transnational resistance. Globalization can therefore be oppressive or resistant, conservative or emancipatory.[13] All of these issues, I would add, are imbricated in Global North/South and race/ multicultural/ coloniality issues: "participatory democracy" is an answer to "master race democracy," biodiversity is linked to the natural commons, to cultural diversity and the intellectual agency of indigenous peoples and the natural commons, a transnational working-class solidarity depends on transcending racism and xenophobia, and so forth.

32

TERMINOLOGICAL REFLECTIONS

After this long journey across nations, worlds, and globes, it is now time to come to a few (necessarily inconclusive) conclusions about our basic terms. We can begin with the Worlds. Some scholars find philosophical value in the World, referring especially to the Heideggerian idea that art "discloses" the world. Heideggerians turn the substantive into a verb—the World Worlds—and a gerund—"worlding." (Edward Said, in a very different way, speaks of "worldliness" as a way to a profoundly secular and cosmopolitan approach to literature). Among those scholars who defend the Heideggerian approach are Pheng Chea in his *What is a World: On postcolonial literature as World Literature*[1] and Daniel Yacavone in his *Film Worlds: A Philosophical Aesthetics of Cinema*, where he postulates three kinds of responses to filmic worlds: the cognitive-diegetic, the sensory-affective, and the formal-aesthetic.[2] The "World Studies: Approaches, Paradigms, and Debates Conference," held at the University of Hong Kong in June, 2016, meanwhile, assigned itself the ambitious task of analyzing a multiplicity of academic-theoretical "Worlds," with separate panels on World Literature, World History, World Music, World Cinema, World Knowledge, World Multilingualism, and World Art. Yet despite a title which attracted scholars from around the world, many of the participants at the conference expressed discomfort with "the World." It was as if some of the participants were reincarnating Littlechap, the character in the stage musical, who whenever something went wrong, would scream: "Stop the World—I Want to Get Off!" While some participants favored the Heideggerian neologism "worlding," as a salutary desubstantialization of the noun "World," many remained unconvinced.[3]

In a very different context, meanwhile, Rey Chow has advanced other objections about the World in World Cinema: As in the case of "World Literature" she writes:

> ... the term "world" is precisely the problem. For those working in non-Western cultural contexts, words such as international, universal, global,

transnational, and so forth—and I would put the term "world" in their midst—have always signified the Euro-American West and a move out of one's native culture toward this West.[4]

Chow further notes an ironic turnabout, by which the term "World" has at times completely reversed its meaning, moving from basically signifying "Western literature plus," to now signifying precisely the opposite—*non*-Western literature. Thomas Elsaesser, meanwhile, calls World Cinema a "symptom of neo-colonialism in the cultural sphere... another name for a cinema that 'others' the other, even if the other colludes in the othering..."[5] Bhaskar Sarkar, finally, dismisses the concept of "World Cinema" as useless and redundant: "If it is taken to mean non-Hollywood or non-Anglophone cinemas [then it reiterates] a tendentious us/them binary—with its implications of an imputed cultural centers and its secondary peripheries. On the other hand, if it includes all cinemas, it becomes a pointless tautology."[6] (None of which, to my mind, invalidates most of the work performed under the World Cinema rubric).

In various essays and in the edited volume, *Design for the Pluriverse*, Arturo Escobar offers an alternative to the word "World," proposing instead "pluriverse"—a pluralization of "universe"—as a key to open up ways of doing and creating that are more attuned to the common interest and to the earth. Within this approach, the World is "made up of multiple worlds, multiple ontologies or reals that are far from being exhausted by the Eurocentric experience or reducible to its terms."[7] Escobar cites the Zapatista dictum—"*un mundo onde quepan muchos mundos*" (a world into which many worlds can fit) to evoke a way of "worlding" called the pluriverse that looks "attentatively from the perspective of the manifold relations that make this world what it is" [providing] "a tool to first, make alternatives to the one world plausible to the one-worlders, and second, provide resonance to those other worlds that interrupt the one-world story."[8]

Although the words "World," "Transnational," and "Global" are sometimes used interchangeably, and although excellent work has been performed under all three rubrics, they nevertheless still harbor nuances of use and meaning. Yet the terms do not name hostile camps or ideological enemies and at times are substitutable for each other. Alone among our three key terms, "World" is, at least implicitly, an honorific; it elevates a literature, or a writer, into its ranks through the equivalent of a literary Oscar. World Literature a la Damrosch is invested in appraising the quality of literature as meriting the status and aura of World Literature, a status which derives from its: 1) putative universality (sometimes covertly premised on Western norms of what constitutes universality) and its 2) aesthetic excellence (also sometimes dependent on Western norms). World Literature analyses—again with exceptions—are sprinkled with aesthetic compliments to the texts in question. The academic stars become our guides through the literatures of the World, welcoming us into an international symposium of gifted writers (and inferentially readers), a kind of aristocracy of literary sensibility. "Transnational" and "global," in contrast, are more usually more analytical than evaluative in tone, while "postcolonial," is, finally and irrevocably, political.

While the World Art categories—"World Literature," "World Cinema," "World Music"—designate specific bodies of work, "Transnational" and "Global" are ad hoc analytic concepts applicable on some level to virtually any texts and processes. All three terms can be used as adjectives to modify a noun, but Transnational and Global need postfixes or definite articles to function as nouns—Transnational*ism*, Transnational*ity*, Global*ity, the* Global, etc. Although "transnational" and "global" lend themselves to the "ization" prefix—globalization, transnationalization—"World does not, although we find an exception in the French neologism "mondializacion." While "transnational" has an affinity for non-state actors like NGOs and infra-national and supra-national movements, the word "international" tends to be related to nation-states in the post-World War II period.

There are also differences of assumed scale. Although the World Art terms (World Literature, World Music, World Film, etc.) would seem to address the entire world in geographical, demographic, social, and artistic terms, they usually focus only on a tiny segment of that world. "Transnational" is the most elastic and multi-scalar of the terms, since it can refer, on the smallest scale, to infra-national minority cultural movements or to the relations between small-scale indigenous nations, which yet might develop connections with parallel movements abroad, or to cross-border cultural connections and interactions ranging from those between just two sites, or to the regional-transnational phenomena such as the pan-movements (pan-African, pan-indigenous, etc). Global is the broadest term in that it pertains to claims made not about national trends but rather about "spottable" trends potentially involving much of the globe.

In terms of their political valence, keywords like "World" and "Transnational" and "Global" cannot be fixed through any essential definition; they are all conjunctural, modifiable, and often merge at the margins. However, each code arguably has its left, right, and centrist wings. Speaking schematically, the "World" could be said to tend centrist through its association with liberal humanism, although this varies with the art or discipline or even the theorist in question. To indulge in what is probably an unverifiable claim, one might say in comparative terms that Nagib's "World Cinema," for example, tacks to the left of Damrosch's "World Literature." The "global," finally, tilts right in that the term emerged first in business studies in the 1970s and exploded in the post 1989 era of globalist euphoria and is thus associated with neo-liberal globalization, the Washington Consensus, and what the French call *la pensée unique* and the "neo-liberal vulgate" (Bourdieu/Wacquant).

Fatally entwined with its derivative "globalization," the word "global" evokes for many a tacit alignment with the powerful, i.e. with that charmed circle of individuals and agencies, the legendary "masters of the Universe" who actually benefit from global reach and power. For some, the toxicity of "globalization" is such that it requires prophylactic adjectives alerting the user to collateral effects, rather like those pharmaceutical commercials where ominous warnings—"may cause depression, suicidal thoughts, and even death"—overshadow the supposed salutary effects of the medicine. Put differently, the word globalization is often seen by the left as so fatally entwined with "globalization" that any progressive inflection of the term requires qualifiers like "alter-globalization" to get rid of the bad odor of triumphalist neo-liberalism. But for that very same reason the "global" can be reverse-engineered, and taking a global, planetary approach to contemporary life can hardly be considered a priori reactionary. As we have seen with the Toby Miller et al. volume *Global Hollywood 2*, the "global" can be invoked as a term of critique.

While I find all the terms useful and have provided a rubric for excellent work, I have found the concept of the transnational to be the most flexible and productive. Rather than define the transnational as a historical stage, or corpus of texts, or a set of aesthetic traits, it is more productively seen as a multidimensional critical grid or conceptual framework. Henry Jenkins, Sam Ford, and Joshua Green prefer "transnational" to "global" because it recognizes the "uneven nature of... flows."[9] For me, the transnational represents less a stage in artistic development than a turn within intellectual history. Despite its first usage in relation to "transnational corporations," the "transnational turn" in media and cultural studies has come to be seen by some analysts as potentially more methodologically and theoretically progressive than the alternative terms. Like postcolonial studies, but unlike World Literary studies, the transnational turn quietly embeds the terms and concepts associated with a long series of earlier theoretical "turns"—the linguistic turn, the structuralist turn, the poststructuralist turn, followed by the postcolonial, the cultural, the feminist, the queer, and the digital turns.

The word "transnational" suggests a wide variety of movements and interdependencies—the regional, the diasporic, the exilic—that can be figured as alongside, underneath, and beyond the national. The transnational theoretically allows, but does not guarantee, more in the way of cross-border affinities, lateral relationalities, and historically specific connectivities. At the same time, it is useful to perform commutation tests—the linguistic mechanism whereby one substitutes signifiers to chart changes in the signified—where we "try out" the different terms in different contexts. For example, "trans" is a prefix rather than a substantive and therefore combines easily with "ization" formulations, such as "transnationalization," while it would be more awkward to say "worldization," although Said, as mentioned earlier, speaks of a "worldly" literary theory and Pheng Cheah enlists the Heideggerian term "worlding." At the same time, "transnational" is not automatically synonymous with "progressive;" the question of its political valence remains open. Both Globalization and alter-Globalization are transnational. Both the Corporate TV ads for Apple, and the radical music videos of the Puerto Rican group Calle 13, are thematically and aesthetically "transnational;" the question is a political one.

As an analytical prism, the term transnational calls attention to multiple cross-border entanglements even in periods prior to the widespread use of the term. Thus the transnational can be seen retrospectively as existing *within* the national. While the role of European immigrants within silent-era Hollywood is well-known, the role of Greeks in early Egyptian cinema, or of Germans and Iraqi Jews in silent Indian Cinema is less familiar. The transnational has an appealing modesty; it acknowledges the national rather than erase it, seeing transnationality not in terms of a constituted corpus but rather as a process that operates under and behind and across national lines. At the same time it opens up onto a wide variety of movements and interdependencies—the regional, the diasporic, the exilic, the indigenous—without making an ill-considered leap to "the universal." Unlike "World" and "Global," it allows for a coalition of trans-concepts: transnational transgender studies, transnational transectional studies, queer transnationalism and so forth. The transnational is polyandrous; it "mates" easily with other "studies" and projects such as transnational queer studies, transnational feminism, and transnational digital activism, potentially forming what Deleuze, in a different context, called an assemblage of minoritarian becomings.

What might be called the "battle of the prefixes" also brings up the issue of sequencing. One is tempted to discern a pattern across instances and fields whereby intellectual progress moves from "multi" (implying additive enumeration) to "inter" (implying a modicum of interaction) to "post" (implying supersession) to "trans" (implying a mutually transformational dynamism). But this idea of an automatic sequence is questionable since in some cases the "inter" came before the "multi," as was the case with corporations, at first "inter" and then "multi." The commonality in most of the sequencings is that the "transnational" tends to be the last term standing, precisely because it conjures up movement, change, and transition, inscribing the national while also going beyond it, without jumping to a totalizing, all-encompassing "global" or "World." As Aihwa Ong points out in *Flexible Citizenship*, "trans" does not only mean "beyond" and "outside of." For her:

> *Trans* denotes both moving through space or across lines, as well as changing the nature of something. Besides suggesting new relations between nation-states and capital, transnationality also alludes to the transversal, the transactional, the translational, and the transgressive aspects of contemporary behavior and imagination that are incited, enabled, and regulated by the changing logics of states and capitalism.[10]

For Ong, a transnational grid is more likely than the "global" to capture the particular articulations of the local and the global which produce "multiple modernities" in various parts of the world. Ong deploys "globalization" to refer to corporate strategies and reserves "transnational" to refer to the cultural specificities of global processes. Within this perspective, she criticizes Appadurai's insistence on the "global production of locality"—and one can add its converse, "the local production of globality"—as blind not only to the ways that nations and states are still bound to each other but also to the agency of the local in differently figured regimes of power.

The word "transnational" offers two signal advantages denied both the "global" and the "world," to wit, its two basic components—the "national" which acknowledges the cultural thickness and historical density of "nation" and the political agency of the nation-state—and the "trans" which moves beyond it. As Nataša Ďurovičová puts it, "in contradistinction to 'global,' a concept bound up with the philosophical category of totality...the intermediate and open term 'transnational' acknowledges the persistent agency of the state... At the same time, the prefix 'trans' implies relations of unevenness and mobility."[11] The term also mates easily with other descriptors, generating Hess and Zimmerman's "adversarial transnationalism,"[12] Lionnet and Shih's "minor transnationalism," Marciniak's "transnational film feminism, and Mette Hjort's "plurality of cinematic transnationalisms." The term "transnational is especially well-suited to an age where totalizing and universalizing discourses have come under suspicion, in comparison with a World which comes redolent of a complacently old-fashioned form of humanism.

As historically situated utterances, the political valence of the terms varies widely in function of historical context, disciplinary formation, and psycho-social investment. Buffeted by the slings, and arrows of history as "that which hurts" (Jameson) a word like "global" can simultaneously evoke both the top-down globalization of film production and distribution embodied in the Hollywoodeanization of the world, and the counter-hegemonic "globalization-from-below" practices embodied in diasporic, indigenous, exilic and transnational feminist film practices. Shaken by the cross-winds of history, the terms become invested with utopian hopes and dystopian fears, careening between foreboding and celebration. It is at that point that spatial metaphors of "central" and "peripheral" and "top-down and bottom-up" are called upon to specify the political drift of the term in question. While some terms are conceived to be intrinsically oppositional—e.g. "postcolonial critique," "minor cinema," "counter-cinema" and so forth—others, such as cosmopolitanism, are so imbued with the aroma of class elitism, that they need a funky deodorant word such as "pop" or "vernacular" to counteract the word's toney connotations. Yet it does make sense to speak, as Arjun Appadurai does, of an oxymoronic "vernacular cosmopolitanism." "Critical postcolonialism," in contrast, would be redundant, while other terms are beyond all political redemption. One could conceivably speak of "subaltern imperialism" but not of "bottom-up imperialism" or "progressive racism."

In sum, we need not reify any of the terms or endow them with a preternatural power that turns them into all-purpose one-size-fits-all explanatory principles. globalization explains everything! Transnationalism is always progressive! All the terms are appropriate in some cases. To ban any of them would be to resemble Tlon, the character in the Borges story, who decides to replace all nouns with their corresponding adjectives. The terms are not the object of a Darwinian *Survivor*-like struggle; none deserves to be "voted off the island." At the same time, no term can be considered as inherently "innocent." The "transnational," for example, cannot escape the gravitational force field of "transnational corporations." It is notable in this sense that some book titles, such as the invaluable Nataša Ďurovičová and Kathleen Newman collection *World Cinemas, Transnational Perspectives* (2010), paratactically mingle "World" and "Transnational," yet the title's first term seems to designate a corpus of films, or a cluster of industries, while the second term seems to refer to a methodological/analytical prism or "perspective." David Martin Jones suggests a hybrid "transworld cinemas." Nor should we look for verbal panaceas for historically shaped aporias. Rather, we can see each of the cognate terms as historically situated, as enabling, or discouraging, certain lines of thought or research. Each term sheds its quantum of light, and excellent work has been performed under all the various rubrics. Each term serves a purpose. It is not a zero-sum lexical game exalting one term means eliminating the others. Each term—World, Transnational, Global—comes with historical baggage, cultural associations, and social intonations. Each nudges us in specific directions.

33

TOWARD A "TRANS" METHODOLOGY

In this book I have tried to manifest and perform a method, only partially realized here, which would be *transnational* on all levels, "all the way down" as the saying goes, in terms of the transnational affiliations of the scholars and directors referenced, in terms of the transnational nature of the films, movements. and genres studied, and in the translingual and the transnational character of the scholarship, theories, and methodologies deployed. A transformative approach to what is variously called World Literature, World Cinema, Global media, Transnational Cinema, and so forth, I would further suggest, could benefit from being thought through from a flexible method pithily summarized by a series of "trans" concepts that bring the advantage of implying movement and transition from one state to another.

The most obvious trans-word, 1) is of course the word foregrounded in the title—"transnational." But the approach to these topics would ideally be, 2) *transdisciplinary*, in drawing on a range both of disciplines in the humanities (literature, philosophy, history), and the social sciences (anthropology, political science, sociology), along with the transdisciplines (cultural studies, ethnic studies, critical race studies, media studies, gender studies and so forth). The disciplines, after all, are also "in bed" with one another.

The approach would also be 3) *transtextual* (with a nod to the work of Gerard Genette) in interweaving, as I have partially done here, intertextual lineages across national borders, both in terms of films and the discourses about them, looking back and forward and sideways to the texts' innumerable interlocutors.

The approach would also ideally be 4) *translinguistic* (with a nod to Bakhtin/Voloshinov) in treating film and media texts and practices not as signs and signifiers within a synchronic system but rather as "situated utterances," impacted by their historical moment, their geographical location, and the vicissitudes of reception.

The method, would also be 5) *transartistic.*" This text is at least partially "transartistic" in that it treats a number of arts—literature, cinema, and music. But cinema as a medium is inherently transartistic, in the sense that the audio-visual media have the tremendous advantage of being multi-track, consisting, at least prior to the advent of the digital, in Christian Metz' already mentioned "five tracks," each of which, as we have seen before, makes potentially available the arts affiliated with that track: the music track potentially inherits the entire history of music; the image track embeds and rearticulates the history of visual representation and the pictorial arts; the sound track absorbs the history of theater, speech and performance, and so forth. All media, in this sense, have been endlessly enriched by their dialogue with all the other arts. In this sense, film has a millennial rather than a single-century history, since it inherits all the temporal arts (music, narration, etc.) and spatial arts (painting, photography) not only within but also across national traditions. Digital media expand these possibilities exponentially, since they facilitate and even encourage the combination of arts and media into new configurations.

The approach would also be, 6) *transsectional*, in that it attempts to transnationalize and "mediatize" Kimberle Crenshaw's generative concept of social-ethnic "intersectionality"—i.e the ways in which the various axes of social stratification—nation, gender, race, ethnicity, sexuality, and so forth—are interconnected and mutually impacting. It would also add to the "mantra" other social categories such as religion, along with another set of real-life trans-words and phenomena that have entered the lexicon, and which have huge contemporary relevance, and which involve a different kind of border-crossing: 7) the *transgender* and the *transsexual*.

The approach would also, with nods to Andre Gaudreault and Henry Jenkins, 8) *trans-mediatic*, in that the corpus studied would not be composed only of feature films or even feature documentaries but rather drawn from the broadest possible spectrum of audio-visual-digital arts and media. Defying all attempts to be corralled into essentialist definitions, the media's famed "specificity" consists precisely in its being *non*-specific and thus capable of cannibalizing the most heterogeneous materials. Rather than exalt the feature film as the ontological quintessence of cinema over and above all of other forms and genres, the work here has suggested, or hinted, that we would do well to include television, interactive documentaries, music video, filmed performance, cable TV satire, sketch comedy, Internet parodies, online games, web-series, and social network activism etc.) in our analyses.

I have also attempted to be 9) *transregional*, in that the basic conceptualization of the topic is not around regions per se—in the manner of a compartmentalizing Area Studies which sees Areas as specific places (for example the continents of African Studies and Latin American Studies). Rather, the conception involves cross-border movement across spaces and broad concepts and processes which, thanks to colonial karma and postcolonial hybridities, are now relevant to *all* the regions. Middle Eastern media organizations like Al Jazeera, for example, are no longer just "in" the Middle East any more than CNN is only "in" Atlanta. Only essentialist and compartmentalized thinking would separate Latinos from Latin America, African Americans from the Afro-diaspora, Arabs in the Middle East from Arabs in the Americas, Indians in India from the non-resident Indians (NRIs), and the Black Atlantic from the Black Pacific.[1] Nor do I see the transnational in Hegelian temporal and stagist terms as an inexorable progression *from* the national *toward* the transnational. Rather, I see the transnational as offering an analytical prism that can even be applied retroactively to only apparently national cinemas that were always already directly or covertly shaped by transnational energies and histories.

My hope, in this sense, has been to "deprovincialize" the debates in spatial-geographical-cultural terms by drawing theories and strategies not only from the theorists and cultural producers of Europe and the United States but also from Latin America, Africa, Asia, the Middle East, and the indigenous world. It is not a question of expanding the list of nations through a policy of "tolerant" inclusion; rather, it is a question of discerning the mutual imbrication of all the worlds that goes back centuries or even millennia. In the present, the various regions will be seen as thoroughly within the postcolonial logic of "we are here because you were there." The Middle East is "in" the Americas—there are more Lebanese in Brazil than in Lebanon, for example—just as the Americas, all too conspicuously, are "in" the Middle East.[2] Thus regions can no longer be boxed into hermetically sealed compartments. The question is not only one of the exchange of cultural products but also one of transnational intersubjectivity, and the multi-directional intercourse of national and transnational imaginaries.

The approach would be 10) *transcultural*, in aiming to be culturally polycentric and inclusive, premised on the radical equality of persons in rights and the inherently interlinked character of all human societies. There is "more in heaven and earth," I have tried to suggest, than is dreamed of within the "major" canons of Eurocentrism, nation-centrism, Hollywood-centrism, and Feature Fiction Film-centrism. Furthermore, all these trans-methods can combine and have a multiplier effect. What happens, for example, if one maps inter/trans-sectionality across transnationality, or transmediality across transdisciplinarity? The point is mutual and reciprocal relativization so that the diverse cultures and communities and methodologies and epistemologies placed in play should come to see the limitations of their own social and cultural perspectives. In Bakhtinian language, each art, medium, and disciplines offer is own "exotopy" or critical distance, its own "excess seeing," hopefully coming not only to see the "other medium" or discipline's point of view, but also, through a salutary estrangement, to see how it is itself seen by others. I am obviously not suggesting that this book has even come close to achieving the "trans-ization" of World Literature, World Cinema, Transnational Film/Media, Global Media and the like—the provincial limitations of my coverage must be manifest to any informed reader—it only points in that direction. True trans-ization can only be a collective project, one that takes into account all the versions of the commons—natural, literary, cultural, cinematic, disciplinary, artistic, mediatic, and political.

NOTES

Introduction

1 John Durham Peters, *The Marvelous Clouds: Towards a Philosophy of Elemental Media* (Chicago: The University of Chicago Press, 2015), 178.
2 While I was working on the final corrections of my manuscript, I encountered a book—Shekhar Deshpande and Meta Masaj's *World Cinema: A Critical Introduction* (London: Routledge, 2018)—that does extremely well what I am not trying to do here—i.e. a book that offers an extremely thorough, insightful, and multidimensional analysis of the current state of World Cinema and World Cinema Studies in all their aspects—historical aesthetic, authorial, industrial, spectatorial, etc.
3 Thomas Elsaesser, "Double occupancy and small adjustments: Space, place and policy in the New European Cinema since the 1990s," in *European Cinema: Face to Face with Hollywood*, Amsterdam: Amsterdam University Press (2005), 108–130.
4 I owe this evocative phrase to my friend Esther Hamburger.
5 See Eddy Fougier, *Parlons Mondialisation* (Paris: La Documentation française, 2017).
6 Naomi Klein, *No is Not Enough: Defeating the New Shock Politics* (London: Allen Lane, 2017), 80.
7 Slavoj Zizek, *Welcome to the Desert of the Real* (London: Verso, 2002), 83.
8 See Amartya Sen, "How to Judge Globalism," *American Prospect*, Jan 1, 2002, cited in Paul Jay, *Global Matters: The Transnational Turn in Literary Studies* (Ithaca: Cornell, 2010), 39.
9 John Durham Peters, op. cit., 8.
10 Ibid.
11 Ibid., 20.
12 Siegfried Zielinski, "*Toward an Archaeology of Hearing and Seeing by Mechanical Means* (Cambridge, MA: MIT, 2008).
13 See Erkki Huhtamo and Jussi Parikka, *Media Archaeology* (Berkeley: University of California Press, 2011), 3.
14 See William Powers, *Hamlet's Blackberry* (London: Harper, 2010).
15 For a deeply informed account of the manifold forms of writing prior to the arrival of Europeans in the Americas, see Gordon Brotherston, *Book of the Fourth World: Reading the Native Americas through their Literature* (Cambridge: Cambridge University Press, 1992).
16 See Jussi Parikka, *A Geology of Media* (Minneapolis: University of Minnesota Press, 2015), 4–5.

17 See Charles C. Mann, *1491: New Revelations of the Americas before Columbus* (New York: Knopf, 2006).
18 See Anibal Quijano, *Coloniality of Power, Eurocentrism and Latin America. Nepantla*, No. 3 (Durham, North Carolina: Duke University Press, 2000); Mary Louise Pratt, *Imperial Eyes: Travel Writing and Transculturation* (New York: Routledge, 1992); and Vandana Shiva, *Monocultures of the Mind: Perspectives on Biodiversity and Biotechnology* (London: Zed Books, 1993). See also Ella Shohat and Robert Stam, *Unthinking Eurocentrism: Multiculturalism and the Media* (New York: Routledge, 1994).
19 See Thomas King, *The Inconvenient Indian* (Minneapolis: University of Minnesota Press, 2013).
20 Jason W. Moore, "Ecology, capital, and the nature of our times," *Journal of World-Systems Analysis* 17 (1) (2011), 108–147.
21 See Robert Stam and Ella Shohat, *Race in Translation: Culture Wars around the Postcolonial Atlantic* (New York: NYU Press, 2015).
22 Ibid.
23 See Jung-Bong Choi, "Introduction: Of transnational-Korean cinematrix," in *Transnational Cinemas* 3 (2) (2012).
24 See Friedrich Kittler, "Toward an ontology of media," in *Theory, Culture, and Society* 26 (2009), 182.
25 John Durham Peters, op. cit., 104.
26 From the Introduction by Joshua Neves and Bhaskar Sarkar, eds., *Asian Video Cultures: In the Penumbra of the Global* (Durham: Duke University Press, 2017).
27 Ibid.
28 Or capitalism with a lecherous face in the case of DSK, where the real scandal was less sexual than ideological, the fact that a "socialist party" would choose a former head of the IMF as its candidate.
29 Cited in See Peter Linebaugh, *The Magna Carta Manifesto: Liberties and Commons for All* (Berkeley: U.C. Press, 2008), 4. The original lines went: "He robbed the whole nation / He claims all forests are his. Did his father come and plant?"
30 Ibid.
31 Peter Linebaugh, *Stop, Thief: The Commons, Enclosures, and Resistance* (Oakland, CA: PM Press, 2014), 1.
32 Peter Linebaugh, *The Magna Carta Manifesto*.
33 Cited in Hardt/Negri, *Commonwealth* (Cambridge, MA: Harvard, 2009), 350
34 On the forest commons, see Peter Linebaugh, *The Magna Carta Manifesto*.
35 See Benjamin Peters, "Introduction" to Benjamin Peters, ed., *Digital Keywords: A Vocabulary of Information Society & Culture* (Princeton: Princeton University Press, 2016), p. xiv.
36 Armand Mattelart, *Transnationals and the Third World: The Struggle for Culture* (South Hartley, MA; Bergin and Garvey, 1983), p. 150.
37 See Fredric Jameson, *The Political Unconscious: Narrative as a Socially Symbolic Act* (Ithaca: Cornell University Press, 1981).
38 See V. N. Volosinov, *Marxism and the Philosophy of Language* (Cambridge: Harvard University Press, 1973). This text is sometimes attributed to Bakhtin. See also my *Subversive Pleasures: Bakhtin, Cultural Criticism, and Film* (Baltimore: Johns Hopkins Press, 1989).
39 Jane Gaines, "White Privilege and Looking Relations," *Race and Gender in Feminist Film Theory, Cultural Critique*, 4 (Autumn 1986), 59–79.

1 Goethe and *Weltliteratur*

1 Cited in David Damrosch, *What is World Literature?* (Princeton: Princeton University Press, 2003), 12.
2 See Preface to Theo d'Haen, David Damrosch, and Djelal Kadir, *The Routledge Companion to World Literature* (New York: Routledge, 2012), xviii.
3 See Arjun Appadurai, *Modernity at Large* (Minneapolis: University of Minnesota Press, 1996).

4 See Martin Bernal, *Black Athena: Afroasiatic Roots of Classical Civilization*, Volume 1: *The Fabrication of Ancient Greece, 1785–1985* (New Brunswick: Rutgers University Press 1987.
5 See Margaret Anne Doody, *The True Story of the Nove*l (New Brunswick: Rutgers University Press, 1996).
6 Ibid.
7 See *The Routledge Companion to World Literature* (New York: Routledge, 2012), 148.
8 Eckermann, *Conversations with Goethe*, 1835; quoted in David Damrosch. *What Is World Literature?* (Princeton: Princeton University Press, 2003), 1, 12.
9 Ella Shohat and I argue for a "polycentric" approach to history and art in our *Unthinking Eurocentrism: Multiculturalism and the Media* (New York Routledge, 1994).
10 Michel Foucault, "Of other spaces: Utopias and heterotopias," *Diacritics* 1 (1) (Spring, 2016).
11 See Emily Apter, *Against World Literature: On the Politics of Untranslatability* (London: Verso, 2013).
12 Rene Wellek, "The Name and Nature of Comparative Literature," in *Discriminations: Further Concepts of Criticism* (New Haven: Yale University Press, 1970), 3–36.
13 Franco Moretti, "Conjectures on World Literature," in Christopher Prendergast, ed., *Debating World Literatures* (London: Verso, 2004), pp. 148–162.
14 Emily Apter: *Against World Literature: On the Politics of Untranslatability* (London: Verso, 2013), 3.
15 Cited in Jing Tsu, "World Literature and National Literature," in Theo D'haen, David Damrosch, and Djelal Kadir, The *Routledge Companion to World Literature* (London: Routledge, 2012), 199.

2 The theory of World Literature

1 Theo D'haen, David Damrosch, and Djelal Kadir, *The Routledge Companion to World Literature*, 5
2 Ibid., 15.
3 Ibid., 78.
4 Damrosch, *What is World Literature?*, 49.
5 Ibid., 127.
6 David Damrosch, *How to Read World Literature* (Malden: Wiley-Blackwell, 2009), 4.
7 Ibid., 52.
8 Ibid., 281.
9 See Mikhail Bakhtin and Pavel Medvedev, *The Formal Method in Literary Scholarship* (Cambridge: Harvard University Press, 1985).
10 See *The Routledge Companion to World Literature* (New York: Routledge, 2012), 283
11 Karl Marx and Freidrich Engels, *The Communist Manifesto* (New York: Bantam Books, 1992), 22.
12 Ibid., p. 32
13 "Conjectures on world literature," *New Left Review* 1 (2000), 56.
14 Of course, one might argue in Moretti's defense that, given Western hegemony, unidirectional diffusion is exactly what one might expect.

3 From World Literature to alternative modernisms

1 Moretti, "More Conjectures," 52.
2 Moretti, 154.
3 Jacques Rancière, *Film Fables* (Oxford/New York: Berg, 2006), 117.
4 Moretti, 771.
5 From Oswald de Andrade, "Marcha das Utopias," cited in Beatriz Azevedo, *Antropofagia—Palimpsesto Selvagem* (Sao Paulo: CosacNaify, 2016), 63.
6 "A Crise da Filosofia Messianica" is included in Oswald de Andrade, *A Utopia Antropofágica* (Sao Paulo: Globo, 2001).

7 See Herbert Marcuse, *Eros and Civilization: A Philosophical Inquiry into Freud* (Boston: Beacon Press, 1955).
8 For an English version of the "Cannibalist Manifesto," see Leslie Bary's excellent introduction to and translation in *Latin American Literary Review* 19 (38) (July–December 1991).
9 Beatriz Azevedo, *Antropofagia—Palimpsesto Selvagem* (Sao Paulo: CosacNaify, 2016).
10 Antonio Candido, *Literatura e Sociedade* (Sao Paulo: Companhia Editora Nacional, 1976), 128.
11 Augusto de Campos, "Revistas re-vistas: Os Antropofagos," *Revista da Antropofagia* (Sao Paulo: Abril, 1976).
12 In the era of mass shootings, to say, for example, that the "ultimate surrealist act would consist of firing a gun randomly into a crowd" no longer sounds as daring and provocative as it once might have.
13 On the ethnic-essentialist problems both with "the Latins" and with the "Anglo-Saxons," see Robert Stam and Ella Shohat, *Race in Translation: Culture Wars in the Postcolonial Atlantic* (New York: NYU Press, 2012).
14 Emily Apter, *Against World Literature: On the Politics of Untranslatability* (London: Verso, 2013), 2.
15 Ibid., 138.
16 Ibid., 43–44.
17 See Larry Rohter, "After a Century, a Literary Reputation Finally Blooms," *NYT* (Sept 12, 2008).
18 Quoted in Casanova, *La Republique Mondiale des Lettres* (Paris: Seuil, 1999), 388 (all translations of Casanova are mine).
19 Ibid., 394.
20 Ibid., 67.
21 Ibid.
22 Ibid., 218.
23 Koch-Grunberg was the inspiration for the first ethnologist character in the Columbian film *The Embrace of the Serpent*.
24 See Theodor Koch-Grunberg, *Do Roraima ao Orinoco*, Vol. 1, trans. Cristina Alberts-Franco (Sao Paulo: EUSP2005), 62.
25 See Tele Porto Ancona Lopez, ed. Mario de Andrade, *Macunaíma: O Heroi sem Nenhum Carater*, cited in Lucia Sa, "Part II: "Macunaíma and the Native Trickster," Woodrow Wilson International Center for Scholars, Special Report (Nov 2008), 3.
26 Lucia Sa, op. cit. 3.
27 Playing on "trance" and "trans," I speak of "trance-modernism" in *Keywords in Subversive Film/Media Aesthetics* (London: Wiley-Blackwell, 2015).
28 S.N. Bennet and D. Blundell "First Peoples." *Cultural Studies* 9:1–12 (1995).
29 Isabel Allende, *Eva Luna* (New York: Bantam, 1989), 300–301.
30 See Lawrence Venuti, *The Scandals of Translation: Towards an Ethics of Difference* (London: Routledge, 1998), 160–161.
31 It would be revealing, in this sense, to see if World Literature has counter-acted the decline of language learning in the Global North, or only exacerbated it by emphasizing literature in translation, where translation usually means English translation. There seems to be a trend of a small group of multilingual cosmopolitans, at least in the Anglophone worlds, becoming the guides for often monolingual students and readers. A philologically inflected Comparative Literature, with its insistence that scholars "know the original language" of the literatures being studied, tended to favor only intra-European polylingualism, and thus remained provincial.
32 See Gayatri Spivak, *Death of a Discipline* (New York: Columbia University Press, 2003).
33 See Chris Andre, "World Literature and Economic Hegemony," in *Paroles Gelees* (1996), 77.
34 Sanja Bahun, "The Politics of World Literature," in Theo D'haen, David Damrosch, and Djelal Kadir, op. cit., 377.
35 Djelal Kadir, "To world, to globalize—comparative literature's crossroads," *Comparative Literature Studies* 41 (1) (2004), 1–9.

4 The cosmopolitanism of the Periphery

1 Mário de Andrade, *Poesias Completas* (Sao Paulo: Martins, 2013), 32–33.
2 I use the word "minoritarian" rather than "minority" because the latter term naturalizes what is historically produced and ideologically constructed through a project which constructs some groups as "major" and others as "minor." "Minoritarian" in our view calls attention to the manufactured aspect of "minorities." Groups that are considered "minorities" were often "majorities" elsewhere or at another time, for example prior to conquest or colonization (e.g. the relation between Chicanos and Mexico).
3 For a comprehensive discussion of these alternative aesthetics up through the 1990s, see Robert Stam and Ella Shohat, *Unthinking Eurocentrism: Multiculturalism and the Media* (London: Routledge, 1994), especially chapters 8 and 9.
4 Ramon Chao, op. cit., 183.
5 Ibid., 166.
6 Casanova, op. cit., 330.
7 Quoted in Casanova, 33.
8 Ibid.
9 See Werner Sollers, ed., *Multilingual America: Transnationalism, Ethnicity, and the Languages of American Literature* (New York: NYU Press, 1988).
10 Stephen Slemon argues this point in his essay "Magic realism as polstcolonial discourse," in *Hispania*, 38 (2) (May 1955), 188.

5 Columbus, *El Nuevo Mundo*, and Postcolonial Studies

1 Jodi A. Byrd, "Mind the Gap," in Federico Luiseti et al., eds., the *Anomie of the Earth: Philosophy, Politics, and Autonomy in Europe and the Americas* (Durham: Duke University Press, 2005), 119.
2 Adam Smith, *The Wealth of Nations* (New York: Random House, 1937), 557.
3 Marx and Engels, *The Communist Manifesto* (1848) cited in Andre Gunder Frank, *Re-ORIENT* (Berkeley: University of California Press, 1998), 13.
4 A.G. Frank and B.K. Gills, eds., *The World System: Five Hundred Years or Five Thousand?* (London: Routledge, 1993).
5 Oswald de Andrade, quoted in Beatriz Azevedo, op. cit., 83.
6 Nandita Sharma and Cynthia Wright, "Decolonizing resistance, challenging colonial states," *Social Justice* 35 (3) (2008–9), 121.
7 Brett Christophers, "Ships in the night: Journeys in cultural imperialism and post-colonialism," *International Journal of Cultural Studies* 10 (3) (September 2007), 285.
8 Ella Shohat first made this point in her essay "Notes on the postcolonial," *Social Text* (1992).
9 See Jane Gaines, "White privilege and looking relations: Race and gender in feminist film theory," in *Cultural Critique* 4 (Autumn 1986).
10 Aijaz Ahmad, "Jameson's rhetoric of otherness and the national allegory," *Social Text* 17 (Fall 1987), 3–25.
11 In terms of the book's emphasis on the multiple 1492s and the centrality of the indigenous question. The coloniality/modernity project takes an approach in many ways similar to the one we outlined in *Unthinking Eurocentrism: Multiculturalism and the Media* (New York: Routledge, 1994).
12 See Homi K. Bhabha. *The Location of Culture* (London/New York: Routledge, 1994).
13 *The Routledge Companion to World Literature*, 212.
14 See Tim Watson, "Improvements and Reparations at Mansfield Park," in Robert Stam and Alessandra Raengo, eds., *Literature and Film* (Oxford: Blackwell, 2005).
15 See Jonathon Arac, "Edward W. Said, "The Worldliness of World Literature," in Theo D'haen, David Damrosch, and Djelal Kadir, eds., *The Routledge Companion to World Literature* (London: Routledge, 2012), 117.
16 See Bruce Robbins, "Uses of World Literature," *The Routledge Companion to World Literature*, 384.

17 Ibid., 383.
18 Paul Chaat Smith, *Everything You Know about the Indian is Wrong* (Minneapolis: University of Minnesota Press, 2009), 71.
19 John Durham Peters, op. cit., 106.
20 I am thinking of the "Biblical radicalism" of figures like Ernest Cardenal, Leonardo Boff, and Juan Stam, who emphasize Moses as the liberator of the enslaved from the Jewish Bible, and who find radical egalitarianism, radical communitarianism, and radical pacificism in the words of Jesus and the Apostles. See H. Mark Roelofs, "Liberation Theology: the Recovery of Biblical Radicalism, in *The American Political Science Review* 62 (2) (June 1988), 549–566.
21 Paul Chaat Smith, op. cit., 22.
22 See Arturo Escobar, *Sentir-pensar con la Tierra* (Cauca: Universidad de Cauca, Columbia, 2012).

6 French postcoloniality and *litterature-monde*

1 See Pascale Casanova, *La Republique Mondiale des Lettres* (Paris: Seuil, 1999), 49.
2 Pierre Bourdieu, "Deux impérialismes de l'universel," in C. Fauré and R. Bishops, eds., *L'Amérique des Français* (Paris: François Bourin, 1992), 149–155.
3 Guiart quoted in Benoît de L'Estoile, *Le Goût des Autres: De L'Exposition Coloniale aux Arts Premiers* (Paris: Flammarion, 2007), 198.
4 Ella Shohat and I attempt to deconstruct the false binarism between two fictions—"Les Latins" and "Les Anglo-Saxons"—in our book *Race in Translation*.
5 Anouar Abdel-Malek, "Orientalism in Crisis," in Alexander Lyon Macfie, ed., *Orientalism: A Reader* (New York: NYU Press, 2001), 51.
6 See Abdallah Laroui, *La Crise des Intellectuels Arabes: Traditionalisme ou Historicisme?* (Paris: François Maspero, 1974).
7 Pascale Casanova, *La République Mondiale des Lettres* (Paris: Seuil, 1999), 49.
8 *The Routledge Companion to World Literature* (New York: Routledge, 2012), 235
9 See Georges Balandier, *Sociologie Actuelle de l'Afrique Noire: Dynamique Sociale en Afrique Centrale* (Paris: PUF, 1971).
10 Marie-Claude Smouts, ed., *La Situation Postcoloniale: Les Postcolonial Studies dans le Débat Français* (Paris: Sciences Po, 2008), 24–25.
11 Rada Iveković, "Langue Coloniale, Langue Globale, Langue Locale," *Rue Descartes* 58 (2007), 28–29.

7 Sibling disciplines

1 Thomas Doherty (2008), cited in Toby Miller, *Television Studies: The Basics* (New York: Routledge, 2010), 35.
2 While working on my dissertation in 1973–1974, I myself had the privilege of studying with Christian Metz, Raymond Bellour, Michel Marie, Pascal Bonitzer, and Thierry Kuntzel and my U.C. Berkeley advisor Bertrand Augst.
3 Astruc's essay was first published in *Ecran Français* (No. 144, 1948) and is included in Peter Graham, ed., *The New Wave* (London: Secker and Warburg, 1969), 17–23.
4 On the relation of these optical devices to 19th-century fiction, see Kara Marie Manning, "Moving Words/Motion Pictures: Proto-Cinematic Narrative in Nineteenth-Century British Fiction" (2016), available Dissertations, 906. http://aquila.usm.edu/dissertations/906.
5 I discuss *Madame Bovary* and its various adaptations at length in my *Literature through Film: Realism, Magic, and the Art of Adaptation* (Oxford: Blackwell, 2005), 144–190.

8 From literature to film

1 Alain Badiou, *Cinema* (Oxford: Blackwell, 2005), 79.
2 *The Routledge Companion to World Literature* (New York: Routledge, 2012), 380.

3 I first made these arguments in "Beyond Fidelity," an essay included in James Naremore, *Film Adaptation* (New Brunswick: Rutgers University Press, 2000) and subsequently elaborated them in "The Theory and Practice of Film Adaptation" in Robert Stam and Alessandra Raengo, eds., *Literature and Film* (Oxford: Blackwell, 2004).
4 See Mitchell Stephens, "Which communications revolution is it anyway?" *Journalism Quarterly* 75 (1998), 9–13.
5 Youssef Ishaghpour notes the paradox that the first "speaking film, *The Jazz Singer*, takes as its subject a central ceremony of a religion—Judaism—founded exclusively on the word and on the prohibition of the image. See "La Parole et l'interdit des Images: *Le Chanteur de Jazz* et les Juifs de Hollywood," in Jacques Aumont, ed., *L'Image et la Parole* (Paris: Cinemateque française, 1999), p. 141.
6 Linda Hutcheon, op. cit., 176.
7 Thomas Leitch, ed., "Introduction" to *The Oxford Handbook of Adaptation Studies* (New York: Oxford University Press, 2017), 2–6.
8 Quoted in Kamilla Elliot, *Through the Looking Glass* (2001), a dissertation written for the English Department at the University of California, Berkeley.
9 Lawrence Lessig, *Remix: Making Art and Culture Thrive in the Hybrid Economy* (New York: Penguin, 2008).

9 The cinema and the World Literature canon

1 See Lucy Mazdon, "Disrupting the Remake: The Girl with the Dragon Tatoo," in Iain Robert Smith and Constantine Verevis, eds., *Transnational Film Remakes* (Edinburgh: Edinburgh University Press, 2017), 27.
2 In the context of South Africa, Keyan and Damien Tomaselli lament "literature departments offering modules to huge undergraduate courses that read film as a topic, often without reference to film theory, production practice, or disciplinary epistemology." See Keyan and Damien Tomaselli, "The In-disciplining of Film Theory, Media Studies and the Disciplining of Practice," in Maria Dora Mourao et al. eds., *The 21st Century Film, TV, and Media School: Challenges, Clashes, Changes* (Sofia, Bulgaria: Cilect, 2016), 154.
3 See Marty Gould, "Teaching Adaptation," in Thomas Leitch, *The Oxford Handbook of Adaptation Studies* (New York: Oxford, 2017), 625.
4 Ibid., 627.
5 Ibid., 628.
6 See Linda Hutcheon, op. cit., 4.
7 Some of the mistakes in judgement: Sully Prudhomme Nobel Prize in 1901, and *Driving Miss Daisy* for Best Picture in 1989.
8 See Eli Lee Carter, *Reimagining Brazilian Television* (Pittsburgh: University of Pittsburgh Press, 2018).
9 Ph.D. dissertation for the Spanish/Portuguese Dept. at University of California, p. 5.

10 The gains of (film) translation

1 Fascinatingly, in this same period, analytic "ordinary language" philosophers were trying to go beyond language and metaphor within philosophy by appealing to mathematics.
2 See Rick Altman, ed., *Cinema/Sound*, in *Yale French Studies* 60 (1980).
3 Marciniak and Bennett, op. cit., 52
4 See Tim Bergfelder, "National, transnational, or Supranational cinema? Rethinking European film studies," *Media, Culture, Society* 27 (2001), 315.
5 See Abe Mark Nornes, *Cinema Babel: Translating Global Cinema* (Minneapolis: University of Minnesota Press, 2008), 234.
6 Ibid., 235.
7 See Alexander Beecroft, *An Ecology of World Literature* (London: Verso, 2015), 6.

8 Ibid., 256.
9 Ibid., 296.
10 See Zeynep Dadak's thus far unpublished Ph.D. dissertation in the Cinema Studies Department at NYU, entitled "A Maudlin Cinema: Arabesk Film and Culture in Turkey" (2014).
11 Ibid.
12 Nicholas Oughton and Jean-Paul Jarry, "Learning Cinematography at Film School: Old Ways, New Directions," in Maria Dora Mourao et al., eds., *The 21st Century Film, TV, and Media School: Challenges, Clashes, Changes* (Sofia, Bulgaria: Cilect, 2016), 282.

11 Adaptation, remix, and the cultural commons

1 Thomas Leitch, ed., *Oxford Handbook of Adaptation Studies* (New York: Oxford University Press, 2017).
2 See Henry Louis Gates, op. cit.
3 See Souleymane Bachir Diagne, *Open to Reason: Muslim Philosophers in Conversation with the Western Tradition* (New York: Columbia University Press, 2018).
4 Henry Louis Gates, *Signifying Monkey: A Theory of African-American Literary Criticism* (London: Oxford, 1988).
5 Houston Wood, *Native Features: Indigenous Films from Around the World* (New York: Continuum, 2008), 169.
6 Ella Shohat and I elaborate on this concept in our *Unthinking Eurocentrism: Multiculturalism and the Media* (London: Routledge, 1994), 351.
7 For a wide-ranging and transnational discussion of Shakespeare in film, see Mark Thornton Burnett, *Shakespeare and World Cinema* (Cambridge: Cambridge University Press, 2013).
8 *Ahram* Online, November 14, 2011, referenced January 20, 2017.
9 M.M. Bakhtin, "Discourse in the Novel," in *The Dialogical Imagination* (trans. Caryl Emerson and Michael Holquist) (Austin: University of Texas Press, 1981), 421.
10 Quoted in Michael Cook, *A Brief History of the Human Race* (New York: Norton, 2003), 196–197.

12 From adaptation to remix

1 Jay David Bolter and Richard Grusin, *Remediation: Understanding New Media* (Cambridge, MA: MIT Press, 1999).
2 Alain Badiou, *Cinema* (Paris: Nova, 2010).
3 J.D. Peters, op. cit., 326.
4 See Hutcheon, op. cit.
5 Henry Jenkins, *Convergence Culture: Where Old and New Media Collide* (New York: New York University Press, 2006), 2.
6 See Aram Sinnreich, *Mashed Up: Music, Technology, and the Rise of Configurable Culture* (Boston: University of Massachusetts Press, 2010).
7 Ibid., 71–73.
8 See Kamilla Elliott, *Rethinking the Novel/Film Debate* (Cambridge: Cambridge University Press, 2003).
9 Ibid.
10 Haun Sassy, "Exquisite Cadavers Stitched from French Nightmares," in *Comparative Literature in an Age of Globalization* (Baltimore: Johns Hopkins University Press, 2006), 31.
11 David Damrosch, "World literature in a postliterary age," *Modern Language Quarterly* 74 (2) (June 2013).
12 Ibid., 160.
13 Ibid., 162.

14 In teaching, given the danger that the source texts themselves might get completely lost in the swirl of intermedial variations in the form of revisionist remixes and mashups, I find it essential in pedagogical terms to insist on close readings of the source texts, even if only in the form of extracts, to give students a vivid close-up sense of the stylistics of the novel in comparison to the stylistics of the adapting film. I find it productive, for example, to counterpoint particular literary passages—Don Quixote and the windmill, Robinson Crusoe and the footprint, Emma Bovary at the Vaubyessard Ball—with the extremely varied ways in which the same passages have been adapted across a wide spectrum of media.
15 See Henry Jenkins et al., *Confronting the Challenges of Participatory Culture* (Cambridge, MA: MIT Press, 2009), 8.
16 For an illuminating study of new internet-based literary pedagogy, see the Henry Jenkins et al.'s book *Reading in a Participatory Culture: Remixing Moby Dick in the English Classroom* (New York: Columbia University Teacher College Press, 2013).
17 See "The Littlest Don Quixotes versus the World," *New York Times* (June 24, 2018), Opinion Section, 5.
18 Hutcheon, op. cit., 92.
19 See Robin Pogrebin, "In Walden Video Game, the Object is Stillness," *The New York Times* (2/25/2017), A-1–11.
20 A capstone project by one of my senior students at NYU-Abu Dhabi (Luis Felipe Morales Novarro), entitled "Material Fictions: A Borgesian Approach to Digital Access to Information" explored how Borges' "speculative fictions" about libraries, memories, archives and encyclopedias help us understand archival research, critical analysis, and the programming of media objects in the post-digital world.
21 If any of the students, and here I must break the frame, or any reader of this book, were to make a successful film based on these ideas, I would not ask for a cut but only for a modest acknowledgement in the credits.

13 World cinema

1 See Tom Gunning, "Shooting into Outer Space," in Matthew Solomon, ed., *Fantastic Voyages of the Cinematic Imagination: Georges Méliès's Trip to the Moon* (Albany: SUNY Press, 2011), 109.
2 See *Time-Image*, 117.
3 From Jose Miguel Palacios' Ph.D. dissertation, "Passages of Exile: Chilean Cinema 1973–2016," written the Cinema Studies Department at New York University.

14 The theory of World Cinema

1 From Michael Talbott's Ph.D. dissertation for the Cinema Studies Department at NYU, entitled "Familiar Difference: Film Funds, Film Festivals, and World Cinema," defended May 2015.
2 Although Ella Shohat and I did not think of ourselves as World Cinema scholars and did not invoke the term "World Cinema," a number of scholars, notably Dudley Andrew and Shekhar Deshpande and Meta Mazaj, have retroactively, and to our mind very generously, called ours *Unthinking Eurocentrism* the "first and key textbook on world cinema." See Shekhar Deshpande and Meta Mazaj's wonderfully comprehensive *World Cinema: A Critical Introduction*, op. cit., 3.
3 Lucia Nagib, "Towards a Positive Definition of World Cinema," in Stephanie Dennison and Song Hwee Lim, eds., *Remapping World Cinema: Identity, Culture, and Politics in Film* (London: Wallflower, 2006), 35.
4 See Lucia Nagib, Chris Perriam, and Rajinder Dudrah, *Theorizing World Cinema* (London: I.B.Tauris, 2012), xxii.
5 Ibid.
6 Dudley Andrew, "An atlas of world cinema," *Framework* 45 (2) (Fall 2004), 9–23.

7 Andrew presented this paper at the "World Studies: Approaches, Paradigms, and Debates" Conference, The University of Hong Kong, Hong Kong, June 23–25, 2016.
8 See Shekhar Deshpande and Meta Mazaj, op. cit., passim, where they flesh out these concepts with sharp arguments and rich detail.
9 From Michael Talbott's Ph.D. dissertation for the Cinema Studies Department at NYU, entitled "Familiar Difference: Film Funds, Film Festivals, and World Cinema," defended May 2015.
10 Ibid.
11 Elsaesser in L. Nagib and C. Mello, eds., *Realism and the Audiovisual Media* (London: Palgrave Macmillan, 2009).
12 See Thomas Elsaesser, "Film Festival Networks: The New Topographies of Cinema in Europe," in *European Cinema: Face to Face with Hollywood* (Amsterdam: Amsterdam University Press, 2005), 21.
13 Ibid.
14 Ibid., 306.
15 I would like to thank Dale Hudson for this insight.
16 Thomas Elsaesser, *European Cinema*, 494.

15 World music and the commons

1 J.D. Peters, op. cit., 111.
2 See the Introduction to Bernd Herzogenrath, ed., *Travels in Intermedia[lity]: ReBlurring the Boundaries* (Hanover: Dartmouth College Press, 2012). In his essay for the volume, Jens Schroter delineates four models of Intermediality: synthetic, formal, transformational, and ontological.
3 Christopher Small, *Musicking: The Meanings of Performing and Listening* (Middletown, CT: Wesleyan University Press, 1998).
4 Ibid., 6.
5 Ibid., 307.
6 Charles Keil and Steven Feld, *Music Grooves: Essays and Dialogues* (Chicago: University of Chicago Press, 1994), 265–66.
7 J.D. Peters, op. cit., 302.
8 Kevin Kelly, *The Inevitable* (New York: Random House, 2016), 66.
9 Kevin Kelly, op. cit., 74.
10 Ibid.
11 Both Paul Simon and Michael Jackson collaborated with the Bahian Afro-Bloco Olodum; does it matter that the former is white and the latter black, or are the asymmetries the same?
12 Steven Feld, "A sweet lullaby for world music," *Public Culture* 12 (1) (2000), 151.
13 Stephen Feld, "My Life in the Bush of Ghosts: 'World Music' and the Commodification of Religious Experience," in Rob W. White, ed., *Music and Globalization: Critical Encounters* (Bloomington: Indiana University Press, 2912), 40.
14 David Byrne, "Crossing Music's Borders: I Hate World Music," *The New York Times* (9/3/1999).
15 Ibid.
16 From the *Africa Film & TV News Flash* Edition 167, 7 August 2002, cited in T. Hoefert de Turegano, "Transnational Cinematic Flows: World Cinema as World Music?" cmsw.mit.edu/mit2/Abstracts/wcwmart2.
17 *Aesthetic of the Cool: Afro-Atlantic Art and Music* (New York: Periscope, 2011), 7.
18 Aram Sinnreich, *Mashed Up: Music, Technology, and the Rise of Configurable Culture* (Amherst: University of Massachusetts Press, 2010), 71.
19 Bill Ivy and Steven Tepper, "Cultural Renaissance or Cultural Divide?" *Chronicle Review*, May 19, 2006, B6.

16 Transmedial music in Latin America

1. See Paul Gilroy, *After Empire: Melancholia or Convivial Culture?* (London: Routledge, 2004).
2. In one instance, the American musician Taj Mahal alerted Brazilian musician Jorge Bem (later Jorge Benjor) that Rod Stewart had plagiarized the melody of his "Taj Mahal" in his "Do You Think I'm Sexy? Stewart in his memoir admitted to "unconscious plagiarism" and ended up devoting the royalties for the song to UNICEF.
3. At a protest rally protesting what leftists see as a soft *coup d'état*, Caetano performed a medley of his songs, where the protestors seamlessly integrated the slogans of the day— "Fora Temer" (Down with Temer) and "O Racismo nao passara" (Racism won't pass) into the gaps of the music.
4. Jose Miguel Wisnik, *"O Som e o Sentido"* Uma Outra Historia da Musica (Sao Paulo: Companhia das Letras, 1989).
5. Jose Miguel Wisnik, "A Gaia Ciencia: Literature e Musica Popular no Brasil," in *Musica* (Rio: Funarte, 2016).
6. Ibid., 26.
7. See Roberto Schwarz, "Verdade Tropical: Um Percuro de Nosso Tempo," in Marcos Lacerda, ed., *Musica* (Rio: Funarte, 2016) The challenge for Caetano is how to absorb what is valid in North American music without being colonized by it. Caetano reminds us that American music could not possibly dominate Brazil "because popular American music has always had to compete not only with Cuban rhumba, Argentinian tango, and the Portuguese fado, but with Brazilian music, which had never been vanquished commercially by the imported product."
8. Caetano Veloso, *Verdade Tropical* (Sao Paulo: Companhia das Letras, 1997), 105 (translation mine).
9. Quoted in Francisco Elinaldo Teixeira, "Incidencias e Avatares de um Cine-ensaio no Brasil, in Francisco Elinaldo Teixeira, ed., *O Ensaio no Cinema* (Sao Paulo: Hucitec, 2015).

17 The transnational turn

1. Ernest Gellner, *Nations and Nationalism* (Oxford: Blackwell, 2006), 6.
2. Aihwa Ong, *Flexible Citizenship: The Cultural Logics of Transnationality* (Durham: Duke University Press, 1999), 4.
3. Juan Pinon, "Corporate Transnationalism: The US Hispanic and Latin American Television Industries," in Arlene Davila and Yeidy M. Rivero, eds., *Contemporary Latina/o Media: Production, Circulation, Politics* (New York: New York University Press, 2014), 21.
4. Nestor Garcia Canclini, *Consumers and Citizens* (Minneapolis: University of Minnesota Press, 2001), 3.
5. Mel van Elteren, "Cultural Globalization and Transnational Flows of Things American," http//www.intechopen.com/books.
6. See Ernest Gellner, *Nations and Nationalism* (1983).
7. See Anthony D. Smith, *The Ethnic Revival* (Cambridge: Cambridge University Press, 1981).
8. Kaplan and Grewal, "Transnational Feminist Cultural Studies: Beyond the Marxism/Poststructuralism/Feminism Divides," in Caren Kaplan, Norma Alarcon, and Minoo Moallem, eds., *Between Woman and Nation* (Durham: Duke University Press, 1999), 358.
9. Inderpal Grewal and Caren Kaplan, eds., *Scattered Hegemonies: Postmodernity and Transnational Feminist Practices* (Minneapolis: University of Minnesota Press, 1994).
10. See Hito Steyerl, *The Wretched of the Screen* (Berlin: Sternberg Press, 2012).
11. Samir Amin, *Spectres of Capitalism* (London: Zed, 1999), 45.
12. Bourdieu speaks of these issues in *The Logic of Practice* (Cambridge: Polity, 1990).
13. Max Weber, "Politics as a Vocation," in H.H. Garth and C. Wright Mills, eds., *Essays in Sociology* (New York: Macmillan, 1946), 26–45.

18 Transnational cinema

1 Stephen Crofts, "Concepts of National Cinema," in John Hill and Pamela Church Dixon, eds., *The Oxford Guide to Film Studies* (Oxford: Oxford University Press, 1998).
2 Andrew Higson, "The Limiting Imagination of National Cinema," in Mette Hjort and Scott MacKenzie, eds., *Cinema and Nation* (London: Routledge, 2000).
3 Paul Willemen and Valentina Vitali, *Theorizing National Cinema* (London: BFI, 2006).
4 See Mette Hjort, "On the Plurality of Cinematic Transnationalism," in Nataša Ďurovičová and Kathleen Newman, eds., *World Cinemas, Transnational Perspectives* (London: Routledge, 2010).
5 Ibid., 13–14.
6 See Paul Julian Smith, "Transnational Cinemas: The Cases of Mexico, Argentina, and Brazil," in Lucia Nagib and Rajinder Dudrah, eds., *Theorizing World Cinema* (New York: I.B.Taurus, 2012), 70.
7 See Mette Hjort, *Small Nation: Global Cinema: The New Danish Cinema* (Minneapolis: University of Minnesota Press, 2005) and Mette Hjort and Duncan Petri, eds., *The Cinema of Small Nations* (Bloomington: Indiana University Press, 2007).
8 See Thomas Elsaesser, "Double occupancy: Space, place and identity in European cinema of the 1990s," *Third Text* 20 (6) (November 2006), 647–658.
9 See Elizabeth Ezra and Terry Rowden, eds., *Transnational Cinema: The Film Reader* (London: Routledge, 2006), 1.
10 See John Hess and Patricia Zimmerman, "Transnational Documentaries: A Manifesto," in Elizabeth Ezra and Terry Rowden, eds., *Transnational Cinema: The Film Reader* (London and New York: Routledge, 2006), 99.
11 Will Higbee and Song Hwee Lim, "Concepts of transnational cinema: Towards a critical transnationalism in film studies," *Transnational Cinemas* 1 (1) (2010).
12 See Françoise Lionnet and Shu-Mei Shih, eds., *Minor Transnationalism* (Durham: Duke University Press, 2006), 5–6.
13 See Nestor Garcia Canclini, *Culturas Hibridas: Estrategias para entrar e salir da la modernidad* (Mexico City: Grijalbo, 1990).
14 Shohini Chaudhuri, *Contemporary World Cinema: Europe/Middle East/East Asia/South Asia* (Edinburgh: Edinburgh University Press, 2005), 3.
15 Randal Johnson, "In the Belly of the Ogre: Cinema and the State in Latin America," in John King, Ana M. Lopez and Manuel Alvarado, eds., *Mediating Two Worlds: Cinematic Encounters in the Americas* (London: BFI) 207.
16 Joana Page, "The Nation as the mise-en-scene of filmmaking in Argentina." Published online on August 20, 2006.
17 See Jungbong Choi, "Introduction: Of transnational-Korean cinematrix," *Transnational Cinemas* 3 (2) (2012).
18 Ibid.

19 The coefficient of transnationality

1 Paul Kerr, "Babel's network narrative: Packaging a global cinema," *Transnational Cinema* 1 (1) (2010).
2 See Deborah Shaw, "*Babel* and the global Hollywood gaze," *Situations: Project of the Radical Imagination* 4 (1) 2011, 11–31.
3 Deborah Shaw, "Deconstructing and reconstructing transnational cinema," in *Contemporary Hispanic Cinema*, indb 48, (3/14/2013) 51.
4 Johann Andersson and Lawrence Webb, eds., *Global Cinematic Cities: New Landscapes of Film and Media* (London: Wallflower, 2016), 6.
5 Saskia Sassen, *The Global City: New York, London, Tokyo* (Princeton: Princeton University Press, 1991).
6 Ibid., 8.

7 See Mikhail Bakhtin, "Forms of Times and of the Chronotope in the Novel," in *The Dialogic Imagination: Four Essays by M. M. Bakhtin*, translated by Caryl Emerson and Michael Holquist (Austin: University of Texas Press, 1981).
8 Hye Jean Chung, "Media heterotopia and transnational filmmaking: Mapping real and virtual worlds," *Cinema Journal* 51 (4) (Summer 2012).
9 Hye Jean Chung, op. cit., 88.
10 Ibid., 109.

20 Transnational reception, gender, and aesthetics

1 Robyn Citizen, for example, has taken a transnational approach to the portrayals of black Americans and mixed-race Japanese in Japanese cinema, where blackness is both stigmatized through a sense of superiority at once Japanese and Western, and at the same time posited as a case of two fellow victims of European racism. She speaks of the "contentious triangulated relationship" between white Americans, black Americans, and the Japanese. See Robyn Citizen, "Projecting Blackness: Japan's Cinematic Encounters with the black-American Other (1946–1993)," as-yet-unpublished Ph.D. dissertation in the Cinema Studies Department of New York University.
2 See Robert Stam, *Tropical Multiculturalism: A Comparative History of Race in Brazilian Cinema and Culture* (Durham: Duke, 1997) and with Ella Shohat, *Race in Translation: Culture Wars around the Postcolonial Atlantic* (New York: NYU Press, 2012), and Ella Shohat, *Israeli Cinema: East/West and the Politics of Representation* (Austin: University of Texas Press, 1989; updated edition with a new postscript chapter, I.B.Tauris, 2010.
3 While the Egyptian director-in-the-film in Chahine's *Alexandria Why?* fantasized about Hollywood Babylon, the Beur/Banlieue directors, at least in an early period, dreamed of recreating something like the black film community of Spike Lee's Brooklyn in the banlieux of Paris.
4 See Katarzyna Marciniak, Aniko Imrre, and Aine O'Healy, eds., *Transnational Feminism in Film and Media* (London: Palgrave, 2007).
5 Ibid.
6 Patricia White, op. cit., 7.
7 Ibid., 22.
8 Ibid., 4.
9 See Alison Butler, *Women's Cinema: The Contested Screen* (London: Wallflower, 2002), 21.
10 In a later period, a director might only slowly become aware of his own aesthetic allegiances, as occurred with Chyam Benegal's discovery that he had long adhered to a kind of pan-rasa aesthetic without being consciously aware of it. I base this opinion on a conversation with Benegal the Subversive Cinema Festival in Zaghreb in 2013.
11 Iain Robert Smith and Constantine Verevis—*Transnational Film Remakes* (Edinburgh: Edinburgh University Press, 2017.
12 Jon Tsuei, cited in Smith and Verevis, op. cit., 1.
13 Ibid., 2.
14 See Rashna Wadia Richards, "Translating Cool," in Smith and Verevis, op. cit.,11.

21 Transnational film schools and pedagogy

1 See Xie Fei, "A Half-Century as a Teacher of Film Directing," in Maria Dora Mourao et al., eds., op. cit., 258–279.
2 See Maria Dora Mourao et al., eds, *The 21st Century Film, TV, and Media School: Challenges, Clashes, Changes* (Sofia, Bulgaria: Cilect, 2016), 227.
3 Quoted in Esther Hamburger, "In a World of Screens," in Maria Dora Mourao et al., op. cit., 84.
4 James Schamus, "A Rant," in op. cit., 257.
5 Justin Wyatt, "Marketing Marginalized Cultures," in J. Lewis, ed. *The End of Cinema as We Know It* (New York: NYU Press, 2001), 70.

6 Katarzyna Marciniak and Bruce Bennett, eds., *Teaching Transnational Pedagogy* (New York: Routledge, 2016).
7 Ibid., 157.
8 Sylke Rene Meyer, "Politics of Narrative," in Maria Dora Mourao et al., eds., *The 21st Century Film, TV, and Media School: Challenges, Clashes, Changes* (Sofia, Bulgaria: Cilect, 2016), 254–255.
9 Quoted in Gwynne Edwards, *A Companion to Luis Bunuel* (Woodbridge, U.K.: Tamesis [Boydell & Brewer], 2005) 90.
10 Jane McGonigal, *Reality is Broken: Why Games Make Us Better and How They can Change the World* (New York: Penguin, 2011), 14.

22 Minor cinema, the indigene, and the state

1 Ibid.
2 She made this remark when her film *Open Bethlehem* was screened at NYU in Abu Dhabi in the spring of 2016.
3 See Ella Shohat, "Columbus, Palestine and the Arab Jews," in *Taboo Memories* (Durham: Duke University Press, 2006).
4 Deborah Danowski and Eduardo Viveiros de Castron, *Ha Mundo por Vir? Ensaio Sobre os Medos e os Fins* (Florianopolis: Cultura e Barbarie and Sao Paulo: Insituto Socioambiental, 2017), 145 (translation mine).
5 See Ronald Niezen, *The Origins of Indigenism* (Berkeley: University of California Press, 2003) 4.
6 Randolph Lewis, *Alanis Obomsawin: The Vision of a Native Filmmaker* (Lincoln: University of Nebraska Press, 2003) 175.

23 The rise of the "woods"

1 David Bordwell, Janet Staiger, and Kristin Thompson, *The Classical Hollywood Cinema: Film Style and Mode of Production to 1960* (London: Routledge, 1988), 384.
2 Ibid.
3 See Stephen Crofts, "Reconceptualizing National Cinema/s in Valentina Vitali and Paul Willemen," in *Theorizing National Cinema* (London: BFI, 2006), 44–58.
4 Cited in Marciniak, op. cit., 141.
5 Anandam P. Kavoori and Aswin Punathambekar, eds., *Global Hollywood* (New York: New York University Press, 2008), 1.
6 Ashish Rajadhyaksha, "The Bollywoodization of the Indian cinema: Cultural nationalism in a global arena," *Inter-Asia Cultural Studies* 4 (1) (2003).
7 See Despande and Mazaj, op. cit., 22.
8 Henry Jenkins, et al., 266.
9 S. Lash and C. Lury, *Global Culture Industry: The Mediation of Things* (Cambridge: Polity, 2007), 4.
10 Courtney Brannon Donoghue, "Sony and local-language productions: Conglomerate Hollywood's strategy of flexible localization for the global film market," *Cinema Journal* 52 (4) (Summer 2014), 3–27.
11 Ibid., 27.
12 Eleftheria Thanouli, "Narration in world cinema: Mapping the flows of formal exchange in the era of globalization," *New Cinemas: Journal of Contemporary Film* 6 (1) (2008).
13 For an excellent anthology of such criticism, see Matthias Krings and Onookone Okome, eds., *Global Nollywood: The Transnational Dimensions of an African Video Film Industry* (Bloomington: Indiana University Press, 2013).
14 See Manthia Diawara, *African Films: New Forms of Aesthetics and Politics* (Munich: Prestel, 2010), 190.
15 Jonathon Haynes, "Neoliberalism, Nollywood, and Lagos," in Andersson amd Webb, op. cit., 67.

16 Jonathon Hayes, "The Hollwood Diaspora," in *Global Nollywood*.
17 See Alessandro Jedlowski, "From Nollywood to Nollyworld," in *Global Nollywood*.
18 Jontathon Haynes, *Nollywood: The Creation of Nigerian Film Genres* (Chicago: University of Chicago Press, 2016), 15.
19 Manthia Diawara, op. cit., 179.
20 See John L. Comaroff and Jean Comaroff, "Criminal justice, cultural justice: The limits of liberalism and the pragmatics of difference in the new South Africa," *American Ethnologist* 31 (2) (2004).
21 Brian Larkin, "Degraded images, distorted sounds: Nigerian video and the infrastructure of piracy," *Public Culture* 16 (2), (2004), 310.
22 Ibid.
23 The recent trials of Bill Cosby remind us of the perils of over-investing in a mediatic "positive image" which can be undone by events.
24 Tom Engelhardt, *Ambush at Kamikaze Pass: Racism in the Media* (Boston: New England Free Press, 1971).
25 Haynes, "Nollywood", 211.
26 Diawara, op. cit., 113.
27 Ibid., 185.

24 Globalization, political economy, and the media

1 Rosalind Galt and Karl Schoonover, eds., op. cit.
2 Roy Stafford, *The Global Film Book* (London: Routledge, 2014), 13.
3 Ibid., 36.
4 See Adam Kirsch, *The Global Novel: Writing the World in the 21st Century* (New York: Columbia Global Reports, 2016).
5 Jan Nederveen Pieterse, "Periodizing globalization: Histories of globalization," Global Studies 6 (2) (2012).
6 Jan Nederveen Pieterse, "What is global studies?" in *Globalizations* 10 (4) (2013), 499–514.
7 Deborah Danowski and Eduardo Viveiros de Castro, *Ha Mundo por Vir: Ensaio Sobre os Medos e os Fins* (Florianopolis: Cultura e Barbarie and Sao Paulo: Insituto Socioambiental, 2017), 145 (translation mine).
8 Peter Linebaugh, *Stop, Thief*, 140.
9 Djelal Kadir, *Columbus and the Ends of the Earth* (Berkeley: University of California Press, 1992), 66.
10 See Vandana Shiva, *Monocultures of the Mind* (London: Zed Books, 1993).
11 See Sean Cubitt, *Finite Media: Environmental Implications of Digital Technologies* (Durham, NC: Duke University Press, 2017), 65.
12 Arturo Escobar, "Latin America at a Crossroads: Between Alternative Modernizations, Postliberalism, and Postdevelopment," Lecture at the Center for Latin American and Caribbean Studies, New York University, October 29, 2009.
13 See Toby Miller and Marwan Kraidy, *Global Media Studies* (Cambridge: Polity, 2016), 31.
14 See Toby Miller, Nitin Govil, John McMurria, Ting Wang, and Richard Maxwell, *Global Hollywood 2* (London: BFI, 2005).
15 Quoted in ibid., 50.
16 One exception is Etihad Airlines, which programs Arabic, European, Indian, and Asian films in their air-borne cinemateque, and where French films are listed, in a kind provincialization of Europe, under "World Cinema."
17 The caricature consists in the implicit denial that progressive film theory, criticism, and importantly, pedagogy, can have progressive political effects in decentering Hollywood, promoting activist filmmaking, deprovincializing students (i.e. spectators), future filmmakers and policy makers. After all, half of the collaborators in the book come from a film studies background and somehow seem to have escaped the pernicious effects of "screen studies."

18 Statistics cited in Johann Andersson and Lawrence Webb, eds., *Global Cinematic Cities: New Landscapes of Film and Media* (London: Wallflower, 2016), 6.

25 Aquatic tropologies

1 See Hayot essay in *The Routledge Companion to World Literature*, 227.
2 See John Durham Peters, op. cit., 54.
3 Vilem Flusser as summarized by Peters, in op. cit., 97.
4 Peters, op. cit., 97.
5 Raymond Williams, *Television: Technology and Cultural Form* (London: Routledge, 1974).
6 Henry Jenkins, *Convergence Culture: Where Old and New Media Collide* (New York: New York University Press, 2006), 2.
7 Paper presented as a plenary lecture at the Brazilian Association of Anthropology in Salvador Bahia, April 14–17, 1996.
8 Kathleen Newman, "Notes on Transnational Film Theory: Decentered Subjectivity, Decentered Capitalism," in Nataša Ďurovičová and Kathleen Newman, eds., *World Cinemas, Transnational Perspectives* (New York: Routledge, 2010), 9.
9 See Inderpal Grewal and Caren Kaplan, *Scattered Hegemonies: Postmodernity and Transnational Feminist Practices* (Minneapolis: University of Minnesota Press, 1994), 12.
10 See Walter Benjamin, "Surrealism," in *One-Way Street* (London: Verso, 1979), 225.
11 Ramon Labato, *Shadow Economies of Cinema: Mapping Informal Film Distribution* (London: Palgrave, 2012).
12 Shekhar Deshpande and Meta Mazag, *World Cinema: A Critical Introduction* (London: Routledge, 2018), 56.
13 Bhaskar Sarkar, "The Pedagogy of the Piratical," in Katarzyna Marciniak and Bruce Bennett, eds., *Teaching Transnational Pedagogy* (New York: Routledge, 2016), 192.
14 Brian Larkin similarly argues that "in many parts of the word, media piracy is not a pathology of circulation media forms but its prerequisite … the only means by which certain media—usually foreign—are available." Brian Larkin, *Signal and Noise* (Durham: Duke, 2008), 240.
15 Sarkar, in Katarzyna Marciniak and Bruce Bennett, eds., op. cit., 195.
16 Joseph Straubhar, "Beyond Media Imperialism: Assymetrical Interpendence and Cultural Proximity."
17 Joseph Straubhaar, *World Television: From Global to Local* (Thousand Oaks: Sage, 2007), 199.
18 Roland Robertson, "Glocalization: Time-Space and Homogeneity-Heterogeneity in Mike Featherstone et al., eds., *Global Modernities* (London: Sage, 1995), 10.
19 Piotra Zalewski, "As Turkey Turns," originally in *Slate*, cited in Toby Miller and Marwan M. Kraidy, op. cit., 140.
20 Juan Pinon, "Corporate Transnationalism: The US Hispanic and Latin American Television Industries," in Arlene Davila and Yeidi M. Rivero, eds., op. cit., 36.
21 See Arlene Davila and Yeidy M. Rivero, *Contemporary Latina/o Media: Production, Circulation, Politics* (New York: New York University Press, 2014), 2.
22 See Siegfried Zielinski, *Deep Time of the Media* (Cambridge, MA: MIT, 2006), 32.
23 John Durham Peters, op. cit., 165.
24 Ibid., 332.
25 Ibid.
26 See Tung-Hui Hu, *A Prehistory of the Cloud* (Cambridge, MA: MIT Press, 22015), 90.
27 See Jennifer Holt and Patrick Vondereau, "Where the Internet Lives," in Lisa Parks and Nicole Starosielski, eds., op. cit.,82.
28 Quoted in Jennifer Holt and Patrick Vondereau, ibid.
29 See Richard Maxwell and Toby Miller, *Greening the Media* (Oxford: Oxford University Press, 2012), 29.
30 See Lisa Parks and Nicole Starosielski, eds., *Signal Traffic: Critical Studies of Media Infrastructures* (Urbana: University of Illinois Press, 2015), 1.

26 Technologies of intermedial flow

1 Kelly, op. cit., 61.
2 Ibid., 65.
3 Ibid, 80.
4 For an eloquent alert to some of these dangers for cine-literate culture, see Wheeler Winston Dixon's invaluable book *Streaming: Movies, Media, and Instant Access* (Lexington: University of Kentucky Press, 2013).
5 Kelly, op. cit., 13.
6 See Nestor Garcia-Canclini, "From the Public to the Private: The 'Americanization' of Spectators," in Acbar Abbas and John Nguyet Erni, eds., *Internationalizing Cultural Studies* (Oxford: Blackwell, 2005), 267.
7 Linda Hutcheon, *A Theory of Adaptation* (New York: Routledge, 2006), xix.
8 See Dale Hudson and Patrica Zimmerman, *Thinking through Digital Media: Transnational Environments and Locative Places* (New York: Macmillan, 2015).
9 Nicolas Bourriaud, *Relational Aesthetics* (Paris: Les Presse du Reel, 2002).
10 See Costas Constandinides, *From Film Adaptation to Post-Celluloid Adaptation: Rethinking the Transition of Popular Narratives and Characters across Old and New Media* (New York: Continuum, 2010), 24–25. Constandinides acknowledges getting the term "post-celluloid adaptation" from my book *Literature through Film*, but he goes much farther with the subject.
11 Kelly, op. cit., 196.
12 See Henry Jenkins, Sam Ford, and Joshua Green, *Spreadable Media* (New York: NYU, 2013), 2.
13 The term "etats generaux" refers to the French Revolution and the "Estates General" of 1789.

27 Globalization

1 See Fredric Jameson, *Postmodernism, or, the Cultural Logic of Late Capitalism* (Durham, N.C., Duke University Press, 1991), p. 25.
2 See F. Jameson, *The Geopolitical Aesthetic: Cinema and Space in the World System* (London: BFI, 1992), 23.
3 For a fairly comprehensive list as of 2005, see Tom Zianiello, *The Cinema of Globalization* (Ithaca: Cornell University Press, 2007).
4 See Jacques Rancière, *Le Spectateur Emancipe* (Paris: La Fabrique, 2008), 81.

28 Transoceanic currents

1 Ella Shohat and I discuss the various racialized chromatic versions of the Atlantic in our *Race in Translation: Culture Wars in the Postcolonial Atlantic*. One of our earlier contemplated titles was *The Black, Red and White Atlantic*. Shohat and I discuss the Sephardi-Moorish Atlantic in "Tropical Orientalism: Brazil's Race Debates and the Sephardi-Moorish Atlantic," in Paul Amar, ed., *The Middle East and Brazil: Perspectives on the New Global South* (Bloomington: Indiana University Press, 2014), 119–161.See also Ella Shohat, "The Sephardi-Moorish Atlantic: Between Orientalism and Occidentalism," Preface essay in *Between the Middle East and the Americas: The Cultural Politics of the Middle East in the Americas* (co-edited with Evelyn Alsultany) (The University of Michigan Press, 2013), 42–63.
2 A major figure in Brazilian whiteness studies is cultural studies scholar Liv Sovik, a Swiss-American who has lived and taught in Brazil for decades. In *Here No One Is White*, Sovik points to the invisibility of Brazilian whiteness, in a situation where the supervalorization of whiteness goes hand in hand with the slighting of blackness, along with a probing analysis of the cultural politics of Brazilian popular music. See *Aqui Ninguém é Branco* (Rio de Janeiro: Aeroplano, 2010).
3 See Jigna Desai, *Beyond Bollywood: The Cultural Politics of South Asian Diasporic Film* (London: Routledge, 2004), 31.

4 I refer to a conference held in Palermo in June 2018, co-organized by Awam Amkpa and Deb Willis, and with the artistic collaboration of Wole Soyinke, entitled "Resignifications: The Black Meditteranean."
5 Ella Shohat and I develop the idea of "intercolonial narcissism" in the already mentioned *Race in Translation: Culture Wars in the Postcolonial Atlantic.*
6 See Nacira Guenif-Souilamas, ed., *La Republique Mise a Nu par son Immigration (The Republic Exposed by its Immigration)* (Paris: La Fabrique, 2006).
7 See Linda Tuhiwai Smith, *Decolonizing Methodologies: Research and Indigenous Peoples* (Chicago: University of Chicago Press, 1999).
8 See Paul Chatt Smith, *Everything You Know about the Indian is Wrong* (Minneapolis: University of Minnesota Press, 2009), p. 37.
9 Jodi Byrd, *Transit of Empire*, 11.
10 See "Indians Grieve over Picture Shows," in *Moving Picture World* (July 10, 1911).
11 I gesture all too briefly toward such analyses in my *Tropical Multiculturalism: A Comparative History of Race in Brazilian Cinema and Culture* (Durham: Duke University Press, 1997) and in (with Ella Shohat) *Race in Translation: Culture Wars in the Postcolonial Atlantic* (New York: NYU Press, 2011).
12 The 2014 Conference, organized by Awam Amkpa and Gunja Sengupta, was entitled, "How Migration Makes Meaning," and included talks by Amir Al-Islam, Herman Bennett, Sugata Bose, Gwyn Campbell, Henry Drewal, Cheryl Finley, Marisa Fuentes, Michael Gomez, Bayo Holsey, David Ludden, Liz McMahon, Alessandra di Maio, Maaza Mengiste, José Moya, Sam Pollard, Caryl Phillips, Ed Rugemer, Ella Shohat, Robert Stam, Deb Willis and Hollian Wint.
13 Shohat argues that while the relation between Israel and the Palestinians is a colonial relation, the situation is anomalous in the sense that Zionism claimed to be a liberation movement analogous to other liberation movements, and also constituted a colonialism, unlike French and British colonialism, for example, without a metropole.

See Ella Shohat, *Israeli Cinema* (Austin: University of Texas Press, first published in 1989 and reprinted with a new Afterward in 2010).

29 Global indigeneity and the transnational gaze

1 Alcida Rita Ramos, *Indigenism: Ethnic Politics in Brazil* (Madison: University of Wisconsin, 1998).
2 Faye D. Ginsburg, "Indigenous media: Faustian contract or global village," in *Cultural Anthropology* 6 (1) (1991).
3 For an illuminating analysis of Caetano's work, including of "O Indio," see Guilherme Wisnik, *Caetano Veloso* (São Paulo: PubliFolha, 2005).
4 See James Clifford, *Returns: Becoming Indigenous in the Twenty First Century* (Cambridge, MA: Harvard University Press, 2013).
5 See Dustin Tahmahkera, *Tribal Television* (Chapel Hill: University of North Carolina Press, 2014), 146.
6 Here I cite and generally draw on an excellent and witty source on Canadian Aboriginal Television and its use of humor, the remarkable book by Dustin Tahmahkera, *Tribal Television: Viewing Native People in Sitcoms* (Chapel Hill: University of North Carolina Press, 2014).
7 See Faye Ginsburg, "Embedded aesthetics: Creating a discursive space for indigenous media," *Cultural Anthropology* 9 (3) (1994), 365–382.
8 Quoted in S. Baldur Hafsteinsson and Marian Bredin, eds., *Indigenous Screen Cultures in Canada* (Winnipeg: University of Manitoba Press, 2010), 130.
9 See Kyra Landzelius, ed., *Native on the Net* (London: Routledge, 2006), 292.
10 See Ivana Bentes, *Midia-Multidao: Esteticas da Communicacao e Biopoliticas* (Rio de Janeiro: Mauad), 2015.
11 See Renato Rosaldo, "Imperialist nostalgia," *Representations*, 26 (Spring 1989).
12 See Ivana Bentes, op. cit.

13 For an excellent analysis of the Xuxa show, and of the role of the Indian within the Brazilian imaginary generally, see Tracy Devine Guzmán, *Native and National in Brazil: Indigeneity after Independence* (Durham: University of North Carolina Press, 2013).
14 Corinn Columpar, *Unsettling Sights: The Fourth World on Film* (Carbondale: Southern Illinois Press, 2010), xiv.
15 See Edouard Glissant, *The Poetics of Relation* (Ann Arbor: University of Michigan Press, 2010).
16 See Thomas King, op. cit., 218.
17 See Chadwick Allen, *Blood Narrative: Indigenous Identity in American Indian and Maori Literary and Activist Texts* (Durham: Duke University Press, 2002).
18 John Locke, "Second Treatise of Government," in *The Selected Political Writings of John Locke*, ed. Paul E. Sigmund (New York: Norton, 2005), sec. 32.
19 See Larry J. Zimmrman et al., "Cyberspace Smoke Signals: New Technologies and Native American Ethnicity," in Claire Smith and Graeme Ward, eds., *Indigenous Cultures in an Interconnected World* (Victoria: University of British Columbia Press, 2000), 79.

30 The media's "deep time" and the planetary commons

1 *The Routledge Companion to World Literature*, see 249 and Dimock, 2006, 3, 4.
2 De Haen et al., op. cit., 326.
3 For example, Moretti speaks of the "planetary" in his *Conjectures on World Lit*, p. 148.
4 See Gayatri Spivak, *Death of a Discipline* (New York: Columbia University Press, 2003), 72.
5 Rob Nixon, "The Anthropocene: The promise and pitfalls of an epochal idea," in *EdgeEffects*, 3/8.2017.
6 See Depesh Chakravarty, "The climate of history: Four theses," in *Critical Inquiry* 35 (97) (2009).
7 Macarena Gomez-Barris, *The Extractive Zone: Social Ecologies and Decolonial Perspectives* (Durham: Duke University Press, 2017).
8 Deborah Danowski and Eduardo Viveiros de Castro, *Ha Mundo por Vir? Ensaio sobre os Medos e os Fins* (Is there a World to Come? Essay on Fears and Ends) (Sao Paulo and Florianopolis: Cultura e Barbarie and ISA, 2017), 16.
9 Ibid., 118.
10 Ibid., 35.
11 Davi Kopenawa and Bruce Albert, *La Chute du Ciel: Paroles d'un chaman yanomami* (Paris: Plon, 2010).
12 Danowski and Viveiros de Castro, op. cit.
13 Peter Szendy, *L'Apocalypse Cinema: 2012 et autres fins du Monde* (Paris: Capricci, 2012).
14 Neil Shubin, *The Universe Within: The Common Roots of Rocks, Planets and People* (New York: Pantheon, 2013), 190.
15 Gilles Deleuze, *Cinema 2: The Time-Image*. Trans. Hugh Tomlinson and Robert Galeta. London: The Athlone Press, 1989. p. 102.
16 John Dunham Peters, op. cit., 385.
17 From MSS of David Martin-Jones, *Cinema against Doublethink: Ethical Encounters with the Lost Pasts of World History* (London: Routledge, forthcoming 2018).
18 James Hansen, *Storms of my Grandchildren* (New York: Bloomsbury, 2009), ix.

31 The commons and the globalized citizen

1 See "U.S. Delegation disrupts Accord on Breast Milk," *New York Times* (7/9/2018), A- and the follow-up article in the *NYT* on 7/10/2018. The *Times* article pointed out that the marketing of milk substitutes had led to more than 60,000 deaths in low- and middle-income countries in the single year of 1981 alone, because the mothers would mix the formula with contaminated water. In the present, the same administration that has separated immigrant mothers from their children also tries to separate infants from their own mothers' milk.

2 Apter, op. cit. 16.
3 Ursala K. Heise, "World Literature and the Environment," in Theo D'haen et al., eds., op. cit., 405.
4 James Clifford, *Returns: Becoming Indigenous in the Twenty First Century* (Cambridge, MA: Harvard University Press, 2013), 20.
5 Cited in Wimock, op. cit., 175–176.
6 Ibid., 177.
7 Ibid., 178.
8 Antonio Negri and Michael Hardt, *Declaracao: Isto nao e um Manifesto* (Sao Paulo: CIP, 2016).
9 Ibid., 41.
10 See Andrew Ross, *Creditocracy: And the Case for Debt Refusal* (New York: Or Books, 2016).
11 Quoted in Linebaugh, op. cit., 245.
12 Hardt and Negri, op. cit., 73.
13 Boaventura de Sousa Santos, *Reinventar as Esquerdas* (São Paulo: Boitempo), 2016 (translation mine).

32 Terminological reflections

1 Pheng Chea, *What is a World: On Postcolonial Literature as World Literature* (Durham: Duke University Press, 2016).
2 Daniel Yacavone in his *Film Worlds: A Philosophical Aesthetics of Cinema* (New York: Columbia University Press, 2015).
3 Even Dudley Andrews, often seen as an advocate of World Cinema, acknowledged in his paper "China and Africa in the Changing World of World Cinema" that the term had lost ground to its competitors "Global" and "Transnational," and that he was calling the field "World Cinema" only as a "convenience."
4 In Bruce Bennett and Katarzyna Marciniak, "coda," in Katarzyna Marciniak, Aniko Imre, and Aine O'Healy, eds., *Transnational Feminism in Film and Media* (London: Palgrave, 2007).
5 Thomas Elsaesser, *European Cinema: Face to Face with Hollywood* (Amsterdam: Amsterdam University Press, 2005), 509.
6 Bhaskar Sarkar, "Postcolonial and Transnational Perspectives," in James Donald and Michael Renov, eds., *Sage Handbook of Film Studies* (London: Sage, 2008).
7 See Arturo Escobar, "Thinking-feeling with the Earth: Territorial struggles and the ontological dimension of the epistemologies of the South," *Revista de Antropologia Iberoamericana* 11 (1) (Jan-April 2016).
8 Ibid.
9 See Henry Jenkins et al., *Spreadable Media*, 259.
10 See Aihwa Ong, *Flexible Citizenship: the Cultural Logics of Transnationality* (Durham: Duke University Press, 1999), 4.
11 See Nataša Ďurovičová, "preface," in Nataša Ďurovičová and Kathleen Newman, eds., *World Cinemas, Transnational Perspectives* (London: Routledge, 2010), ix.
12 See John Hess and Patricia Zimmerman, "Transnational Documentaries: A Manifesto," in Elizabeth Ezra and Terry Rowden, eds., *Transnational Cinema: The Film Reader* (London and New York: Routledge, 2006) 99.

33 Toward a "trans" methodology

1 On the Middle East and the Americas, for example, see Ella Shohat and Evelyn Alzultany, *Between the Middle East and the Americas: The Cultural Politics of Diaspora* (Ann Arbor: University of Michigan Press, 2013).
2 See Hess and Zimmerman, op. cit., 3.

INDEX

Note: 'n' indicates chapter notes.

4.44 Last Day on Earth (dir. Ferrara) 222
100% Arabica (dir. Zemmouri) 44, 153

Abdel-Malek, Anouar 53
Aboriginal filmmaking *see* indigenous filmmaking
Aboriginal People's Television Network (APTN), Canada 211, 213
activism 9, 53, 56, 149, 161–62, 213, 220, 226
Adaptation (dir. Jonze) 66
adaptation, film 61, 62, 64–68, 81–82, 87–90, 173; music videos 116–17; remixes 91–99, 248n14; studies 66, 92–94, 98, 99, 111, 248n14; world literature canon 69–74
Adena culture 18
Adichie, Chimananda Ngozi 173
aesthetics 21, 22, 24–25, 35, 36–39, 61, 64, 138–39, 143, 149, 152–54, 245n4, 252n10
Afolayan, Kunle 29
African languages 79
African literature 17, 54, 55–56, 74
African music, polyrhythms 25
African theater collaboration 85–86
African transnationality 149
African-American music 110–11, 117–18
Africans 18
Afro-diaspora 92, 111, 117, 119, 124, 149
Afro-indigenous culture 28, 37

Afromodernity 174
Against World Literature (Apter) 29
Age of Stupid, The (dir. Armstrong) 224–25
Ahmad, Aijaz 44–45
Akomfrah, John 202
al Ahmad, Jalal 7
Alexander, M. Jacqui 132
Algeria 42–44
Allen, Chadwick 219
Allen, Woody 19, 30, 33, 99
Allende, Isabel 33
Almanac of the Dead (Silko) 38
Almereyda, Michael 87
Alphabet 184
Alquist, Lloyd 149–50
Altman, Rick 77
Amata, Jet 172–73
Amazon (company) 63, 183–84
Amazonian indigenes 168; filmmaking 213–14, 217
Amazonian legends 38
Amin, Samir 23, 105, 133
Amkpa, Awam 206
Anderson, Benedict 130
Andersson, John 144
Andre, Chris 34
Andrews, Dudley 104, 105–7, 259n3
Andromeda Strain, The (dir. Wise) 67
"Anglo-Saxons, les" 52, 245n4
Annales School 23, 178
Anthropocene 221–22

anthropophagy 26, 27–28, 86, 125
anti-colonial discourse 42, 44, 55
anti-colonialism 134
anti-corporeality, and film adaptation 65–66
Antilles Francophone literature 54
antinomies, term 11
anti-slavery movement 134
apartheid 114
Appadurai, Arjun 10, 17, 131, 186, 235
apparati 63
Apple 184, 190
Apter, Emily 18, 19, 227
aquatic metaphors 185–90, 191, 202, 226
Arab films 72, 81
Arab intellectuals in France 53
Arab literature 17
Arac, Jonathon 47
Araujo, Joel Zito 204
Arca dos Zo'e, A (VNA film) 214
archaic modernism 32–33
Argentinian cinema 139–40
Aristophanes 94–95
Armstrong, Franny 224–25
Arnold, Matthew 21
Around the World in Eighty Days (Verne) 22
Art of the Motion Picture, The (Lindsay) 64
arts, the 2, 5, 110, 152–53
Asian cinemas 109
Asmat (dir. Yimer) 202–3
Astruc, Alexandre 60, 245n3
Asturias, Miguel Angel 38
Atanarjuat: The Fast Runner (dir. Kunuk) 210
Ateliers Varan, Paris film school 159
Atlantic Studies 202–6, 256n1
Atlas of the European Novel (Moretti) 105, 106
"Atlas of World Cinema, An" (Andrews) 105–7
Auerbach, Erich 19, 221
Austen, Jane 46–47, 88, 96–97
Australian indigenous cinema 210–11, 218
Australian indigenous land rights 219–20
Austrian literature 33
autonomization 58
avant-garde 26, 27, 32, 37, 39, 92
Avatar (dir. Cameron) 161–62, 166, 213
Azevedo, Beatriz 27
Aztec literature 20

Babel (dir. Iñárritu) 141–42
Bacalov, Luis 143
Badiou, Alain 64, 91
Baetens, Jan 65
Bahrani, Ramin 201
Bahun, Sanja 34

Bakhtin, Mikhail 13, 14, 22, 31, 41, 44, 65, 76, 87–88, 106, 129, 145–46, 155, 161, 223
Balandier, Georges 55
Balibar, Étienne 55
Balzac, Honoré de 93
Bamako (dir. Sissako) 197
Bande a Part (dir. Godard) 206
Bandele, Biya 173
banks 4, 5, 178
Bannon, Steve 133–34
Barclay, Barry 218
Barnosky, Anthony 221
Baskhar, Sandar 10
Battle in Seattle (dir. Townsend) 198
Battle of Algiers, The (dir. Pontecorvo) 43–44
Bazin, Andre 58
Beecroft, Alexander 80
Beijing Film School 157
Bekolo, Jean-Pierre 29
Belgrade Department of World Literature 65
Bellour, Raymond 193
Benin, masks 25
Benjamin, Walter 33, 63, 126, 187
Bennett, Bruce 160
Bentes, Ivana 214–15
Beowulf 95
Bergfelder, Tim 77
Berlin Film Festival 107–8
Bernal, Martin 17
Beyonce 114
Bhabha, Homi 45, 55, 244n12
Bible 17, 49, 94, 245n19
Bichlbaum, Andy 199
Bildung 22
binarisms 24–25, 140, 245n4
Birds, The (dir. Hitchcock) 222
Black and White in Color (Julien) 204
Black Atlantic Cinema 204
Black Atlantic Studies 202, 203–4, 206
black British art movements 43
black British cultural studies 46
Black Cinema 149
black movements in France 52–53
Black Orpheus (film) 14
Black Pacific Studies 206
Black Panther movement 149
black popular music 112
Black Skin, White Masks (dir. Julien) 42–43
Black Venus (dir. Kechiche) 57
Bloom, Harold 30, 34
Blur 117–18
Boal, Augusto 123
Boccaccio, Giovanni 17

Bolivian cinema 180–81
Bolivian indigenous rights 226
Bollain, Iciar 180
Bollywood 89, 169–72
Bolter, Jay David 91
Bonanno, Mike 199
Booker Prize 74
border crossing 1–2, 3, 14, 20, 22, 29, 87–88, 101, 142, 147–55, 238
borderlessness 23
Bordwell, David 169, 193
Borges, Jorge Luis 69, 248n20
Bossa Nova 122
Bourdieu, Pierre 51, 58
Bourriaud, Nicolas 193
Bran Nue Dae (dir. Perkins) 210–11
Bras Cubas (Machado) 30
Brathwaite, Kamau 10
Braudel, Fernand 23, 178
Brazil 25–28, 32, 36, 123–24, 148, 179, 256n2; *indio technizado* 168; Modern Art Week, Sao Paulo, 1922 26; Sony do Brazil 171; Video in the Villages 214–16
Brazilian cinema 14, 109, 120, 127, 143
Brazilian documentaries 217
Brazilian film adaptations 72
Brazilian garbage film genre 196–97
Brazilian indigenous culture 32–33
Brazilian indigenous media 208–10, 214
Brazilian literature 30–34, 45, 120, 154
Brazilian modernism 26–28, 38, 154, 211
Brazilian music 115, 120–27, 143
Brazilian rap 203
Brazilian telenovelas 188
Brazilian television 72, 88, 216
Brazilian theater 86
Brazilian women filmmakers 151–52
Brecht, Bertolt 63, 123
Brenez, Nicole 102
Bride and Prejudice (dir. Chadha) 88, 96–97
British Film School, London 157
British imperialism 26, 45
Brown, Robert E. 112
Buarque de Holanda, Chico 122–23
Bucy, Matt 67
Bunuel, Luis 70, 161
Burd, Jodi A. 40
Butler, Alison 152
By Any Media Necessary (Jenkins et al.) 200
Byrd, Jodi 205
Byrne, David 29, 114, 115–16, 125

cable television 183
Cahiers du Cinema (journal) 59–60
Caillois, Roger 161
Cameron, James 161–62, 166, 213
Cameroonian cinema 29
Campos, Augusto de 28
Canaan 17
Canada, Aboriginal People's Television Network (APTN) 211, 213
Canadian indigenous comedy 211–12, 257n6
Candido, Antonio 28
Cannes Film Festival 107, 184
Cannibal Manifesto 27, 28
canon, the 17, 63, 69–74, 84–90, 112
Capellen, George 111
capitalism 3, 5, 13, 22, 23, 27, 34, 40, 131–34, 178, 217–18, 224, 227; savage 5, 214n28
Carelli, Vincent 217–18
Carib revolution 27–28
Caribbean cosmopolitanism 37
Caribbean literature 54
Caribbean postcolonial theory 45, 46, 47
Caro Diario (Moretti) 153
Carpentier, Alejo 37, 119
Caribbean literature 74
Carriere, Jean-Claude 41
Carter, Eli Lee 73
Carvalho, Luis Fernando 73–74
Cary, Joyce 76
Casanova, Pascale 31, 36, 38, 47, 51, 52, 54, 106
Castaway (dir. Zemeckis) 71
Cave of Forgotten Dreams (Herzog) 62
Celso, Jose 86
Cendrars, Blaise 32
center and periphery see core and periphery
Centre Americain d'Etudes du Cinema, Le (later *Le Centre Parisien d'Etudes Critiques*) 60
Centro Sperimentale di Cinematographia, Il 157
Certeau, Michel de 84
Cervantes, Miguel de 17
Cesaire, Aime 149
Chabrol, Claude 157
Chadha, Gurinder 88, 96–97
Chakravarty, Depesh 221
Chan, Euan 137
Chapelle, Dave 144
Chaudhuri, Shohini 104, 139
Chea, Pheng 230, 233
Cher 143
Cherokee literature 86
Chickasaw 40
Chilam Balam (myth) 38
Chilean exile cinema 102

China 3, 18, 48, 134, 185; Beijing Film School 157
Chinese cinema 137
Chi-raq (dir. Lee) 94–95
Chirgilchin group 129
Choderlos de Laclos, Pierre 116
Choi, Jung-Bong 10, 140
Chow, Rey 230–31
Christopher, Brett 42
chronotope concept 145–46
Chung, Hye Jean 146
Churchill, Ward 27
Cinema after Babel, The (Shohat, Stam) 78
Cinema Babel (Nornes) 78–79
Cinema Falado (dir. Caetano) 126
Cinema Novo 25, 73, 109, 127
cinema *see* transnational cinema
cinemas and digital technologies 192–93
cinematique francaise, la 59
cinephilia 192
circulation 189; cinema 62–63, 69, 103–4, 106; literature 21, 22, 29–31, 69; *see also* distribution
cities, global 144–45
Citizen, Robyn 252n1
City of God (Lins) 93
Cixous, Helene 29
Claernout, David 67
class, social 42, 45, 66, 96, 148
classical music 110–11, 119–20
Clifford, James 210, 227
climate change 179, 221
cloud storage 189–91
Coelho, Paulo 21
Cohen, Margaret 19
Coldplay 116
collaboration 114–16, 120, 128, 249n11
colonial modernity 40
colonial theory 167
colonialism 8, 26, 41, 43, 48–50, 52, 56, 57, 70, 74, 78, 114, 124, 130, 134, 150, 172, 203, 207, 211; intercolonial narcissism 78, 203, 257n5
colonialisms 26
coloniality 7, 8, 24–25
Coloniality/Modernity Project 26, 28, 46, 49, 244n11
Color Adjustment (Riggs) 204
Columbus, Christopher (1492 conquest) 40–41, 48, 179–81, 211, 244n11
Comaroff, Jeff 174
Comaroff, John 174
commerciality 112
commons, the 12–14, 26, 27, 38, 41, 226–29, 241n29; digital 188; indigenous 31–32, 212, 218–19; literary 84–85, 95–96; musical 117–18, 121, 128–29; planetary 221–25; privatization of 3, 180–81, 226; term 12
Commonwealth, British 45, 47
communism 13, 22–23, 40
commutation tests 11
comparative linguistics 18
comparative literature 17, 46, 243n30
Concierto Barroco (Carpentier) 37, 119
configurability 118
Constandinides, Costas 193, 256n10
Contemporary World Cinema (Chaudhuri) 104
content 63, 190
contradictions 11
Coogan, Steve 95
Copeland, Aaron 113
copyright 117–18, 179–80; *see also* intellectual property rights; piracy
core and periphery theory 14, 23–25, 28, 30–31, 33–39, 45, 114, 172, 178–79, 242n14; term 235
Corporation, The (dir. Archer; Abbott) 198
corporations 23, 41, 130–31, 134, 198–201; big tech 183–84; *see also* enclosure; globalization
Correia, Jose Celso Martinez 86
Corumbiara (dir. Carelli) 217
Cosby, Bill 254n23
cosmopolitanism 22, 35–39, 106
Costa, Thiago da 215–16
Costa-Gavras 198
Creditocracy (Ross) 228
Crenshaw, Kimberle 147–48, 238
Creole consciousness 28
Crise des Intellectuels Arabes, La (Laroui) 53
Crisis of Messianic Philosophy, The (Oswald) 27
Crofts, Stephen 136, 169
Croll, Angus 99
cross-bordering *see* border crossing
Cuaron, Alfonso 88
Cuba, *La Escuela Internacional de Cine y Television* 157
Cuban literature 37
Cubitt, Sean 180
cultural capital 34, 57, 108
cultural industries 63, 170–71
cultural studies 21, 57
Culture and Imperialism (Said) 46–47
curatorial me 118
Curtius, Ernst 19

Dada 26, 28
Dadak, Zeynep 81

Daedalus, Stephen 22
Dafora, Asadata 85
Damrosch, David 16, 18–19, 20–22, 42, 46, 47, 52, 66, 69, 72, 84, 88, 93, 105
Dangerous Liaisons (Choderlos de Laclos) 116
Danowski, Deborah 179
Darwish, Mamoud 207
Davila, Arlene 189
de Andrade, Mário 30–33, 36
de Castro, Eduardo Belo 167–68
de Castro, Eduardo Viveiros 179
de Gaulle, Charles 52, 54
de Moraes, Raymundo 32
De Sousa Santos, Boaventura 229
dead media 6
Death of a Discipline (Spivak) 34
debt 228
Deckard, Sharae 46
de-colonial, term 26
decolonization 8–10, 26, 41, 42, 44, 48, 71, 132
deep media 5–6, 48
deep Remixability 2
deep state 134
deep time 5–6, 38, 64, 110, 221–25, 227
Deleuze, Gilles 101, 163, 224
Deloria, Philip J. 228
Delta Studies 202
democracy 18, 229
Denis, Claire 61
Denmark, National Danish Film School 157
Denowski, Deborah 222
Dependency Theory 9, 23, 31, 181–82, 188
deprovincialization 20, 31, 239
derivation 7, 11, 25–26
Derrida, Jacques 25, 55, 69, 91
Desai, Jigna 202
Deshpande, Shekhar 107
deterritorialization 131
development, term 107–8
D'haen, Theo 16
Diagne, Souleymane Bachir 86
Diary of a Mad Black Woman (TV series) 95
Diawara, Manthia 173, 174, 175, 202
dichotomous thinking 65
Dickens, Charles 88, 92
digital, term 189
digital commons 13, 224–25
digital divide 159, 193
digital economy 191
digital era 5, 83, 113, 118, 196, 220
digital media 91–93, 97–99, 192, 238, 248n20; cloud storage 189–90; term 2, 5–6

digital technologies, intermedial flow 191–95
digital turn 67, 138, 145–46
Dimock, Wai Chee 221, 227
Diogenes (journal) 53
Dion, Celine 116
discourse 41–43, 53–54, 55, 66, 107–8
Disney 70–73
dissemination 91
distribution 182, 184; tentpole releases 176; web-based cinematic 225; *see also* circulation
Divine Intervention (dir. Suleiman) 165
Do You (scholar) 88
Don Quixote (Cervantes) 17, 36, 98, 116
Donoghue, Courtney Brannon 171
Doody, Margaret Anne 17
Doughty, Ruth 136, 160
dubbing 77–78, 80, 81
Dudrah, Rajinder 105
Duras, Marguerite 76
Ďurovičová, Nataša 235
Dylan, Bob 115, 124

Eastern Europe 24
economics 23
Ecuador indigenous rights 226
Education of the Filmmaker, The (Hjort) 158
Edwards, Greg 98
Egypt, ancient 17, 18; Pyramid texts 20
electric guitars 115
Elias, Amy J. 221
elitism 16, 18, 111; *see also* class
Elliott, Kamilla 92
Elsaesser, Thomas 3, 11, 104, 108–9, 138, 145, 231
Embrace of the Serpent, The (dir. Guerra) 243n23
Emmerich, Roland 109
Emmy Awards 72
emulation/emigration model 109
Encerclement (film) 198–99
enclosure 12–13, 84, 109, 117–18, 180, 188, 224, 227
"End of Postcolonial Theory?, The" (PMLA) 50
Engelhardt, Tom 175
Engels, Friedrich 22–23, 224
English language 33–34, 45, 63, 78–80, 243n30
environment, the 27, 190; *see also* Anthropocene; climate change
epic rap battles 149–51
Escobar, Arturo 50, 181, 231

Escuela Internacional de Cine y Television, La, Cuba 157
Esquive, L' (dir. Kechiche) 95–96
essay-films 196–97
Essman, Sussie 200
estrangement 69, 84, 88
Ethiad Airlines 254n16
Ethiopia 18
ethnic music, term 54
ethnicity 42, 44, 115; transnational 144
ethnocentrism 31, 85
Euripides 95
Eurocentrism 7–9, 16, 20, 23, 26, 29, 169
Eurochronology problem 17
European Cinema (Elsaesser) 109
Eva Luna (Allende) 33
Even the Rain (dir. Bollain) 180–81
Ezra, Elizabeth 139

Fables of Bidpai 17
Facebook 184
Faden, Eric 72–73
"Fair[y] Use Tale" (remix video) 72–73
fan subtitling 78
fan-made music videos 116
Farsi 18
federated phase in world cinema 106–7
Feld, Stephen 114, 115
feminism 27, 148; transnational 132, 134, 151–52
feminist studies 132
Ferrara, Abel 222
Fielding, Henry 17, 67–68
film, term 2, 196
film adaptation *see* adaptation
film festivals 107–8, 138, 156, 173, 208
film production, tech companies in 183–84
film schools 156–62, 254n17
film theory 60
filmmaking 157, 158, 193–94
filmo-biography 72
financial crisis 4
First Australians (TV series) 211
First World 44–45; *see also* Global North
Flaubert, Gustave 62, 88–90, 99, 161–62
Flexible Citizenship (Ong) 234
folklore 25
Fond de l'Air est Rouge, Le (*A Grin without a Cat*, dir. Marker) 101
Ford, Sam 233
form/material binary 30–31
Foucault, Michel 18, 55
Fourth World 45, 165
France 9, 29, 30, 31; Paris 51, 52–53, 60, 61, 96, 145

Francophone cinema 52, 172–73
Francophone literature 47, 51, 74
Francophonie, la 52, 54
Frank, Andre Gunder 5, 23
Frankfurt School 63
Frayling, Christopher 206
Freire, Paulo 159, 160
French cinema 77–78, 106, 254n16, 206
French colonialism 42–44
French film adaptations 95–96
French film schools 157–58
French film theory 60–61
French imperialism 26
French intellectuals 45
French music 112
French New Wave 59, 60, 68, 157
French "Oriental" studies 53
French postcoloniality 51–57
French women filmmakers 151–52
Fuentes, Carlos 38
funding, cinema 107, 139, 173
Furtado, Jorge 196–97
futur anterieur 33
Futurism 26, 32

Gabriel, Peter 29
Gaines, Jane 14, 43
Galt, Rosalind 176
Games of Love and Chance (Marivaux) 95–96
Gandhi, Mahatma 149–51
Garbo, Greta 76
Garcia Canclini, Nestor 131, 139, 192
Garza, Armida de la 136, 141
Gates, Henry Louis 85, 86
gaze 43, 87, 114, 175; looking relations 14, 147–55; transnational 208–20
geist 91
Gellner, Ernest 132
gender 42, 44, 133–34, 151–52
Genette, Gerard 67
genres, transnationality 147, 152–53
German language films 77, 79
German literature 23
Gesamtkunstwerk (total artistic synthesis) 113
Ghost in the Shell (dir. Saunders) 154–55
Gil, Gilberto 121, 123–25, 126–27
Gilbert, John 76–77
Gilgamesh Epic 20
Gills, Barry 5
Gilroy, Paul 10, 119
Ginsburg, Faye 208
Glaineuses, Les (Varda) 84
Glissant, Edouard 29, 47, 54
global, term 10–11, 13, 21, 176–77, 231–36

Global Bollywood (Kavoori; Punathambekar) 170
global cinema phase 107
global cities 144–45
Global City, The (Sassen) 145
Global Cultural Industry (Lash; Lucy) 170–71
Global Film Book, The (Stafford) 176
Global Hollywood 2 (Miller et al.) 182, 183, 233
global indigeneity 208–20
global literature 176–77; term 10
global media 69, 120, 146, 176–84, 221–25, 237, 239; discourse 185–86; studies 177–78, 182; term 1–3, 8–9, 14, 177
Global North 4, 134–35, 186, 188; -Global South power relations 7–9, 23, 25, 29–30, 34, 48, 135, 169, 188–89, 222
Global South 4, 22, 25, 26, 36, 39, 52, 73, 87, 107–8, 119–29, 135, 169–71, 186, 188, 197
global village, term 11
Global Weimar moment 4
globalization 3–7, 11, 22, 34, 42, 47, 71, 78, 87, 88, 97, 102, 107, 131–33, 136–37, 139, 176–87, 196–201, 226–29, 258n1; studies 177–78; term 232–33, 234
Globalization Tapes, The (dir. Oppenheimer) 199
glocalization 189
Glover, Danny 198
Godard, Jean-Luc 157, 206–7
Goethe, Johann Wolfgang 16–19, 20, 22–23
Gold, Jack 71
Gomez-Barris, Marcarena 222
Google 69, 91, 184
Gould, Marty 71
Govil, Nitin 182, 183
"Graceland" (Simon) 114
Graeber, David 12
Graham, James 46
Graham, Zoe 158–59
Gramsci, Antonio 121
Grandy, Sandy 226–27
Grapes of Wrath (Steinbeck) 116
Gravesend (dir. McQueen) 199
Great Expectations (dir. Cuaron) 88
great time 87–88
Greco-centrism 17–18, 20
Greece, ancient 17–18, 35
Greek, ancient 20
Greek literature 123
Greek tragedy 121–22
Green, Joshua 233
Greening the Media (Maxwell) 190
Grewal, Inderpal 132, 151, 187

Grusin, Richard 91
Guarani-Kaiowá people 217
Guattari, Félix 163
Guenif-Soulimas, Nacira 203
Guiart, Jean 52
guitars, electric 115
Gupta, Sanjay 155
Guzmán, Patricio 223–24

Habibi, Emile 165
Haine, La (dir. Kassovitz) 44
Haiti, King Henri Christophe 37
Haitian revolution 85
Half of a Yellow Sun (dir. Bandele) 173
Hall, Stuart 152
Hamlet (dir. Almereyda) 87
Hamlet (Shakespeare) 86–87, 98
Hanks, Tom 71
Hannerz, Ulf 186
Hansen, James 224
Hardt, Michael 13, 227–29
Harvey, David 12
Haynes, Jonathon 173, 174, 175
Heart of Darkness, The (Conrad) 70
Hegel, Georg Wilhelm Friedrich 18, 26
hegemonizing hermeneutic 34
hegemony 8, 29, 30, 34, 79–80, 115, 163, 165, 166, 182–84, 242n14
Heidegger, Martin 126, 230
Heise, Ursula K. 227
Heliodorus 17
hermeneutics 47
Herzog, Werner 61
Hess, John 139, 235
heteroglossia 44
hierarchies 8, 18, 23, 31, 48, 54, 80
Higbee, Will 139
high/low art 112, 113–14, 122
Highsmith, Patricia 77
Higson, Andrew 136
Hill, Charlie 211
Hindu literature 38
hip-hop 25, 117–18, 150–51
Hitchcock, Alfred 77, 222
Hjort, Mette 96, 136–38, 158, 160, 180, 235
Hoefert de Turegano, T. 116
Hollywood 63, 66, 70, 80, 87, 105–6, 107, 108–9, 154–55, 169–75, 182–83, 187–88
Holquist, Michael 17
Holt, Jennifer 190
Holtmeier, Matthew 160
Hombres de Maiz (Asturias) 38
Homeland (TV series) 161
Homo Ludens (Huizinga) 161

homophobia 148
Horse's Mouth, The (dir. Neame) 76
How Tasty was my Frenchman (dir. dos Santos) 78
How to Read World Literature (Damrosch) 20–22
Hu, Tung-Hui 190
Hudson, Dale 192
Huhtamo, Erkki 6
Huizinga, Johan 161
Hulu 183
humanism 21–22
Hutcheson, Linda 66, 98, 192
hybridity 37, 168
hypotexts 67

Iberian imperialism 26
iconophobia 65
identities 29
If Hemingway Wrote JavaScript (Croll) 99
Ikpeng people 215
Iliad, The (Homer) 123
Illusions Perdues (Balzac) 29
immigration films 174
imperialism 42, 53, 181–82
imperialisms 26
In the Future they Ate from the Finest Porcelain (dir. Sansour) 165
Inca, *quipus* 6
"Indian, the" (Veloso) 208–10
Indian cinema 69, 78, 96–97, 170, 176; "third way" 88–90; *see also* Bollywood
Indian literature 17
Indian postcolonial studies 46, 48
Indian *rasa* aesthetics 20
"Indians" in world culture 205–7
Indians on TV (VNA TV series) 215
Indie Screenings 225
indigeneity, global 210–11
indigenism, term 165
indigenous cinema 163–68
indigenous comedy 211–12, 257n6
indigenous cosmopolitanism 38
indigenous critique 166–67
indigenous filmmaking 211–18
indigenous language films 78, 79
indigenous languages 38
indigenous literature 38
indigenous media 33, 208–11; movements 138–39, 214
indigenous myths and legends 25, 31–32, 38
indigenous peoples 4, 8, 24, 28, 38, 45, 135, 179, 181; communal land rights 41, 218–20, 226–28; notion of the "Indian" 204–7

indigenous science 50
indigenousness 26, 27
indio tecnizado (high-tech Indian) 27–28
Indus Valley 18
innovation 35, 38, 39, 160–61
institutions 25, 111, 114
intellectual commons 13
intellectual property rights 179–80, 187–88
intercolonial narcissism 78, 203, 257n5
intermedia 91
intermediality 14, 110, 249n2
international, term 102
International Association of Film and Television Schools (CILECT) 158
internationalism, term 102
Internet 4, 6, 21, 23, 78, 91, 98–99, 159, 190, 191–92, 194, 220; *see also* digital era
intersectionality 147–48, 238
intertextuality 66–67, 91
intertitles 76, 77
Intrus, L' (Nancy; dir. Denis) 61
Inuit filmmakers 212
Iranian cinema 14
Ishaghpour, Youssef 246n5
Islam 44, 86, 148, 203
Isle of Flowers (dir. Furtado) 196–97
Israel 134, 257n12
Israeli cinema 138
Italian Neo-Realism 59, 100, 156–57
Italian Renaissance 17
iTunes 183
Iveković Rada 56
Ivens, Joris 100–101
Ives, Charles 113
Ivey, Bill 118

Jackson, Michael 124
Jamaica Accords of 1976 3
Jamaican English 80
Jamaican music 124
Jameson, Fredric 196
Japanese anime 154–55
Japanese cinema 252n1
Jay-Z 114
jazz 120
Jazz Singer, The (dir. Crosland) 246n5
Jedlowski, Alessandro 174
Jenkins, Henry 91, 97, 185, 194, 233
Jewish Bible 17, 94
Jews 8, 18
Joaquim (dir. Gomes) 120
Joglar, Rene Perez (El Residente) 127–29
Johnson, Randal 139
Jolie, Angelina 143
Jones, David Martin 105, 160, 236

journals, radical film 59–60
Judaism 124
Jules et Jim (Truffaut) 117
Julien, Isaac 42–44, 204
Jungle Book, The (Disney) 67

Kaante (dir. Gupta) 155
Kadir, Djelal 16, 34, 47, 179
Kadrey, Richard 6
Kant, Immanuel 22
Kaplan, Caren 132, 151, 187
Kaufman, Deborah 180
Kavoori, Anandam P. 170
Kayapo: Out of the Forest (documentary) 213
Keats, John 5, 13
Kechiche, Abdellatif 57
Kechiche, Allouache 95–96
Kelly, Kevin 113, 191–92
Kerr, Paul 142
Kiarostami, Abbas 170
Kikuyu language 79
King, Martin Luther 149–51
King, Thomas 7, 211, 219
Kirsch, Adam 176–77
Kittler, Friedrich 10
Klein, Naomi 5, 12
Koch-Grunberg, Theodor 31–32, 243n23
Kopenawa, Davi 222
Kraidy, Marwan 182, 183
Kubrick, Stanley 93–94
Kundera, Milan 83
Kunuk, Zacharias 212

Labato, Ramon 187
labor 5, 146
Laboratory for Third World and African Studies, University of Paris VII 52
Labyrynth of Solitude (Paz) 38
Lacan, Jacques 55
Lakoff, George 10
Landzelius, Kyra 212
Lang, Jack 178
Langlois, Henri 59
Langton, Marcia 218
Larkin, Brian 174, 255n14
Laroui, Abdallah 53
Las Casas, Bartolomé de 41
Lash, S. 170–71
Latin America 9, 24, 25, 28, 49; *Latinité* 28; term 28–29, 243n13; *see also specific countries*
Latin American cinema 139, 205
Latin American cosmopolitanism 36, 37, 39
Latin American filmmakers 101
Latin American literature 74

Latin American media 189
Latin American music 128
Latin American postcolonial theory 45
Le Pen, Marine 4
Lee, Ang 66
Lee, Spike 95–96
left, the 52, 53, 115, 133
leftist filmmaking 100–101
Leitch, Thomas 66, 71, 84
Lennon, John 23
Lennox, Annie 116
Leone Have Sept Cabecas, Der (dir. Rocha) 78
Lessig, Lawrence 188
Life of Brian, The (Monty Python) 94
Life of Pi (dir. Lee) 176
Lim, Song Hwee 139
Lindsay, Vachel 64
Linebaugh, Peter 12, 179, 180
Lins, Paulo 93
Lionnet, Françoise 54, 163, 235
Lispector, Clarice 29
literature *see* world literature
litterature-monde 54–57
logophilia 65
Lolita (Nabokov) 21, 116
looking relations 14, 147–55
Lord of the Rings [*of Free Trade*]*, The* (trailer) 78
Loridan, Marceline 100
Lucy, C. 170–71
Luiselli, Valeria 98

Macbeth (Shakespeare) 85
Machado de Assis, Joaquim Maria 29, 30
Macunaíma: The Hero without Character (De Andrade) 30–33
Madame Bovary (Flaubert) 62, 88–90, 99, 161–62
magic realism 30, 33, 36–39, 165
Mahfouz, Naguib 87
major, term 163
Man Friday (dir. Gold) 71
Man without Qualities, The (Musil) 33
Manifesto Canibal Dada 28
Manovich, Lev 2
Mansfield Park (Austen) 46–47
Mansfield Park (dir. Rozema) 46–47
"Many Moons" (Monae) 113–14
Maori filmmaking 218
Maori language 87
Marche des Beurs, Paris 149
Marciniak, Katarzyna 160, 235
Marcuse, Herbert 27
Mardi Gras: Made in China (dir. Redmon) 141

Marivaux, Pierre de 95–96
Mark, Karl 40
Marker, Chris 101, 194
marketing 21, 34
markets, world 22–23
Marley, Bob 124
Marlowe, Christopher 22
Martel, Lucretia 117
Martel, Yann 176
Martí, José 9
Martin-Jones, David 224
Martirio (dir. Carelli) 217–18
Marx, Karl 12, 22–23, 224
Marxism 22, 23, 27, 133, 178, 197
Marxizing 22
mashups 91, 94
Master and the Divine, The (dir. da Costa; Teserahu) 215–16
matriarchy 27, 28
Mattelart, Armand 5, 13
Maxwell, Richard 182, 183, 190
Maya Memsaab (dir. Mehta) 88–90
Mazaj, Meta 107, 187
Mazdon, Lucy 70
MC Lars 97–98
McGonigal, Jane 161–62
McGuire, Anne 67
McKay, Adam 201
McLuhan, Marshall 11, 91
McMurria, John 182, 183
McQueen, Steve 199
"Mean Sketels" (mashup) 80
Medea (Euripides) 95
media, term 2, 5–7, 12
media convergence 91–92
Media Imperialism 188
media studies 10–11, 65, 110, 185
medium, term 110
Medium Cool (dir. Wexler) 198
Mehta, Ketan 88–90
Melancholia (dir. von Trier) 222–23
Melies, Georges 70
melodrama 153
Melville, Herman 97–98
Memmi, Albert 101
Merchant of Venice, The (Shakespeare) 87
meritocratic assumptions 34
Meso-America 18
Mesopotamia 17, 18, 20
metaphors 10–11, 51; aquatic 185–90, 191, 202, 226; literary Stock Market 36
metrocentrism 23
Metz, Christian 2, 238
Mexican indigenous culture 38
Mexican literature 38

Mexican telenovelas 188
Mexico 130; border films 200–201; Montezuma figure 37
Meyer, Sylke Rene 161
MGM studios 109
Miami 189
Microsoft 184
Middle Ages 35
Middle East 148
Mignolo, Walter 28
migration, transoceanic 202–3
Miller, Toby 182, 183, 190, 233
minor, term 163
minor transnational cinema 163–68
Minor Transnationalism (Lionnet, Shih) 163
minor world cinema 163–65
minoritarianism 148–49, 244n2
Minority Cinema, term 104
minor-language films 79
Mirror of Production, The (Baudrillard) 27
Moby Dick (Melville) 19, 97–98
Moderato Cantabile (Duras) 76
modernism 33, 61; Brazilian 26–28, 38, 154, 211
Mohanty, Chandra 132
Monae, Janelle 113–14
Monde Diplomatique, Le 133
Moore, Jason W. 7
Moorish culture 35
Moraes, Vinicius de 122
Moraru, Christian 221
Moretti, Franco 19, 23, 29, 30–31, 33, 35, 36, 46, 105, 106, 221, 242n14
Moretti, Nanni 153
Morris, Meeghan 11
Motorcycle Diaries (Salles) 108
Moutout, Jean-Marc 198
movements 9, 102, 149
Mr. Robinson Crusoe (dir. Sutherland) 70
multicultural turn 10
multilingualism 34, 38, 243n30
music videos 114, 116–17, 128–29, 134
musical commons 110–18
musical instruments 115
musicals, Western 218–19
Musil, Robert 33

Nagib, Lucia 104–5, 151
Nancy, Jean-Luc 61
Nation Estate (dir. Sansour) 164
nationalism 22, 51–52, 134
nation-state, the 42, 131–32, 134, 136, 140, 163–68
Native American comedy 211–12, 257n6

Native Americans 168, 205–6; commons 227–28
nativism 4, 11
naturalism 37–38
Negri, Antonio 13, 33, 227–29
Nelson, Blake 87
neo-colonialism 26, 50
neo-imperialism 80
neo-liberalism 5, 34, 71, 158, 184, 186
Netflix 183–84
network narratives 141–42, 225
Neves, Joshua 10, 11
New Wave cinema 59
New Wave movements 157
New Wave transnational textuality 154
New York Times, The 183–84, 258n1
New York University: Department of Cinema Studies 59; Tisch School of the Arts 157
Newman, Kathleen 235
Ngugi wa Thiongo 79
Niblett, Michael 46
Nigerian cinema 29; film piracy 187; Nollywood 170, 172–73
Nixon, Richard 3
Nixon, Rob 221
Nobel Prizes in literature 72, 74, 246n7
Nollywood 169–70, 172–75
Nornes, Abe Mark 78–79
Norton Anthology of World Literature, The 34
Norton Anthology of World Masterpieces, The 20
Nostalgia for the Light (dir. Guzmán) 223–24
Notre Musique (dir. Godard) 206–7
novels 17, 24, 92–93, 119, 126; film adaptations 64–67, 69–71, 75, 77, 81–82, 87–88, 173; global 176–77
Nowell-Smith, Geoffrey 104
nuclear weapons 134
Nuevo Mundo, El 40–50

O (dir. Nelson) 87
O Espirito da TV (The Spirit of Television, VNA film) 214
Occupy Movement 226–27
Oceanic Studies 202
Odyssey, The (Homer) 17, 32, 67, 121, 123
Oedipus Rex (Sophocles) 21
Of Oz the Wizard (Bucy) 67
One Night the Moon (dir. Perkins) 218, 219
Ong, Aihwa 131, 234
online teaching 160
opera 112
Opera of the World (Diawara) 202
Oppenheimer, Joshua 199

Orchid Thief, The (film) 66
organic intellectuals 121
Orientalism (Said) 48, 53
Orphic intellectuals 121
Oscars 71–72, 170, 183, 246n7
Ostrom, Elinor 12
Oswald de Andrade, José 26–27, 40–41, 86
Othello (Shakespeare) 87
Oxford Handbook of Adaptation Studies (Leitch) 84
Oxford History of World Cinema, The (Nowell-Smith) 104
oxymoron 11, 33

Page, Joana 139
Palacios, Jose Miguel 102
Palestinian cinema 29, 138, 163–65
Palestinian poetry 207
Paley, Nina 194–95
Palimpsests (Genette) 67
Pamela (Richardson) 17
para-modernisms 33–34, 37
parasitism, and film adaptations 66
Parikka, Jussi 6–7
Parks, Lisa 190
patents, term 179
paternalism 30, 52, 54, 108
patriarchy 27, 134
patronage 52, 107
Payne, Tom 12
Paz, Octavio 38
PDQ Bach 118
pedagogy 156–62, 254n17
Pedagogy of the Oppressed (Freire) 159, 160
Perec, Georges 67
performers, nationality of 143–44
Perkins, Rachel 210–11, 218
Perriam, Chris 105
Persian literature 38
Peru, Quipu Project 6
Pessoptimist, The (Habibi) 165
Peters, Benjamin 13
Peters, John Durham 2, 5, 10, 48, 91, 110, 113, 185, 189–90, 224
Peterson, Wolfgang 109
Petrie, Duncan 158
philology 17, 19
philosophy 18, 60–61
Picasso, Pablo 25
Pieterse, Jan Nederveen 177–78
Pindorama, Tupi Ur-matriarchy 27, 28
Pinon, Juan 189
piracy 187–88, 255n14
planetary discourse 221–25
Planetary Turn: The (eds. Elias; Moraru) 221

Plato 17
Playtime (dir. Tati) 131
poetry 121, 123
Polish film translations 76
political commons 13
political economy 7, 23, 28, 176–84
political films 196
polycentrism 18, 105, 107, 242n9
polyphony, cultural 33
Popol Vuh (Mayan myths) 38
popular culture 21, 57, 66
popular music 110, 112, 113, 119–22, 143
Porter, Michael 145
Portuguese language 36, 86; cinema 73–74
post-colonial, term 26, 231
post-colonial cinema, term 104
post-colonial critique 41–43, 47–50
post-colonial discourse 14
post-colonial postnationalism 43
post-colonial studies 20, 40–50, 52, 53, 55–57, 56
Postcolonial Studies and World Literature (Graham; Niblett; Deckard) 46
post-colonial theory 37, 41–43, 45, 49, 50, 53–55, 57, 167–68
post-colonialism 26, 39, 50, 55
post-coloniality 51–57, 172
post-Marxism 178
post-modernism 32, 37
Postmodernism, or, The Cultural Logic of Late Capitalism (Jameson) 196
post-structuralism 42, 55
post-synchronization 77–78, 81
power 25, 29, 31, 34, 48, 51, 52, 63, 80, 114, 130, 187–89; *see also* Global North-Global South power relations
Power, William 6
Practice of Everyday Life, The (de Certeau) 84
Pratt, Mary Louise 7, 186
prestige 51, 64, 138, 157
Pride and Prejudice (Austen) 88, 97
primitivism 27–28
Prinop: My First Contact (indigenous film) 214
privatization 3; of water 180–81, 226
productivism 27
progress 26–27
property 12, 23, 26
prosumers/produsers 194
proto-cinema 61–62
proto-colonialism 49
proto-imperialism 49
proto-postcolonial studies 53
Proust, Marcel 60, 92
provinciality 22

publishing 36, 63
Puerto Rico 127–29
Punathambekar, Aswin 170
Pure Necessity, The (dir. Claernout) 67
Purple Rose of Cairo, The (Allen) 99

quality 107
Quijano, Anibal 7
Quipu Project 6

Rabbitson Crusoe (Disney) 70–71
race 42–43, 45, 52, 54, 57, 148
Race in Translation (Shohat; Stam) 55, 254n1
racial discrimination 203–7
"Racial Draft" sketch (Chapelle) 144
racism 8, 148, 211
radical film movements 59
radical film theory 59–60
radicalism 166
Rajadhyaksha, Ashish 170
Ramayana 194–95
Rancière, Jacques 13, 24–25
Raoni (Kayapo leader) 213
rap 117, 149–51, 203
"Rappa" (Brazilian rapper) 203
Reagan, Ronald 3, 5
realism 108
reality 161–62
Reality is Broken (McGonigal) 161
Rear Window (dir. Hitchcock) 43
rebellion 101
Red Atlantic 204–7
Reeves, Keanu 143
Reino de Este Mundo, El (Carpentier) 37
religion 42, 44, 124, 147
remakes 138, 154–55
remediation 91
Remix (Lessig) 67
remixes 67, 72–73, 91–99, 117–18, 127
representative regime 24–25
republican colonialism 56–57
Republique Mondiale des Lettres, La (Casanova) 51, 52
resistance 163
Resnais, Alain 60
revolutionary nostalgia 33
rhetoric 11
Richardson, Tony 67–68, 95
Rickard, Jolene 167
Riggs, Marlon 204
right, the 133, 148
"Rise of the Rest" in cinema 170, 183–84
Rivera, Alex 199–200
Roach, Joe 10
Robbe-Grillet, Alain 81

Robbins, Bruce 48
Robertson, Roland 189
Robinson Crusoe (Defoe) 17, 70–71
Robinson Crusoe (dir. Bunuel) 70
Robinson Crusoe (dir. Hardy; Miller) 70
Robinson Crusoe on Mars (dir. Haskin) 70
Rocha, Glauber 25, 78, 126, 154
Rodney, Walter 197
Roman Empire 49
Romeo and Juliet (Shakespeare) 86
Rosaldo, Renato 214
Ross, Andrew 228
Rouch, Jean 159
Routledge Companion to World Literature, The (d'Haen; Damrosch; Kadir) 16, 65
Rowden, Terry 139
Rozema, Patricia 46–47
Rushdie, Salman 17
Russia 71
Russian Formalism 58
Russian State University of Cinematography, Moscow (VGIK) 156–57

Sahlins, Marshall 27
Said, Edward 21, 46–47, 48, 55
Salles, Walter 108
Salles Gomes, Paulo Emilio 25
sampling 91, 117–18
Sanskrit 18
Sansour, Larissa 164–65
Santiago, Silviano 45
Sarkar, Bhaskar 11, 187–88, 231
Sassen, Saskia 145
Saussy, Haun 92
Sauvy, Alfred 44
Scattered Hegemonies (Grewal; Kaplan) 132
Schamus, James 158, 200
Schickele, Peter 118
Schoonover, Karl 176
Schroter, Jens 249n2
Schwarz, Roberto 143
sciences 49–50
Scorsese, Martin 107
Seattle anti-globalization protests, 1999 4
Second World 44–45, 132
self-awareness 11
self-empowerment 228
Selwyn, Don 87
Sen, Amartya 5
Sengupta, Gunja 206
Sepulveda, controversy 41
Seshpande, Shekhar 187
sexism 148
sexuality 42–44

Shadow Economics of Cinema (Labato) 187
Shakespeare, William 22, 85–87
Shakuntala (Kalidasa) 21
Sharma, Nandita 41
Shaw, Deborah 136, 141, 142, 160
Shelley, Percy Bysshe 12
Shih, Shu-Mei 163, 235
Shining, The (dir. Kubrick) 93–94
Shiva, Vandana 12, 180
Shock Doctrine, The (dir. Winterbottom; Whitcross) 198
Shohat, Ella 8, 9, 41, 55, 78, 105, 144, 242n9, 244n8, 245n4, 256n1, 257n12
Shubin, Neil 223
Shuckoff, Peter (Nice Peter) 149–50
silent films 73, 76–77, 106, 153
Silko, Leslie Marmon 38, 227
Simon, Paul 29, 114
Simone, Nina 110
Sindbad the Philosopher 17
Sinnreich, Aram 92, 117
Sissako, Abderrahmane 197
Sita Sings the Blues (dir. Paley) 194–95
Sithengi Film Festival 116
Sivan, Eyal 206
Sixpence None the Richer 116
slavery 24, 41, 46, 47, 57, 70, 111, 124, 134, 203, 227–28
Sleep Dealer (dir. Rivera) 199–200
Slemon, Stephen 244n10
Slumdog Millionaire (dir. Boyle; Tandan) 14
Small, Christopher 110–11
Smith, Adam 40
Smith, Anthony 132
Smith, Iain Robert 154
Smith, Paul Chaat 48, 205
Smith, Paul Julian 137–38
Smouts, Marie-Claude 56
Snitow, Alan 180
Social Darwinism 71
social networking 192
socialism 45, 100, 102
Socialist Bloc 44
socialist internationalism 23
Society for Cinema Studies 58
solidarity 103
song-essay-poems 126–27
song-poems 123
Sons of Gandhi (group) 210
Sontag, Susan 22, 29, 30
Sony Pictures Entertainment, Local Language Productions (LLPs) 171
Soulimas-Guenif, Nacira 148
sound, cinematic 76–77
Sound and Sense (Wisnik) 122

soundtracks 81
South African film/literature studies 246n2
South Asia 24, 46
South Korean cinema 137, 184
Southern Europe 24
sovereignty 167
Soviet Union 3–4, 44, 132
Sovik, Liv 256n2
Soyinke, Wole 175
Space Exodus, A (dir. Sansour) 164
spaghetti Westerns 206
Spivak, Gayatri 34, 47, 55, 221
Springsteen, Bruce 116
Stafford, Roy 142, 176
stagism 18, 26
Stam, Robert 8, 9, 41, 55, 59, 78, 105, 144, 242n9, 245n2, 245n4, 256n1
Starosielski, Nicole 190
Steinbeck, John 116
Stephens, Mitchell 65
Sterling, Bruce 6
Sterne, Laurence 95
Steyerl, Hito 133
Still Waters in a Storm (school) 98
Stoneman, Rod 158
storytelling, collective 212
Strain Andromeda, The (dir. McGuire) 67
Strangers on the Train (dir. Hitchcock) 77
strategic traditionalism 33
Straubhaar, Joseph 188–89
streaming 184, 191–93
Suassuna, Ariano 73–74
subjects/citizens, contemporary 227–28
subtitles 76–79
Suleiman, Elia 29, 165, 198
Sumerian poetry 20
surrealism 26, 37, 243n12
Sur-Realismo 154
Sur-realismo Magico 25
"Survivor" (Reality Show) 71
sweding 91
Swiss Family Robinson (dir. Annakin) 70
syncretism 37, 120
Syria 17, 145
Szendy, Peter 223

Tagore, Rabindranath 69
Talbot, Michael 103–4, 107, 108
Tanzanian cinema 174
Tati, Jacques 131
Te Tangati Wahi Rawa o Wenitit (dir. Selwyn) 87
Teaching Transnational Pedagogy (eds. Marciniak; Bennett) 160
telenovellas 88, 188–89

television 73, 184, 188–89, 216; narrative innovation 160–61; studies 176
temporalities 33, 37
Tepper, Stephen 118
terminological technologies 13
terminology 13
Teserahu, Divino 215–16
texts, sacred word of 65
Thanouli, Eleftheria 171–72
Thatcher, Margaret 3, 5
theater 85–87, 95–96
Theorizing World Cinema (Nagib; Perriam; Dudrah) 105
Third Cinema 128
Third World 8–10, 20, 52, 54, 71, 100, 132, 157; theory 44–45
Third World Cinema, term 104
Third Worldism 52–53, 55
Thirst (dir. Kaufman; Snitow) 180
This is not a Manifesto (Negri; Hardt) 227–29
Thompson, Kristen 193
Thompson, Robert Farris 10, 117
Thoreau, Henry David 98–99
Three Worlds model 44–45
Through Other Continents (Dimock) 221
"Thug Notes" (web series) 98
Time-Image, The (Deleuze) 224
Tom Jones (dir. Richardson) 67–68, 95
Tom Jones (Fielding) 17, 67–68
top-down and bottom-up, terms 235
Townsend, Stuart 198
TradeMarkG 118
Traffic (dir. Soderbergh) 141
trance-modernism 32, 113, 243n27
trans, term 234–35, 237
transartistic method 237–38
transartistry 2, 122, 125–28
transcultural approach 239
transdisciplinary approach 237
transformations 87–88, 93
transgender approach 238
translation: film 69, 72, 75–83; literature 33–34, 243n30; *see also* adaptation
translational transnationalism 29
translinguistic approach 237
transmediality, world music 110, 116–17, 119–29
trans-mediatic approach 238
trans-methodology 237–39
transnational, term 10, 12, 13, 21, 23, 139, 231–36
transnational approach 237–39
transnational cinema 136–141, 143–145, 151–153, 188; term 1–3, 8–9; *see also* world cinema

Transnational Cinemas (journal) 136, 141
transnational corporations 4–5, 131
transnational emotion and affect 148–49
transnational feminism 132, 134, 151–52
Transnational Film Remakes (eds. Smith; Verevis) 154–55
transnational film schools 156–62
transnational gaze 208–20
transnational literature, term 10
transnational media flows 188–89
transnational reception 152
transnational resistance 229
transnational turn 10, 130–35
transnationality 39, 48, 125, 128, 163, 166; coefficient of 141–46; looking relations 147–55; term 131, 133
Transoceanic Black Studies 206
transoceanic studies 202–7
transregional approach 238–39
transsectional approach 238
transsectionality 147–48
transsexual approach 238
transtextual approach 237
transtextuality 26, 39, 67; theory 86
tricontinental movements 9
Tristram Shandy (dir. Winterbottom) 95
Tropicalia 121, 125–27
Truffaut, François 117
Trump, Donald 4, 133–34, 168, 199, 226
Trumpism 71
Tsuei, Jon 155
Tudors, The (TV series) 14
Tunisia, Jasmine revolution 101–2
Tupi language 78
Tupinamba peoples 86
Turkey 24, 189
Turkish cinema 81
Turkish telenovelas 80
Turtle Island, indigenous North America 18
Turtles, The 143
Tzara, Tristan 28

Ulysses (Joyce) 21
Unbearable Lightness of Being, The (Kundera; dir. Kaufman) 83
Une Femme est une Femme (dir. Godard) 206
United Kingdom 46, 145; Film Council, Britishness test 142
United States of America: American Studies 10; avant-garde cinema 109; hegemony 80, 182–84; imperialism 26, 49, 70, 115; indigenous land rights 219; as inevitably mestizo (*fatalmente mestizo*) 35; minority culture 149; movements in 9–10; nationalism 51; New York 145; race and class 148
universality 22, 147
Unthinking Eurocentrism (Shohat; Stam) 41, 105, 144
Ur-sprache 18

Vacavone, Daniel 230
value, cinematic 106
van Elteren, Mel 131
Varda, Agnes 84
Veloso, Caetano 35, 121, 125–27, 133, 208–10
Venuti, Lawrence 33–34
Verevis, Constantine 154
Vertigo Sea (Akomfrah) 202
video games 93, 98–99, 161–62
Video in the Villages, Brazil 214–16
video-on-demand *see* streaming
Villa-Lobos, Heitor 113
Violence des Echanges en Milieu Tempere (dir. Moutout) 198
Vitally, Valentina 136
Viveiros de Castro, Eduardo 222
Von Trier, Lars 222–23
Vondereau, Patrick 190
Voodoo Macbeth (dir. Welles) 85–86
voyeurism 43

Waiapi people 214
Walden (Thoreau) 98–99
Wall Street 186
Wallerstein, Emmanuel 23
Wang, Ting 182, 183
Warnell, Phillip 61
Warrior, Robert 167
water privatization 180–81, 226
Watson, Tim 47
"We the Economy" (Web Series project) 200–201
Wealth of Nations, The (Smith) 40
web series 97, 98
Webb, Lawrence 144
Weekend (dir. Godard) 206
Wellek, Rene 18
Welles, Orson 85–86
Weltkinematographie, term 103
Weltliteratur 16–19, 23
Weltmusik 111
Wenders, Wim 170
Wessels, Chelsea 160
West Africa 24
Western Canon, The (Bloom) 34
Western "we" 22
Westernization 81, 155

Westerns, American 206
Westocentrism 7–8, 25, 29, 34
Wexler, Haskell 198
What is Cinema? (Bazin) 58
"Wheel of Mash" (TradeMarkG) 118
Whitcross, Matt 198
White, Patricia 151
white backlash 4, 8, 148
White Mythologies (Young) 55
whiteness 115, 175, 256n2
Whiteness Studies 202
Wild Life (animation) 71
Willemen, Paul 136
Williams, Raymond 87, 149, 152, 185
Winterbottom, Michael 95, 198
Wire, The (TV series) 160–61
Wise, Robert 67
Wisnik, Jose Miguel 121–22
Woman on Top (dir. Torres) 142
women filmmakers 151–52
Women's Cinema (Butler) 152
Women's Cinema, World Cinema (White) 151
Wong Kar-Wai 143
Wood, Houston 87
"Woods" (Hollywood, Nollywood, Bollywood) 169–75
Woolf, Virginia 66
world, term 10, 13, 16, 18, 21, 40, 47–48, 230–32, 234–36
world cinema: circulation 62–63, 69, 103–104, 106; emergence of 103–109; end of the world in 222–225; international pre-history of 100–102; phase 107; studies 58–63, 104, 136, 138; term 8–9, 16, 103–105, 230–232; theory 104–105; trans-ization of 237, 239; and world literature 58–63, 69–74; and world music 112, 113, 116–117, 119–120, 123, 126–129; *see also* transnational cinema
World Cinema Foundation 107
World Cinemas, Transnational Perspectives (Ďurovičová; Newman) 235
world literature: circulation 21, 22, 29–31, 69; classics 6, 92–94, 97–99; film adaptations 64–68, 75, 77, 81–88, 95–96; history of 17–18; studies 58–63; system 23; term 1–3, 8–9, 18–19, 231–32; theory 20–23, 64–65; trans-ization of 237, 239; *Weltliteratur* 16–19; and world cinema 58–63, 69–74; and world music 112–14, 116–17, 119–20, 123, 126–29. *see also* novels
World Literature in Theory (anthology) 47
World Literature Today (journal) 47
world music 29, 52, 110–18, 143; term 1–2, 9, 14, 16, 54, 111–12, 114, 115, 119; transmediality of 119–29; and world cinema 112, 113, 116–17, 119–20, 123, 126–29; and world literature 112–14, 116–17, 119–20, 123, 126–29
World Republic of Letters, The (Casanova) 47, 106
World Social Forum 56
World Systems Theory 23, 40, 221–22
World Television: From Global to Local (Straubhaar) 189
World Trade Center attack, 2001 4
World Trade Organization 179–80, 199
world-historical peoples 18
worlding 230–31, 233
Wretched of the Earth, The (Fanon) 42–43
Wright, Cynthia 41
Wright, Richard 56
Wrong Man, The (dir. Hitchcock) 77
Wyatt, Justin 158

Xavante people 215–16
Xi Jinping 185
Xie Fei 157

Yale French Studies, "Cinema/Sound" (Altman) 77
Yes Men films (Bichlbaum; Bonanno) 199
Yimer, Dagwami 202–3
Young, Robert 46, 48, 55
"Young Turks" 59
YouTube 149–50, 184, 194, 211, 220

Zelig (dir. Allen) 19, 33
Zemmouri, Mahmoud 44, 153
Zielinski, Siegfried 6, 189
Zimmerman, Patricia 139, 192, 235
Zizek, Slavoj 5, 12
Zo'e people 214–15

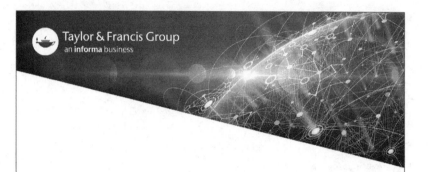